THE RESTORATION OF JUSTICE IN POSTWAR HESSE, 1945–1949

THE RESTORATION OF JUSTICE IN POSTWAR HESSE, 1945–1949

Andrew Szanajda

LEXINGTON BOOKS

A division of
ROWMAN & LITTLEFIELD PUBLISHERS, INC.
Lanham • Boulder • New York • Toronto • Plymouth, UK

LEXINGTON BOOKS

A division of Rowman & Littlefield Publishers, Inc.
A wholly owned subsidiary of The Rowman & Littlefield Publishing Group, Inc.
4501 Forbes Boulevard, Suite 200, Lanham, MD 20706

Estover Road, Plymouth PL6 7PY, United Kingdom

British Library Cataloguing in Publication Information Available

Library of Congress Cataloging-in-Publication Data
Szanajda, Andrew, 1967–
The restoration of justice in postwar Hesse, 1945-1949 / Andrew Szanajda.
p. cm.
Includes bibliographical references and index.
ISBN-13: 978-0-7391-1870-2 (cloth : alk. paper)
ISBN-10: 0-7391-1870-6 (cloth : alk. paper)
1. Justice, Administration of—Germany—Hesse—History. I. Title.
KK5049.S93 2007
347.43'41009044—dc22

2006033272

Printed in the United States of America

∞™ The paper used in this publication meets the minimum requirements of American National Standard for Information Sciences—Permanence of Paper for Printed Library Materials, ANSI/NISO Z39.48-1992.

For Joyce

Contents

Acknowledgments

I WISH TO ACKNOWLEDGE MY GREAT indebtedness to Professor Peter Hoffmann, Professor of German History at McGill University, who encouraged me to work independently until my book was ready for submission, and for providing incisive criticism at appropriate times. Great thanks are also respectfully and humbly offered to Herr Professor Bernard Diestelkamp, Professor Emeritus at the Johann Goethe University in Frankfurt-am-Main, and to Herr Doktor Rolf Faber, Leitender Ministerialrat at the Thüringen Ministry of Justice, for providing me with advice during our illuminating, albeit brief, discussions. They were instrumental in helping me identify and confirm the key features of this work.

Special thanks also to Dr. Detlef Mühlberger, lecturer in German history at Oxford-Brookes University, for stiffening my backbone by providing me with much needed encouragement in the course of the research. My gratitude is also extended to the very professional staff at the *Hessisches Hauptstaatsarchiv*, as well as to the equally professional staff of the *Bundesarchiv* in Koblenz. My research in Germany was made possible by the *Institut für Europäische Geschichte*, which secured the necessary funding.

Special thanks are offered for patient and very helpful assistance provided by Frau Jutta Ries at the Institute library in procuring literature material for this book, along with Dietmar Schönfeld, Ries Roowaan, and Wolfgang Fritzsche for their significant efforts. Thanks are especially due to the interlibrary loan staff at the McLennan Library of McGill University, who endured many infuriating requests while doing an excellent job of procuring sources for my research. Great thanks are extended to John Pope for providing constructive advice and criticism during the writing stage.

Introduction

THE PURPOSE OF THIS BOOK IS TO EXAMINE the restoration of the justice system in postwar Hesse, a new land in the U.S. occupation zone, during the postwar Allied military occupation of Germany (1945–1949). The unconditional surrender of the National Socialist regime reduced Germany to a mere geographical entity[1] at the beginning of the occupation, when the jurisdictions of all governmental institutions had ceased to function as a consequence of the surrender.

Supreme authority was vested in the Allied occupation powers[2] until the Federal Republic of Germany was established. Germany was governed by the Allied military government, run by the four occupation powers at the national level and by separate military government administrations representing those occupation powers in their respective occupation zones. Allied aims for the postwar reconstruction of Germany were to be implemented by separate military government administrations in each zone. German administrations of justice were reconstructed within the restored *Länder*, or states, of the U.S. zone,[3] in keeping with the Potsdam Protocol principle of decentralising the German political structure and the development of local responsibility, which was believed to be conducive to democratisation.[4] *Land* Hesse was created at the beginning of the occupation and formed out of former *Land* Hesse on the right bank of the Rhine[5] and parts of the Prussian provinces of Kurhesse and Nassau.[6]

The reconstruction of postwar Germany took place under the military government administrations at the national, zonal, and *Land* levels, which exercised supreme executive, legislative, and judicial power at those levels. Since the jurisdiction of the U.S. military government was limited to only one of the four zones, the task of the postwar reconstruction of the German government and its affiliated institutions was limited to the *Land* level, while policy-making for the national level was dependent upon the cooperation of the other three occupation powers.[7]

The task of postwar reconstruction was undertaken during the period of transition from the National Socialist totalitarian *Unrechtsstaat* to the restoration of constitutional government, or *Rechtsstaat.* Policies for the reconstruction of the justice system and other tasks to be implemented within the individual *Länder* of the U.S. zone were drafted at the national level, under the auspices of the Allied Control Council, while the U.S. military government functioned at the zonal and *Land* levels. The reconstruction of the justice system in the U.S. zone took place under the supervision of the U.S. military government, which established a Military Government Office in each *Land* within its zone.

The process of reconstructing the German *Land* governments and judicial organisations in the U.S. zone began with the creation of the *Länder.* Common measures for the U.S. zone as a whole were later introduced by representatives of the reestablished *Länder* governments and representatives of the zonal U.S. military government, while the German governments at the *Land* level in the U.S. zone were substituted for the national government.[8] The *Länder* of the western zones were incorporated into a federal system of government in September 1949, when the Federal Republic of Germany was created[9] and the functions and powers of the *Land* judicial organisations were affirmed in the federal constitution.

The function of the justice system within a state is to promote an orderly social life as an institution of the state. That is accomplished by applying laws enacted by the government of the state, which organises and governs the judicial organisation in accordance with its interests.[10] In that respect, laws enacted by the political power in a democratic state are to serve two simultaneous functions that can't be separated: 1) safeguarding the social order as a state institution, and 2) serving as a moral authority by fulfilling the interests of justice.

The second function was negated during the National Socialist regime, in the interest of extending the first, thereby corrupting the nature of the law.[11] Those two functions underlay the reconstruction of the justice system and the reestablishment of the supremacy of the law, based on the principle of the rule of law, which can be characterised by five general concepts.

First, the government of a state can't exercise arbitrary power over the individual. An individual can only be subject to legal proceedings in the event of a distinct breach of the law.[12] The role of a constitutional government is therefore to safeguard individual civil rights that are embodied in its constitution.[13] Second, a government based on the rule of law maintains the concept of legal equality. Every person in the state is subject to one body of law, administered by law courts.[14] Third, the general principles of the constitution, such as the rights of individuals, are maintained through judicial decisions made in individual cases brought before the law courts.[15] Fourth, the principle of judicial independence is inexorably bound to the concept of the *Rechtsstaat.*[16] A judge is to be responsible only to the law, and not subject to any outside influences. Fifth, the executive, legislative, and judicial powers of the state are divided, thus preventing the government, the legislature, or the judicial organisation from overstepping their assigned jurisdiction.[17] This separation of various branches of government prevents arbitrary abuse of the power of the state, as was the case during the National Socialist regime, in which a centralised dictatorship was created through the concentration of legislative, executive, and judicial power into one body.

The judicial organisation of a constitutional government functions independently from the state executive. Individual courts make decisions in cases within their jurisdiction, based on the application of law and dependent upon the content of each individual case. In the case of postwar Germany, that included the criminal, civil, labour, and administrative courts, as well as their respective appellate courts. Each of those judicial organisations was governed by laws and statutes that defined their constitution and their respective responsibilities.[18]

The restoration of a *Rechtsstaat* in postwar Germany also required three additional elements: restoring the material preconditions for a judicial organisation and eliminating National Socialist influences from German law, restoring a judiciary that would apply those material preconditions according to the rule of law, and restoring the independence of *Land* judicial organisations that would be permanently administered by German authorities without being subject to the supervision of the occupation powers.

The first of those preconditions required the establishment of a fully functional justice system. That entailed restoring a judicial organisation, consisting of ordinary law courts and specialised courts with a system of appeals courts to provide an extensive guarantee of legal recourse, maintaining the principle of judicial independence to ensure that the courts were free from executive control, and applying the body of law based on general concepts of the rule of law to maintain the principles of justice.

The second precondition required the acceptance of the *Rechtsstaat.* The third precondition required the lifting of U.S. military government supervisory control over the restored *Land* judicial organisation after the preconditions had been fulfilled at the end of the military occupation. Increasingly greater judicial responsibility was transferred from the military government to German authorities during the occupation, until the full-fledged independence of the German state and its affiliated institutions was attained.

The first part of this book will provide an overview of the justice system under the National Socialist regime. German institutions were subordinated to the National Socialist *Gleichschaltung* (synchronisation). This process legalised and institutionalised a complete ordering of state and society in Germany under the guidance, supervision, and direction of the NSDAP, without it being hindered by parliamentary opposition or being subject to public opinion.[19] It's been argued that the greatest impact of the National Socialist programme on German institutions was on the judicial organisation, since basic rights that had been guaranteed by the Weimar constitution were rendered meaningless under the National Socialist regime.[20]

Since an independent judicial organisation would have impeded the authoritarian power of the National Socialist regime, the justice system was politicised and made to serve the interests of the regime.[21] The *Rechtsstaat* was thus destroyed and the justice system was turned into an instrument of policy to accomplish the goals of National Socialism.[22] Statutes were enacted to introduce a new conception of the law based on the political ideology of the regime. The independent authority of the judicial organisation was systematically undermined as the arbitrary rule of the dictatorship took precedence over the rule of law.[23] Authority over the justice system was also transferred from the *Länder* to the *Reich* government, and was thus *gleichgeschaltet* (synchronised), or integrated, into the apparatus of the National Socialist regime.[24]

The second part of the book will discuss wartime preparations for military government in postwar Germany. Military planning agencies prepared guides to be used by the military civil affairs units that would initiate the first stage of the military government administration while political policy was prepared at the governmental and international levels, paving the way for the occupation objectives for postwar Germany. While political planning set forth the general principles for the restoration of justice, military planning drafted the initial measures for the implementation of those principles.

The third part of the book traces the development of the postwar restoration of Germany's judicial organisation in Hesse during the military occupation, which involved restoring a Ministry of Justice and a judicial organisation in each *Land* within the U.S. occupation zone. A series of military government enactments at the outset of the occupation established the principles for organisation and the responsibilities of the German justice system. The objectives of the western occupation powers were proclaimed through statements issued by the military government at the national and the zonal levels, in the form of proclamations, directives, and laws governing occupation policy. The National Socialist judicial organisation and its corruption of the German justice system were abolished. A provisional extraterritorial military government judicial organisation was established to maintain the security and interests of the occupation powers. A German judicial organisation was restored under the leading authority of the *Land* Ministry of Justice, which resumed its function, in accordance with German and occupation law. The restoration of justice in occupied Germany involved abolishing laws and courts that would be unacceptable in a democratic constitutional state, and restoring responsibility to a reconstructed German judicial organisation, under the supervision of the U.S. military government, exercising supreme authority to ensure compliance with occupation objectives.

The fourth and last part of this book will examine the human element of the reconstruction of justice—the reinstatement of the judicial personnel who were to staff the justice system during its reconstruction and an examination of the policies governing the denazification of judicial personnel. The concept of denazification was considered one of the preconditions for the postwar rehabilitation of Germany. This process[25] entailed the unusual situation of prosecuting individuals on the basis of their membership in a formerly legal political party, the NSDAP, or their activities within that party or its affiliated organisations.[26]

Former members of the NSDAP and its affiliated organisations were judged on the basis of presumptive guilt—membership was considered as constituting evidence of adherence to the National Socialist regime and its ideology. The basic objective of the denazification programme in all professions was to determine who was a former National Socialist and to prevent these individuals from occupying positions of influence in postwar Germany.[27]

U.S. military occupation authorities and German authorities operating under the supervision of the U.S. military government established elaborate regulations for dealing with individuals who had served as jurists under the National Socialist regime, just as they did with members of all other professions. Judgment was based on schematic categories of presumptive guilt. German jurists in the National Socialist regime were dealt with as an anonymous bloc of individuals. The experience of denazification in Hesse demonstrated the same problems and difficulties that were evident in the U.S. zone as a whole. The thorough denazification of the judicial personnel that had been envisaged at the beginning of the occupation wasn't accomplished, since the approach to implementing that objective proved to be impractical.

1

Law and Justice in National Socialist Germany

THE NSDAP REORGANISED THE POLITICAL order and the justice system in Germany in order to establish its hegemony over the state, and to reorganise society on the basis of National Socialist conceptions. According to the constitution of Weimar Germany, the elected *Reichstag* was the legislature; the government, subject to the confidence of the elected representatives in the *Reichstag*, represented the executive; and the justice system was operated by independent courts that were subject only to the law. Under Nationalist Socialism, those formerly independent state functions were united to implement the will of the *Führer*.[1]

The essence of National Socialist political theory was based on unity and integration under the executive authority of the state. The executive was to be unimpeded by checks upon its authority by legislative assemblies as governments are in other constitutional states. In turn, the state, as a unified entity without internal dissensions to impede its progress, was itself dependent upon the existence of a leader. The unified executive consisted of the leader of the state and the NSDAP, acting as the vanguard of the nation. The unity of the state under the authority of a dictatorship was achieved through the *Gleichschaltung* process, or political "synchronisation."

The purpose of the process was to remove all of the conflicting social and political forces that could impair the domination of the unified executive.[2] In order to achieve that purpose, the elements of a constitutional government, including the separation of powers, judicial control of the administration, judicial independence, the fundamental rights of citizens, the impartiality of the civil service, and all other measures provided by the constitution against arbitrary actions by the legislative, executive, and judicial branches of the government upon the individual, were eliminated.[3] The regime accrued extended powers through legislation establishing a dictatorship and supplanting the principles of the *Rechtsstaat*—a constitutional government subject to the rule of law. German law befitting a *Rechtsstaat* was incompatible with National Socialist ideology, and was therefore destroyed as part of the National Socialist "revolution."

Constitutional government in Germany was subverted through superficially legal means. Although the Weimar constitution wasn't formally abolished, it was placed in abeyance through National Socialist legislation. Subsequent enactments institutionalised the establishment of a dictatorship. The provisions of the "*Reichstag* Fire Decree" of 28 February 1933 suspended fundamental individual rights on the basis of Article 48 of the Weimar Constitution.[4] Rather than being in force for the duration of a state of emergency, as provided by Article 48, the decree remained in force for the duration of the National Socialist regime.

The basis of the decree allowed for the political power of the *Führer* to become the basic law of the regime, a move through which the authority of the judicial organisation and the civil service were circumvented.[5] The decree also opened the way for additional legislation directed at what were classified as political offences, leading to the suppression of all potential opposition to the regime. All political gatherings and demonstrations could be dissolved, and all political newspapers and other such publications were banned. The circulation of political publications was made illegal. Anyone who received an illegal political publication and didn't submit it to the police or report whoever had circulated it was subject to prosecution.[6]

The subverting of the authority of the constitution and the suppressing of all political opposition facilitated the creation of a dictatorship that was essentially established through legislation. The principle of the separation of state powers was subverted by the Enabling Act of 24 March 1933, which allowed the NSDAP to suspend the legislative procedure prescribed by the constitution and allowed the national government to enact legislation that deviated from the constitution.[7] Whereas the constitutionality of legislation in the Weimar Republic was ensured by parliamentary proceedings and the law conforming to the principles of the constitution,[8] the Enabling Act empowered the NSDAP government to rule by decree and contravene the principles of constitutional government with impunity.

Subsequent legislation established the NSDAP dictatorship by ordering the dissolution and prohibition of all political parties other than the NSDAP,[9] making the state and the NSDAP one and the same[10] and concentrating political leadership into the hands of the *Führer* by combining the offices of *Reich*

President, *Führer*, and *Reich* Chancellor.[11] Hitler was thereafter designated "*Führer* and *Reich* Chancellor," a move by which he assumed supreme political authority.

The office of *Reich* Chancellor had been subject to the limitations associated with governmental office, but Hitler's position as *Führer*, representing the will of the nation, overrode all other authority.[12] The concentration of central political authority was extended further by the dissolution of the *Länder* legislatures and by absorbing their functions into the national government administration.[13]

The reorganisation of the political order was used to promote the interests of the National Socialist regime in the administration of justice. Since the precepts of the rule of law were incompatible with those interests, the National Socialist regime used its political authority to introduce a new conception of justice through a series of legislative enactments. The National Socialist concept of justice was to be administered through the existing judicial organisation that had been in existence prior to the establishment of the regime, as well as National Socialist extraordinary courts that served the direct purpose of upholding the interests of the regime. That new conception of state and law resulted in the subjugation of German society by the National Socialist regime and the undermining of the independence of the justice system through its subordination to the political authority of the state.[14]

All spheres of the law were to be interpreted in accordance with the spirit of National Socialism.[15] Although civil law wasn't modified when it didn't directly affect the interests of the state,[16] the administration of criminal justice was characterised by an increasing "politicisation," which the regime eventually turned into an instrument of terror through both judicial and extra-judicial measures.[17]

The Basis of National Socialist Justice

National Socialist legal theory was based on point 19 of the NSDAP programme of 1920, demanding the institution of a so-called German law to replace the basis of Roman law, which in the opinion of national Socialist ideologues supposedly reflected "a materialist world order."[18] Hence, an entirely new conception of justice in Germany was to be created, based on National Socialist ideology.[19]

The National Socialists objected to the legal principles governing the constitutional rule of law, such as equality before the law, and the principle that only actions considered crimes were to be declared as such by a law.[20] According to National Socialist ideology, the fundamental values of the law were the protection of the national community (*Volksgemeinschaft*) and "safeguarding the life of the nation."[21] That interpretation of the law was illustrated by Hitler's expression of contempt for the judiciary and "juridical scruples," which, in his view, hindered the exigencies of "*national survival*." Hitler told the world, "I shan't let myself be hampered by juridical scruples. Only necessity has legal force."[22]

National Socialist legal theory postulated that the law of "necessity" arose from the *Volk* (nation) as the source of law. The primary function of the law was thereby to uphold and protect the *Volksgemeinschaft*,[23] which was to be protected by the state, serving as the instrument for applying the law. The *Volk* was represented by the NSDAP for the purpose of its leadership, which was responsible for articulating its desires and defending its interests. As the representative of the will of the *Volk*, the NSDAP was also responsible for promulgating the law and ruling the state.[24]

To implement the will of the *Volk*, the NSDAP instituted the leadership principle (*Führerprinzip*), by which all authority emanated from Hitler, who was responsible only to the *Volk* as the supreme embodiment of its will.[25] According to National Socialist ideology, all the political power of the "German race" was united in the hands of the *Führer*; and as a consequence, all law was derived from that source.[26] The will of the *Führer*, as the ultimate source of the law, was issued through governmental statutes, ordinances, or edicts.[27]

The interpretation of the law and the administration of justice were subjugated to National Socialist ideology. In contrast to the traditional justice system, by which a judgment was based on deductive reasoning according to the evidence of a case presented as fact and the interpretation of recorded statutes with a reasonable sense of objectivity, justice in National Socialist Germany was also to be administered in accordance with unwritten laws. The legality of Hitler's will as unwritten law, which actually represented the interests of the NSDAP, ostensibly emanated from the interests of the nation. Hitler disclosed his purposes for the law in a speech to the *Reichstag* concerning the enactment of the "Enabling Law," stating that the government of the "National Revolution" had a duty to protect the nation from elements that consciously and intentionally acted against the nation's interests. Equality before the law was only to be granted to those who supported the national interest and "didn't fail to support the Government while the centre of legal concern was the nation rather than the individual."[28]

National Socialist legislation abolished the principle of *nullum crimen sine lege* that had governed the justice system before the National Socialist regime was established. The principle dictated that an individual could only be prosecuted for an act considered illegal according to the provisions of a law prescribing a penalty for criminal actions.[29] The retroactive sanction of the murders of *Sturmabteilung* (SA) leaders as enemies of the state on 30 June and 1 and 2 July 1934[30] demonstrated the arbitrariness with which the interests of the regime could be pursued.Those criminal actions were legalised retroactively, since the political leadership considered them "necessary for the self-defence of the State."[31]

The principle of *nulla poena sine lege* was officially suspended through the "Law to Change the Criminal Code on 28 June 1935," which introduced a new conception of the justice system. Judges were obliged to impose penalties according to "healthy popular emotions" (*gesundes Volksempfinden*), rather than "merely" according to the provisions of the law as it was written.[32] Actions could therefore be considered offences against the state according to that analogy, rather than strictly according to the facts of the case, thus enabling National Socialist ideology to be applied as law.[33] That law subverted the spirit and method of interpreting criminal law by empowering judges to pass judgments and impose penalties for actions not defined as criminal according to recorded statutes.[34] Any action that violated so-called "healthy popular emotions" was to be prosecuted, although there were no specific legal provisions to deal with such "violations." Since the leadership of the regime determined what those "emotions" were supposed to be, the arbitrariness of the leadership as the embodiment of the nation was made a principle of law.[35] Criminal law was thus marked by the severity of its application and the scope of political offences.

In contrast to the "liberalistic" notion that criminals deserved humanitarian treatment, the regime emphasised meting out harsh sentences.[36] That in itself was a perversion of justice, since it's been argued that "the most extreme justice is the greatest injustice."[37] Defendants in criminal cases were to be considered enemies of the state.[38] All criminal actions were considered offences against the nation, thus transforming the administration of criminal justice into a political instrument.[39]

Legislation intended for the implementation of ideological goals, such as preserving the "Aryan" race as a focal point of National Socialism, was put into practice through anti-Semitic legislation.[40] The most notorious were the Nuremberg Laws of 15 September 1935, which defined citizenship according to racial and civil qualifications.[41] The principle of equality of all people before the law was thus substituted with the notion of racial homogeneity.[42] A widespread example of not affording Jews the protection of law followed the so-called *Kristallnacht* of 8 November 1938. Those who took part in that anti-Jewish pogrom weren't brought to trial for their actions,[43] and Jews were denied the right to claim legal compensation for the destruction or damage of their property.[44] A series of laws and ordinances also blocked Jews from various occupations,[45] made their property subject to state control, limited their freedom of movement, eliminated claims for public assistance, and prohibited their access to cultural activities and education.[46]

The meaning of civil law procedure was changed from the protection of the individual to the protection of the "way of life of the German nation."[47] The decline of the former civil law principles were marked by the practices of expropriating property, mainly without compensation; and the depriving of Jews of their civil law rights.[48] The first practice was indicative of the fact that the principle of equality before the law had been redefined on the basis of race;[49] and the second was indicative of the undermining of property rights and the disposal of assets.[50]

Although wide areas of civil law remained unchanged,[51] some parts of civil law were changed in accordance with the concepts of the National Socialist state. For example, revised marriage law forbade marriage between German citizens or persons of "related blood" and those with "foreign blood" as defined by the "Law for the Protection of German Blood and Honour" of 15 September 1935, which was instituted to preserve "national health" (*Volksgesundheit*).[52] Other examples included legislation concerning hereditary farms and inheritance. The revised law on hereditary farms set forth new provisions for the organisation of agricultural life and racial qualifications for farmers,[53] and a new law regarding testaments decreed that the manner of disposing bequeathed property would be annulled if the person leaving the inheritance contravened "healthy popular emotions."[54]

The most concerted attempt to perpetuate the National Socialist reconstruction of the law was undertaken by the Academy of German Law (*Akademie für Deutsches Recht*), whose purpose was to develop a concept of justice in accordance with National Socialist ideology.[55] The academy was to participate in legal education and research while working in close cooperation with the NSDAP and state legal agencies.[56] Hans Frank, the academy's president,[57] believed that the academy could contribute to creating an authoritarian *Rechtsstaat* based on National Socialist legal principles representing the interests of the *Volksgemeinschaft*.[58]

The academy was composed of an increasing number of committees that were to undertake various tasks, such as developing ideas to lay the groundwork for the National Socialist reorganisation of all existing law and its codification. However, in practice, its influence was negligible.[59] The academy failed to produce a proposed National Law Code (*Volksgesetzbuch*) that would have replaced the civil code,[60] and most of the proposals drafted by the academy's various committees weren't applied in the justice system.[61] The efforts to formulate a justice system based on National Socialist principles of law were subordinated to the arbitrariness of the authoritarian *Führerstaat*.[62] Hence, the justice system in National Socialist Germany was permeated with legislative and extralegal abuses of the law, rather than being wholly restructured.

The Coordination and Function of the Administration of Justice

The transfer of judicial sovereignty from the *Länder* to the *Reich* was the most incisive change of the judicial organisation in National Socialist Germany.[63] The justice system that had been organised among the German *Länder* during the Weimar period was transferred to the jurisdiction of the national government as part of the National Socialist *Gleichschaltung*, thus bringing it under the control of the regime.

Administrative matters concerning the justice system were concentrated in the *Reich* Ministry of Justice. Policies concerning judicial personnel and administration in the various *Länder* were thus unified[64] at the national level. In contrast to the pre-1933 situation, when judges were either appointed by the responsible *Land* minister or minister-president or elected to office in Hamburg and Bremen, the *Reich* minister of justice recommended candidates for judicial office who were then appointed to office by Hitler.[65] The unification of judicial organisations also cleared the way for state interference in court proceedings throughout Germany. The state was empowered to interfere in pending court procedures by allowing the *Reich* president to halt criminal proceedings and to grant reprieves.[66] Legal practice, in accordance with the precepts of National Socialist ideology, was reinforced through the control of the various organisations of jurists. Associations of jurists were reorganised to ensure their conformity to National Socialist ideology. All jurists were compelled to join the German Legal Front (*Rechtsfront*), founded on 1 June 1933 and consisting of organisations involved in promoting and protecting the law as an instrument for organising all German jurists.[67] The leading element of that broad organisation was the *Bund Nationalsozialistischer deutscher Juristen*[68] (BNSDJ), which integrated all professional judicial organisations to "unite and cleanse the entire German legal profession in order to fulfill the promise of the Party Program in returning Germany to a governance of indigenous racial law."[69] Jurists who didn't join that organisation risked being considered an enemy of the regime.

The dissolution of the former judicial associations and their incorporation into the BNSDJ gave the National Socialist regime a free hand to supervise, train, and "align" the judiciary with the appropriate political orientation, or National Socialist *Weltanschauung*.[70] The training work of the organisation wasn't particularly successful, consisting of strictly compulsory attendance of lectures that were generally sketchy. On the other hand, its supervision and spying functions placed jurists in danger[71] of coming under suspicion for disloyalty to the regime.

Most jurists joined the BNSDJ as a substitute for belonging to the dissolved former professional organisations, since it appeared, at least in the beginning, to be a way of avoiding the political action of joining the NSDAP and also as a way of avoiding any further demands or pressures without actually making any thoroughgoing commitment to the regime.[72] On the other hand, their membership in professional organisations made them subject to the jurisdiction of "honour courts," which adjudicated in matters concerning professional offences and breaches of National Socialist principles that were penalised as professional offences. For example, one honour court expelled a lawyer from the profession for having refused to give the "voluntary" Hitler salute.[73]

Jurists who were members of the NSDAP were also subject to the jurisdiction of the NSDAP party courts.[74] Those courts were responsible for maintaining discipline among the members of the NSDAP and its affiliated organisations. Members of those organisations were responsible for upholding their duties toward *Führer*, nation, and state, and were to be tried for any violation of those duties.[75]

Standards for the admission of lawyers and their conduct within the profession were also redefined on the basis of National Socialist legislation. The "Law Concerning the Admission of Lawyers," promulgated on 7 April 1933, contained the provisions of the "Civil Service Law," including the so-called "Aryan clause" that excluded "non-Aryans" from practicing law. Anyone who had participated in Communist activities was likewise barred from appointment.[76] Newly appointed lawyers were to swear an oath of allegiance to Hitler in the execution of their duties.[77] Their supervision was reinforced by establishing probationary periods for new lawyers of at least one year, and up to several years in exceptional cases, at the discretion of the *Reich* Minister of Justice.

The decision for the appointment of lawyers rested with the *Reich* Minister of Justice, in agreement with the *Reichsführer* of the *Bund Nationalsozialistischer Deutscher Juristen.*[78] In practice, that meant admission to the bar association became a privilege granted by the state to loyal supporters of the government, rather than a right earned by an individual based on the results of the bar examination.[79] Lawyers were thereafter subject to discipline and supervision for political reliability in the practice of the profession.[80] Honour courts were established in every local bar association chamber (*Rechtsanwaltskammer*) to adjudicate in offences against the discharge of duties. Potential penalties included warnings, reproaches, monetary fines of up to RM 5,000, or expulsion from the profession.[81]

The National Socialist regime brought enormous pressure to bear upon both the functioning and the organisation of the justice system. Although the independence of the judiciary wasn't formally abolished, the tenure of judicial office was directly influenced by political considerations. National Socialist civil service legislation put pressures on judges to join the NSDAP or one its affiliated organisations in order to demonstrate loyalty to the regime. The preponderance of political considerations contravened the practice of maintaining the impartiality of court proceedings by redefining the principle of judicial independence. The principle had previously meant that judges were subject solely to the force of the law in pronouncing judgments and that they were guaranteed the permanent security of their office. They couldn't be removed from office or transferred on the basis of pronouncing judgments that didn't contravene the law.[82] Judicial independence was henceforth to serve as a vessel of the National Socialist conception of law and state, rather than following the constitutional principle of the separation of law and state.[83] In practice, that meant the role of judges was reduced to safeguarding the ideology of the regime and carrying out its orders.[84]

Judges remained subject to the criminal code provision on the perversion of the course of justice (Art. 336) if they didn't administer justice according to the spirit of National Socialism, such as failing to deviate from the former principles of justice by applying the law on the basis of "healthy popular emotions."[85] The tenure of judicial office was also made contingent upon their political reliability. This ensured their conformity in applying National Socialist ideology to the administration of justice. Political reliability became a condition for civil service appointment, which, in practice, was more important than technical qualifications.[86]

Nonconformists and other such unsuitable jurists were initially expelled from the judiciary under provisions of the "Law for the Reconstruction of the Professional Civil Service" of 7 April 1933.[87] Individuals who didn't demonstrate loyalty to the government or lacked the appropriate political predispositions or heritage, such as members of leftist political parties or "non-Aryans," were dismissed from government service.[88] The law was a direct affront to the principle of judicial independence,[89] but that was irrelevant in view of the conception of the state that the National Socialist regime intended to establish. The extent of the implementation of the law was demonstrated in a statement released by the Prussian Minister of Justice on 18 February 1934, which noted that only 374 judges remained in their positions out of 1,034 who had previously been judges in Berlin.[90]

The law of 7 April 1933 was later extended by the "German Civil Service Law" of 26 January 1937,[91] which stated that civil servants who didn't demonstrate sufficient guarantees of support for the National Socialist state were to be dismissed.[92] It was thus no longer sufficient to belong to the NS-Rechtswahrerbund (NSRB)[93] to allay suspicion of disloyalty to the regime. Civil servants were also responsible for observing occurrences within the civil service that could be considered offensive to the NSDAP, and for reporting such occurrences.[94] The appointment of new judges who were loyal to National Socialism was to be approved by a representative of the *Führer*.[95] Judges were to apply the law in accordance with political considerations, rather than being guided solely by their responsibility to the law, and thereby to exercise the will of the state in order to demonstrate their political reliability. They were obliged to follow National Socialist legal theory under the new judicial oath of office, introduced on 20 August 1934.[96] Judges thereafter swore loyalty and obedience to the *Führer* and to adhere to the law, which, in practice, meant exercising the will of the *Führer* as his representatives in the justice system.[97]

The role of the judge was to administer the law as a representative of the National Socialist state in order to uphold the interests of the nation.[98] Judges were to act as followers of the *Führer*, and thereby to apply the law with the internal conviction of the political will of the nation and the state leadership in protecting the security of the nation, as if Hitler himself were hearing the case.[99] Judicial independence was to be understood as being rooted in National Socialism and loyalty to the *Führer* as the supreme judge, which meant that judges couldn't act upon their consciences in contradiction to healthy popular emotions, the NSDAP programme, and the announcements of the *Führer* in addition to the law.[100] Judges remained formally independent by being bound solely to the law insofar as they adhered to the values of the *Volksgemeinschaft* or will of the *Führer*. Judges were thus obliged to pronounce sentences on the basis of the law as it was written, as well as according to vague National Socialist legal theory, which was based on emotions rather than facts, and unfamiliar to most judges.[101] Whether or not they were convinced National Socialists, the regime continually viewed judges with suspicion about whether they conformed to National Socialist standards in the administration of justice.[102]

Political considerations also distorted the role of lawyers. The National Socialist conception of law dictated that a lawyer take the interests of the state into account, rather than the interests of the client.[103] Before the National Socialist regime was established, the office of the public prosecutor (*Staatsanwaltschaft*) was responsible for examining witnesses and defendants, to determine how an offender had violated the law according to the statutes, and to determine the appropriate penalty.[104] As was the case with judges, public prosecutors in the National Socialist regime were turned into servants of the state whose first interest was loyalty to the *Führer* and his will as the embodiment of the law.[105] Public prosecutors seldom played an active role in court proceedings, since judges anticipated their questions.[106]

The role of defence counsel was also undermined in court proceedings that had lost their former impartiality. Although defence counsellors could at least ensure that the defendant underwent the proper course of court proceedings,[107] they were responsible for defending the interests of the state before those of the defendant.[108] They were always faced with the danger of being called to account for remarks made during court proceedings in political cases.[109]

Rather than attempt to influence trial proceedings solely through factual arguments, the defence was only to emphasise personal factors. In one such example, a defence counsel attempted to undermine the evidence presented by the plaintiff, a member of the NSDAP, by questioning his loyalty to the NSDAP. The defence argued that since the person had told neighbours that he wanted his son to join the *Wehrmacht* rather than the Waffen SS, the elite military corps of the NSDAP, his loyalty was too suspect for his evidence to have any credibility.[110] The defence counsel could otherwise attempt to plead for a reduced sentence on the basis of a defendant's upright personality, lack of previous convictions, or respectable work record,[111] or on the basis of what the court considered a defendant's genuine repentance.[112] The mercy of the court could be acquired on the basis of a defendant's demonstrated support for the National Socialist regime, such as early membership in the NSDAP.[113]

Criminal law was applied with increasing severity and frequency from the beginning of the National Socialist regime, and reached a culminating point of extreme severity during the Second World War, when it took on the character of an instrument of terror and annihilation.[114] The brutality with which the law could be applied was characterised by the number of offences that were punishable by death during the regime, which was raised from three to forty-six.[115] Criminal courts were charged with the task of securing the power of the state on the home front during World War II,[116] which, in practice, meant upholding the interests of the regime by using the force of law and by addressing wartime exigencies.

A defendant in a criminal case could only be allowed defence counsel in certain types of cases, such as at a main hearing before an *Oberlandesgericht* or a *Landgericht*, if the defendant was deaf or mute, or if the severity or complexity of the case made the participation of defence counsel necessary, either for the entire course of the proceedings or in part.[117] Defence counsel was ordinarily no longer permitted to serve in trials before an *Amtsgericht* in the interest of sparing personnel[118] who could be made available for the war effort.

That law also simplified court proceedings, in order to raise the efficiency of the courts[119] by accelerating proceedings. Jury courts, which previously had been staffed with reliable jurors appointed by the NSDAP executive or its representatives, were abolished altogether, in the interest of sparing personnel for the war effort.[120] The functions of jurors were thereafter assumed by judges.[121]

Legislation was enacted for the purpose of prosecuting offences specifically relating to wartime conditions. Anyone who destroyed or hoarded vital raw materials, finished products, or money was to be imprisoned, or in serious cases sentenced to death.[122] Courts were to pronounce sentences of imprisonment or death in cases of exploiting air raid conditions to commit a crime or misdemeanour, and death sentences for cases of arson or other serious crimes that undermined the defence effort, as well as imprisonment for criminal actions committed while exploiting wartime conditions, or a death sentence when actions were deemed especially reprehensible according to healthy popular emotions.[123] Individuals normally subject to the ordinary judicial organisation could be subject to trial in a military court if they had taken part in a criminal offence in which a person subject to military court jurisdiction was also implicated.[124] The *Führer* or the supreme commander of the *Wehrmacht* could order court proceedings to be resumed after a court had passed a verdict.[125] Anyone who endangered national defence, such as by destroying, abandoning, or damaging weaponry or equipment, or by damaging the work of an important enterprise necessary for that purpose, was to be sentenced to at least six months to life in prison, or in serious cases to death. Whoever participated in or supported a pacifist organisation, had contact with a prisoner of war in a manner that violated healthy popular emotions, or was involved in collecting or transmitting news on military affairs was to be imprisoned.[126]

The guarantee of judicial independence was abolished altogether upon the outbreak of the Second World War.[127] The government decreed that all civil servants could be transferred to another office or kept out of retirement whenever it was deemed necessary.[128] Hitler later declared himself "supreme judge" on 26 April 1942, claiming the ultimate authority to supervise the justice system. Rather than administer justice solely according to the letter of the law, judges were made responsible for administering justice as representatives of the interests of the nation. Judges could be removed from office if they didn't "recognise the needs of the hour."[129] The *Reichstag* passed a resolution stating that the *Führer* was unconditionally empowered to use whatever means necessary to urge every German, including every soldier and judge, to fulfill duties that would enable the nation to achieve victory. Any violation of those duties would be met with an unconditional removal from office, rank, or position.[130] The passing of this resolution cleared the way for unlimited state interference in the functions of the judiciary.

The passing of this resolution eradicated the last vestiges of the formality of judicial independence.[131] It entrenched the idea that the will of the people, as expressed through the *Führer*, overrode the provisions of legislation in order to uphold the interests of the nation in all circumstances. That declaration also indicated that a considerable number of judges up to that date had not conformed to Hitler's will in the administration of justice.[132] Although relatively few judges were dismissed on the basis of the 26 April 1942 resolution, mainly due to wartime personnel shortages, it raised the uncertainty of each individual judge's tenure of office.[133] Hitler issued a special decree on 20 August 1942 that authorised Otto Thierack, the *Reich* Minister of Justice, to deviate from existing laws and construct a National Socialist justice system that would further "bring the administration of justice into conformity with the needs of the regime."[134]

The primacy of law in the justice system had become practically redundant as the exigencies of state security surpassed knowledge of the law and its application. A new height of the regime's interference in the justice system was reached by Hitler's *Reichstag* speech of 26 April 1942, culminating in the issuing of the "Judges' Letters."[135] These were documents sent to judges and prosecutors by Thierack after 7 September 1942, in which he presented what he considered to be exemplary court decisions,[136] followed by an evaluation statement criticising or praising each decision.[137] Judges were expected to become more familiar with the National Socialist conception of administering justice by following those examples and to pass suitable sentences accordingly.[138] Since the court decisions were publicised, judges were made aware that their decisions could be publicly reprimanded for not being in accordance with the National Socialist conception of the law. They could also face a worse possibility—that the Ministry of Justice would deem them "politically unreliable."[139]

"Lawyers' Letters," introduced on 1 October 1944, served the same purpose as "Judges' Letters," instructing lawyers to comply with the priority of upholding the interests of the nation over those of the individual. These letters were specifically aimed at lawyers acting as defence counsels.[140] The letters' purpose was to familiarise lawyers with court decisions pertaining to wartime necessities, and to thereby save time by dispensing with unnecessary work from pending court cases, such as matters relating to counter-objections, appeals, and legal remedies.[141] The administration of justice was supervised to ensure that it conformed to the demands of the regime, and court decisions could be rescinded in view of that purpose. Hitler always regarded the judiciary of ordinary law courts with suspicion, and depended upon "law-enforcement" organisations that weren't restricted by laws or regulations for the regular judicial process.

The judiciary and the bar association were continually supervised by the *Geheime Staatspolizei* (*Gestapo*) and the *Sicherheitsdienst* (SD) to ensure that the disposition of cases was politically in accordance with the standards of National Socialist justice. The purpose of the SD, as the intelligence branch of the SS, was to investigate the relationship between various spheres of public life and the state while the *Gestapo* dealt with more specific political matters. The

Gestapo initially investigated antistate activities in Prussia, but spread throughout Germany as the separate *Land* political police forces were consolidated under the control of *Gestapo* headquarters in Berlin. In turn, the *Gestapo* was later incorporated into the *Schutzstaffel* (SS), which then assumed control over all police matters in Germany.[142]

The purpose of the political police was to function as an instrument for suppressing political opposition to the state, as well as for "correcting" the justice system in matters that weren't openly expounded in the law.[143] Acting as a state agency that was independent of the rules of the civil administration, the *Gestapo* held the authority to circumvent judicial decisions by arresting individuals and sending them to concentration camps or special *Gestapo* prisons without trial for an indefinite period.[144] Pastor Martin Niemöller, for example, and others like him who opposed the regime, was brought to a concentration camp immediately after having been acquitted by an ordinary law court.[145]

Defendants who received sentences that the political authorities considered too mild were transferred to the custody of the *Gestapo*. The practice of "correcting" court decisions took place with increasing frequency after the beginning of the Second World War.[146] Since "outright" acquittals commonly resulted in the subsequent arrest of the accused by the *Gestapo*, judges and lawyers in the ordinary judicial organisation would sometimes protect the accused by "agreeing" to imprisonment sentences that were essentially unlawful. However, taking that course of action could be beneficial for the accused, since they would be incarcerated in a judicature prison rather than a concentration camp.[147]

Another form of what could be considered judicial resistance was to pronounce appropriate sentences while promoting one's loyalty to the regime by disguising verdicts with National Socialist platitudes.[148] While fair trials and independent judgments weren't guaranteed by law and were solely contingent upon the personality of the individual judge,[149] there were judges who didn't accept the precepts of National Socialism in the administration of justice. The SD reported in October 1942 that virtually all judges were to be reproached for not pronouncing judgments that concurred with the prevailing political circumstances. It was therefore considered necessary for the political police to obstruct judicial independence.[150]

Both the police and the criminal justice system were responsible for maintaining the security of the internal national order (*Volksordnung*), and the common basis for their activity was political correctness. Whereas both institutions were to work toward the same objective, criminal courts often pronounced judgments that the political police considered inadequate in view of political necessities. As a result, the police began to counteract those judgments with increasing frequency.[151] Hence, the judiciary was responsible for administering justice according to the National Socialist perspective, which was ensured by the political police, to compensate for the shortcomings of the judiciary. In contrast to the former practice of judicial independence, judges remained independent as long as they remained aware of the National Socialist spirit of the law and administered justice accordingly.

Administrative and Labour Courts

The subjugation of the justice system to the National Socialist regime affected the specialised branches of the justice system as well as the ordinary law courts. Since the National Socialist *Gleichschaltung* was to encompass all branches of the German state and society, individual rights and individuals in positions of authority, such as judges, were overshadowed by the authority of the regime, which sought to impose its conception of state and society upon all judicial institutions. As a consequence, the functions of the labour and administrative judicial organisations were reoriented toward serving the state, rather than serving to protect the interests of individuals in labour disputes and grievances lodged against the state.

The concept of the law as a state institution for the protection of individual interests conflicted with the National Socialist regimentation of state and society, and therefore couldn't be maintained. The responsibility of the administrative courts, which had been responsible for the judicial protection of civil rights, inevitably conflicted with the National Socialist regime. Judges were to be guided by their acceptance of the "national order" and public interest, as defined by the state leadership, rather than the rights of the individual and the separation of state and society.

Since it was presumed that the *Führer* and his followers were united, conflicts of interest between state and society were theoretically "abolished." Hence, their continued existence was acceptable, as long as administrative court judges adjudicated in accordance with the National Socialist concept of state and society.[152] Therefore, those courts remained in place, while relinquishing certain types of cases, such as examining arrests by the *Gestapo* or so-called "political cases" that were "understood" to be outside of their jurisdiction and emphasising that what was considered the common good outweighed individual rights.[153]

The "Prussian Law Concerning the *Gestapo*" of 10 February 1936 stated that its orders couldn't be reviewed by the administrative courts.[154] The right of the individual to protection under the law was increasingly undermined as governmental and police actions were frequently exempted from review by a law court. Legal review was eliminated from the state matters that the National Socialist leaders had determined to be "political."[155] Administrative court jurisdiction was therefore adjusted to the new situation, and the protection of the individual under the law was displaced by the extended political power of the regime over the individual.[156]

The function of the labour courts was also redefined in accordance with the concepts of the National Socialist state. Labour relations were reorganised to represent the "old Germanic community of leader and follower," rather than a liberal philosophy based on individual and collective contracts governing employer-employee relations. Employers and employees were to compose a "community," working jointly for the interest of the nation—the National Socialist state—rather than being organised as business and labour, which both held political power that could represent potential resistance[157] to the state.

The reorganisation of labour relations made the labour courts practically redundant. Wage agreements could no longer be concluded after the trade unions were dissolved on 2 May 1933, and industrial actions were proscribed. Disputes in industrial relations were transferred to state labour trustees.[158] Labour was recast into a new conception, by which labour was a social duty rather than an individual right.[159] A labour trustee, appointed by the *Reich* Minister of Labour, was entrusted with dealing with labour relations in every enterprise,[160] and the German Labour Front (*Deutsche Arbeitsfront*) was established to replace the trade unions.[161]

The system of labour courts was later effectively eliminated through the "Law for the Organisation of Labour" of 20 January 1934, or National Socialist "Labour Charter."[162] The previous decrees that had regulated employer-employee relations, such as collective agreements, arbitration, the Works Council Law, and Section 152 of the Industrial Code guaranteeing freedom of organisation, were displaced by that law. Democratic employee representation was abolished, and the organisation of labour was shifted to individual enterprises, in which employers and employees were redefined as leaders and followers. The community within the enterprise (*Betriebsgemeinschaft*) was to further the interests of the enterprise, and thereby the nation.[163] Common interests within the enterprise were to be maintained by social honour courts, which prosecuted violations of the rights and duties of followers and leaders. They were to safeguard the social honour, fulfilling the responsibility of duty to the enterprise community, which was to govern relations between leaders and followers in every enterprise.[164]

Labour disputes could be adjudicated by the amended labour courts law of 10 April 1934.[165] However, labour courts could no longer deal with disputes regarding the freedom of coalition, collective agreements, works councils, economic organisations, strikes, and lockouts, since those types of disputes were obsolete. The labour courts henceforth basically dealt with disputes between individual employers and employees or between two workers.[166] The division of jurisdiction between the labour and the social honour courts depended upon the intention of a violation. Social honour courts had jurisdiction in disputes involving wages, working hours, or inadequate housing conditions, if those cases had resulted from "unsocial motives, abuse of authority, and malicious intent." On the other hand, labour courts maintained jurisdiction over cases involving "honest differences of opinion" or "underpayment made in good faith." Consistently paying wages below rates according to the collective rules, irregular payment, and neglecting to pay insurance fees were considered "malicious exploitation of labour with abuse of authority, unless the employer was unable to pay."[167] In addition to limiting the jurisdiction of the labour courts and National Socialist measures for purging and "synchronising" the justice system, lay representatives and judges in the labour courts were replaced by individuals who were loyal adherents to the regime.[168]

The National Socialist Extraordinary Courts

Cases directly concerning opposition to the National Socialist regime were removed from the jurisdiction of ordinary law courts. The most significant aspect of the administration of justice in National Socialist Germany was its role in the suppression of actual or alleged hostility toward the regime. New state institutions were created for that purpose, circumventing the judicial organisation. Article 105 of the Weimar Constitution, guaranteeing free access to ordinary law courts and prohibiting extraordinary courts,[169] was abrogated as part of the process of subordinating the judicial organisation to political exigencies.

Extraordinary courts were established to deal with alleged offences committed against the National Socialist regime. Jurisdiction over such offences was held by extraordinary courts: the "People's Court" (*Volksgerichtshof*) and the special courts (*Sondergerichte*). The extraordinary courts adjudicated in those types of cases while the ordinary law courts remained in place. Whereas law courts in a *Rechtsstaat* served as a check upon arbitrary actions of the executive in the interest of upholding justice, their authority was undermined in the National Socialist state in the interests of political expediency.[170] The political leadership relied upon those courts to satisfactorily meet its demands in the adjudication of what it considered to be political cases.[171]

Cases of treason were initially in the jurisdiction of the Supreme Court (*Reichsgericht*)[172] until those cases were transferred to a "People's Court" (*Volksgerichtshof*). The *Volksgerichtshof* was established on 26 April 1934 to try all cases of high treason, treason, and attacks against the state and members of the national or *Land* governments.[173] The primary cause for the establishing of that court was Hitler's dissatisfaction with the outcome of the *Reichstag* fire trial. Hitler had hoped to exploit that trial to demonstrate the existence of a Communist conspiracy,[174] but most of the Communist defendants in the trial were acquitted.[175] The underlying purpose of that court was to suppress political opposition to the regime and to familiarise German society with the concept of National Socialist justice. Rather than prosecuting defendants for their actions, the court convicted them on the basis of their attitudes toward National Socialism. Any defendant who didn't demonstrate support for the regime was considered a traitor.[176]

The *Reich* Chancellor appointed the members of the court, which consisted of two professional judges, screened for their loyalty to the regime, and two or three lay assessors serving as judges who possessed special knowledge about the "defence against subversive activities" or were "intimately connected with the political trends of the nation." The president of the court, one of the two presiding judges, was to approve the defence counsel. The evidence presented by the defence could be refused, and decisions of the court couldn't be appealed.

According to Heinrich Parrisus, a senior prosecutor of the *Volksgerichtshof*, the purpose of that court "was not to dispense impartial justice 'but to annihilate the enemies of National Socialism.'"[177] In practice, the purpose of the court was to terrorise the public through severe penalties, secret proceedings, and the abrogation of most of the rights of the accused, who wasn't allowed to choose defence counsel.[178] The president of the court selected defence counsellors who were invariably politically reliable members of the NSDAP.[179]

Whereas the *Volksgerichtshof* dealt with the most outstanding actions of opposition to the regime, the *Sondergerichte* heard cases of various types of real or apparent opposition. The *Sondergerichte*, composed of three judges and defence counsel appointed by the court, were initially set up in each *Oberlandesgericht* district.[180] In general, the jurisdiction of those courts extended to all actions considered hostile to the NSDAP, the government, and later, to the continuation of the Second World War. Their initial jurisdiction extended to all offences committed under the conditions of the "*Reichstag* Fire Decree" and the "Decree to Protect the Government of the National Socialist Revolution from Treacherous Attacks" of 21 March 1933. Its judgments couldn't be appealed.[181] The jurisdiction of those courts was defined by a series of legislative enactments dealing with political offences. They were responsible for adjudicating acts of political violence, which were subject to sentences of up to fifteen years, life imprisonment, or death.[182]

Their jurisdiction over political offences[183] was widely extended by the "Law of 20 December 1934 against Insidious Attacks upon the State and Party and for the Protection of the Party Uniform." Anyone who made a false statement offending the welfare of the national government or the esteem in which it was held, the political leadership, the NSDAP, or any of its affiliated organisations, was subject to imprisonment ranging from three months to two years.[184] Instigating revolt, arousing alarm or terror among the population, or causing difficulties for the *Reich* abroad could be penalised with imprisonment ranging from three years to life, or in exceptional cases, the death penalty.[185]

Their jurisdiction in dealing with political offences was extended by the "Law for the Guarantee of Peace Based on Law" on 13 October 1933, which prescribed the death penalty, imprisonment for up to fifteen years, or life in prison for anyone who attempted to kill or sanctioned the killing of a judge, public prosecutor, police authority, or any other state official out of political motives.[186] Their jurisdiction was later extended to criminal as well as political offences by the ordinance of 20 November 1938.

These courts were authorised to deal with any act that the public prosecutor believed aroused the public, or if the gravity or baseness of the crime called for immediate prosecution by the *Sondergerichte*. Such cases were removed from the jurisdiction of the *Schwurgerichte* (*Landgerichte* with a jury) and the *Amtsgerichte*.[187] Hence, the administration of justice on the basis of "healthy popular emotions" in criminal cases was extended, further undermining the function of the ordinary law courts. After the outbreak of the Second World War, those courts were established in every *Landgericht* district and assumed jurisdiction over all cases presumed to seriously endanger public order and security.[188] The *Reich* Minister of Justice, Otto Thierack, explained that the courts were initially established to serve as "sharp weapons of the state leadership (*Staatsführung*) for sentencing political criminal offences" or "summary courts-martial of the home front."[189]

Upon the beginning of World War II, their jurisdiction was extended through the ordinances of 1 September 1939[190] and 5 December 1939.[191] An ordinance of 21 February 1940 extended their jurisdiction in dealing with all offences that the prosecuting authorities considered necessary for immediate adjudication by those courts—acts that were severe or reprehensible, aroused popular indignation, endangered public order and security, or contravened enactments relating to the implementation of the Four-Year Plan.[192] The wartime ordinances extended the jurisdiction of the *Sondergerichte* with the power of imposing the death sentence for offences such as intentionally circulating news from foreign radio broadcasts that endangered the defence effort,[193] civilian plundering of evacuated buildings and areas,[194] violent crimes, or armed assaults and threats.[195] An increasing number of death sentences, especially after the beginning of the war, indicated the severity with which the law was applied. The number of death sentences passed by all law courts were as follows:[196]

1933–39: 664
1940: 250
1941: 1,292
1942: 3,641
1943: 5,336
1944: 4,264

Those courts were able to function flexibly and rapidly, by not being required to conduct a pretrial investigation or to open a trial by determining that the charges introduced by the prosecution were justifiable. The extent of the evidence to be considered was decided by the court itself,[197] and defence attorneys couldn't question the proof of the charges. Verdicts were enforceable immediately, and there was no right of appeal.[198]

The characteristics of the *Sondergerichte* thus violated the legal principle of due process and fulfilled the desire of National Socialist authorities for pronouncing harsh sentences rapidly. In practice, it signified intimidating the public through arbitrary psychological terror, operating like the courts of the Inquisition.[199] The number of those courts was greatly increased as the workload increased to an extraordinary extent during the war, since their jurisdiction extended over all significant criminal cases.

The *Sondergerichte* had a strong deterrent effect during the first years of their operation, since their rapid and severe sentencing was feared. As a result, the emphasis on the administration of criminal justice was transferred from the ordinary law courts (*Amtsgerichte* and *Landgerichte*) to the *Sondergerichte* in the course of their development, to the extent that they became considered a special part of the criminal justice system, and ordinary criminal courts correspondingly lost their significance as the jurisdiction of the *Sondergerichte* was extended. Some criminal courts had hardly any work, while the *Sondergerichte* were constantly overburdened with cases that threatened to slow down the rate of adjudication. The initial deterrent effect of the *Sondergerichte* thereby became diluted, since they were responsible for hearing relatively insignificant minor offences, such as illegal animal slaughter and illegal fishing by foreigners.

The extension of their jurisdiction and the increase in the number of those courts resulted in various difficulties. Many of their judgments weren't uniformly consistent. For example, a person accused of the theft of weaving materials was considered to have committed an act offensive to the nation (*Volksschädlingstat*) and was sentenced to four years in prison, while a very similar case, heard by another chamber at the same *Sondergericht*, was sentenced to only eight months.

Many judges who had been drawn from the ordinary law courts to serve in the *Sondergerichte* lacked suitable qualifications—especially political qualifications—that judges had possessed during the early years of operation. A great number of judges serving with a *Sondergericht* by July 1943 had never been members of the NSDAP. In addition to the types of cases that were to be heard by those courts, the one essential difference, in contrast to the ordinary administration of criminal justice, was that there was no right to appeal their decisions.[200]

The primary purpose of the National Socialist extraordinary courts was to apply the law in cases in which the state had a direct interest, rather than to administer actual justice. The former principles of justice were suspended in their adjudication of political offences that had been removed from the jurisdiction of ordinary courts, which weren't entrusted with that function. The extraordinary courts represented how the National Socialist regime intended justice to be administered according to the unwritten law of National Socialist justice—no real or apparent opposition to the National Socialist regime would be tolerated. Any resistance was considered a political offence that contravened the National Socialist conception of justice, by which all individuals who contravened the demands of the regime were subject to prosecution.

Conclusion

The National Socialist regime reorganised the political order and the justice system in order to bring society under its complete control. As a consequence, the precepts of the rule of law were disregarded to serve that purpose. The purpose of the law in National Socialist Germany was redefined in accordance with the concepts of the regime and was used to advance the regime's demands rather than the common interests of state and society.

Justice, according to the rule of law in a liberal-democratic society, is based upon the relative objectivity of existing laws that govern a society of individuals equally and that protect their interests as well as those of the state. That notion was incompatible with the ideology of the National Socialist regime, which redefined the society of National Socialist Germany as a national community united by virtue of "race," and the common interests of individuals in that national community, which were expressed through the will of the political leadership of the regime. Hence, the application of law was directed toward the interests of the regime while the interests of individuals were secondary.

The principal purpose of National Socialist justice was to bring pressure to bear upon society to ensure its conformity to the regime. As a result of such intimidation, people feared being brought before courts that had been given the duty of suppressing opposition to the regime. Jurists engaged in the administration of justice at the time of the National Socialist takeover, and subsequent jurists who entered into its service, were compelled to function in accordance with the demands of the regime and its conception of the law.

Whether jurists had any actual commitment to the National Socialist regime depended upon the individual. There were few jurists who had been members of the NSDAP or its affiliated organisations before 1933. Of the 7,000 judges in Prussia, for example, only 30 had been members of the NSDAP before January 1933.[201] On the other hand, the changed political situation led to a dramatic increase within a short period of time. More than 54 percent of judges and prosecutors were members of the NSDAP by 1938, and more than 90 percent by 1945.[202]

It's unclear whether they genuinely accepted the precepts of National Socialism or were merely safeguarding their interests by joining the NSDAP. Individuals employed in the civil service were never officially required to become members of the NSDAP,[203] and membership in the NSDAP or one of its affiliated organisations wasn't a prerequisite for joining the civil service until after 28 February 1939.[204] Individuals who joined the NSDAP could thus have been prompted by opportunism[205] rather than outright force. Joining the NSDAP also followed personal considerations, such as being dependent upon financial or professional considerations in the interest of acquiring employment or promotion,[206] as well as in merely maintaining one's livelihood by allaying suspicion of disloyalty to the state.

There were also other factors that brought pressure upon the judiciary to demonstrate loyalty to the regime. Terror and self-preservation hindered open opposition to the regime. Resistance, and the potential to stage a putsch, required organisation and instruments of power, which were held by the military rather than the judiciary.[207] Resistance by the judiciary against the state was therefore limited to actions within the justice system.

It's been argued that most judges preserved their independence, even though they were members of the NSDAP, and many judgments demonstrated that they followed their conscience through passive resistance in the dispensation of justice.[208] No evidence has been uncovered of judges who were imprisoned in concentration camps due to their sentencing decisions, or of any similar cases that affected public prosecutors.[209] However, judges were forcibly transferred to new duties for not sentencing according to the spirit of National Socialism.[210] There were many lawyers who were determined to preserve the law in the face of the injustice of the regime,[211] as well as judges who resisted the regime at great personal risk.[212] Not all criminal court judges were National Socialist "blood judges."[213]

Since the body of law was permeated rather than completely recast with National Socialist concepts, everyday court business continued, with political interference in the administration of justice in trivial criminal cases and in wide areas of civil law. The worst examples of National Socialist administration of justice—cases of excessively severe sentences that made a mockery of justice, such as those passed by the *Volksgerichtshof*—were represented by so-called "political" cases. Judges had to apply the law, and in some cases interpreted the law restrictively in order to avoid passing unjust sentences or to mitigate the severity.[214]

Instances of what authorities considered overly mild judgments took place in both the *Sondergerichte* and the ordinary criminal courts.[215] On the other hand, it cannot be denied that judges and prosecutors exercised a dangerous authority over defendants in view of the draconian sentences imposed during the National Socialist regime.[216] The administration of criminal justice in spheres of National Socialist policy terrorised the population through alarmingly harsh sentences that were imposed with increasingly barbaric severity during the Second World War.[217]

Whether or not German jurists, either quantitatively as a whole or qualitatively individually, could be considered implicated with the National Socialist regime was to be determined after the end of the Second World War, when the justice system was reconstructed with jurists who could be entrusted with resuming their functions. The collapse of the National Socialist regime and its institutions opened the question of how the effects of the "synchronisation" or "nazification" of the justice system were to be eliminated and the elements of the *Rechtsstaat* restored. The reconstruction of the *Rechtsstaat* entailed the task of restoring the judicial institutions that had been in place prior to the establishment of the National Socialist regime, and the more complex matter of staffing the postwar justice system.

2

Planning for Military Government and the Postwar Restoration of Justice

PLANNING FOR THE RESTORATION OF JUSTICE in postwar Germany began during the Second World War in the wider context of the Allied war aim to destroy the National Socialist regime. Political representatives of Allied governments and Allied military planning staffs drafted plans and policies for the reconstruction of postwar Germany. U.S. planning for the postwar Germany took place in the American government departments that prepared political policy, while military civil affairs personnel drafted plans for the nonmilitary aspects of the administration of territories that would be occupied by Allied military forces.

The main principles guiding the planning of policy for the reconstruction of justice in Germany included: abolishing the NSDAP, eradicating National Socialist legislation, removing National Socialists from the judicial organisation, and restoring the justice system that had been in place before the National Socialist regime was established. The political objectives and military civil affairs plans for the reconstruction of Germany drafted during the Second World War later formed the basis of policies implemented during the postwar Allied military occupation.

Political Planning for Postwar Germany

Political planning for the postwar occupation of Germany took place within and between the governments of the "Big Three" Allied nations—the United States, the United Kingdom, and the Soviet Union. Leaders and foreign ministers of the three major Allies discussed postwar political planning for Germany while they met to discuss the coordination of military strategy. The first concrete progress on the question took place at the Moscow Conference of Foreign Ministers (18 October–1 November 1943).

On 23 October 1943, the U.S. Secretary of State, Cordell Hull, presented policy proposals for discussion in a memorandum produced by the U.S. State Department, titled "The Political Reorganization of Germany." That memorandum included four principal goals: empowering the UN with supreme authority in Germany, establishing an inter-Allied Control Commission to supervise the terms of surrender, placing Germany under occupation by the military forces of the Big Three Allies, and removing all Nazi officials and eliminating all vestiges of National Socialism.[1]

Since the purpose of the meeting was to prepare an agenda for the subsequent Teheran Conference of the heads of state of the Big Three Allies, the foreign ministers didn't attempt to reach any formal decisions concerning post-surrender planning. They only confirmed that their governments would act jointly in matters pertaining to the defeat of Germany and its allies and to post-surrender policy-making.[2]

The discussion of that document was merely informal. Cordell Hull later stated before the U.S. Congress that arriving at a complete and rapid understanding on matters arising from post-hostilities planning required further study of possible recommendations for dealing with the non-military problems related to the administration of enemy territories. The most practical instrument for that task would be an inter-governmental commission to advise the governments of the Big Three Allies.[3]

The combined instrument for inter-Allied post-surrender planning was to be coordinated by the European Advisory Commission (EAC), established in the Moscow Protocol of 1 November 1943. The EAC was charged with the task of making joint recommendations for the surrender terms the Allies would impose on the European Axis states and for control arrangements that would ensure the execution of those terms.[4] The U.S. government would provide technical advice to the U.S. representative on the EAC, John G. Winant, the U.S. Ambassador to London. The source of that advice was the Working Security Committee (WSC),[5] a subcommittee operating within the State, War, and Navy Departments, established on 21 December 1943, to coordinate their views and to draft instructions for Ambassador Winant by supplying him with background studies, policy recommendations, and directives.[6]

The EAC began its deliberations on 14 January 1944, and eventually produced the general terms through which Allied postwar objectives in Germany would be implemented. The terms were set forth in three key documents. On 25 July 1944, the EAC adopted a draft instrument for the terms of the unconditional surrender of Germany,[7] and on 14 November 1944, the EAC adopted further agreements for the implementation of those terms.

Germany and Berlin were to be divided into occupation zones allocated to the U.S., the UK, and the Soviet Union.[8] Supreme authority would be exercised through the Allied control machinery, composed of representatives of the three occupation powers "acting jointly in matters affecting Germany as a whole"[9] and upon instructions from their governments in their respective zones of occupation.[10] The documents provided terms that later formed the basis of the Allied military occupation of Germany, but Allied policies that were to be carried out during the occupation weren't established at this time.

Although the EAC formulated plans for the problems that would require the most urgent consideration immediately following the surrender, it didn't reach any agreement concerning specific policies to place into effect through the Allied administration of Germany.[11] For example, the WSC issued a memorandum to Ambassador Winant on 16 September 1944, setting forth general military and political policies to be implemented during the Allied occupation of Germany. In the sphere of justice: the key laws and decrees that had established the political structure of National Socialism and the implementation of its ideology and objectives were to be abolished, the Supreme Allied Authority was to suspend all discriminatory German laws and would take action to annul such laws, extraordinary National Socialist courts were to be abolished, and National Socialist personnel were to be removed from the German justice system, which was to be restored to as rapidly as possible.[12] However, agreements concerning surrender terms, zones of occupation, and control machinery were to be concluded before that memorandum could be discussed by the EAC.[13]

Although Ambassador Winant and his staff produced several policy directives dealing with substantive issues concerning the occupation and the military government in postwar Germany,[14] the EAC wasn't responsible for formulating such policy, since its purpose was to draft plans, rather than to function as an intergovernmental decision-making body.[15] The WSC received papers from Ambassador Winant dealing with major postwar policy questions, but discussion in the U.S. government on the substance of those policy recommendations was delayed until August 1944.[16]

The political planning organisation for relaying U.S. government plans to the international level and inter-Allied postwar planning was in place by late 1943, although the policy-*making*, rather than planning, machinery was established thereafter. There was also a lack of systematic coordination between the development of foreign policy and military planning.[17] While planning at the governmental level formulated political policies for postwar Germany, military planners drafted instructions for dealing with civil affairs during the occupation.

Military Planning for the Postwar Occupation of Germany

The office of the Chief of Staff to the Supreme Allied Commander (COSSAC) organised the initial military planning for the postwar occupation of Germany. A Post-hostilities Planning Section was formed under COSSAC to determine the responsibilities of the commander-in-chief during the interval between the end of hostilities and the institution of a civil administration in the occupied areas. Planning for post-hostilities civil affairs functions in the occupied territories that had begun under COSSAC was absorbed into the newly organised Supreme Headquarters, Allied Expeditionary Force (SHAEF)—the combined British-American military operations command staff that superseded COSSAC in January 1944.[18] Military civil affairs planners drafted studies concerning the occupation of Germany without coordination with governmental agencies in the U.S. and the UK that were charged with the same function.[19]

Whereas Allied political planning for postwar Germany was undertaken by the EAC,[20] military planning for civil affairs was charged to a "German Country Unit" that was established in March 1944 as a "Special Staff" subsidiary of the SHAEF (G-5) Civil Affairs Division.[21] Since instructions regarding policies to be applied in occupied Germany weren't dispatched from the political policy-makers to the military planning authorities, the German Country Unit took precedence in the planning for the nonmilitary aspects of the occupation of Germany.[22] That unit produced the *Handbook for Military Government in Germany: Prior to Defeat or Surrender*, published in its final draft in December 1944.[23] The *Handbook* was to serve as a comprehensive military government manual for Germany by providing advice and direction to the civil affairs units.[24]

Civil affairs planning for the occupation of Germany became increasingly pressing at that time, since the plans and organisation for the military government of Germany were to be completed before D-Day in order for the military government personnel to become familiar with their mission.[25] General Eisenhower, the Supreme Commander of SHAEF, therefore requested the preparation of guidance for civil affairs planning. The Combined Civil Affairs Division (CCAD), a civil affairs planning subcommittee of the UK-U.S. Combined Chiefs of Staff (CCS),[26] formulated a directive for military government administration during the pre-surrender period entitled "Combined Directive for Military Government in Germany Prior to Defeat or Surrender," or CCS 551.[27] The directive was dispatched to General Eisenhower by the CCS on 28 April 1944 while combined Allied military government policies prior to the surrender of Germany hadn't been forwarded from the EAC or G-5 of SHAEF.[28]

CCS 551 addressed the general conditions of military government administration assumption of supreme authority in Germany occupied by SHAEF forces. The SHAEF commander was to be vested with supreme legislative, executive, and judicial authority in all occupied territories, and was charged with three main tasks while serving in that capacity: 1) abolishing the NSDAP and its affiliated organisations; 2) eliminating National Socialist laws and courts from the German justice system; and 3) ensuring that no National Socialist of importance or member of the German general staff was retained in or appointed to any position of authority.[29]

Those objectives represented the essence of military government denazification planning.[30] The directive also provided guidance on the administration of justice in Allied-occupied Germany. The SHAEF commander was authorised to establish military courts to maintain law and order in the occupied territories. Courts would be established in accordance with appropriate regulations concerning their jurisdiction. National Socialist personnel would be removed from German courts. The functions of German courts would be suspended until they could be reopened under predetermined regulations and measures for their supervision and control could be introduced. Extraordinary National Socialist courts and National Socialist laws were to be abolished permanently.[31] While CCS 551 defined military government policy, definitive guidance for the application of military government legal functions was outlined in military government manuals, such as the *Handbook for Military Government* and the *Technical Manual for Legal and Prison Officers.*

The *Handbook for Military Government in Germany* provided instructions for various military government operations that would be undertaken upon the occupation of German territory by SHAEF forces prior to Germany's surrender or defeat. Measures pertaining to legal objectives included general instructions for the eradication of National Socialist influences from the German justice system, the restoration of law and order, and the safeguarding of Allied forces and UN interests.[32]

The terms in the *Handbook* regarding the staffing of German institutions called for the removal of all active National Socialists and sympathisers, or any individuals deemed likely to oppose Allied interests and principles, from government or civil service offices, without exception, including for administrative convenience or expediency. They were to be substituted with non-National Socialists, or military government personnel as a temporary measure, if no suitable German personnel could be found. German public officials who had belonged to National Socialist organisations were automatically to be removed from office. All reinstated German personnel would be screened through questionnaires (*Fragebogen*) providing detailed and specific information concerning their participation in the activities of the

NSDAP or its affiliated organisations, which then would be verified by other sources of information, such as military government counterintelligence, NSDAP and police records, or informers.[33]

The purposes of the military government were to be proclaimed through military government legislation. German legislation containing NSDAP doctrines was to be abolished, while German laws that didn't conflict with military government policies and legislation would be maintained.[34] The *Handbook* provided the military government with the initial proclamation, laws, and ordinances that were to be promulgated by SHAEF military commanders upon the occupation of any area.

Legislative measures dealing with the administration of justice in SHAEF-occupied Germany included SHAEF Military Government Proclamation No. 1 on "Establishment of Military Government," SHAEF Military Government Law No. 1 on "Abrogation of Nazi Law," SHAEF Military Government Law No. 2 on "German Courts," SHAEF Military Government Law No. 6 on "Dispensation by Act of Military Government with Necessity of Compliance with German Law," SHAEF Military Government Ordinance No. 1 on "Crimes and Offences," and SHAEF Military Government Ordinance No. 2 on "Military Government Courts."[35]

Military government courts would be established as soon as it was practicable, to enforce military government legislation and to protect the interests of the Allied forces and the UN.[36] German courts would be suspended upon the occupation of enemy territory. The judicial organisation in each territory was to be reorganised as soon as possible upon the establishment of the military government in the area.[37] German courts would be reopened at the discretion of Army Group Commanders, subject to military government regulation, supervision, and control.[38]

The military government was to exercise the following powers over the German judicial organisation: 1) the power to dismiss any German judge; 2) the right to attend any court session; 3) the power to review the decisions of German courts; 4) the power to nullify, suspend, or modify sentences rendered by those courts; and 5) the power to assume jurisdiction over any class of cases or particular cases for military government courts.[39] All National Socialist special courts, such as the People's Court, would be abolished.[40]

The *Handbook* was supplemented by the SHAEF *Technical Manual for Legal and Prison Officers*. Whereas the *Handbook* was to provide information and guidance for military government detachments in SHAEF-occupied Germany, technical manuals were to be used by specialist officers.[41] The technical manual restated the principles set forth in the *Handbook*, provided terms for procedures in the conduct of military government court trials in occupied Germany, and provided directions for reopening German courts.[42] The manual set forth policies for the denazification of justice, such as preventing the application of discriminatory laws and the reorganising of the German justice system to eliminate National Socialist elements and doctrines. Legislation was to be enacted by SHAEF in occupied Germany for the implementation of those measures, which would, in turn, be promulgated by SHAEF Army Group commanders.[43]

All German courts in the occupied territories were to be closed, and all National Socialist personnel were to be eliminated from the justice system. Military courts were to be established in the occupied territories as soon as practicable, to maintain order and the security of Allied forces. National Socialist courts would be abolished, and all other German courts would be closed until the military government had secured judicial personnel who could be relied upon to administer justice without National Socialist principles and doctrines, in conformity with the objectives of the military government. Jurisdiction over cases affecting the interests of the military government would be withdrawn from German courts and assumed by military government courts.[44]

The handbooks for use by SHAEF military government detachments in occupied Germany outlined military government policy and functions, while the long-term Allied political policy for postwar Germany remained forthcoming. Military government detachments were to establish "an adequate system for the administration of justice" in the territories under SHAEF control as the occupation progressed on the basis of the SHAEF Directive and the two handbooks. That system was to provide for the promulgation of military government legislation (proclamations, ordinances, etc.) and the establishment and operation of military government courts. Effective control over German courts was to be established through the presidents and prosecutors of the German regional appeals courts (*Landgerichte*). The effective control of the German justice system by the *Reich* Minister of Justice in Berlin would be progressively terminated in proportion to the territories occupied by SHAEF troops.[45]

The provisions contained in the handbooks were implemented during the Allied invasion of western Germany. The justice system in the territories occupied by Allied forces was established by military government detachments that began to operate in western Germany following SHAEF tactical forces advancing into Germany.[46] SHAEF forces, under General Eisenhower's command, entered western Germany in September 1944. General Eisenhower issued an interim directive to the 21st and 12th Army Groups on 10 September 1944, ordering Field Marshal Montgomery and General Bradley to establish a military government as soon as they occupied German territory, and empowering army group commanders to enforce the terms of surrender, to take the necessary steps to establish order, and to eliminate traces of National Socialism.[47] Military planning for occupied Germany prevailed until Allied political policy on postwar Germany was established in 1945.

The Establishment of the Allied Occupation Objectives

The initial occupation directives were supplemented by policy deliberations at the international level.[48] Whereas the EAC documents laid the basis for the Allied military occupation of postwar Germany, questions concerning Allied objectives for the occupation remained unresolved. The political leaders of the Big Three Allies set forth the basis for the postwar occupation of Germany at the Yalta Conference (3–11 February 1945). They agreed to the surrender plans for Germany that had been formulated by the EAC, and proclaimed the broad postwar aims of disarmament, demilitarisation, and denazification. Those aims were to be implemented by the military governments of four occupation powers. They were to be represented in an Allied Control Council coordinating uniform policies for Germany as a whole. Germany would be partitioned into separate zones of occupation, which would be governed by the military governments of the Big Three Allies and France.[49]

Representatives of the U.S. War, Navy, State, and Treasury Departments, and the Foreign Economic Administrator, which composed the Informal Policy Committee on Germany,[50] set forth policy instructions for the military government in the U.S. occupation zone. That committee held its first meeting on 15 April 1945 to prepare a summary of U.S. policy for Germany in the initial post-defeat period. The committee drafted a summary of policies regarding the military government of Germany, which served as the basis for a directive to the Commander-in-Chief of the United States Forces of Occupation. That directive, JCS 1067, was completed on 26 April and sent to the U.S. Joint Chiefs of Staff (JCS), and then sent to the Commander-in-Chief of U.S. Forces in Germany, General Eisenhower, to provide guidance for the U.S. military government.[51]

The directive was to succeed CCS 551 as a policy statement in providing guidance for the U.S. military governor in occupied Germany and the military government civil affairs operations in the occupied territories, addressing short-term objectives of a military nature immediately following the surrender until long-term policies could be determined.[52] It remained the basic policy directive for the U.S. military government until common Allied policies were established for Germany as a whole.[53]

Eisenhower was ordered to dissolve the NSDAP and its affiliated organisations and institutions, and to abrogate all laws, decrees, and regulations purporting to establish the political structure of the National Socialist regime. All members of the NSDAP who had been more than nominal participants in its activities, all active supporters of National Socialism and militarism, and all individuals considered hostile to the Allied occupation were to be removed and excluded from public office or positions of importance in quasi-public and private enterprises that had been under the direction of the state, the NSDAP, or its affiliated organisations. They weren't to be retained in office in the interest of administrative necessity, expediency, or convenience.[54] All extraordinary courts, such as the *Volksgerichthof* and the *Sondergerichte*, were to be abolished immediately, while all German criminal, civil, and administrative courts were to be closed until all vestiges of National Socialism and National Socialist personnel had been eliminated.[55]

The Second World War in Europe ended with the unconditional military surrender of National Socialist Germany on 7 May 1945. That military surrender instrument was followed by the "Berlin Declarations" of 5 June 1945, which proclaimed the military and political surrender of Germany. The 5 June Declarations established the structure of a joint Allied military government administration in Germany, which included the forces under SHAEF command and those of the Soviet Union. The Allied military government superseded the German government through the unconditional surrender, and Allied control machinery was to remain the provisional political and administrative structure of Germany for the duration of the occupation.

The first declaration proclaimed that the four occupation powers would assume supreme authority in Germany, and presented the terms for unconditional surrender. Germany's resources were to be subordinated to the disposal of the Allied occupation authorities, and various measures were to be taken to ensure the complete disarmament, demilitarisation, and denazification of Germany. The second declaration outlined the boundaries of the Allied occupation zones in Germany and Berlin. Each zone would be placed under the authority of a commander-in-chief of the respective occupation power governing the zone. An Inter-Allied Governing Authority, consisting of the four Allied military commanders in Berlin, would jointly direct the administration of Berlin. The third declaration defined the Allied control machinery in Germany. The commanders-in-chief of the four occupation zones would hold supreme authority in their respective zones. Their authority would be subject only to their own-governments and to an Allied Control Council. The four commanders composed the Allied Control Council and would act in concert in matters affecting Germany as a whole. A Coordinating Committee, composed of the deputies of the four commanders, would be responsible for advising the Control Council, administering the execution of its decisions, transmitting decisions to appropriate German agencies, and supervising the activities of those agencies.

A Control Staff, consisting of twelve separate directorates, would function as the provisional administration of Germany. The administration of Berlin would be under the direct authority of an Inter-Allied Governing Authority, which would be subject to the direction of the Control Council. That control machinery would be maintained for the duration of the Allied military occupation when Germany would carry out the basic requirements of the unconditional surrender.

The task of the reconstruction of justice in Germany as a whole was charged to the Legal Directorate of the Control Council, which would prepare legislation for approval and enactment by the Control Council or the Coordinating Committee.[56] The Legal Directorate consisted of the Directors of the Legal Divisions representing each of the four occupation zones, subcommittees performing various functions, such as a Committee on the Reopening of German Courts, and Working Parties on the German Criminal Code and on the Repeal of National Socialist Laws.[57]

Having announced their plans for the military occupation and control of postwar Germany, it was necessary for the Allies to establish the practical characteristics of their administration.[58] Allied political policy-makers set forth the objectives of the postwar reconstruction of Germany at the Potsdam Conference (17 July–2 August 1945). The conference affirmed Allied aims that had been proclaimed at the Yalta Conference and set forth objectives to be implemented in postwar Germany by the occupation powers.

The U.S. delegation at Potsdam introduced the provisions outlined in JCS 1067, which formed the basis of discussions on major policies at the conference. Representatives of the Big Three Allies produced the "Proposed Agreement on the Political and Economic Principles to Govern the Treatment of Germany in the Initial Control Period," or the Potsdam Protocol, which outlined uniform policy provisions for postwar Germany concerning problems to be dealt with to meet the general objectives of the postwar occupation. Those objectives included political and economic controls, disarmament, demilitarisation, and denazification, to be fulfilled jointly under the supreme authority of the four occupation powers[59] and implemented under the authority of the Allied Control Council.

The Allied Control Council was empowered with enacting legislation to implement the objectives. Allied military governments were to be established in the separate zones of occupation. The commander-in-chief of each occupation zone would exercise supreme authority in accordance with directives received from his own government and would implement Allied Control Council policy decisions in his respective occupation zone.[60]

The Potsdam Protocol provided the Control Council with a charter for implementation of the joint political reconstruction, supplementing the terms of the Yalta Protocol and the Declarations of 5 June 1945.[61] Among the objectives set forth were terms for the reconstruction of the justice system in occupied Germany. Occupation objectives pertaining to the denazification of Germany included: the elimination of the NSDAP and its affiliated organisations; dissolving National Socialist institutions; preventing National Socialist activity and propaganda; abolishing National Socialist laws; arresting war criminals and National Socialist leaders, as well as the leading officials in National Socialist organisations and institutions, and bringing them to justice; and removing "all members of the NSDAP who had been more than nominal participants in activities[62] from public, semi-public, or important private positions of responsibility and replacing them with individuals deemed capable of assisting in the development of democratic institutions."[63]

The objective for the restoration of justice in Germany was to reestablish the rule of law. That included calling for the abrogation of all National Socialist laws, with the additional provision that no form of legal discrimination would be tolerated, and for the reconstruction of a democratic justice system.[64]

The reconstruction of postwar Germany was to be undertaken under the authority of the Allied Control Council, enacting legislation for Germany as a whole for the various tasks of reconstruction based on the principles set forth in the Potsdam Protocol. The four zones were, in fact, treated entirely separately by the Control Council, as if they were separate states, and their respective administrations were the exclusive concern of the occupation power.[65]

The U.S. military government was originally organised as the U.S. Group, Control Council (USGCC), which absorbed the U.S. element of the German Country Unit in August 1944 to prepare for the future operations of the Allied Control Council.[66] It would serve two purposes: as a U.S. planning agency for the occupation of Germany prior to the actual occupation, and as the top-level U.S. military government headquarters in Germany.[67]

On 30 August 1945, Proclamation No. 1 of the Allied Control Council proclaimed that the Council had been established and had assumed "supreme authority in matters affecting Germany as a whole," as stated in the Declaration of 5 June 1945. Any orders that had been issued under the authority of the commanders-in-chief in their zones of occupation to date would remain in force.[68] The Allied Control Council, the Coordinating Committee consisting of their deputies, and the twelve directorates of the Control Staff were established in August 1945.[69]

Conclusion

The Allied war aim of destroying the National Socialist regime in the administration of justice was to be accomplished by abolishing the laws and courts that had supported the regime and by restoring a judicial organisation with an independent judiciary.[70] SHAEF military civil affairs units took precedence in wartime planning for eliminating National Socialist influences in the German justice system. Their plans were adopted by political authorities as general principles of Allied policy that were to be implemented under the authority of a military government administration in postwar Germany.

Long-term policies for the various tasks of reconstruction were concluded at the Potsdam Conference. The tasks were to be administered by the Allied Control Council, which would operate as the provisional national government of Germany and direct joint occupation objectives through military government administrations governing the zones under their control. The provisions presented in CCS 551 and the *Handbook* defined military government responsibilities in SHAEF occupied territories until Allied government policy-makers issued additional directives that would supersede them.[71]

3

The Reconstruction of a Postwar Administration of Justice

RECONSTRUCTING THE GERMAN JUSTICE system was an integral part of the transition from the National Socialist dictatorship to a *Rechtsstaat*—a state based on the concepts of equality before the law and the protection of the individual from arbitrary and oppressive actions of the state and its officials.[1] German political and judicial institutions ceased to function at the end of the Second World War, when the unconditional surrender and collapse of the National Socialist regime created a political vacuum that was filled by the supreme authority of the Allied occupation powers. Those institutions were restored during the postwar military occupation, under the auspices of the occupation powers.

The development of those institutions in the U.S. zone took place at the *Land* level, where decentralised German political and administrative structures were created[2] at the outset of the occupation. The establishment of a constitutional state with a justice system based on the precepts of the rule of law entailed a twofold problem: eradicating National Socialist legislation, and determining the methods to be applied by the occupation authorities in the process of reconstructing the German justice system.

The Allied military governments assumed the responsibilities of all the governmental functions and established a provisional justice system with their own laws and courts. U.S. military government authorities initially provided the sole source of law and political authority in what became *Land* Hesse, until German *Länder* governments were restored in the U.S. zone. Whereas the U.S. military government purged National Socialist influences from the justice system and supervised the process of its reconstruction, the *Länder* governments continued the work of reconstruction by enacting the laws to be applied by each independent *Land* justice system.

The occupation powers set forth the functions of the German justice system during postwar reconstruction. The collapse of the German government essentially removed the basis of state sovereignty, and consequently eliminated the jurisdiction of the German judicial organisation.[3] Since the unconditional surrender had eliminated all German governmental institutions, the occupation powers established the extent of the jurisdiction of German courts. Measures for implementing the reconstruction of justice and for eradicating the influences of National Socialism were expressed through the enactment of both Allied Control Council and military government legislation. German court jurisdiction was widened during the occupation, through either amendment of occupation law or administrative revision of the categories of cases to be withdrawn from the jurisdiction of German courts.[4]

The Introduction of Occupation Law

The abolition of the National Socialist justice system began immediately upon the Allied invasion of western Germany in September 1944. SHAEF military forces imposed a standstill of justice[5] upon their advance into Germany. SHAEF military government detachments introduced the initial framework for a provisional military justice system, on the basis of five key documents introduced on 18 September 1944, which went into force immediately upon the occupation of Germany by SHAEF forces[6]: SHAEF Proclamation No. 1; SHAEF Military Government Law No. 1 on "Abrogation of Nazi Law;" SHAEF Military Government Law No. 2 on "German Courts;" SHAEF Military Government Ordinance No. 1 on "Crimes and Offences;" and SHAEF Military Government Ordinance No. 2 on "Military Government Courts."[7]

Proclamation No. 1 set the basis for the Allied war aim of destroying the National Socialist regime, declaring the establishment of the military government in Germany and vesting SHAEF Supreme Commander, General Eisenhower, with supreme executive, legislative, and judicial powers within the occupied territories as the Military Governor. The military government pledged to overthrow the National Socialist regime and to eliminate its oppressive laws and NSDAP institutions. Military government courts were to be established to maintain the law in occupied territories.[8]

All German courts were suspended at the outset of the occupation, since they couldn't be trusted after "six years of war and twelve years of National Socialism had reduced the German judiciary to such a feeble and corrupt state."[9] U.S. military government courts administered justice in their place. SHAEF legislative enactments that had set the basis of occupation law were retained in the U.S. zone after zonal military government administrations were established in the summer of 1945, and remained in force for the duration of the military occupation.

The process of eliminating the influences of National Socialism in the body of German law began with Military Government Law No. 1. That law ordered the abolition of nine fundamental National Socialist enactments that had contributed to maintaining the policies and doctrines of the NSDAP. The law also prohibited the application of whatever other laws would perpetuate injustice or inequality, or had been applied in accordance with National Socialist doctrines, such as sentencing for offences determined by analogy.[10] Its adjoining Regulation No. 1 nullified the ordinances and regulations that had been issued for the execution of the enactments abolished in Law No. 1.[11]

In terms of the actual application of German law, Military Government Law No. 2 ordered the temporary suspension of all German ordinary law courts, administrative courts, and labour courts until the U.S. military government had directed when and to what extent the criminal and civil courts would resume their operations, subject to whatever conditions occupation authorities considered necessary. The normal jurisdiction of the German justice system was suspended until further notice, while cases or groups of cases were removed from the jurisdiction of German courts and assumed by U.S. military government courts.

The extraordinary National Socialist courts, the *Volksgerichthof* and the *Sondergerichte*, were permanently abolished. Additional terms were set forth governing the function of ordinary German courts when they were reopened. The military government claimed the power to dismiss any German judge or prosecuting attorney, to disbar any lawyer or notary from practice, and to supervise the proceedings of and to review, modify, or commute the decisions of German courts.[12]

The power to commute or modify sentences represented the greatest form of intervention into the independence of the German justice system.[13] The initial legal basis for the intervention of occupation power in the German justice system was imposed[14] to ensure that the German judicial organisation complied with the policies of the occupation powers.[15]

Military Government Ordinance No. 1 set forth a series of forty-three offences against the military government that could be tried by military government courts, and defined how a person could be considered an accessory to criminal actions.[16] Military Government Ordinance No. 2 established military government courts and provided for their jurisdiction, powers of sentence and composition, the rights of the accused appearing before those courts, trial records, and rules of trial proceedings.[17] Military Government

Law No. 6 of 4 October 1944 on "Dispensation by Act of Military Government with Necessity of Compliance with German Law" empowered the military government to undertake any actions on its own authority, making all such actions legal and effective, superseding all existing requirements under German law,[18] thus establishing the military government as the supreme source of legislative and judicial authority in occupied Germany.

SHAEF military government detachments issued instructions for the application of criminal law by German judges[19] prior to the reopening of German courts, instructing judges to obey and enforce all military government proclamations, laws, ordinances, notices, and regulations; to bring whatever matters could be of concern to the military government to the military government authorities, including matters having political or military significance or likely to affect public order; to comply with existing German law and all instructions and regulations concerning the administration of the courts; to observe the limitations on the jurisdiction of German courts imposed under Art. 6 of Military Government Law No. 2[20] and any other additional sections of the German Criminal Code that required prior authorisation from the military government; and not to pass unduly harsh sentences. Judges were also instructed that their authority to act in their official capacity was entirely provisional, and that they and other court personnel were subject to review at any time. Any attempt to perpetuate the lawlessness and abuses of the National Socialist regime or to perpetuate National Socialist ideology would be severely punished.[21]

Those instructions set new standards for the postwar justice system. Their primary purpose was to maintain the application of German law in accordance with the standards that had been in place prior to modifications of the law and practices in the administration of justice, especially those preventing the pronouncement of cruel or excessive penalties that had been introduced by the National Socialist regime.[22] Whereas the initial military government and Allied legislation regarding the application of German law forbade the application of National Socialist principles, each individual judge was responsible for upholding the abolition of National Socialist legislation when pronouncing judgments and was expected to abide by the restrictions on German court jurisdiction.

The Allied occupation of Germany had a twofold effect on the German justice system: 1) the institution of a foreign court jurisdiction operating alongside the German judicial organisation, and the limitation of the latter's jurisdiction; and 2) the control of the German administration of justice, which allowed for intervention in the activities of the German judicial organisation. The extent of the supreme authority of the occupation power determined the extent of its court jurisdiction or judicial power, and thereby limited the jurisdiction of the German judicial organisation. Occupation court jurisdiction was exercised separately in the western occupation zones by military government courts established by the occupation powers.[23]

Until all aspects of National Socialism had been eliminated from the German justice system, the responsibilities of German judicial personnel and the extent of German court jurisdiction would be limited under the predominance of Allied occupation law.[24] The military government followed the principle that "the law of the occupied territory at the time of the occupation continues in effect as amended, annulled, suspended, or modified through military government legislation or by legislative action of competent German authorities acting in the exercise of power conferred upon them by Military Government."[25] This situation was an effect of an accepted principle of international law, by which every military occupation power introduced its law and formed a "*cordon judiciaire*" around itself,[26] setting forth a body of law that remained separate from the law of the occupied territory.

SHAEF legislation that was retained in the U.S. zone formed the basis of occupation law, which was later supplemented by Control Council legislation that governed Germany as a whole. The Allied occupation powers extended their jurisdiction in the justice system as a consequence of their exercise of supreme authority in Germany, and to prosecute the goals of the occupation. The jurisdiction of the Allied occupation powers therefore extended beyond their direct interests.[27]

Whereas U.S. military government courts applied the jurisdiction of occupation law to maintain the interests of the military government in the occupied territory, those courts also applied German criminal law until German court jurisdiction was restored[28] to its normal extent. Certain restrictions were thus imposed upon the jurisdiction of the German judicial organisation in view of those circumstances. In principle, the extent of the jurisdiction of military government courts was unlimited. They were responsible for the prosecution of all individuals in the occupied territory according to the provisions of the law of war, occupation law, or German criminal law that would normally fall under the jurisdiction of German courts. In contrast, the extent of the jurisdiction of German courts was limited in view of the provisions of Ordinance No. 2 and Law No. 2.[29]

The U.S. Military Government Provisional Administration of Justice

Legislative reform was carried out in the political context of the occupation, in which the military government constituted the sole and supreme political and legal authority in occupied Germany. The initial legal measures enacted under the authority of the Control Council or the U.S. military government in the form of proclamations, laws, and ordinances served as temporary expedients for the administration of justice, since the German judicial organisation and political authority had temporarily ceased to exist.

A provisional justice system, based on the system of military government courts, began to operate in occupied Germany in September 1944 to maintain order and the security of Allied troops[30] in the wake of battlefield conditions and the legal vacuum created by the initial military government legislation.[31] Until German courts were reopened, those courts appropriated the functions of the German justice system and upheld the law[32] in the occupied territories.

Military government courts were established at the outset of the occupation as an emergency measure,[33] operating with a set of laws, judicial organisations, and trial procedures to guide them, as defined by Ordinance No. 2. All offenders violating military government legislation were brought to trial, regardless of how slight the charge, and faced severe sentences.[34]

Justice was to be administered by U.S. military government legal officers exercising the following responsibilities: 1) preventing the operation of National Socialist laws; 2) reorganising the German system of justice; 3) promulgating military government legislation; and 4) establishing and operating military government courts to maintain law and order in the occupied territories. The military government courts initially assumed complete responsibility for adjudicating criminal cases involving Germans and other civilians. Those courts didn't deal with civil cases, which were reserved for German criminal courts whenever conditions would allow them to reopen.

The cases brought before a military government court were based on the nature of the offence and the extent of the court's jurisdiction. U.S. military government summary courts adjudicated minor offences, with the power to impose sentences of up to one year's imprisonment, a fine of up to a thousand dollars, or both. More serious offences, such as counterfeiting or bribery, were brought before an intermediate court, which could impose sentences of up to ten years' imprisonment, fines of up to ten thousand dollars, or both. The most serious offences, such as murder, looting, sabotage, and espionage, were tried by a general court, which could impose fines of an unlimited amount or a death sentence.[35] Those courts dealt with cases involving UN nationals,[36] U.S. civilians, and Germans who had violated U.S. military government or Control Council laws, ordinances, or decrees.[37]

U.S. military government courts were regarded as the most important instruments for shaping relations between the German population and the occupation forces. They were to enforce the authority claimed by military government legislation and to exemplify the difference between National Socialism and democracy by giving fair and impartial trials to all who stood before them. The first military government courts were set up during the Rhineland campaign. The first summary and intermediate courts began to operate in Kornelimünster in September and October 1944.[38] There were 343 military government courts in operation from the beginning of the occupation, which had tried more than 15,000 cases by July 1945, more than two-thirds of which dealt with minor offences against the occupation, such as curfew and travel restrictions.[39]

The jurisdiction of the U.S. military government courts extended to all violations of military government enactments, German law that remained in force, and the laws and usage of war. Hence, the extent of their jurisdiction was practically unlimited. They held jurisdiction over all persons in the occupied territories, including German and foreign civilians other than Soviet citizens in the U.S. zone,[40] and held concurrent jurisdiction with courts martial and military commissions over civilians serving with the U.S. military who were subject to military law. UN nationals and liberated prisoners of war were subject to their respective service laws.[41] U.S. military government courts could try cases of offences cited in the German Criminal Code, and were limited to the extent of their powers rather than German law.[42]

Military government courts in Hesse during the spring and summer of 1945 dealt mainly with cases arising from movement restrictions, curfew violations, theft of U.S. military property, and the illegal possession of firearms.[43] By September 1945, most of the cases coming before the general and intermediate courts throughout the U.S. zone involved unlawful possession of firearms and falsification of the denazification *Fragebogen*. Military government courts in September 1945 dealt with the following types of cases: curfew violations and travel restrictions (25 percent), illegal firearms possession (6 percent), theft (12 percent), unlawful possession of Allied property (5 percent), cases of false statements (2 percent), and "cases involving acts to the prejudice of the good order of the interests of the Allied Forces" (25 percent).[44]

Other offences arising from the current circumstances of maintaining law and order in a period of civil unrest were dealt with under the sweeping charge of "conduct prejudicial to the good order of military government," by which military government courts could administer justice in cases that weren't specifically governed by an existing statute. That especially applied to displaced persons—individuals who'd been taken to Germany during the war against their will—who were often guilty of committing serious crimes after they'd been liberated.[45]

The unarmed or ill-equipped German police were virtually powerless against armed bands of displaced persons who were subject to the jurisdiction of the U.S. military government courts. It was reported to the bishopric of

Limburg-an-der-Lahn that about 10,000 displaced persons from eastern Europe residing in the local *Landgerichtsbezirk* seriously threatened peace and order and public security with frightening forms of criminality, including many cases of armed robbery, in which people were wounded or killed.[46] Representative of the problem was the fact that the first twelve death sentences handed down by military government courts in Hesse were imposed on displaced persons who had committed armed robbery and murder.[47]

Specific legal objectives were set forth for promoting a democratic administration of justice and to guide U.S. military government legal officers in the execution of their duties. Those objectives were: 1) restoring and maintaining law and order; 2) assuring the equality of justice under the law for all; and 3) reorganising the German judicial system according to the principles of democracy.

It's been argued that military government courts also had a signal effect for democratisation by providing Germans with practical demonstrations of the application of justice in accordance with the law, the maintenance of the protection of civil rights, and the institution of judicial independence.[48] Military government courts afforded Germans a place where they could witness the work of the occupation power, as participants in the court proceedings, witnesses, or spectators. Germans from all classes of society came into direct contact with the military government in those courts, allowing Germans to test the meaning and significance of the protection of their newly acquired democratic rights and safeguards.[49]

The military government courts functioned throughout the occupation, serving the interests of the military government in occupied Germany before and during the restoration of the German judicial organisation in each of the *Länder* of the U.S. zone. In addition to prosecuting offences against the interests of the Allied forces and administering justice under the terms of military government laws, the responsibility of the military government courts also extended to assuming German court jurisdiction to maintain peace and order under military government administration. That also included prosecuting criminal offences that didn't directly affect the interests of the Allied forces, such as offences against the lives and property of German citizens, for as long as the German criminal courts were closed. The exercise of court jurisdiction was therefore divided between German and U.S. military government judicial organisations. The military government courts held a wider jurisdiction than the German courts that had been reopened by that time and assumed responsibility for cases that would have fallen under German court jurisdiction under normal circumstances.[50]

Further legislative measures enacted in the U.S. occupation zone concerning the administration of justice mainly dealt with defining the jurisdiction of the U.S. military government courts.[51] The military government judicial organisation in the U.S. occupation zone thus functioned as an institution of the military occupation, while the permanent German judicial organisations that had been established at the *Land* level in the U.S. zone followed the creation of the *Länder*.

The Creation of *Land* Hesse

U.S. military forces first entered Hesse on 22 March 1945 at Nierstein on the east bank of the Rhine. The advance continued with further inland exploitation of the military bridgehead that had been established by the next day and other bridgeheads along the Rhine. The German garrison at Darmstadt, the first major city in Hesse to fall under Allied control, surrendered on 24 March 1945. Wiesbaden and Frankfurt-am-Main capitulated on 28 March, Fulda on 2 April, and Kassel on 4 April.

The first phase of the military occupation of what would become the new *Land* Hesse after the surrender was completed by early April 1945. The *Oberlandesgericht* in Frankfurt-am-Main and the subordinate courts over which it had exercised appellate jurisdiction officially ceased to operate on 29 March 1945 as Military Government Law No. 2 went into effect.[52] The first U.S. military government detachment in Hesse arrived in Darmstadt on 26 March.[53] Military government detachments were established across Hesse by the end of April 1945, which included legal officers responsible for the administration of justice in the occupied territories. Military government units assumed the various functions of administration in a state of virtual anarchy ensuing from the disintegration of local German government, since its officials had fled before the Allied military advance, along with the German troops, often taking the public records with them.

German administrations at the *Regierungsbezirk* level were initially established by military government detachments in Hesse in April 1945.[54] The work of establishing the military government headquarters for Hesse began in Wiesbaden in mid-July 1945. The headquarters would exercise governmental jurisdiction roughly corresponding to both the former *Regierungsbezirk* government in Kassel and the former *Land* Hesse government in Darmstadt.[55]

In accordance with the policy of decentralising the German political and economic structure and to encourage the development of local democratic responsibility, U.S. military government authorities reestablished *Land*,

Regierungsbezirk, and local governments throughout the U.S. zone in the summer of 1945. *Land* governments were established with capitals in Munich, for Bavaria; Stuttgart, for northern Württemberg-Baden [the southern halves were included in the French occupation zone]; Darmstadt, for Hessen-Nassau; and Marburg, for Hesse. The military government authorised the provisional German governments at Darmstadt and Marburg to organise single ministries to deal with the affairs of both *Länder* wherever necessary.[56]

German authorities had planned to form the state of Greater Hesse by incorporating the former territories and governments of *Land* Hesse, with Darmstadt as its capital, and the Prussian province of Hessen-Nassau, which had consisted of two regional governments (*Regierungsbezirke*), centered in Wiesbaden and Kassel.[57] The organisation of the new *Land* Hesse was initiated following discussions in late June 1945 between Walter L. Dorn, a member of the Office of Strategic Services, and Gerhard Anschütz, a constitutional lawyer who had produced plans for a united greater Hesse in 1919–20. Those plans had been officially submitted to a *Länder* conference in 1928, but had been blocked by Prussia's opposition.[58]

The territories of former *Land* Hesse, on the right bank of the Rhine, and parts of the Prussian provinces of Kurhessen and Nassau were combined to form a single and cohesive new *Land* that was to be called *Groß-Hessen*,[59] or Greater Hesse. Study and discussion between military government and German officials had determined that the consolidation wouldn't violate local historical integrity or traditions, and would form a basic economic, political, and geographical unit. Formation of the new state would also establish a basic unit in a future federal system of government, while the former *Land* Hesse was considered too small to require or support a *Land* government, as was Nassau, which had been included in the U.S. occupation zone. That development also marked a step toward accomplishing the U.S. military government objective of decentralising the governmental structure of Germany, and eliminating the predominance of Prussia, which had previously prevented the federalisation of Germany.[60]

Pressing administrative tasks made it necessary to form local governments in the U.S. zone before parliamentary assemblies could be elected.[61] The U.S. zone was subdivided into three *Länder* that were formed under U.S. Military Government Proclamation No. 2 of 19 September 1945, constituting the territories of Bavaria, Württemberg-Baden, and the new *Land* of Greater Hesse.[62] Each of those *Länder* was established as the highest German administrative unit in the U.S. zone.[63]

Proclamation No. 2 marked a new stage in the legislative development of postwar German self-government, clearing the way for the reconstitution of *Land* administrations exercising legislative and executive powers under the authority of the respective *Land* U.S. military government, as well as under the limitations imposed by the military government at the zonal level and the Control Council[64] at the national level. The jurisdiction of German legislative authority was restricted by the U.S. military government, which in turn would transfer legislation to be applied by the German judicial organisation.

Proclamation No. 2 assigned full legislative, executive, and judicial powers to the separate *Land* governments, subject to the authority of the U.S. military government and to the provision that the exercise of those powers wouldn't conflict with actions taken by the Control Council or by any central German authority established by the Control Council, either before or after the promulgation of the Proclamation.[65] The U.S. military government would supervise the various tasks of postwar reconstruction in the separate *Länder* of the U.S. zone.[66] All military government laws and ordinances that had been introduced from the beginning of the occupation remained in force in three *Länder*.[67] The governments of the *Länder* would represent the reconstruction of justice[68] thereafter, insofar as the powers conferred upon the *Land* governments would enable them to enact measures for that purpose.

The supreme authority of the U.S. military government administration was subdivided among the newly created *Länder*.[69] The military government was divided into regional *Land* military government administrations on 1 October 1945, when the USGCC was redesignated as a policy-making rather than a planning organisation—the Office of the Military Government, United States (OMGUS),[70] composed of staff organised into divisions, serving various functions of the occupation and coordinating their work with the Allied Control Council.[71] OMGUS coordinated its functions with the Control Council and operated in the U.S. occupation zone in coordination with regional *Land* military government offices in Bavaria, Baden-Württemberg, and Hesse, receiving its instructions from the central OMGUS office in Berlin, and then transmitting them to the *Land* governments.[72]

The Director of the Legal Division of the Office of the Military Government for Germany (U.S.) in Berlin was responsible for policy and the supervision of legal affairs in the U.S. zone.[73] While that division functioned as an element of the Control Council at the national level, its organisation and related functions were duplicated in the *Land* Military Government Office for Hesse. An Office of Military Government for Greater Hesse was established in Wiesbaden on 8 October 1945, under the command of Lieutenant-Colonel James R. Newman, replacing the military government detachment for Hesse (the E-5 military government detachment). The *Land* military government for Hesse would guide the creation of responsible German self-government upon finding suitable and trained personnel to staff the new *Land* government. The Civil Administration branch of the military government chose qualified German personnel to compose a rump cabinet of the new government,[74] which was appointed and sworn into office on 16 October 1945 by Lieutenant-Colonel Newman, the Director of the *Land* Office of the Military Government. Professor Karl Geiler was sworn in as minister-president[75] of the newly established *Land* Greater Hesse.

The basic organisation of the government was completed on 1 November 1945, consisting of a cabinet of eight ministers, headed by the minister-president and his deputy.[76] The authority of the German civil administration at the *Land* level was emphasised by granting them full legislative, executive, and judicial powers, subject only to the supervision of the U.S. military government, while the *Land* minister-president was responsible to the director of the *Land* office of the military government.[77]

A skeletal government was formed for the new *Land*, under the supervision of the regional military government, which held provisional governmental authority until a full-fledged constitutional government could be formed. The validity of *Land* legislation at that stage depended upon the approval and promulgation of the *Land* minister-president. Existing German law was to remain in force until it had been repealed or suspended by new legislation enacted either by the Allied Control Council or the U.S. military government.[78]

The provisional *Land* government enacted a provisional constitution for Greater Hesse on 22 November 1945, which essentially described the *Land* government as it was operating at that time[79] and maintained that the extent of its governmental jurisdiction was limited by the Office of the Military Government for Greater Hesse.[80] Before a *Land* constitution was in place and it was possible to establish a permanent legislative process, governmental powers were to be exercised solely by the minister-president of the *Land*, appointed by the U.S. *Land* military government.[81] *Land* minister-presidents promulgated the approved laws in their respective *Länder* by decree,[82] subject to the approval of the U.S. military government.[83]

The task of making the state machinery function was left to the minister-presidents and their cabinets, to meet the demands of the occupation power "to fashion an emergency roof over the collapsed house."[84] The director of the *Land* military government office examined all *Land* legislation to determine whether any provisions conflicted with military government policies or would have a substantial effect outside the area of its limited application. Having examined the legislation, the director could either approve, suspend, or repeal the legislation, or refer the matter to a higher authority—either the zonal U.S. military government command in Frankfurt-am-Main or the national military government headquarters in Berlin.[85]

The most significant legislation by decree during the period of provisional government was for reconstructing the political-administrative machinery of the *Land* in order to restore the status of the self-governing political entities.[86]

Such legislation included providing for elections in the townships (*Gemeinde*)[87] and the structure of their organisation,[88] organising the county (*Landkreis*) structure,[89] electing representative bodies and officials,[90] formulating laws for electing a constitutional convention[91] that would take up the task of drafting a new *Land* constitution to replace the provisional one of 22 November 1945, and electing a *Land* parliament[92] to replace the provisional government that had been appointed by the military government.

The provisional government of Hesse set forth its goals upon its formation. One of its primary objectives was to lay the foundation of the new *Land*, based on the principles of democracy and the rule of law. The basis of the new *Land* was thus in complete contrast to the nature of the National Socialist state, in which forcible interventions in all spheres of society were possible, due to the absence of democratic controls.

Hesse was to be a *Rechtsstaat*, with its own state authority, founded upon and limited by a system of laws. The legal foundation of the new *Land* was to be established upon the restoration of the security of law, equality before the law, and the fair dispensation of justice. Those principles were to be ensured by a free and independent judiciary, by the restoration of the principles of civil rights, and by an equally incorruptible civil service.[93] The endeavour to put those principles into practice began with the reconstruction of the legal institutions of the state and the promulgation of appropriate legislation to direct the implementation of the principles.

Allied Control Council Measures for the Restoration of Justice

Control Council measures for the reconstruction of justice in Germany were essentially a continuation of those that previously had been introduced by the military government in the U.S. zone. Legislative reforms continued at the national or Control Council level, adopted on a quadripartite basis and carried out in the four occupation zones by their respective military governments. These reforms took place concurrently with the development of political life and judicial organisation at the zonal and *Land* levels. Control Council laws dealing with the abolition of National Socialist laws and the liquidation of National Socialist institutions and extraordinary courts were drafted in the summer of 1945, supplementing the general laws and orders that had been issued by the U.S. military government in the previous months. The Control Council's Legal Division then made further studies to determine the nature and extent of further legislation.[94]

Control Council Law No. 1 of 20 September 1945 was the first measure for the denazification of German law at the national level. The law was enacted in accordance with the Potsdam Protocol provision concerning the abolition of National Socialist legislation, and substantially dealt with the same content as

Military Government Law No. 1 in abrogating National Socialist legislation that had related to the establishment of the political structure of the National Socialist regime.[95] Any legislation of a political nature enacted after 30 January 1933 was automatically repealed. Any person applying or attempting to apply future German enactments that favoured any person with National Socialist connections or discriminated against any person on the basis of race, nationality, religious beliefs, or opposition to the NSDAP or its doctrines would be subject to criminal prosecution.[96]

Military Government Law No. 1 and Control Council Law No. 1 therefore included a general "suspending clause" that prohibited German courts from applying discriminatory provisions in any German law, at least for as long as the German judiciary remained under military government supervision.[97] German courts thus assumed responsibility for applying German law in view of the standards set by the general suspending clauses introduced by military government legislation.[98] Whereas the application of National Socialist principles in the law was expressly forbidden as of the beginning of the occupation, the Control Council remained engaged in the lengthy and continuing task of repealing specific enactments within the body of German law.

Specific National Socialist laws were abolished through Control Council legislation, which superseded zone legislation issued by zone commanders and German enactments,[99] thus extending the initial SHAEF military government legislation to all four occupation zones. Military Government Law No. 5 of 4 October 1945 on the "Dissolution of Nazi Party," by which the NSDAP, fifty-two of its affiliated organisations, and eight paramilitary organisations, such as the SA, the SS, and the SD, were abolished and declared illegal,[100] was extended by Control Council Law No. 2 of 10 October 1945 on "Providing for the Termination and Liquidation of the Nazi Organizations" in Germany as a whole. That law abolished the NSDAP and sixty-two of its affiliated organisations and outlawed their reconstitution.[101]

The Control Council set forth the basis for a democratic justice system under Control Council Proclamation No. 3 of 20 October 1945 on "Fundamental Principles of Judicial Reform." The proclamation called for the restoration of equality before the law; restoring the rights of the accused; restoring judicial independence by declaring that judges were free from executive control and responsible only to the law; prohibiting the administration of justice on the basis of crime "by analogy" and "sound popular emotions;" abolishing National Socialist courts, such as the *Volksgericht* and the *Sondergerichte*; and quashing the sentences of individuals who had been convicted under the National Socialist regime on political, racial, or religious grounds.[102]

In accordance with the proclamation, Control Council Law No. 4 of 30 October 1945 on the "Reorganization of the German Judicial System" reestablished the constitution and responsibilities of the ordinary law courts. The law reestablished the jurisdiction of German courts as it had operated during the Weimar period, according to the Law Concerning the Structure of the Judiciary of 27 January 1877 in the version of 22 March 1924.[103] District courts (*Amtsgerichte*[104]), regional appellate courts (*Landgerichte*[105]), and supreme courts of appeal (*Oberlandesgerichte*[106]) were to be restored in each *Land* and were to maintain their specified jurisdiction in all criminal and civil cases involving German citizens and appellate jurisdiction. Hence, the responsibilities of German courts were generally to be defined in accordance with the legal situation that had been in place before 30 January 1933. However, aligning the responsibilities of German courts in accordance with that law remained at the discretion of the occupation power.[107]

Each occupation power was empowered with withdrawing selected criminal and civil cases from the jurisdiction of German courts, in addition to separating its interests from the jurisdiction of the German judicial organisation. The jurisdiction of German courts was extended to all criminal and civil cases, except criminal offences committed against the Allied occupation forces; offences involving citizens of Allied nations and their property; crimes directed toward reestablishing the National Socialist regime and the activity of National Socialist organisations; or criminal cases involving military or civilian personnel who were citizens of Allied nations.[108]

Military government courts could also exercise jurisdiction in civil cases if a case involved an amount exceeding the value of RM 2,000, which Control Council Law No. 4 had set forth as the greatest amount that could be handled by an *Amtsgericht* in civil cases.[109] The prosecution of offences was to be left to the jurisdiction of German courts when the nature of the offence didn't compromise the security of the Allied Forces.[110]

U.S. military government and Control Council legislation defined the power of the military government to supervise the work of the reopened German courts and limited the jurisdiction of German courts while military government courts were in place. Military Government Law No. 2, applicable in the U.S. occupation zone and the U.S. occupation sector in Berlin, and Control Council Law No. 4 of 30 October 1945, applying in Germany as a whole, set forth the original basis for matters that lay outside the jurisdiction of the German judicial organisation.[111] Those matters mainly involved two types of cases: 1) those involving crimes and offences committed by individuals who would normally be subject to trial in a German court, and 2) criminal cases involving offences against occupation law. Cases involving occupation forces, or any UN or nationals serving with or accompanying occupation personnel, were excluded from the jurisdiction of German courts.[112] Limitations were thus imposed upon the jurisdiction of German courts in criminal and civil cases, depending upon the status of the parties involved in the offence or dispute.

The rule of law lacked the element of the full restoration of judicial independence.[113] Judicial independence was restricted in order to ensure that the judiciary complied with the concepts of the rule of law in the administration of justice. Military Government Law No. 2 allowed for far-reaching intervention, which affected the normal operation and internal affairs of the German justice system, while at the same time, judicial independence was to be promoted as long as German judges complied with the objectives of the military occupation powers.[114] The occupation powers maintained unlimited power of supervision over German courts, such as the power to remove a judge from office and to examine judgments by German courts, which effectively limited the German judicial independence set forth under Proclamation No. 3.

The restoration of an independent judiciary was the most important element in reinforcing law and justice in postwar Germany, which was to fulfill the spirit and precepts of a *Rechtsstaat* upon the reestablishment of state institutions. The dispensation of justice that was restored in Germany served those ideals, although under a different form of law, introduced under the occupation regime, in which the application of Control Council and zonal military government law took precedence over German law.[115] The principle of judicial independence, the freedom of a judge to administer justice without interference from executive control, was one of the main occupation objectives in the sphere of legal reconstruction.[116] It was the avowed policy of the U.S. military government to foster the independence of the German judiciary by allowing courts the freedom to interpret and apply the law, and to limit military government control to "the minimum consistent with the accomplishment of the aims of the occupation."[117]

U.S. military government policy was to avoid interfering in the operation of German courts, except in cases involving the serious interests of occupation authorities.[118] In stark contrast to the National Socialist justice system, the restoration of judicial independence implied that judges were to remain politically neutral and impartial.[119] Whereas the government enacted legislation, judges were to pronounce judgments strictly in accordance with the impartiality of the law, thereby preserving the rule of law.[120]

Control Council Proclamation No. 3 and Control Council Law No. 4 set forth the fundamental principles of reform that were to govern the restoration of justice in Germany as a whole, and the principles for the reconstruction of the German judicial organisation through which those principles were to be implemented.[121]

The implementation of Control Council Law No. 4, bringing the jurisdiction of German courts into conformity with its terms, remained at the discretion of the military government in each zone.[122] That opened the way for divergence in the implementation of law in the four occupation zones, which was further complicated by the fact that the coordination of divergent decisions among the various courts of appeal, either in an occupation zone or in Germany as a whole, was lacking, due to the absence of a supreme court, such as the *Reichsgericht*, since the terms of the Potsdam Protocol on decentralisation hadn't allowed for central German administrations to be reestablished.[123]

The Reconstruction of a *Land* Judicial Organisation

A new judicial organisation was to be established in the newly created *Land* Hesse after all German courts were closed.[124] The reopening of the German courts became a pressing task as the military government judicial organisation became overburdened with cases.[125] The first *Amtsgerichte* and *Landgerichte* began to operate throughout Germany at the end of May and early June 1945 in order to help alleviate the workload of military government courts.[126] The next major step in restoring the German justice system was the reconstruction of a permanent judicial organisation in each *Land*.

The restoration of a German judicial organisation in what was to become *Land Groß-Hessen* began with the reopening of the first *Amtsgerichte* in Limburg on 4 June 1945, and in Wiesbaden on 11 June 1945.[127] The military government instructed the leading judges of the *Amtsgericht* (*aufsichtsführende Richter*) to open the court, to recommend judicial personnel to be reinstated by the military government, and to adhere to stated responsibilities, subject to certain limitations. They were to hear criminal cases that dated from just before and just after the beginning of the military occupation to the time the courts were reopened.

Jurisdiction in criminal matters was restricted in certain cases, such as those outlined in Instructions to Judges No. 1.[128] All offences of a political character and certain types of civil cases were removed from the jurisdiction of these courts until the approval of the military government was provided. The courts were otherwise to handle matters affecting the maintenance of public order, and to strictly adhere to all military government proclamations, laws, ordinances, notices, and regulations. All matters of interest to the military government, such as violations of military government regulations, cases of political or military significance, and cases affecting public order, were to be reported to the military government on a weekly basis. Any attempt at continuing the lawlessness and arbitrariness of the National Socialist regime or the maintenance of the National Socialist *Weltanschauung* in the administration of justice was to be penalised severely.[129] The U.S. military government issued instructions to the newly appointed *Landgericht* president in Frankfurt-am-Main on 28 July 1945, directing that he select personnel for the court and subordinate *Amtsgerichte* in that area of jurisdiction (*Landgerichtsbezirk*). Judges in every court were to be provided with a copy of the Instructions to Judges No. 1 and the instructions for *Amtsrichter*, and were to become familiar with the guidelines and regulations issued by the military government. The *Landgericht* president was to exercise supervision and disciplinary authority in accordance with German law at his discretion, subject to military government instructions, over all judicial personnel in the area of jurisdiction, until authority could be assumed by the president of an *Oberlandesgericht*.[130]

Until that authority was relinquished, the *Landgericht* president directed the reorganisation of the judicial system by providing the local government with recommendations as to which *Amtsgerichte* were to resume functioning, the allocation of judicial personnel and distribution of business for those courts, and the staffing and distribution of business for the *Landgericht* in Frankfurt-am-Main once it was reopened.[131]

By August 1945, military government legal officers had reopened German courts at the *Amtsgericht* level in most communities of the U.S. zone, dealing with lesser criminal and civil cases, as well as a number of *Landgerichte*, with jurisdiction over broader areas and over more serious criminal and civil cases.[132] Military government detachments continued to reopen additional German courts throughout September 1945.

The first *Landgericht* in what had become *Land* Greater Hesse was opened in Frankfurt-am-Main on 18 October 1945.[133] Civil litigation had begun to be heard in August 1945, although criminal cases constituted most of the courts' business.[134] More than two-thirds of the courts scheduled to reopen in Hesse were in operation by the time the Ministry of Justice began to operate at the end of October 1945.[135] Seventy-nine *Amtsgerichte* and seven *Landgerichte* were functioning in Hesse by 21 December 1945, making the reorganisation of the judicial organisation in Hesse virtually complete.[136] By the end of December 1945, 98 percent of the *Amtsgerichte* and all eight *Landgerichte* in Hesse were open, leaving the *Oberlandesgericht* in Frankfurt-am-Main as the only remaining high court left to be opened.[137]

While the first German courts were opened as a matter of expediency, a permanent *Land* judicial organisation was to be reestablished as part of restoration of German state institutions. The long-term occupation objective of restoring responsibility to German judicial authority was to be served by what could be considered a blueprint for the structure of all German judicial organisations in the *Länder* of the U.S. zone. The structure of the postwar justice system in each *Land* was outlined in the "Plan for the Administration of Justice in the United States Zone," issued in October 1945 by the Control Council Legal Division and forwarded to the regional Military Government headquarters for implementation[138] in Hesse, Württemberg-Baden, and Bavaria.[139]

The plan set forth provisions for the establishment of a justice system, operated by German authorities in the U.S. zone on the basis of the Potsdam Protocol provision of reorganising the justice system in accordance with the principles of democracy and equality before the law; the military government policy of establishing and maintaining the independence of the German justice system; and German assumption of responsibility for the establishment and function of Germany's justice system while under the supervision of the military government.[140]

The implementation of the provisions of the plan rested with authority of the *Land* ministers of justice. Whenever possible, former provisions governing the judicial organisation and the administration of court jurisdiction under German law were to be taken into account.[141] New legislative developments also could be applied by the postwar German judicial organisation, as defined under the plan.[142]

The plan required that a minister of justice would function as the leading administrator of the justice system in each *Land*,[143] exercising the duties that formerly had been performed by the *Reich* minister of justice for Germany as a whole.[144] Those duties included opening the courts; handling administrative matters concerning the judicial organisation, such as the appointment of personnel and organising the practical functions of their offices; supervising all judicial personnel functions, such as the handling of transactions with the military government; and recommending legislation.[145] The power of the minister of justice to appoint judicial personnel and judicial independence, as defined in the plan, was provisional, since the military government retained the power to appoint or dismiss any judge under the terms of Military Government Law No. 2.

In the interest of maintaining judicial independence,[146] the plan also contained the provision that the minister of justice was prohibited from intervening in the judicial functions of judges.[147] Disciplinary courts for all judicial personnel were to be established at the *Landgerichte* and one *Oberlandesgericht* in each *Land*. Disciplinary court jurisdiction was to be handled by the disciplinary chambers of the *Landgerichte* and the disciplinary senate at the *Oberlandesgericht* for Hesse in Frankfurt-am-Main, consisting of three judges, with jurisdiction over court presidents, vice-presidents, judges of the *Oberlandesgericht*, and the general state prosecutor.

Appeals from disciplinary chambers would be presented to appellate courts (*Rechtsmittelgerichte*). Their jurisdiction extended over all civil servants, as well as prosecutors, notaries, and legal advisors. Appeals against decisions of the disciplinary senate would be transferred to a larger senate, consisting of five judges. Until local professional associations of lawyers and notaries could be reestablished, the *Landgericht* presidents were responsible for supervising the professional conduct of lawyers and notaries, and were authorised to impose disciplinary measures.[148]

The plan stipulated that the traditional jurisdictions of German courts were to be maintained and provided a structure for the reorganisation of the judicial system in each *Land*. Five *Oberlandesgerichte*, appeals courts of the second instance, were to be opened in the three *Länder* of the U.S. zone, exercising appellate jurisdiction over the appeals courts of the first instance, or *Landgerichte*, which were to exercise appellate jurisdiction over the county courts, or *Amtsgerichte*. One *Oberlandesgericht* was to be established for the newly formed *Land* of Hesse, operating in the former *Oberlandesgericht* for Frankfurt-am-Main, with adjoining seats occupied by a vice-president in Darmstadt and Kassel.[149]

Eight *Landgerichte* were to be set up: in Frankfurt-am-Main, Wiesbaden, Darmstadt, Gießen, Limburg, Hanau, Marburg, and Kassel. Seventy-one *Amtsgerichte* and twenty-five *Amtsgericht* branch offices were to be reopened, along with nine additional locations where the *Amtsgerichte* were to be in session.[150] The *Landgerichte* were to hold appellate jurisdiction over the *Amtsgerichte* in their appropriate areas of jurisdiction, or *Landgerichtbezirke*. Public prosecutors' offices were to be established at the location of the *Oberlandesgericht* and the *Landgerichte*.[151]

The jurisdiction and functions of German courts were established by German law, with certain modifications arising from Military Government Law No. 2 (Art. 6 on the limitations of German court jurisdiction), Military Government Instructions to Judges No. 1, the organisational provisions of the plan, and other directives enacted by the military government.[152] The jurisdiction of the *Amtsgerichte*, as criminal courts of the first instance, was reduced to crimes punishable by prison sentences to a maximum of five years, or penitentiary sentences of up to two years. In civil cases, they were to act as the courts of first instance, in which the value of the disputes didn't exceed RM 1,500.[153] Court jurisdiction had been regulated by Art. 23 of the *Gerichtsverfassungsgesetz* of 27 January 1877.

The *Landgerichte* were defined as courts of the first instance in criminal cases that superseded the jurisdiction of the *Amtsgerichte*, depending on the extent of the potential penalties, as well as acting as appeals courts for the decisions of the *Amtsgerichte*. As civil courts, the *Landgerichte* were to deal with all civil and commercial cases of the first instance that lay outside the jurisdiction of the *Amtsgerichte*, as well as serving as the appeal authority for those courts.

Modifications were made to the appeals courts by abolishing parts of the *Gerichtsverfassungsgesetz* of 1877. The plan abolished the division of chambers for civil and criminal matters in the *Landgericht* and the *Oberlandesgericht* senates, and prohibited the creation of special chambers for civil and criminal matters. The greatest difference was the reform of the *Oberlandesgericht*. That court was made responsible for hearing criminal, as well as civil, appeals cases from the *Landgericht*, thus making the *Oberlandesgericht* strictly a supreme appeals court, taking the place of the former *Reichsgericht*, which had functioned at the national level.[154] The local military government detachment in each *Land* supervised the function of those courts.[155]

Operation of the postwar German judicial organisation at the *Land*[156] level was directed by the newly established *Land* Ministry of Justice,[157] which assumed the authority that formerly had been exercised by the *Reich* Ministry of Justice[158] at the national level. The transfer of direct responsibility for the judicial organisation to the *Land* minister of justice also represented the first step toward the restoration of judicial sovereignty.[159] The minister of justice, whose powers and responsibilities were outlined in the plan, was to function as the leading authority of the *Land* justice system.[160] The minister was charged with handling the administrative affairs of the judicial organisation, the operation of the courts, and the appointment of judges, subject to the approval of the military government, and was also responsible for the disciplinary supervision of legal personnel, submitting monthly reports to the *Land* military government office.[161]

The U.S. military government instructed the minister-president of Hesse to establish a *Land* Ministry of Justice on 15 October 1945, in which the *Land* minister of justice would be correspondingly charged with the supervision of that ministry, subject to the supervision and approval of the military government. That included the exercise of administrative control over judicial and administrative personnel and the temporary appointment of personnel.[162]

Even though the plan provided for the reorganisation of the ordinary law court system, additional measures were introduced regarding the other branches of the justice system. The *Land* minister of justice was to assign matters concerning Rhine navigation to the jurisdiction of the appropriate *Amtsgerichte*, subject to the prior approval of the military government. Labour courts weren't to be reopened at that time. The function of the labour courts, as established in the provisions of labour court law, were to be assumed by the *Amtsgerichte* and *Landgerichte* as required.[163] Since the plan didn't include provisions for courts to review administrative and labour disputes or constitutional controversies, those branches of the judicial organisation and their function in each *Land* of the U.S. zone were developed separately.[164] Further developments of the *Land* judicial organisation would take place upon the reconstitution of a permanent *Land* government, which would succeed the provisional government.

The Establishment of the *Länderrat*

The reconstruction of German political life in the U.S. zone began at the *Land* level. Governmental jurisdiction in the U.S. zone was divided between the military government and the reconstituted German government at the *Land* level. It soon became apparent after the creation of the *Länder* in the U.S. zone that certain governmental functions that formerly had been exercised by the government at the national level, such as administrative services, exceeded the scope of the *Land* governments, while others required coordination on a zonal basis.[165] In order to coordinate the reconstruction work in the three *Länder*, a *Länderrat* was created in Stuttgart on 5 October 1945, under the auspices of the U.S. military government, to represent the common interests of the *Länder* of the U.S. zone and to coordinate the interests of the *Länder* and the regional offices of the military government.[166]

General Lucius D. Clay, deputy military governor of the U.S. zone, opened the first meeting of the *Länderrat* on 17 October 1945, in which he stated that the *Länderrat* was to serve as a provisional central authority to coordinate legislation whenever uniformity in the zone was necessary. However, it wasn't to serve as a legislature or an executive for the U.S. zone.[167]

The joint responsibility of the representatives of the three *Länder* was to facilitate the decision-making for the various tasks of the zonal reconstruction by coordinating their common interests, which would otherwise be undertaken by a national government.[168] Although the *Länderrat* didn't possess legislative power, uniform legislation for the three *Länder* of the U.S. zone was drafted in the *Länderrat* and promulgated by each *Land* minister-president until full-fledged *Land* legislatures were established following the adoption of *Land* constitutions.[169]

The *Länderrat* consisted of the minister-presidents of Hesse, Württemberg-Baden, and Bavaria, serving to coordinate discussion and policy-making on matters of common concern to the three *Länder*. The minister-presidents were assisted by a staff of German functionaries and experts and a permanent secretariat in Stuttgart, serving as a steering committee for preparing the agenda of matters for discussion.[170] The *Länderrat* was a new legislative authority for the *Länder* of the U.S. zone. It was created because of the lack of a central German government. Representatives of the *Land* governments at the *Länderrat* worked under the supervision of U.S. military government officials from the Regional Government Coordinating Office (RGCO), which was directly responsible to the U.S. deputy military governor,[171] while *Land* military government directors supervised the work of German officials at the *Land* level.[172]

The representatives of the RGCO held a twofold function: conveying military government policy to German authorities, either at the various *Länderrat* committees they attended or through the secretariat; and informing OMGUS and *Land* military government offices about the work of the committees.[173] The *Länderrat* wasn't vested with executive authority, since its decisions were to be promulgated as legislation in each *Land* by the minister-president, which remained subject to the approval of the *Land* military government to ensure that all legislation conformed to military government policy.[174] In practice, the adoption of legislative measures by the *Länderrat* served as uniform legislation for the U.S. occupation zone, but its decisions and those of individual minister-presidents were promulgated separately by the minister-presidents of each *Land*.[175]

Legislation that would be applied on a zonal basis could emanate from either of the two sources of authority. Proposals for *Länderrat* legislation were to be submitted to the Regional Government Coordinating Office and then sent to OMGUS headquarters in Berlin with its recommendations for approval, along with simultaneous notification to the *Land* military government offices or they could be drafted by U.S. military government authorities and then sent to the *Länderrat* for consideration as legislation in the *Länder* of the U.S. zone.[176]

In the interest of maintaining unity of legislation in the U.S. zone, legal matters of common concern to the *Länder* were dealt with by a *Länderrat* Legal Committee, composed of the ministers of justice of the *Länder* formed on 4 December 1945. The purpose of the committee was to examine and approve new legislation proposed by the *Land* governments, as well as to examine proposed amendments to existing legislation, such as removing National Socialist influences, before forwarding the legislation to the *Länderrat*.[177]

The ministers of justice deemed it important to enact uniform legislation in the three *Länder*, thus maintaining continuity with German *Reichsrecht*, or national law. It was also desirable to avoid duplication of work at the separate ministries and the military government. The committee planned to discuss all important matters pertaining to the reestablishment of independent German legislation and the judiciary. Subjects of discussion at that time included such things as the transfer of cases to German courts when German legislation would cover all crimes being handled by military government courts, the trial of war criminals in German courts, and the drafting of a uniform German denazification law that would emphasise the individual examination of former National Socialists.[178]

The legal committee functioned as one of the *Länderrat* technical committees,[179] with the minister of justice for Greater Hesse acting as chairman. That committee drafted and issued all legislation within the *Länderrat* machinery, in which roughly sixty permanent or semi-permanent committees handled various functions.[180] All *Länderrat* decisions were forwarded to the Regional Government Coordination Office and then transferred to OMGUS headquarters in Berlin for review and approval,[181] unless the legislation had been approved on the spot by the military governor, who was present at the monthly meetings.

Laws adopted by the *Länderrat* could be rejected by the U.S. military government if they didn't serve to accomplish a basic occupation objective or violated democratic principles.[182] Every law drafted in the *Länderrat* and approved by the military government would be promulgated by the minister-presidents for their respective *Land*[183] until *Land* constitutions could be adopted and state parliaments formed.

The Reconstruction of a German Constitutional Government in Hesse

The provisional *Land* government of Hesse had initially been installed to serve until a permanent *Land* constitution could be adopted to form the basis of the state, establishing a free and independent judiciary and placing limitations upon the exercise of governmental power. The authority of the *Land* military government was to be limited to exercising supervisory control over the German constitutional *Land* government.[184] The relationship between the U.S. military government and the newly constituted *Land* governments was established under the terms of a new policy directive, promulgated on 30 September 1946, defining the powers to be retained by the military government and the relationship between *Land* military government offices and German *Land* civil governments.

U.S. occupation policy required increasing German self-government, which was brought about through the elections of *Länder* governments and the adoption of *Land* constitutions. Although constitutional government was established in each *Land*, the *Land* governments didn't become fully independent, since certain powers were reserved by the military government.[185] The military government maintained its supreme authority to accomplish its objectives and could intervene in the activity of the *Land* government,[186] and military government proclamations, laws, enactments, orders, and instructions remained in force.

Occupation objectives were to be met by means of observation, inspection, reporting, advising, and through military government courts. Intervention of the U.S. military government in the function of the *Land* government was to be limited to disapproval of economic, social, political, and governmental activity that clearly was considered in violation of the objectives of the occupation, or to removing public officials whose public activities violated those objectives.[187]

The new *Land* constitutions of the three *Länder* in the U.S. occupation zone determined the separation of executive, legislative, and judicial powers that previously had been assumed by the military government under the terms of the unconditional surrender, by which those powers had been vested in the military government. The Civil Affairs Division of the U.S. military government formulated a programme for the drafting and adoption of *Land* constitutions in January 1946, directing each minister-president to appoint a *Land* constitutional commission to research necessary material to be placed at the disposal of elected constitutional assemblies, which then would draft and approve the new constitution for each *Land*, to be reviewed by the U.S. military government[188] for final approval prior to promulgation by the elected *Landtag* (state parliament).

Delegates from all the *Land* political parties were elected on 30 June 1946 to form a constitutional commission to draft a new *Land* constitution,[189] which later would be approved in a referendum.[190] The commissions in the three *Länder* completed their work in October 1946, which was subsequently reviewed and approved by the military government and the U.S. State and War Departments.[191] The constitution was officially adopted by the constitutional commission by a vote of eighty-two to six, with two abstentions,[192] and ratified by a referendum in Hesse on 1 December 1946.[193] A new *Land* parliament was elected on the basis of that referendum on the same day.[194]

The *Land* constitution organised the future political life of the state[195] (*Staatsleben*), conferring full legislative powers upon the *Land* government, maintaining the principle of the separation of powers,[196] and establishing parliamentary government, by which legislative power was assigned to the *Landtag* and to the people.[197] The adoption of the *Land* constitution marked a step toward the establishment of a permanent *Land* executive and legislature. The responsibility for promulgating *Länderrat* legislation in each *Land* was conferred upon the elected *Landtag*, provided it wasn't rejected by the U.S. military government.[198]

The primary function of the military government regarding the legislative process in the U.S. zone was to review the enactments of the German *Land* legislatures (*Landtage*), which possessed broad legislative authority in local and regional matters.[199] In the interest of U.S. policy-makers and to maintain maximum decentralisation, as postulated in the Potsdam Protocol, governmental authority was concentrated at the *Land* level, in accordance with the *Land* constitutions. The *Land* governments therefore superseded the *Länderrat*, which had no direct executive authority[200] and served only the legislative function of drafting laws to be implemented by the *Land* governments.

The *Land* constitution set forth new terms governing judicial organisation. National Socialist perversions of law and justice were outlawed. There was to be no punishment other than on the basis of law; no individual would be deprived of their right to trial and could only be tried by a regularly appointed judge; and all extraordinary courts were expressly forbidden. Legislative authority would be expressed through the courts. Judges were declared to be independent, subject solely to the authority of the law.[201]

A Supreme Constitutional Court (*Staatsgerichtshof*) was to be established and charged with the task of defending the provisions of the constitution.[202] The *Staatsgerichtshof* was to judge the constitutionality of legislation, the violation of fundamental rights, the integrity of popular elections, and cases involving constitutional disputes arising from the constitution or laws.[203] It was also empowered to remove judges from office, upon the request of the *Landtag*, if they didn't exercise the functions of their office in accordance with "the spirit of democracy and social understanding."[204]

Terms of the Plan for the Administration of Justice and U.S. military government directives for the implementation of that plan in Hesse were rescinded on 21 July 1947. The *Länder* constitutions laid the basis for a reorganisation of German judicial organisations that corresponded to the principles of democracy, justice according to the law, and equality before the law for all citizens.[205]

The Plan for the Administration of Justice previously had served as the basis for the reconstruction of German court jurisdiction prior to the adoption of the *Land* constitutions, but had become obsolete. The establishment and implementation of German administration of justice became the responsibility of German authorities, while remaining subject to the Control Council, the U.S. military government, and German legislation and regulations dealing with the administration of justice, such as the receipt of monthly reports on the operations of German courts. The *Land* government was also free to modify the provisions of the plan, in whole or in part, at its discretion.[206]

The minister of justice questioned whether changes to the current *Land* judicial organisation were desirable at that time, two years after the collapse of the National Socialist regime and the redrawing of *Land* boundaries. Changes up to that time had always dealt with considerations of expediency and pressing demands of the moment.

Potential changes to be considered included whether the locations of the *Landgerichte*, the *Landgerichtbezirke*, and the *Amtsgerichtsbezirke* that had been introduced upon the formation of Hesse corresponded to the present situation or whether modifications were necessary, and whether the opening of new courts was desirable or necessary.[207] The plan effectively became redundant, but the *Land* government supplemented the original provisions that remained in effect.[208]

New terms were introduced for selecting judges in accordance with Art. 127 of the constitution of Hesse,[209] establishing terms for the permanent appointment of judges[210] and replacing the provision for temporary appointments that had been set forth in the plan.[211] New provisions were also introduced for the formation of disciplinary courts at the *Landgerichte* and the *Oberlandesgericht* for the institution of disciplinary proceedings against jurists.[212] The establishment of the constitutional government in Hesse thus led to greater independence from direct influence by the U.S. military government and to a greater responsibility for the judiciary to serve as a safeguard against arbitrary actions by the state.

Questions involving constitutional matters were handled by a constitutional court, established to serve as a check upon public authority and legislation enacted by the *Land* government. The government of Hesse adopted the *Land* Constitutional Court Law on 12 December 1947 to defend the principles of the constitution. Professional judges and lay members were appointed to that court by the *Landtag*, responsible for hearing cases against members of the government or the permanent judiciary.

The law prescribed procedures by which the court was to protect the constitution, to determine the constitutionality of laws and regulations, and to mediate in jurisdictional conflicts between separate levels of government. Any individual or administrative authority could take a case to court if it involved a matter that violated one of the basic rights in the constitution.[213] The jurisdiction of the constitutional court also extended to cases of impeachment for members of the *Land* government who had violated the constitution, cases involving the constitutionality of *Land* legislation, cases involving the integrity of legislative elections, and cases involving judges accused of professional neglect or acting contrary to the constitution.

Unlike the constitutional courts of the other *Länder*, only the constitutional court in Hesse allowed for an individual to bring a case before the court if their fundamental rights had been violated.[214] Reform of the *Land* justice system represented a major innovation that entrenched the protection of civil rights set forth in the constitution.

The establishment of the constitutional court mitigated the ordinary courts' claim of the right to judge the constitutionality of governmental enactments. That had been one of the most dangerous features of the justice system in the Weimar Republic, in which reactionary judges had used that claim to sabotage progressive measures, citing their right of judicial independence.[215]

Administrative Courts

A system of administrative courts would provide a judicial safeguard to affirm the division of the legislative, executive, and judicial powers of the state, thus maintaining the ideal of the *Rechtsstaat* by preventing the exercise of arbitrary action by state authorities. The role of those courts was to adjudicate in controversies concerning the rights of an individual who had been affected by an act committed by a public authority, thus contributing to safeguarding the rule of law by providing for the defence of an individual's constitutional rights, while acting independent of governmental control, as were the ordinary law courts.[216]

At the national level, Control Council Law No. 36 of 10 October 1946 on "Administrative Courts" declared that administrative courts be reestablished throughout Germany and in Berlin. The terms of the structure, jurisdiction, and procedure of the courts were left to the discretion of the respective Allied military government zone commanders and the Allied Kommandatura in Berlin, as long as the legislation guiding the courts didn't conflict with Control Council legislation and policy. National Socialist legislation regarding administrative courts was abolished upon the enactment of that law.[217]

Control Council Law No. 36 confirmed the existing reform of the administrative courts that had already been reopened in the U.S. occupation zone, where the U.S. military government had pressed for a rapid restoration of administrative courts.[218] The *Länderrat* worked in coordination with instructions from the military government to create a uniform regulation for the procedures and jurisdiction of administrative courts in the three *Länder* of the U.S. zone, essentially following the pattern of administrative justice that had been established before 1933.[219]

A panel of German jurists convened in Heidelberg in September 1945 to draft proposed legislation for the procedures and jurisdiction of the administrative court system in the U.S. zone.[220] It was necessary to reorganise the system to achieve uniformity in the three *Länder* and to restore their significance in the administration of justice. The NSDAP had considered administrative courts to be a hindrance to its arbitrary rule, and therefore had limited their responsibility. As a consequence, the legal authority of administrative courts to protect the rights of individuals and public bodies had been almost completely eliminated. The restoration of protection against unlawful actions by state authorities thus became an important task, in view of the past circumstances, in addition to the standardisation of the law[221] governing the structure and responsibility of the administrative courts in each of the three *Länder*. The primary goal for the initial development of the administrative courts was to achieve the complete separation of administrative courts from the administration and personal legal positions of individual judges, as well as to establish a two-tiered system of administrative courts, by which appeals from a first instance court could be heard at a higher level.[222] The revision of the Administrative Code was completed on 17 September 1945, removing all traces of National Socialist ideology,[223] and was then referred to the *Länder* governments for comment.[224] The text of the new administrative code was approved and adopted by the legal committee of the *Länderrat* on 24 April 1946,[225] and was to be promulgated by the minister-president of each *Land*, with the appropriate adjustment for local conditions.[226]

The *Land* military government ordered administrative courts in Hesse to be reopened, according to the terms of the *Länderrat* law enacted on 6 August 1946. The courts were to be reestablished in each *Land* of the U.S. zone and were to conform with the legislation and policies of the military government and the Control Council.[227]

The government of Hesse decreed that administrative courts in Wiesbaden, Kassel, Darmstadt, and an administrative court serving as a special senate at the *Oberlandesgericht* in Frankfurt-am-Main were scheduled to open on 1 September 1946.[228] The *Oberlandesgericht* would hear appeals from those courts.[229] All administrative courts in Hesse were reopened on 15 October 1946,[230] And for the first time[231] since their introduction in the nineteenth century, all administrative courts in the *Länder* of the U.S. zone were regulated uniformly.[232] The conclusive provisions on their composition, responsibilities, and procedures were later set forth in a *Land* law on administrative courts, promulgated on 31 October 1946.[233]

U.S. military government administrative courts officers were instructed to educate people in their occupation zone about the availability of administrative courts for the redress of complaints and grievances against decrees by German governmental agencies or officials, and about "the protection of the citizen against arbitrary use and abuse of power by the German government."[234] The *Land* government decreed that the organisation of administrative courts in Hesse was to consist of an administrative appeals court in Kassel and three administrative courts, situated in Darmstadt, Kassel, and Wiesbaden.[235] The supreme administrative court of Hesse was established in June 1947, thus completing the restoration of the system for procedural and administrative justice in Hesse. It was also a system for procedural and administrative justice, that in the opinion of the Civil Administration experts of the Military Government For Greater Hesse, was better and stronger than ever before.[236]

The central element of administrative court reform lay in the extension of their jurisdiction. The administrative court organisation was made responsible for ensuring the protection of rights in disputes concerning public law outside of constitutional law.[237] The principle of having all incriminating administrative actions subject to legal action had only been implemented in a few German *Länder* in the nineteenth century. The introduction of courts throughout western Germany, the complete organisational separation of the jurisdiction of the administrative courts from the state, and the absolute judicial independence of those courts were considered significant developments of constitutional law in the Federal Republic of Germany.[238]

Labour Courts

Labour disputes in Germany prior to the National Socialist takeover had been dealt with by a system of labour courts, established under the Labour Courts Law of 23 December 1926.[239] New regulations governing the settlement of disputes by labour courts were introduced by Control Council legislation. The regulation of labour relations was restored under Control Council Law No. 40 of 30 November 1946 on "Repeal of the Law of January 20, 1934 on 'The Organization of National Labor," which abolished National Socialist law and all related enactments and ordinances pertaining to its application.[240] That law was later supplemented by Control Council Law No. 56 of 30 June 1947 on the "Repeal of the Law of 23 March 1934, on the Regulation of Labor in Public Administrations and Enterprises," which abolished that law and all its related enactments.[241]

The restoration of an independent labour court organisation wasn't urgent after the unconditional surrender, since organised labour had disintegrated. Therefore, the functions of those courts in the U.S. zone were provisionally assumed by the *Amtsgerichte*[242] until further measures could be implemented to establish a permanent labour judicial organisation. The absence of legislative authority regarding labour relations was replaced by economic legislation, issued by the Control Council, which generally set forth uniform quadripartite principles or standards of labour regulations for Germany as a whole.

The execution and implementation of those regulations was charged to *Land* labour authorities, under the general supervision of the zonal military government.[243] Examples included establishing common wage policies in the four zones, allowing trade unions to negotiate wage adjustments with employers and employers' associations, subject to Control Council policies and the labour offices responsible for authorising any changes in the wage rates.[244] Uniform provisions were also to be introduced for regulating working hours.[245]

A series of Control Council enactments advanced the democratisation and self-government within the organisation of labour, such as making provisions for the creation of federations of democratically organised trade unions uniting each branch of industry.[246] The principle of democratic self-government was reinforced by attaching advisory councils, composed of representatives of workers and employees (*Arbeiter und Angestellten*) and employers to the labour offices established at the *Land* level to advise them on all matters within their jurisdiction.[247] Works councils (*Betriebsräte*) were elected to represent and protect the professional, economic, and social interests of workers and employees in every enterprise.[248] Labour disputes between employees and employers were to be settled through arbitration agencies[249] and labour courts.[250]

Labour courts were established under the terms of Control Council Law No. 21 on "German Labor Courts" of 30 March 1946, which extended the terms of the Plan for the Administration of Justice in the U.S. zone.[251] Pending labour matters were to be handled in German ordinary law courts under the interpretation of that law[252] until labour courts could be established.

The law called for the reestablishment of a system of German labour courts in each of the four occupation zones, and provided terms for the composition, responsibility, and jurisdiction of local and appellate labour courts in certain kinds of disputes, including: 1) those arising from a collective agreement or to the presence or non-existence of such an agreement; 2) disputes concerning working conditions, such as safety or health measures; and 3) disputes concerning the interpretation of agreements concluded between works councils. Judges for these courts were to be selected by panels of representatives drawn from management and labour unions. Provisions of the German Labour Courts Law of 23 December 1926 didn't contradict those of the Control Council law in any way, and therefore continued to be in force.[253] The new German labour courts law was reviewed and approved by the *Länderrat*. Measures for its implementation were then instituted, providing for labour courts of first and second instance to be administered under the labour minister of each *Land*, with assessors from labour and employer organisations. The U.S. military government approved the law in September 1946, subject to the inclusion of certain terms of Control Council Laws No. 21 and No. 22, which were incorporated into the final draft.[254]

Provisions of the new Labour Court Law would be applied in its original form through the *Land* judicial organisation, except that they would operate under the supervision of each *Land* Ministry of Labour, which wasn't to exercise any form of influence on court decisions.[255] The terms of the new German labour courts law were based on the original labour courts law, except for provisions that had been imposed by Control Council Law No. 21, eliminating National Socialist features from court procedures, jurisdiction, and organisation.[256]

Law No. 21 also allowed for the appointment of lay judges in courts of the first instance.[257] Twelve labour courts in Hesse (Darmstadt, Frankfurt-am-Main, Fulda, Gießen, Hanau, Hersfeld, Kassel, Limburg, Marburg, Offenbach, Wetzlar, and Wiesbaden) were reopened on 30 September 1946, along with the labour appeals court (*Landesarbeitsgericht*) in Frankfurt-am-Main,[258] and placed under the jurisdiction of the *Land* Ministry for Labour and Welfare.[259] Labour courts law went into force on 27 August 1947,[260] while regulations concerning their composition, responsibilities, and procedures were officially published on 30 March 1948.[261]

The reconstruction of the labour judicial organisation represented an important aspect of the democratisation of German society. In addition to eliminating National Socialist influences, the restoration of labour courts and organised labour reinforced the role of individual responsibility in the postwar social order. Just as the military government courts had set an example for the administration of justice when the operation of all German courts was suspended, it may be argued that labour courts, like the courts in the other branches of the German justice system, demonstrated firsthand examples of the impartial settlement of disputes under law. Considering that the labour force comprises the majority of the population, it may be surmised that settling labour disputes in accordance with labour legislation administered by independent judges fostered confidence in the postwar justice system.

The Restoration of the Bar Association

The legal profession, like other occupational groups in National Socialist Germany, had been organised as a part of the governmental structure.[262] At the beginning of the occupation, local lawyer associations could be formed on a free and democratic basis, subject to approval by the military government, although they were not permitted to exercise any judicial function. Their main purpose was to provide mutual assistance among their members, to open and maintain legal libraries, to form legislative committees for drafting recommendations to the military government, and generally to support the law courts in their endeavour to reestablish a high level of non-political justice.[263]

Until provisions for the restoration of a bar association were drawn up the reinstatement of lawyers was subject to denazification regulations and to the approval of the local military government detachment, the local *Landgericht* president, and the *Land* minister of justice.[264] The Law on the Organisation of the Bar, or "Lawyers' Code," reestablished the terms for admission of lawyers to the bar association and the organisation and functions of the bar.

The new law was drafted by U.S. Legal Advisor of the Office of Military Government for Germany, Professor Karl Loewenstein, in consultation with prominent German lawyers.[265] It was then reviewed at the *Länderrat*,[266] where it was approved by the ministers of justice and their delegates.[267] The *Länderrat* legal committee approved a draft of the law on 23 July 1946,[268] and the deputy military governor gave his official approval on 6 October 1946.[269]

The law went into force in three *Länder* of the U.S. zone on 1 December 1946. The Chamber of Attorneys, or bar association, was restored, in accordance with the terms of the original law, enacted on 1 July 1878, that had been in place on 30 January 1933.[270] Technical innovations introduced under the National Socialist regime were retained, and the self-government of the bar was extended.[271] The new law retained the provision for internship in office (*anwaltschaftliche Probedienst*) of a year, or six months in special cases, that had been introduced in the *Reichsrechtsanwaltsordnung* of 21 February 1936.[272] The Lawyers' Code also called for the establishment of a Chamber of Attorneys in every *Oberlandesgericht* district, where it would be permanently situated.[273]

Annual elections were to be held for members of the bar to choose a nine-member governing board (*Vorstand*). Apart from administrative functions, the board possessed disciplinary powers over members, in the event of professional misconduct. Disciplinary courts were reestablished to deal with violations of professional duties. The governing board would serve as the court of first instance in deciding such cases. Appeals were to be transferred to a court of appeals, consisting of four practicing lawyers elected by members of the bar and three judges of the *Oberlandesgericht*, appointed by its president.[274]

Every lawyer admitted to practice was to become a member of the Chamber of Attorneys and had to serve in a governmental office for up to a year within three years of their admission. The latter provision would help relieve a shortage of judges and prosecutors in German courts.[275]

Lawyers who'd been unjustly persecuted under the National Socialist regime could clear their records. Any lawyer who'd been sentenced by a disciplinary court of honour after 5 March 1933 could request that their case be reviewed and their sentence annulled if the regulations and standards of judgments in the case hadn't been valid before 5 March 1933.[276] Transitional provisions included terms for the reinstatement of lawyers, according to existing regulations. No lawyers who had been admitted to practice after 9 May 1945 could resume their practices until they'd officially been readmitted to the bar association, unless the military government disapproved their readmittance.[277]

Further provisions specifically addressed the circumstances of the time. The law included penalties to deter disbarred lawyers from resuming their practice, which particularly applied to disqualified former National Socialists.[278] The U.S. military government drafted and inserted a clause into the revised *Rechtsanwaltsordnung*, instructing practicing lawyers to act against abuses of the law.[279] The clause stated that if a member of the bar became conscious of any official action or inaction implying a danger of perversion of the law or contradicting the principle of equality for all before the law, as set forth in Art. 2 of Control Council Law No. 1, the bar association's governing board (*Vorstand der Rechtsanwaltskammer*) was to be informed immediately. In turn, the board was to investigate such matters and make a report to the minister of justice, if the public interest required further measures. The minister would then notify the military government. The obligation to report offences was to take precedence over an attorney's requirement of confidentiality.[280]

Reform of German Law at the *Land* Level

Regulations governing criminal law and procedure in the U.S. zone reverted to those in force in Weimar Germany.[281] On the other hand, emergency legislation was enacted for the administration of criminal justice in Hesse, due to an increase of crime and a shortage of judicial personnel.[282] The significant number of criminal cases and the limited number of judges and reopened courts in Germany at the time required simplification and acceleration of proceedings in criminal cases. The revised accelerated proceedings of criminal procedure (*Strafprozeßordnung*) §212 StPO, §18–20 of the Ordinance of 21 February 1940 was therefore retained in all four occupation zones.[283]

An emergency ordinance was enacted in Hesse on 23 May 1946, allowing for the office of the public prosecutor to abstain from attending a main hearing before an *Amtsgericht*, provided that a sentence wasn't expected to be more than two years in prison. The ordinance was only to remain in force from 1 March 1946 to 31 December 1947.[284] The *Land* government also introduced expedited court proceedings for the prosecution of curfew violations or failure to produce registration identification. With the consent of the accused, an *Amtsgericht* was to pronounce decisions in such cases immediately without the usual procedure of instituting prosecution, participation of the public prosecutor, or protection of a delay period. The procedure in such cases would be applied in accordance with existing legislation governing court procedures.[285] That ordinance was later extended to all misdemeanours.[286] The accused could request to appear before an *Amtsgericht* on the same day the files were presented.[287]

The most notable achievement regarding the reform of the law was the revised *Strafrechtspflegeordnung*, or Code of Criminal Procedure, which was sent to the minister-presidents in February 1946.[288] It was the only example of military government legislation being imposed upon the *Land* governments. Without any previous consultation, the minister-presidents of the *Länder* were ordered to enact the revised text of the code of criminal procedure that had been drafted by military government officials at the Control Council Legal Division. The dictated legislation was justified by the need for reopening German courts to administer criminal justice according to democratic principles.[289] Technical improvements were introduced into the new code, such as substantially strengthening the rights afforded the accused and divesting police authorities of their former power to enact legislation and adjudicate in certain offences.[290]

The U.S. military government recognised the authority of the *Landrat* (equivalent of a county government) and the *Oberbürgermeister* (mayor) to enact police ordinances, to the extent that their authority had existed in German law before the NSDAP came to power, which would extend the responsibilities of the German police and judicial organisation and further relieve military government courts of dealing with minor cases.[291]

Certain types of minor infractions had been handled by the police under Weimar, but that power was extended and abused during the National Socialist regime.[292] As a result, functions involving the administration of criminal justice were to be removed from police jurisdiction, in order to prevent arbitrary abuse. The military government thus ordered the former legislative and judicial power of German police to be eliminated from *Land* law and legal procedures to prevent excessive exercise of police control over the civil population.[293] All existing laws, ordinances, or other legislative enactments giving police the power to legislate or to promulgate enactments with the force of law or to adjudicate criminal offences, to issue penal orders, or to impose penalties for the violation of any law, were to be repealed.

The former legislative powers of the police were transferred to the exclusive control of civil legislative authorities, including the *Bürgermeister*, *Oberbürgermeister*, *Landräte*, *Regierungspräsidenten*, minister-presidents, and ministers of the interior. The former judicial power would revert to the *Amtsgerichte* or any other administrative agency selected or created for that purpose.[294] Infractions against police ordinances in Hesse became governed by law on 16 May 1946, after which, cases involving violations of police ordinances would be brought before an *Amtsgericht*.[295]

A new criminal code was introduced in Hesse by the Law of 21 February 1946, which consisted of two parts: the *Strafgerichtsverfassungsgesetz*, adjusted from the Judicature Act of 1877 (*Gerichtsverfassungsgesetz*) by the *Land* in conformity to Control Council and U.S. military government legislation in matters regarding criminal justice; and the Code of Criminal Procedure (*Strafprozessordnung 1946*), common for the three *Länder*. The code was subsequently amended, in line with local requirements in each *Land*.[296] It introduced regulations for German court proceedings and supplemented the provisional criminal code that comprised occupation law and the provisions of German law that had remained unaffected by occupation law. Criminal jurisdiction was to be exercised by *Amtsgerichte*, through a judge or jury court, by the *Strafkammer* (division of the court for criminal matters) of the *Landgerichte*, and by the *Oberlandesgericht*, serving as the appeals court of highest instance.

The formation of the *Schöffengerichte* (jury courts at the *Amtsgericht* level) and of the *Schwurgerichte* (jury courts at the *Landgericht* level) would take place upon the instruction of the minister of justice.[297] The new criminal code otherwise reaffirmed the principles of the German criminal code that had been in place before 30 January 1933, subject to amendments deemed necessary according to the prevailing conditions in Hesse.[298]

The *Strafrechtspflegeordnung* of 1946, consisting of the new *Strafgerichtsverfassungsgesetz* and *Strafprozeßordnung*, went into force on 1 March 1946, abolishing wartime provisions for the administration of criminal justice.[299] Procedural regulations in subsidiary criminal laws would remain in force, as long as they didn't contradict the *Strafrechtspflegeordnung*, the implementation law, or the laws of the military government. The *Strafrechtspflegeordnung* was to be applied in accordance with the goals and regulations of military government laws—especially Proclamation No. 3 and the Plan for the Administration of Justice in the U.S. Zone. The leading authority of the justice system was the minister of justice, and the *Oberlandesgericht* replaced the functions of the *Reichsgericht*.[300]

Reform of German Law at the National Level

The reopened German courts administered justice according to German law that remained in force, unless aspects of the law or individual laws had been repealed or suspended by the Allied Control Council, the U.S. military government, or a *Land* government.[301] The first Allied Control Council measures in the autumn of 1945 abolished the most notorious examples of National Socialist legislation.

The problem of staging a thorough reform of German law was finding all the National Socialist legislation that would have to be abolished. It would have required enormous legal research, examining individual German laws for National Socialist content, since the number of legislative enactments that had been published in the official law gazette of the Third *Reich* (the *Reichsgesetzblatt*) alone reached five figures.

Initial military government legislative enactments followed the narrow range of legal objectives outlined in the Potsdam Protocol, but wouldn't suffice to bring about a comprehensive reform of German law.[302] Detailed planning for the denazification of German law only began after the occupation had begun,[303] and was implemented in an unsystematic and piecemeal manner. As a result of this while the *Land* governments in the U.S. zone were enacting a postwar body of legislation National Socialist legislation remained in force until it had been expressly abolished.

The Control Council Legal Division considered three approaches for reforming the body of German law. The most convenient and simple approach would have been a wholesale repeal of all legislation that had been enacted after 30 January 1933. However, that wasn't practical, since it would have removed technical innovations that would also serve the purpose of occupation authorities and postwar German governments.[304] For example, the law on juvenile courts of 1943 was maintained, with modifications introduced by the military government in 1945.[305] The denazification of German law was therefore to be limited to eliminating the "political" legislation of the regime. However, there remained the question of how it was to be carried out.

A second approach involved the examination of each legislative topic and every enactment of German law for National Socialist content. That approach was accepted by the Control Council, but new difficulties arose with regard to replacing repealed National Socialist legislation or provisions with new, more appropriate modifications. The basic question was whether the new modifications were to be drawn from the pre-1933 body of German law, if any had existed, or whether new improvements of technique or substance were to be introduced.

If new legislation was to be introduced, the next question concerned whether German authorities or the occupation power should introduce that legislation. The Control Council Legal Division concluded that it would examine individual laws for possible revision. The Ministries of Justice of the *Länder* in the U.S. zone lacked the manpower for the task, and there was no single German agency to operate in the legislative field for Germany as a whole. Legal unity in Germany couldn't be achieved, since there was also no machinery for coordinating the legislation of the seventeen German *Länder*.[306] So military government lawyers undertook the task of the denazification of individual legislative subjects, to be dealt with either at the Control Council or the zonal military government level, selecting subjects at random, without actually determining which subjects were appropriate for either Control Council or zonal legislation.[307]

The occupation objective of the denazification of German law was dealt with systematically at the national level after the Allied Control Council established a quadripartite German Law Revision Committee, which held its first meeting on 21 March 1946.[308] The purpose of the committee was to carry out the spirit and letter of Control Council Law No. 1 and Military Government Law No. 1. The committee was responsible for examining German legislation for making recommendations to the Legal Division for the elimination of National Socialist legislation and the substitution of appropriate provisions where necessary.[309]

The new legislative reform programme was extended from previously formulated occupation policies, which would contribute to the Potsdam Protocol objectives of decentralisation, democratisation, and demilitarisation by stigmatising all provisions relating to the NSDAP in all spheres of the law, with representatives of the four occupation powers each dealing with separate fields of law,[310] and by formulating new provisions to compensate for gaps in the legal structure that could be created when making the necessary repeals.[311]

The U.S. military government enlisted the assistance of the Ministries of Justice of the *Länder* in preparing for the denazification and demilitarisation of German legislation in various fields by requesting them to provide lists of National Socialist enactments. Those lists were also to include recommendations for repealing legislation or provisions by the Control Council, as well as recommendations on which should remain in force.[312] In turn, the *Land* ministers of justice would form their own legislative reform committees, which would be joined by law professors in the U.S. zone and German legal experts.

The Legal Division of the U.S. headquarters in Berlin retained general direction and supervision of the legislative reform work through the German Law Revision Section of the Legislation Branch, established by the midsummer of 1946. In practice, the plan proved unworkable, since the completion of the legislative reform programme would have taken several years of cooperation among the four occupation powers, whose representatives disagreed over political and social divergences, and their work would be dispersed among several German sub-agencies in the four occupation zones, rather than implemented under the authority of a central Ministry of Justice or national parliamentary body coordinating legislative reform. The approach was also beyond the capacity of the quadripartite legal staffs, since a thorough examination of German legislation and the replacement of unsuitable provisions required expert knowledge on virtually all aspects of German life.[313]

A new plan for legislative reform was developed by the Control Council during 1947, by which the entire body of law was to be analyzed to determine whether individual enactments would require outright repeal, partial abrogation, or amendment.[314] Examples of partial abrogation and amendment included purging the most flagrant National Socialist alterations to the criminal code. Sixteen additional laws and auxiliary enactments of substantive and procedural content and related enactments were abolished under Control Council Law No. 11 of 30 January 1946 on the "Repealing of Certain Provisions of the Criminal Code."[315] Law No. 11 also included repealing provisions pertaining to treason and high treason (sections 80 to 94 of the Criminal Code), which could theoretically be used by a future German government to prosecute Germans who had cooperated with Allied authorities[316] when a national court was be reestablished. Apart from the abolition of National Socialist legislation and its principles under the provisions of Military Government Law No. 1, Control Council Proclamation No. 3, and Control Council Laws No. 1 and No. 11, the criminal code essentially remained unchanged.[317] The Criminal Law Committee of the Legal Directorate of the Control Council continued its deliberations of the German criminal code and supplementary laws, and sought the opinions of the *Land* governments and German experts on criminal law to contribute to the reform of German criminal law. *Land* ministers of justice were also advised that the Control Council didn't intend to undertake a thorough reform of German criminal law and that further reform was to be limited to provisions that were expressions of National Socialist or militarist ideologies.[318]

The minister of justice requested leading authorities to report experiences with the 1946 Code of Criminal Procedure, such as whether any regulations required amendment, whether Control Council Law No. 11 had thoroughly eliminated National Socialist conceptions from criminal law, whether additional regulations that could be considered typically National Socialist should be subject to revision, and whether they had suggestions for reforms regarding the elimination of the National Socialist body of thought.[319]

Control Council Law No. 11 was later supplemented by Control Council Law No. 55 of 20 June 1947 on "Repeal of Certain Provisions of Criminal Legislation," which abolished an additional sixteen criminal enactments or parts thereof.[320] Those enactments followed the concentration of the Control Council on repealing statutes of a political nature in the body of criminal law after the initial outright abolition of the most notorious National Socialist statutes under Control Council Law No. 1.[321]

Whereas German criminal law and procedure had been practically amended beyond recognition under the National Socialist regime, civil law, which governs private relations, proved to be the least affected.[322] German civil law in force after the collapse of the National Socialist regime remained virtually unchanged,[323] apart from the repeal of National Socialist provisions.

The Control Council set forth an important reform in the field of civil law by introducing a new marriage law, under the provisions of Control Council Law No. 16 of 1 March 1946,[324] in response to receiving a large number of divorce petitions. That Control Council enactment substantially represented a compromise between the second and third approaches to the denazification of law, which didn't call for outright abolition but required partial reform. For example, Section 55 of the 1938 statute on marriage was retained, allowing for divorce on the grounds of incompatibility, which hadn't been recognised under the Civil Code of 1900. That technical improvement was retained after deleting National Socialist content[325] that was incompatible with Law No. 16 (Art. 79, para. 2).[326]

Divorce cases were by far the most common type of civil case in Hesse,[327] representing approximately 85 to 90 percent of civil cases before the *Landgerichte* by November 1946.[328] Those cases continued to be entered at a rate of almost twenty a day by late summer and autumn of 1947.[329] There were 1,831 divorce cases in Hesse per 100,000 people in 1947, in comparison to 486 in 1937 within the same approximate area[330] in pre-1945 Germany.

Another example of reforming civil law that had been permeated with National Socialist ideology was the deletion of statutory provisions from the rules of succession. Law No. 37 of 30 October 1946 on the "Repeal of Certain Statutory Provisions Relating to Successions"[331] abrogated Art. 48, para. 2 of the law on testaments of 31 July 1938 (*Reichsgesetzblatt* I 1938, p. 973), which had allowed the modification of testaments by courts in the public interest, or for "healthy popular emotions," which, in practice, meant exercising discrimination against disfavoured individuals.[332]

One of the last substantial measures for reforming German civil law by removing National Socialist norms was the repeal of National Socialist hereditary farm legislation by Control Council Law No. 45 of 20 February 1947 on the "Repeal of Legislation on Hereditary Farms and Enactment of Other Provisions Regulating Agricultural Forest Lands."[333] That measure was followed by Control Council legislation that permanently abolished the former National Socialist interference in cultural and spiritual life.

Two other National Socialist laws were repealed under Control Council Law No. 60 of 24 December 1947 on "Repealing Nazi Legislation on Motion Pictures," which abrogated the law of 14 July 1933 establishing a Provisional Film Chamber, and the Motion Pictures Law of 16 February 1934,[334] which empowered the Propaganda Ministry to censor German and imported motion pictures. The repeal also extended to all supplementary laws, ordinances, and decrees.[335]

Control Council Law No. 62 on "Repealing certain Laws, Ordinances and Decrees Promulgated by the Nazi Government concerning Churches" of 20 March 1948 repealed two laws and one decree[336] that had given the state greater power over churches than had ever been exercised in Germany.[337] That was the last Control Council measure concerning the repeal of National Socialist legislation.

Increasing political paralysis hindered the progress of the Control Council[338] toward the settlement of major problems, such as the establishment of economic unity, the creation of a central German government, and measures for the reconstruction of a national German justice system, apart from the task of repealing National Socialist legislation. It may be argued that further progress in restoring justice could only have been made by zonal authorities operating independently at their levels of jurisdiction while the operation of the Control Council as the governing body for Germany as a whole was deteriorating, as demonstrated by the lack of progress in its decision-making.

The Control Council completely ceased to function after 20 March 1948, when Soviet representatives in the Control Council closed its last meeting[339] and didn't return to join delegations from the western occupation powers in further deliberations. Future legislative reform in the U.S. zone would thus be relegated to the U.S. occupation and German authorities at the zonal and *Land* levels, which took place after the operations of the Control Council had been suspended. While the Control Council led the way in eliminating National Socialist influences from German law and issuing principles for the restoration of justice in Germany, German authorities in the U.S. zone produced their own reforms, under the supervision of the military government.

Transfer of Responsibility to the German Judicial Organisation

The military government supervised the function of German courts in order to prevent misuse or abuse of judicial responsibilities after twelve years of National Socialism. The supervision of German courts therefore composed an integral part of the justice system in the U.S. zone, to ensure that German courts would confine themselves to their assigned jurisdiction, wouldn't disseminate propaganda against the military government, wouldn't apply National Socialist laws and concepts of jurisprudence, and that the administration of justice would be kept free from any form of discrimination and would be administered according to military government laws.[340]

At the beginning of the occupation, German courts in each *Landgericht* district submitted weekly reports to the military government. That practice was later amended so that they only reported on a monthly basis.[341] In view of the

U.S. military government's objective to promote democratic principles in the administration of justice without impairing the independence of the courts, the supervision of German courts would be exercised most effectively by the minister of justice.[342]

The minister of justice was responsible for preparing monthly reports, submitted to the Chief Legal Officer of the *Land* military government office. Those reports consolidated all information pertaining to the courts, the office of the public prosecutor, and the personnel thereof in each *Oberlandesgericht* district.[343] The independence of German courts was thus limited by the military government, although the military government didn't generally interfere in their functions.

Direct interference by the military government in a case pending before a German court was possible, but wasn't ordinarily permissible unless specific revisions had been made for it under German law. The military government could only exercise its power directly in reversing or revising a decision in the event of a flagrant violation of military government policy. Routine supervision entailed military government legal officers making unannounced visits to German courts to observe proceedings, regularly inspecting court registers and case files to determine the accuracy of the monthly reports submitted to the *Land* Military Government Office by the minister of justice, and periodically investigating cases in which the public prosecutor had failed to act in order to determine whether cases had been dropped for justifiable reasons.[344]

Although the military government machinery at the *Land* level for that purpose was insufficient due to the lack of trained personnel,[345] the military government was encouraged by the fact that "spot checks" at the courts and offices of public prosecutors in Hesse didn't normally reveal any irregularities.[346] The shortcomings of military government supervision of German courts were also compensated by the work of the *Land* ministers of justice, who were noted to be "first-rate people" and "convinced anti-Nazis."[347]

By the end of January 1946, the restoration of the German judicial organisation was reported to have reached a stage where *Land* ministers of justice could assume direct responsibility for the operation of German courts. Many types of cases that had been handled by military government courts would be transferred to German courts, with the exception of cases involving the illegal possession of firearms.[348] An increasing number of cases were transferred from military government courts once the great majority of German courts had been reopened. The work of the German courts was expedited by merging courts and referring cases to them without the prior approval of *Land* Military Government Headquarters.[349] The reconstructed justice system in Hesse was thus brought to function, but it still remained under military government restrictions.

All ordinary law courts in Hesse had been reconstituted by 23 May 1946, with the opening of the *Oberlandesgericht* for Hesse, which assumed the appellate jurisdictions of the former prewar *Oberlandesgerichte* in Darmstadt and Kassel.[350] The supreme court in the *Land*, which would hear appeals from the *Landgerichte* in criminal and civil cases was thus reopened.[351] However, there remained restrictions on the extent of the *Land* judicial organisation's responsibility, since the U.S. military government maintained supreme judicial authority under occupation law.

The complete restoration of the *Land* judicial system was followed by measures regulating the operation of military government courts as the jurisdictional limitations of German courts were gradually extended, thus establishing greater judicial responsibility as the German judicial organisation operated alongside military government courts.

The first jurisdictional limitations were imposed under Military Government Law No. 2, which forbade German courts from dealing with any case that involved offences "against any order of the Allied forces, or any enactment of the U.S. military government, or involving the construction or validity of any such order or enactment."[352] Violators of military government laws, regulations, and orders were brought before military government courts, or before German courts, when authorised by the Theatre Commander.[353] German courts were thus responsible for adhering to the terms of military government enactments and for applying the law to the extent of their jurisdiction under occupation law. However, German judges were reluctant to apply military government or Control Council legislation, since they believed they had no authority to do so under a literal interpretation of Article VI(10) of Military Government Law No. 2, which stated that German courts couldn't exercise jurisdiction over certain classes of cases unless they'd been expressly authorised to do so by the military government.[354]

Problems regarding the administration and supervision of the German judicial system were addressed by the enactment of additional military government legislation,[355] regulating the relationship between military government courts and the German judicial organisation. The first permitted overlapping of the jurisdictions of the two judicial organisations was the allowance of UN nationals to serve as witnesses in German courts, thus providing evidence for a trial as in any normally functioning court. Previously, court cases involving witnesses who were U.S. nationals could only have been heard in military government courts, even if the offence was being tried under German law.

Regulation No. 2 under Military Government Law No. 2 of 5 July 1946 on "Testimony in German Courts by Persons Subject to United States Military Law and by Persons Associated with the United States Office of Military Government" allowed UN nationals and military and civilian personnel serving with the U.S. armed forces or associated with the military government to appear as witnesses in German courts upon written request by the president of a German court to the appropriate military government or commanding officer. The approval was subject to certain conditions: the testimony couldn't concern a matter that was classified or prejudicial to the interests of the military government or of the U.S. armed forces, and the evidence being sought, such as copies of official papers or reports of inquiries, couldn't be requested or furnished in connection with the testimony. A German court also couldn't issue subpoenas requiring the attendance of witnesses defined by that regulation or hold a U.S. witness, whether military or civilian, in contempt of court. They could, however, make a written request to the superior officer for disciplinary action[356] against military personnel.

Restoring the everyday functions of the German judicial organisation continued by widening its jurisdiction. That included dealing with questions regarding the jurisdiction of German courts, such as the exclusion of German courts from "construing" or interpreting any military government enactment and thereby falling under military government jurisdiction, according to Art. 6 of Military Government Law No. 2, and the denial of German court jurisdiction in all cases involving UN nationals.[357]

Those questions were addressed by Amendment No. 2 to Military Government Law No. 2 of 9 September 1946.[358] The amendment was designed to harmonise the provisions of Art. 6 of Military Government Law No. 2 and of Art. 3 of Control Council Law No. 4, both of which established limitations on the jurisdiction of German courts. However, some of the terms of Military Government Law No. 2 weren't consistent with the Control Council Law, and some of its provisions were obsolete. The purpose of the amendment was to embody modifications of policy, to consolidate and review certain instructions that were issued by the military government regarding the jurisdiction of German courts, and to repeal Amendment No. 1 to Military Government Law No. 2 of 2 March 1946.[359]

German courts could be empowered to assume jurisdiction in a range of cases when expressly authorized to do so "by Control Council or Military Government law, ordinance, or regulation, or by order of the Military Government Director of the appropriate *Land*."[360] That provided the possibility for German courts to apply military government law, as well as opening the way for the transfer of cases from U.S. military government to German courts. Subject to the prior authorisation by the appropriate authority, German courts could hear cases involving the validity of orders issued by the Allied forces, Control Council, or military government enactments; cases over which jurisdiction had been assumed by a military government court or withdrawn from the jurisdiction of German courts; and monetary claims against a German government or any legal entity in existence under public law.[361] German courts could assume jurisdiction in criminal cases that involved any member of the UN, UN armed forces, individuals serving with them or accompanying them, UN nationals, and UN nationals with the status of displaced persons. They could also try offences committed against the citizens of Allied nations or their property, and attempts to reestablish the National Socialist regime or other National Socialist organisations.[362]

Military government courts maintained exclusive civil jurisdiction over cases involving disputes arising from the ownership or operation of automobiles by U.S. nationals in the U.S. zone,[363] while civil cases that could be transferred to German courts included those affecting any member of the UN, the UN armed forces, individuals serving with those forces or the Allied administration of Germany, individuals accompanying them, and cases *against* UN nationals not holding the status of one of the aforementioned categories.[364]

A considerable number of cases brought before military government and German courts involved displaced persons. Most of them were UN nationals, and therefore the legal status of those cases needed to be clarified. The provisions of the amendment decreed that German courts didn't have the legal authority to try those cases, unless the military government issued its approval. Cases involving UN nationals were to be exempted from the jurisdiction of German courts if the case involved a party in a criminal or civil case serving with the military forces of the UN, held an official position or was performing official functions in the Allied administration of Germany, or was a dependent accompanying such an individual.[365] On the other hand, German court jurisdiction was extended to civil cases involving all other UN nationals and stateless persons who were considered displaced persons.[366]

Although the principle of allowing UN nationals to appear before the courts of a conquered nation was inconsistent with the principle of the extraterritoriality of the occupying force, allowing such cases to be handled by German courts followed the exigencies of the situation[367]—to help stem litigation coming before military government courts by transferring them to German courts. German courts also acquired the express authorisation to apply Control Council Law No. 16 of 20 February 1946: the Marriage Law. The provisions and interpretation of the first amendment of Military Government Law No. 2 had specified that German courts couldn't exercise jurisdiction in cases under Control Council Law No. 16 in which a UN national was a party.[368] The first amendment was thereby repealed.[369] The imposition of death sentences by German courts required the consent of the *Land* military government director or the deputy military governor of the U.S. zone, unless the execution was expressly prohibited by the military government within thirty days after the sentence was pronounced.[370]

The amendment to Military Government Law No. 2 made it possible for German criminal courts to adjudicate over members of the Allied military forces, which theoretically extended German court jurisdiction into the sphere of Allied jurisdiction. According to Control Council Law No. 4, however, German courts couldn't exercise criminal jurisdiction in cases against Allied occupation forces (Art. 3a) or in criminal offences involving military occupation personnel or UN citizens (Art. 3c). On the other hand, German courts could adjudicate in such cases if the nature of the offence didn't affect the security of the Allied forces (Art. 3e).

The withdrawal of competence in cases involving UN nationals from the jurisdiction of German courts, including those considered displaced persons, was considerably wider.[371] The limitation of German court jurisdiction was considerably wider for criminal than civil cases, since the removal of civil cases from their jurisdiction wasn't as specific as it had been for criminal cases.[372] In short, the second amendment to Military Government Law No. 2 provided for the U.S. military government to retain jurisdiction over cases involving UN nationals, unless those cases were allowed to be heard in a German court, as well as all cases involving UN nationals considered displaced persons and criminal matters concerning the direct interests of U.S. military forces.

Military Government Ordinance No. 8 on military tribunals for security violations of 10 November 1946 retained the jurisdiction of the military government in protecting its direct interests, stating that individuals who committed acts prejudicial to the security or interests of the U.S. Forces would be tried by a military court appointed by the European Theatre Commander. The ordinance wouldn't affect the application of Military Government Ordinances 1 and 2, which remained in force.[373] Cases involving theft or similar offences committed by German civilians in the employ of the U.S. Forces were to be brought to trial before military government courts, since they directly affected U.S. interests, even though German courts could properly exercise jurisdiction over such cases.[374] German judges were to respect and concur with the letter and spirit of military government laws and ordinances. They were also responsible for determining whether German courts or military government courts should exercise jurisdiction over cases upon examining the status of the affected parties in each case.[375]

The limitations on the jurisdiction of the German judicial organisations weren't to affect the work of the judiciary in pronouncing judgments. The U.S. military government maintained that the independence of the German judiciary was to be fostered while military government controls of the German justice system were in place. The exercise of those controls was to be limited to an extent that was consistent with protecting occupation forces, accomplishing the aims of the occupation, and eliminating undue military government interference in the German administration of justice.

The U.S. military governor ordered that the objectives be charged to the *Land* military government office. The inspection of records, registers, calendars, and files of the *Landgerichte, Amtsgerichte,* and other subordinate courts would only be done by military government legal officers upon the request of or after clearance with the *Land* military government office. Verbal or written instructions to judges, prosecutors, and other judicial personnel, and the removal of cases from German to military government courts required prior clearance from the *Land* military government office. Suspending any official in the German justice system required the prior authorisation of the *Land* military government office. No supervisory action concerning German courts could be taken by Germans or displaced persons employed by the military government, except by order of and in the presence of military government officers. In the event that action was urgently required to prevent a flagrant violation of military government policies, measures would be taken by subordinate offices of the military government, and a report immediately forwarded to the *Land* military government office.[376]

In keeping with safeguarding the interests of occupation forces, German judges and prosecutors were instructed to report cases of a political nature or involving the interests of the military government. Such notification was initially left to the discretion of the individual German official, but was more closely regulated after March 1947, when new regulations defined categories of such cases more precisely, such as cases involving UN nationals and violations of Control Council and military government laws. Those cases were to be reported to the chief legal officer of the *Land*, and served the purpose of improving information about the work of German courts as reported in the monthly court reports submitted by the minister of justice to the *Land* military government office while reducing the level of direct supervisory activity by the military government.[377]

However, the machinery of supervision was undermined by a shortage of American lawyers familiar with German law and procedure. Only three military government officials in Greater Hesse, one of whom wasn't familiar with German law or the language, were charged with supervising some one hundred courts employing some four hundred judicial personnel who were working through nearly 12,000 criminal and 25,000 civil cases per month. In practice, it meant that supervisory control was limited to field inspectors visiting every *Amtsgericht* twice a year and every *Landgericht* three times a year at irregular intervals, while the inspection of files and records was limited to irregular "spot-checking."

Barring the official limitations on the jurisdiction of German courts and the examination of court reports, those courts maintained *de facto* independence in their everyday operations, since they weren't greatly affected by military government power of court supervision.[378] The responsibility for enforcing an impartial and fair justice system thus fell to the minister of justice as chief administrator of the *Land* judicial organisation.[379]

The military government and the *Land* judicial organisation held the responsibility of ensuring standards for postwar administration of justice, which was further reinforced through the involvement of wider public scrutiny. Public opinion, with the benefit of a free press, could act as a safeguard against abuses of judicial authority.[380] Free public opinion could serve as an instrument of democratic control in a sovereign state, controlling all public affairs, just as control of the government is exercised by parliament and control of the state administration is exercised by the judiciary.[381]

A permanent safeguard against potential abuses of the application of law was introduced with the restoration of jury courts, in which professional judges determined a sentence in coordination with lay jurors drawn from the public sector, who would evaluate cases with the equivalent power of a magistrate on the judicial bench, along with the judges presiding over the case.

The minister of justice for Hesse issued ordinances for future locations of jury courts throughout Hesse on 22 October 1946[382] and 25 April 1947.[383] On 17 April 1947, an ordinance on the creation of those courts laid out guidelines for their composition and function, based on the appropriate articles of criminal code. Jury courts were to be formed at the *Amtsgerichte* (*Schöffengerichte*), consisting of one judge and two jurors, the *Landgerichte* (*Schwurgerichte*), consisting of two judges, including the presiding judge, and seven jurors. The decisions pronounced by those courts could be appealed to the *Oberlandesgericht.* The proceedings of those courts were to take place as they would have without a jury. The *Schwurgerichte* were solely responsible for cases involving robbery, extortion, perjury, and willful criminal actions that resulted in death, while the *Schöffengerichte* dealt with criminal cases that were presented to the *Amtsgerichte,* if the sentence could warrant imprisonment in a prison or a penitentiary for more than a year. They also heard other cases, such as those involving negligent action or slander.

Jurors in jury courts at both levels were selected by political parties, trade unions, and mayors of local districts, in order for the jurors to be appropriately representative of the local population and professions. It was also prescribed that no more than three-fourths of either gender could be represented.[384] Some of the *Schöffengerichte* and *Schwurgerichte* in Hesse were established on 1 November 1947, and other jury courts in Hesse were to be reestablished on 1 January 1948.[385] The participation of laymen in judicial proceedings, which had been eliminated under the National Socialist regime was once again made an important factor in the administration of criminal justice.[386]

In the event of a flagrant violation of military government policies by a German court, the military government could intervene directly by either reversing or revising a court judgment. In practice, such intervention seldom occurred in the U.S. zone.[387]

An example of an intervention by the military government took place in the French zone, where Heinrich Tillesen was tried for the murder of Centre Party Reichstag deputy Matthias Erzberger in 1921. Tillesen had been acquitted under an amnesty declared by Hitler on 21 March 1933, and the *Landgericht* in Offenburg upheld the acquittal on 29 November 1946.[388] Although the basis for the amnesty had been repealed by Control Council Law No. 1,[389] the court defended its decision on the grounds that the perpetrator had committed the murder out of "excessive patriotism." French occupation authorities quashed the verdict, removed the judge from office, rearrested Tillesen, and referred the case for a new trial by the *Landgericht* at Konstanz,[390] which sentenced Tillesen to fifteen years in prison.[391]

A case may be made that the judge in the first trial was insensitive to postwar standards for the administration of justice, and it was argued that such an example of a miscarriage of justice was possibly a consequence of the tradition of legal positivism in the German legal environment. According to legal positivism, the law is a manifestation of the authority of the state, recorded in codes and statutes and interpreted by the judiciary in separate cases, in contrast to law based on a system of precedents, as in common law.[392] A law is interpreted solely according to how it's recorded, without questioning the validity of its intrinsic justice by consciously reasoning with the values of democracy and morality.[393]

Legal positivism allegedly made the German judiciary defenceless against laws containing arbitrary or illegal content, because judges considered themselves bound by the principle "law is law," just as "orders are orders" binds soldiers. That meant that judges served the value of upholding the law of the state, without upholding the principles of justice[394] or discerning the discrepancy between positive law promulgated by the legislature of the state and the principles of "natural law" not set forth in definitive provisions.

Although judges are bound by the laws enacted by the executive authority of the state, their obedience to the law can't be compared to soldiers subject to military orders. A judge is obliged to decide what is just. The correct decision is to be made within the context of the standards of the law and justice. A judge who applied laws that contravened the principles of justice also contravened the responsibilities of judicial office, and served merely as an extension of the executive authority.[395] That indictment applied especially to judges who took part in the trials conducted by the *Sondergerichte* and the *Volksgerichtshof*, as well as judges in the ordinary law courts who had protected their personal interests by conforming to the standards of the National Socialist justice system.

After the end of the Second World War, German courts began to deviate from the trend of employing legal positivism by considering the concept of natural law in making their judgments.[396] That method of reasoning was applied by the Wiesbaden *Amtsgericht* in a judgment pronounced on 13 November 1945. The plaintiff in the case had demanded restitution of property expropriated from her parents, who had perished in a concentration camp. The *Amtsgericht* ruled that a restitution complaint was only justifiable if the plaintiff and other related legal heirs were the owners of the property. In that case, the property had been formerly owned by Jews and had been confiscated under the force of National Socialist legislation. Laws dealing with property on the basis of race had been abolished under military government legislation, but there was no defined approach for dealing with the consequences of laws that previously had been in force. The court therefore decreed that there were rights of individuals according to the tenets of natural law, which the state can't rescind through legislation, including the right to private property. Hence, the laws declaring Jewish property forfeit contravened natural law, and therefore had been invalid or unjust from the time they'd been enacted. It followed that the finance office that was holding the property wasn't authorised to dispose of expropriated Jewish property, since it wasn't holding the property with the consent of the rightful owner.[397]

All German law courts were entrusted with administering the law independently. The task of the military government overseeing the restoration of the postwar German judicial organisation and German courts of appeal served the function of highest legal authority, holding the power to revise dubious court decisions, and to ensure appropriate application of the law. The function of hearing appeals from the lower courts became increasingly important during the occupation, since reopened German courts in the U.S. zone passed conspicuously mild sentences that didn't reflect the objective meaning and purpose of sentencing in accordance with the facts in certain cases. This recurring problem, which reached crisis proportions, was considered to be a symptom of the judiciary's reaction to the past, when excessively severe penalties were imposed by courts of the National Socialist regime.[398] The military government could intervene in German court decisions to prevent violations of Control Council or military government enactments or the principles of a democratic justice system, but German appeals courts made the final decisions considering errors in the application of the law or the use of judicial discretion.[399]

Greater Responsibility Conferred upon the *Land* Judicial Organisation

The restoration of constitutional government led to *Land* governments and judicial organisations acquiring greater freedom of action. Indirect government by the U.S. military government ended following the promulgation of U.S. Military Government Proclamation No. 4[400] on 1 March 1947. That proclamation superseded Proclamation No. 2, which had initially established the *Länder* in view of changed conditions and set forth the new U.S. occupation aims at that stage of the military occupation.

Proclamation No. 4 stated that complete legislative, executive, and judicial power existed in the *Länder* of the U.S. occupation zone, and that it was to be exercised by the *Länder* governments in accordance with *Land* constitutions. The authority of the *Land* governments, as defined in the *Land* constitutions, remained subject to certain reservations: international agreements involving the U.S., Allied Control Council legislation, and powers reserved to the U.S. military government in order to execute basic policies of the occupation,[401] such as disallowing *Land* legislatures from dealing with subjects concerning Germany as a whole.[402] The approval and adoption of the *Land* constitution thus extended the legislative jurisdiction of the *Land* government, which was given official sanction under Proclamation No. 4.[403]

Proclamation No. 2 had initially defined the power of the military government and the minister-president acting under its authority. The power of approving and promulgating legislation was conferred upon the *Land* minister-president until democratic institutions could be established, while the legislative, executive, and judicial powers of each *Land* were subject to the authority of the military government.[404] Military government jurisdiction was substantially reduced by Proclamation No. 4 to three fields: international agreements to which the U.S. was a party, four-power legislation, and powers reserved to the U.S. military government for implementing the basic policies of the occupation, which continued unchanged from Proclamation No. 2.[405]

New legislation adopted by the *Länderrat* thereafter would be subject to the prior examination of a military government review board, established under General Order No. 30 of 4 April 1947 to ensure compliance with Proclamation No. 4.[406] Proclamation No. 4 also led to greater autonomy for the German justice system. The military government exercised its control over German courts through supervision, guidance, and regular inspections, to ensure that the administration of justice was carried out in accordance with Allied occupation policy.[407]

Giving greater responsibility to the *Land* legislative and judicial authorities in the U.S. occupation zone was fully endorsed by a new Joint Chiefs of Staff

Directive of 11 July 1947. The new policy directive superseded JCS 1067, which had laid out the policies for the initial post-defeat period, and marked the second phase of reconstruction by reflecting the development of the new situation in Germany since 1945. This policy directive instructed the military government to establish stable political and economic conditions in Germany that would contribute to European recovery.[408] The directive reaffirmed the objective of establishing democracy in Germany, and recognised the importance of both the reestablishment of German self-government and the German governmental agencies assuming direct responsibility for legislative, executive, and judicial powers, while maintaining military security and the purposes of the occupation. All powers and political life were to be established in the *Länder* before a central German government was formed.[409] The supervision of German courts was to be maintained in order to enforce compliance with the principles expressed in Proclamation No. 3, the provisions of Control Council, and U.S. military government legislation. The independence of the restored German judiciary was to be fostered by allowing courts the freedom to interpret and apply the law, and by reducing military government control measures to "the minimum consistent with the accomplishment of the aims of the occupation."[410]

No mention of law reform was made in the new directive, since it may have been believed that the task was considered complete, that it was no longer important, or that legislative reform was no longer considered a function of the U.S. military government.[411] The power of the military government to disapprove German legislation was maintained and was to be used if legislation conflicted with the legislation or policies of the military government.[412] A further concession to German self-government was made when the validity of *Land* legislation was no longer dependent on the approval of the military government.[413]

There was one exception to this general trend of granting more power and jurisdiction to the German authorities. The principle of the extraterritoriality of the military government was maintained while allowing for a progressive number of cases to be handled by German courts. As the U.S. Department of State Bulletin stated, "You may extend the jurisdiction of German courts to all cases which do not involve the interests of Military Government or persons under the protective care of Military Government."[414] That would also serve to reduce the caseload of military government courts by transferring them to German courts.

Although an increase in criminal cases and a shortage of prosecutors led to a large backlog, German courts in Hesse had accelerated their work through the dockets by December 1946. The courts disposed of the current monthly scheduled cases and began to work through the backlog of criminal cases for the first time since the beginning of the occupation.[415] Correspondingly, the greatest reduction of cases handled by military government courts was in Hesse, where military government courts tried 5,457 cases in July 1947 and 1,144 cases in September 1947.[416]

The improvement of the performance of German courts in Hesse was particularly impressive by September 1947, when the courts dealt with a 25 percent increase of additional cases over the preceding month, and a 100 percent increase over September 1946. The acceleration of the denazification of jurists and the employment of refugee lawyers made more personnel available, which consequently enabled the courts to deal with cases more expeditiously.[417]

Meanwhile, the number of trials that were held in Hesse escalated as an increasing number of cases of theft, black market activity,[418] and groups of minor cases continued to be transferred from U.S. military government courts to German courts. On 7 April 1947, German courts were authorised to exercise jurisdiction over cases involving offences against Control Council Law No. 50, "Punishment of the Theft of Unlawful Use of Rationed Foodstuffs, Goods and Rationing Documents" committed by individuals who weren't exempt from German court jurisdiction under Section 10(a) of Military Government Law No. 2.[419]

A directive to the German justice system on 26 July 1947 authorised the transfer of additional categories of minor cases that previously had been in the jurisdiction of military government courts.[420] Those cases included theft or illegal possession of property belonging to a UN national or government under the value of twenty-five dollars, illegally crossing the border of Germany or the U.S. zone by individuals, the illegal transference of property across the border of Germany or the U.S. zone, and failing to produce proper identification. German courts couldn't exercise jurisdiction if the affected individuals in those cases fell outside German court jurisdiction, as set forth in Art. 6, para. 10 of Military Government Law No. 2. They were to transfer such cases to a military government court if they affected the security of Allied military forces or the interests of the military government. German courts were to apply either military government law, such as Military Government Law No. 161 regarding cases of unauthorised movement of persons or property across the boundaries of Germany or the U.S. zone, or German law in trying those cases.[421] By the end of 1947, German courts handled most cases involving unauthorised border crossings, and theft or illegal possession of U.S. property under a certain value.[422]

German court jurisdiction in criminal and civil cases arising from disputes dealing with Rhine navigation was reestablished under Military Government Law No. 9 and Military Government Ordinance No. 16 of 11 July 1947. Law No. 9 designated German courts in Mannheim and Wiesbaden as having jurisdiction over shipping in Württemberg-Baden and Hesse respectively, handling both civil and criminal cases. The function, jurisdiction, and procedure of those courts were established in accordance with the revised Rhine Navigation Act of 1868, the Convention of Mannheim, as it was amended prior to 14 November 1936, specifically repealing the National Socialist law of 30 January 1937 concerning procedure in Inland Navigation cases.

Depending upon the location of the court of first instance, appeals could be conveyed to the Karlsruhe Branch of the *Oberlandesgericht* in Stuttgart or the *Oberlandesgericht* of Hesse in Frankfurt-am-Main. Ordinance No. 16 provided for the establishment of military government courts in Mannheim and Wiesbaden to hear cases involving occupation interests or UN personnel.[423] The *Amtsgericht* in Wiesbaden was designated as the Rhine navigation court for Hesse. The function and jurisdiction of that court were determined by Law No. 9 and existing German legislation governing such cases.[424]

The jurisdiction of military government courts regarding U.S. dependents and UN nationals in Germany was also clarified under Amendment No. 2 to Ordinance No. 2 (Military Government Courts), effective 22 July 1947, confirming that military government courts would deal with violations of army circulars, rulings, and orders, rather than courts-martial. Amendment No. 1 to Ordinance No. 1 (Crimes and Offences) established the maximum penalties for such violations at no more than five years in prison or a fine of no more than RM 10,000 or a corresponding dollar equivalent. The penalty was not to be more severe than a court-martial sentence for similar offences.[425]

Due to the heavy caseload in military government courts and a shortage of experienced military government court personnel to act as judges and prosecutors, a directive of 16 July 1947 ordered a 25 percent reduction in the number of cases handled monthly by 1 November 1947. That would be accomplished by turning cases of a minor nature over to German courts or by the dismissing of the charges when the offence was considered trivial or inconsequential or when the evidence to obtain a conviction was clearly insufficient.[426] Transferring certain types of cases to German courts, which proved capable of handling an increasingly large caseload, and dropping trivial cases resulted in a 40 percent decrease in the number of cases in October 1947 in comparison to the number of cases tried by summary courts in June 1947.[427]

The military government court caseload continued to decrease in early 1948, largely due to the transfer of cases to German courts.[428] On 23 January 1948, the jurisdiction of German courts was extended to deal with cases involving the theft or illegal possession of property of UN nationals or governments, valued at up to one hundred dollars.[429] Since German courts performed satisfactorily in the trial of such cases, more minor cases were transferred to them to further relieve the burden on military government courts.[430]

On 27 April 1948, German courts in Hesse were also empowered to hear cases involving UN nationals and displaced persons considered UN nationals concerning misdemeanours as defined under §§ 407 of the *Strafprozeßordnung*,[431] unless they were members of UN military forces or dependents accompanying them. The accused in those proceedings could file objections with a local military government court that would deal with the case.[432] That was later extended on 24 August 1948 to encompass crimes as well as misdemeanours (*Übertretungen und Vergehen*) committed by individuals within the jurisdiction of the *Amtsgerichte* (section 407 of the *Strafprozeßordnung*).

If the accused demanded a main hearing (*Hauptverhandlung* as defined in section 411 of the *Strafprozeßordnung*), the case would immediately be transferred to a military government court. In such cases, it was emphasised that a German court couldn't impose a penalty amounting to more than 3,000 DM, or the length of imprisonment stated in Art. 407, Part II of the *Strafprozeßordnung*.[433] Those measures brought the exercise of German courts in such cases to a much wider scope under German law, except that the maximum fine a German court could impose couldn't exceed the amount that could be imposed by a military government summary court. The review of such cases by the military government legal division up to the end of 1948 demonstrated satisfactory results by German courts, and no judgments in such cases were suspended.[434]

Further enactments were introduced for cases that had been reserved for trial in the military government courts. On 22 June 1948, the U.S. military governor approved a plan providing for the participation of German authorities in the arrest and extradition of suspected German war criminals and German nationals accused of common crimes in the U.S. zone. Requests for the extradition of both classes of cases would be scrutinised by the military government and, unless rejected, would be forwarded to the minister-president of the appropriate *Land*, who would then forward the results of the investigation, together with his recommendations, to the military government. Cases involving suspected war criminals would be returned to military government authorities, who would make the final disposition of the case in view of the minister-president's report. Cases involving common crimes would be returned to the Military Government Extradition Board for final disposition.[435] The minister-president would order the arrest of the accused after the extradition request was approved.

The jurisdiction of German courts was further extended on 1 August 1948 under Regulation No. 4 of Military Government Law No. 2. German courts were empowered with the authority to deal with claims arising after 8 May

1945 against a German governmental or legal entity, provided the matter didn't involve the Allied Forces, claims against the German *Reich*, unless specifically authorised, or payments from assets that had been held prior to 8 May 1945.[436] German labour courts were also allowed to accept cases involving monetary claims filed against the German government, provided the cause of the claim had taken place after 8 May 1945, which allowed employees at all levels of German government to seek redress in the labour courts.[437]

German courts were later granted jurisdiction over cases involving all violations of Military Government Law No. 53 on "Foreign Exchange Control," except when cases involved the possession of Military Payment Certificates or when cases involved individuals over whom German courts couldn't assert or exercise jurisdiction as defined by Military Government Law No. 2, unless expressly authorised to do so by the military government. The latter types of cases would remain within the jurisdiction of military government courts.[438]

The Reorganisation of the Military Government Judicial Organisation

The transfer of greater responsibility from the military government to German courts was followed by an improvement in the procedures of the military government judicial organisation. Reform of the U.S. military government criminal courts took place upon the initiative of General Clay, the U.S. military governor. General Clay appointed the Administration of Justice Review Board in August 1947 to conduct periodic examinations of the handling of criminal justice in the military government courts.[439]

The military government judicial organisation was examined by William Clark, a former federal judge of the United States Third Circuit Court of Appeals, after January 1948. Clark made recommendations for the reorganisation of the judicial system, which led to the institution of a new system in the U.S. occupation zone.[440] Fundamental principles for the military government courts were extended under Military Government Ordinance No. 23 of 7 January 1948 on the "Relief from Unlawful Restraint on Personal Liberty."[441] Under that ordinance, every person indicted before military government courts in the U.S. zone was formally accorded the fullest extent of the protection of *habeas corpus*—the right to secure speedy judicial determination of the legality of the restraint of personal liberty. The ordinance gave any individual detained or confined by the military government the right to apply for a judicial hearing to determine the legality of the confinement.[442] The military government judicial system was also reorganised. It was no longer necessary for it to be maintained as an emergency measure, as it had been when German judicial organisations in the U.S. zone were restored, especially in view of the problems encountered with the operation of military government courts.

Military Government Ordinance No. 2, which had established military government courts in Germany, hadn't established an integrated system. Every military government court was an individual unit, responsible to the *Land* director of the military government where it was located. The result of this was a lack of uniformity in the separate *Länder*. All military government court personnel were appointed and supervised by *Land* directors through their chief legal officers. The same individual who was responsible for appointing prosecutors and judges was also responsible for reviewing the appeal of all cases in the area, and there was no regular appellate procedure. The system was also weakened by the fact that a number of the judges and prosecutors didn't have legal training or experience.[443] Although all criminal cases tried by those courts were reviewed at the *Land* offices of the military government and all major cases were also reviewed by the OMGUS Legal Division in Berlin, the dispensation of justice was considered excessively dependent upon the capacity of each individual judge.

Although sentencing was fair, for the most part, uniformity of sentencing was lacking and there were cases of undue punishment.[444] As a result, the OMGUS Legal Division made plans to convert the military government court organisation into an integrated and completely civilianised system that would eliminate existing injustices.[445]

The military government established a new military government judicial organisation in the U.S. zone on 18 August 1948 as more categories of criminal cases were restored to German courts, which culminated in a new arrangement between German and U.S. military government courts. The new system, which would only handle cases involving occupation personnel and matters directly relating to the military government,[446] was brought into effect under Military Government Ordinances Nos. 31, 32 and 33. An integrated, zone-wide court system was established as a separate unit of OMGUS and also completely separate from the *Land* military government offices. An Office of the Chief Attorney was created within OMGUS in order to separate the prosecution from the judicial function, consisting of a chief attorney and district attorneys. The system also included a regular appellate procedure,[447] in contrast to the previous system, in which appeals were heard through administrative reviews by military government officials, rather than allowing for judicial appeal of court decisions.[448]

The composition and jurisdiction of those courts were set forth in Ordinance No. 31. The United States Area of Control was divided into eleven judicial districts,[449] with a district court established for each judicial district. Each of those courts consisted of one or more district judges and one or more magistrates, with jurisdiction over all criminal and civil cases, along with a district attorney and one or more assistant district attorneys. The court could impose sentences of up to ten years in prison or death, or a fine of up to ten thousand dollars.

Appellate jurisdiction was held by the court of appeal at Nürnberg, consisting of a chief justice, six associate justices, and a chief attorney, acting for the prosecution. That court served as the highest judicial authority of the entire U.S. Area of Control. The fourth and fifth judicial district courts maintained both civil and criminal jurisdiction as Rhine navigation courts. Each district court exercised exclusive civil jurisdiction over U.S. personnel in cases involving automobiles, the collection of damages and penalties for breaches of contracts, and Rhine navigation.

The jurisdiction of those courts extended to all persons in the U.S. Area of Control, including all non-German civilians serving with or accompanying the U.S. occupation forces, who could be tried for offences against Control Council or U.S. military government legislation or German law. All judges, magistrates, and lawyers in those courts were trained and experienced jurists.

All cases pending before the former military government courts that had been established under Military Government Ordinance No. 2, No. 6, or No. 16 were transferred to the district courts. Their functions were governed by the regulations for the proceedings of the district courts.[450] Separate ordinances governed the procedures of those courts in criminal[451] and civil[452] cases. Jurisdiction over civil cases was divided between military government and German courts. The military government courts and German courts exercised exclusive jurisdiction over cases involving UN or German persons respectively, but shared jurisdiction over cases involving both types of persons.[453]

A board of review was established in the U.S. zone on 10 August 1948 as part of the judicial reorganisation to deal with civil cases concerning the restitution of property. Those cases were to be dealt with according to the terms of Military Government Law No. 59 on "Restitution of Identifiable Property,"[454] which governed the procedures for restitution of property that had wrongfully been seized from its owners between 30 January 1933 and 8 May 1945 "for reasons of race, religion, nationality, ideology, or political opposition to National Socialism."[455] The property would be restored to the former owner or a successor.[456] The board was empowered to review judgments pronounced by the civil division of an *Oberlandesgericht* if a decision violated Law No. 59, and could either affirm or modify a decision, in whole or in part, or remand a case, in whole or in part, back to the German court that previously had heard the case.[457] In practice, that represented the most significant limitation of German civil law, since it concerned numerous cases and large monetary amounts.[458]

Technical improvements to the U.S. military government judicial organisation were complemented with an important reform in the procedure for appointing German judges in Hesse. The *Landtag* enacted a law on the selection of judges on 13 August 1948, which confirmed Art. 127 of the constitution of Hesse. The appointment of judges would no longer be determined by the minister of justice alone, but in accordance with a committee consisting of presidents of the highest courts in the *Land* and a number of representatives from the *Land* parliament.[459]

The military government court of appeal convened in Nuremberg on 10 September 1948. The new U.S. military government courts in Bavaria, Württemberg-Baden, and Hesse were officially opened on 25, 26, and 27 October 1948.[460] The original military government courts in Hesse ceased to operate on 26 October 1948.

The new system of military government courts in Hesse, composed of districts III and IV, with district seats in Marburg and Frankfurt-am-Main, exercised the same criminal and civil jurisdiction as the former military government courts and held civil jurisdiction in collecting fines and forfeitures. They were removed from the supervision of the *Land* military government for Hesse and operated under the authority of the OMGUS Legal Division.[461] The new judicial organisation was a significant improvement over the previous system. The court of appeals provided greater protection for the rights of the accused, and ensured uniformity in the military government's administration of justice.[462]

Toward the Conclusion of the Military Occupation

The German judicial organisation gained increasingly greater responsibility from the beginning of the occupation, but complete independence could only be restored when all military government controls were lifted. While the Potsdam Protocol had established a blueprint for the reconstruction of Germany, diplomatic discussions on the "German Problem" among the occupation powers at the international level led to the development of a new political framework for western Germany.

The failure of the London Conference of the four occupation powers in December 1947 ended expectations that agreement to form a central German government could be reached between the western Allies and the Soviet government.[463] The western Allies therefore developed separate plans for the creation of a West German state. Legal developments in western Germany would be integrated into the structure of that new state, in which a German federal government would be restored at the national level. The apex of the reconstruction of a West German state would be the drafting of a federal constitution, followed by the formation of a German national government.

The three military governors of the western occupation zones conferred with the minister-presidents of the western German states on 1 July 1948 and called upon them to form a national German government.[464] A parliamentary council, consisting of sixty-five delegates from the elected *Land* parliaments, convened at Bonn on 1 September 1948 to draft a Basic Law for the future West German state,[465] which would lay the basis for the constitution of the Federal Republic of Germany. The adoption of a Basic Law for the Federal Republic of Germany and the establishment of federal judicial institutions and a federal government ended the initial phase of the restoration of justice in western Germany.[466]

The Basic Law (*Grundgesetz*), or "Bonn Constitution," ratified the work of the reconstruction of the justice administration in western Germany. It affirmed the restoration of constitutional government in the western German *Länder*,[467] and outlined governmental powers at the national level. The creation of a national German government on the foundation of the western *Länder* and a federal constitution necessitated redefining the relationship between the occupation powers and the national government.[468] That was brought about by drafting an Occupation Statute, which defined the authority of the western occupation powers, subsequent to the creation of the Federal Republic of Germany.[469]

The western Allies introduced the Occupation Statute as a partial substitute for a formal peace treaty between Germany and the Allies as it became evident that the conclusion of such a settlement couldn't be reached in the course of diplomatic negotiations with the Soviet Union. The purpose of the settlement was to introduce a new relationship between the occupation powers and German authorities.[470] The Federal Republic of Germany and participating *Länder* were afforded full legislative, executive, and judicial powers, in accordance with the Basic Law and their respective constitutions. Those powers were subject only to the limitations prescribed in the Occupation Statute.[471]

The occupation powers reserved control over certain fields, in order to ensure that the basic purposes of the occupation were accomplished, including disarmament and demilitarisation; economic controls in the Ruhr; economic questions regarding restitution, reparations, decartelisation, deconcentration, non-discrimination in trade, and foreign economic claims against Germany; foreign affairs questions, such as international agreements to which Germany was a party; displaced persons and refugees; the security and prestige of Allied forces; adherence to the Basic Law and *Land* constitutions; foreign trade and exchange controls; control over internal action concerning national self-subsistence; and control over persons sentenced and imprisoned under the authority of occupation courts.[472]

The military government administrations in the western occupation zones were to be replaced by an Allied High Commission for Germany, consisting of three high commissioners representing each of the western occupation powers. They were to ensure the implementation of occupation objectives in the new West German state according to the provisions of the Occupation Statute.[473]

The Basic Law, or federal constitution, decreed that justice in the Federal Republic of Germany held equal status with legislative and executive power,[474] although those powers served as separate organs, representing the totality of state sovereignty (Art. 20, para. 2): "All state authority emanates from the people. It shall be exercised by the people by means of elections and voting and by specific legislative, executive, and judicial organs."[475]

The rule of law was given practical expression under Art. 19, para. 4, stating that the rights of an individual affected by an act of the public authority was given the right of redress through the courts and Art. 20 para. 3: "Legislation shall be subject to the constitutional order; the executive and the judiciary shall be bound by law and justice."[476]

Hence, judicial office in the Federal Republic of Germany, restored following the collapse of the National Socialist regime, and which had demonstrated consistent disregard for law and justice, was granted a position in the federal constitution it had never before possessed. All of public life was made subject to the control of the law courts.[477] The maintenance of the new standard of justice was laid out in Art. 123, which stated that all law that had been in force prior to the formation of the West German government remained in force, as long as it didn't contravene the principles of the federal constitution.[478]

The responsibility for the administration of justice in the Federal Republic of Germany remained under the jurisdiction of the individual *Länder*. Appeals could be forwarded to appellate courts at the national level.[479] Provisions concerning the administration of justice were stated in a separate section of the Basic Law, in Articles 92–104. All judges were guaranteed independence, subject only to the law (Art. 97), but subject to impeachment in the event of a violation of the constitution (Art. 98). Other safeguards against abuse of the law included provisions for the legal protection of the individual, such as outlawing extraordinary courts (Art. 101, para. 1), retroactive laws (Art. 103, para. 3), and double jeopardy (Art. 103, para. 3).[480]

In accordance with federal principle, the appointment of judges at the *Land* level remained under the jurisdiction of the *Länder* (Art. 98 para. 4). The traditional judicial organisation of lower and intermediary courts also remained under *Land* jurisdiction, while the highest courts in the new Republic were placed under federal jurisdiction and served as the courts of final instance appeals arising from the application of *Land* law (Art. 99).[481]

A Federal Constitutional Court was established to protect the constitution by ensuring that the legislature, executive, and judiciary adhered to the provisions of the Basic Law, and a Supreme Federal Court was mandated, to ensure the uniform administration of justice.[482] The constitutional courts at the state and federal levels and the process of judicial review that it afforded enforced a uniform legal interpretation by the judiciary and all branches of government. The major effect of this was that individual judges could no longer interpret the law any way they chose and make their interpretations sustainable. This process of judicial review essentially undermined the legacy of legal positivism that had underpinned German legal thought and practice prior to and then throughout the National Socialist regime. The constitutional courts supervised the judiciary's interpretations of the constitutional norms to enforce a consistent reading of the constitution on the other branches of government, and to protect the civil rights of German citizens. The old positivist belief of the separation of the realm of law from the realms of politics and ethics was abandoned with the idea that justice could be achieved through the formal mechanical application of codified laws and statutes enacted by the government. The restoration of legal jurisdiction at the national level also served to provide unity to the justice system in Germany,[483] which had previously been divided between the occupation zones and among the *Länder* of the same zone.[484]

The Basic Law and the Occupation Statute went into force simultaneously on 21 September 1949, marking the creation of the Federal Republic of Germany and the end of the military occupation. Allied control in Germany was thereafter exercised by Allied civilian authorities. Although the occupying powers retained supreme authority, the authority exercised through the Allied High Commission was restricted to provisions of the Occupation Statute.[485] The previous disposition of governmental powers was dissolved in view of the division of responsibilities between the *Länder*, the federal government, and the occupation powers. Whereas the *Länder* retained their power of legislation under the terms of the federal constitution, the unification of the western *Länder* in the newly established federal state led to the dissolution of the *Länderrat* and the assumption of its legislative functions by the West German government.[486]

Since court jurisdiction is a product of state sovereignty,[487] foreign jurisdiction over German courts was to be lifted when the Federal Republic of Germany was proclaimed a sovereign state with full-fledged state authority. The newly established national German authorities regained the power of self-government and sovereignty in the administration of justice, except for certain judicial powers reserved by the western occupation powers.[488]

Although the Occupation Statute didn't contain any specific regulations regarding the jurisdiction and independence of the German justice system,[489] its enactment led in practice to a full restoration of the judicial authority of German courts.[490] The supervision of judicial activities became inadmissible when political sovereignty was restored, thus negating the authority of the military government to intervene in the decisions of German courts, which previously had been an official limitation of the independence of the German judiciary. Since the Occupation Statute presented general terms for the new political status of Germany that were more of a political than juridical nature, the extent of the limitations of German court jurisdiction was to be redressed through new legislation.[491]

The Allied High Commission enacted legislation to clarify the delineation between Allied and German judicial responsibility.[492] The right to withdraw a case from German jurisdiction (*evocatio*) that had been imposed under Military Government Law No. 2 was nullified under the Occupation Statute and superseded by HICOG (Office of the High Commissioner for Germany) Law No. 13 of 25 November 1949 on "Judicial Powers in the Reserved Fields."[493] That law defined the new relationship between the prerogative of Allied occupation law necessitated by the enactment of the Occupation Statute,[494] aligning the legal jurisdiction of the western occupation powers with its principles.[495] Except when expressly authorised, German court jurisdiction was only excluded in cases affecting the Allied forces, the Allied High Commission or persons accompanying them or their property, or enactments of occupation authorities. Allied authorities could only intervene in the functions of German courts in cases that directly involved the interests of the occupation, which were specified in the terms of that law and cited in Art. 2 of the Occupation Statute. Such intervention was limited to inspecting court records in cases relating to occupation interests, withdrawing cases directly affecting occupation personnel or matters from a German court, or suspending court decisions in such cases.

Cases directly affecting occupation personnel or matters were assumed by an occupation court that could confirm, nullify, or modify the decision of a German court, or transfer a case to a German court for trial or retrial. Allied enactments in the western occupation zones that had been imposed on the German justice system under occupation law, such as Control Council Law No. 4 and Military Government Law No. 2, were repealed.[496]

The newly established jurisdiction of the occupation courts was confined to cases affecting persons defined according to reserved fields and limited primarily to offences against the security of occupation interests.[497] Those offences included espionage, sabotage, or armed assault against the Allied forces; theft or unauthorised possession of property belonging to Allied forces; or any act that was prejudicial to the security of Allied forces.[498]

In conformity to what was considered to be the "natural law" of occupation, members of the Allied forces, persons officially connected with the Allied High Commission, and their dependents were still officially excluded from German courts in criminal matters and civil affairs, thus leaving certain formal restrictions on German judicial sovereignty.[499] On the other hand, the power of the occupation authority to nullify decisions of German courts in matters that remained within the scope of their jurisdiction, such as the relations between Germans, the power to remove jurists from office, and the power to supervise the German judicial organisation, were rescinded,[500] thus fully restoring the principle of judicial independence to the German justice system.

The U.S. High Commissioner issued a subsequent directive on 28 December 1949,[501] and the *Land* Commissioner for Hesse issued two additional directives on 3 January 1950 that outlined the new jurisdiction of German courts. The first directive extended the jurisdiction of cases involving all citizens of the U.S., the UK, and France, as well as all displaced persons, regardless of their citizenship. The exceptions stipulated in Art 1(b) of Law No. 13[502] remained in force. The directives for Hesse transferred criminal court jurisdiction to German courts, according to the terms of Law No. 13 and the Directive of 28 December 1949.[503]

Law No. 13 set forth a new status governing the division of jurisdiction between German and Allied occupation courts, which remained in place for the remainder of the Allied civilian occupation. Except for criminal jurisdiction over members of the Allied armed forces and their dependents, all jurisdiction was transferred to German courts.[504] All remaining enactments that had been issued by Allied occupation authorities in Germany during the military and civilian occupation periods, including Allied High Commission Law No. 13 and Law No. 14, were repealed when the "Convention on Relations between the Three Powers and the Federal Republic of Germany" of 26 May 1952 and the "Protocol on the Termination of the Occupation Regime in the Federal Republic of Germany" of 23 October 1954 went into force[505] on 5 May 1955. The Allied High Commission and the offices of *Land* Commissioners in the Federal Republic of Germany were abolished.[506]

Conclusion

The restoration of justice was developed gradually in view of the circumstances since there was no structured approach or tested formula[507] for achieving that objective. The process of restoring justice in Germany began with the closing of the justice system and the legislating of National Socialist laws and influences out of existence.

German judicial organisations in the U.S. zone began to operate under the supervision of the *Land* Ministry of Justice and the U.S. military government. The constitution and function of the *Land* justice system in the U.S. zone were regulated under the "Plan for the Administration of Justice." They were further defined by Allied Control Council and U.S. military government legislation, such as Control Council Proclamation No. 3, outlining the principles for postwar administration of justice, and Control Council Law No. 4 and Military Government Law No. 2, setting forth regulations for the composition of German courts and their jurisdictions.

The next phase of the restoration of justice after reopening German courts at the *Land* level was to restore the normal conditions of the justice system, such as extending the jurisdiction and lifting the supervision of German courts, thus fully restoring judicial independence. The restoration of the German justice system was guided under Allied military government legislation,[508] beginning with a standstill of justice, followed by the subsequent reconstitution of the German judicial organisation and the restoration of its functions.

The conditions allowing for the reconstruction of a German judicial organisation into what became *Land* Hesse and the application of denazified German law by the reconstructed judicial organisation was introduced by Allied, U.S. military government, and *Land* legislation suited to local conditions. Allied military government legislation established uniform principles for the administration of justice in Germany, while U.S. military government and German *Land* legislation prescribed the law to be applied by the German judicial organisation at the *Land* level in the U.S. zone.

The greatest deficiency of the legal reconstruction was the absence of a superior court that would coordinate the divergent legal practices of the three *Länder*, which had been endowed with quasi-statehood.[509] Further progress at the national level was made with the unification of the postwar legal situation, in which several different legislative bodies hadn't coordinated their efforts in establishing a common legal system.[510] The *Oberlandesgericht* in Frankfurt-am-Main functioned as the supreme appeal court until 1950, when the Federal Supreme Court assumed appellate jurisdiction at the national level.[511] Both courts were bound to adhere to the provisions of the federal constitution.

The *Land* justice system in Hesse formed part of the judicial organisation of the constitutional state at the national level. The division of jurisdiction between the military government and the German judicial organisation was gradually narrowed as a greater number of cases were transferred to German courts. Safeguards against future violations concerning the interpretation and application of law by judges were introduced into German law while the U.S. military government focused on restoring responsibility to German judges, who would operate within the postwar judicial organisation. An attempt at neutralising National Socialist influences regarding the human element of the legal reconstruction and the denazification of the legal profession took place at the same time as the institutional restoration of the law and the reconstruction of a fully functional German justice system.

4

The Personnel Reconstruction and Dealing with the Past

THE DENAZIFICATION OF THE GERMAN justice system consisted of two main elements that were seen as crucial with regard to forming the basis of a rule of law: first, the material reconstruction with respect to the institutional reconstruction of a German judicial organisation and a reform of the law that had contributed the basis of the National Socialist regime; second, the human element of the denazification of justice—the question of undertaking the reconstruction of the personnel who would staff the restored postwar judicial organisation, and who would administer justice following a denazified body of law brought forth in each *Land* in the U.S. occupation zone. The latter entailed eliminating National Socialist concepts and practices from the body of German law and removing personnel from the legal profession who could be considered to be former National Socialists—those who were considered to have aided and abetted the National Socialist regime in destroying the *Rechtsstaat* by having taken part in administering justice according to the National Socialist conception of the law.

Many of the jurists in the new postwar *Land* of Hesse would be drawn from the ranks of the judiciary who had survived the National Socialist regime and the Second World War, and hadn't been expelled from the profession for political reasons. They would be subjected to the denazification process, just like members of other professions, as well as to specific measures for the legal profession. Denazifying the legal profession faced the same problems that were encountered in the application of the rest of the denazification programme, such as how tangible evidence could be produced to determine whether a candidate for reinstatement in the postwar justice system could be considered to be politically compromised.

The denazification programme in the three *Länder* of the U.S. zone was divided into two main phases: the implementation of the programme by the U.S. military government, then its continuation by German authorities. In both cases, the purpose of the programme was to remove individuals who had been members of the NSDAP or its affiliated organisations from positions of responsibility.

Denazification was considered the most pressing and vital task of U.S. military government field detachments from the beginning of the occupation until March 1946. The responsibility for the implementation of the programme was then transferred to German civil authorities under the supervision of the U.S. military government[1] when the military government considered German local institutions to have been sufficiently revived to allow for their participation.[2]

The denazification of personnel in Hesse, as in the other *Länder* of the U.S. zone, was initially handled by the U.S. military government, in accordance with the political policy stated in the Potsdam Protocol and JCS 1067 and various military government denazification directives. German governmental authorities in the *Länder* of the U.S. zone later assumed the task and were granted the authority to enact denazification legislation that superseded military government legislation. The German programme was administered separately in each *Land*, following the terms of the Law for Liberation from National Socialism and Militarism. In both cases, individuals were defined theoretically as former National Socialists, according to the terms of denazification directives and laws.

The Law for Liberation didn't call for wholesale removals from office. Dismissals were to be based on more specific categories of alleged political implication, and an attempt to judge all members of the NSDAP and its affiliated organisations was maintained. The removal or reinstatement of jurists after the collapse of the National Socialist regime was based on an individual's political record, which was considered to be a part of the qualifications for judicial office. As a result, jurists were brought to account on the basis of their former political affiliation, regardless of their actions and conduct while in office, without any consideration of their motives for having joined a National Socialist organisation or evaluating an individual's guilt according to their conduct in the National Socialist regime.[3]

The First Phase of the Denazification

Military Government Law No. 5 on the "Dissolution of the Nazi Party," introduced upon the entry of SHAEF forces into Germany, provided a general order for the outright abolition of the NSDAP and its affiliated organisations, listing fifty-two organisations that were to be dissolved immediately, including the *NS-Rechtswahrerbund*, and eight para-military organisations, such as the SS and the SA, were slated for abolition at a later date. All organisations and their activities listed in that law were declared illegal.[4]

The removal of jurists implicated by National Socialist affiliation took effect immediately upon Allied occupation of Germany. U.S. denazification policy during the Allied invasion of western Germany was governed by the terms of JCS 1067 and SHAEF military government legislation. Instructions for the implementation of SHAEF policy were included in the *Handbook for Military Government in Germany*,[5] including lists of incumbents of enumerated offices (*Beamtenstellungen*) who had been employed on or after 30 January 1933 and were to be automatically excluded from continuing in or being admitted into public service. The *Handbook*, JCS 1067, and SHAEF legislation served as key documents representing the various functions and powers of the military government during the Allied invasion of Germany while the military government held supreme power as declared under SHAEF Proclamation No. 1.[6]

All jurists in the occupied territories upon the entry of SHAEF troops into Germany were dismissed from their positions by virtue of SHAEF Proclamation No. 1 and Military Government Law No. 2. All German courts were closed, and jurists only could be reinstated by the consent of the military government[7] in accordance with existing denazification provisions.

Difficulties and adverse publicity over the denazification of the local administration in Aachen[8] led to a new SHAEF directive, issued on 9 November 1944, which called for the dismissal of public officials who had joined the NSDAP before 30 January 1933.[9] A directive instituting a revision of policy was transmitted to SHAEF by the Combined Chiefs of Staff, ordering the removal of "ardent Nazis" and "active Nazi sympathizers" from office. Even those who had been retained, as was formerly permissible under the terms of previous directives "on the grounds of expediency or "administrative necessity," were to be dismissed.

However, problems arose involving the interpretation of the terms and their practical application[10] by the military government in the field when suitable replacements couldn't be found for dismissed personnel who hadn't been politically compromised. For example, the examination of 150 *Fragebogen* submitted by jurists in Kurhessen revealed only twenty-five prospects for appointment, of which each was then subject to an interview and an investigation.[11] Locating trained and competent substitutes who were "free from Nazi taint" was one of the greatest obstacles to implementing an "immediate and peremptory Denazification."[12] Another difficulty was that neither JCS 1067 nor the *Handbook*, which was to be used by military government officers for "direction" and "guidance," provided a specific definition of what constituted an "active Nazi."[13] The earlier CCS 551 also hadn't provided military government officers in the field with definitions of what constituted an "active Nazi" or an "ardent sympathizer," simply ordering that they were to be removed from office immediately.[14]

Until clearer definitions and instructions were available, military government officers attempted to fulfill the task of reconstructing German administration to the best of their ability and found pragmatic solutions, which often led to results that diverged from official denazification policy. Most military government detachment commanders were more concerned with restoring a functional local administration than with ideological or judicial hairsplitting, and soon found, that in many cases, nominal or lower level membership in the NSDAP wasn't a certain criterion for the assessment of the individual's political viewpoint.[15] In practice, removal from office or reinstatement at the initial stage of the occupation[16] was predominantly left to the discretion of the military government officer handling the particular case.[17] They decided whether a candidate for reinstatement could be considered trustworthy, rather than mechanically determining the guilt of an individual by the date of that person's entry into the NSDAP or one of its affiliated organisations.

Military government officers in the field were responsible for restoring order at the local level, which required the stop-gap measure of relying upon the cooperation of German administrative officials. That was considered a greater priority than finding qualified individuals as defined by denazification directives. The dismissal of all officials on the basis of former NSDAP membership would have meant that all administration would have ceased, rather than being reestablished as quickly as possible, as had been intended by military government detachments.[18]

Until July 1945, military government detachments were under the immediate jurisdiction of SHAEF tactical commands, which exercised the privilege of interpreting and revising directives issued by military government headquarters. While policy demanded that German personnel be screened for their political records, tactical commanders demanded that German personnel be reinstated, to help restore a functioning administration, to maintain military supply lines, and to provide the local population with basic necessities in order to prevent civilians from interfering with military operations.[19] Military government commanders in the field were more interested in "getting things done" than in engaging in the "tearing down" required by JCS 1067.[20]

The ambiguous initial SHAEF denazification directives left the military government officers without any precise guidance on the meaning of the term "active Nazi," which inevitably led to a wide variety of interpretations in the field, resulting in variances in practice of the denazification procedure in nearly every *Landkreis.*[21] Army group headquarters, following the pattern of operating autonomously in the field improvised by issuing their own denazification directives. In turn, the armies, which were to a large extent also self-sufficient, also formulated their own directives that were then carried out at the corps and division levels. As a consequence, U.S. military government detachments were operating under at least four different denazification directives during the summer of 1945.[22] In those chaotic conditions, some military government detachments removed all individuals who'd had any connection with the NSDAP and its affiliated organisations, while others allowed notorious National Socialists to retain their positions.[23]

Uniformity was established by a new directive, issued 7 July 1945, replacing the previous patchwork of denazification regulations with a list of one hundred thirty-six mandatory removal categories and stating that membership in the NSDAP before 1 May 1937 or holding office in certain affiliated organisations would be considered as having been "active." Membership before that date was therefore to be "cause for mandatory removal or exclusion from 'positions of importance in quasi-public and private enterprises'... and from positions of 'more than minor importance' in public affairs."[24] The removal categories were drafted by the Public Safety Branch of SHAEF, providing terms for the automatic arrest of top-level National Socialists and militarists, and the arrest and screening of others through questionnaires (*Fragebogen*) about an individual's personal history, including questions concerning any former connection to the NSDAP or its affiliated organisations.[25]

Jurists included in automatic arrest categories were leading civil servants of the *Reich* Ministry of Justice, members of the *Reichsgericht* and the *Volksgerichtshof,* presidents and prosecutors of the *Oberlandesgerichte,* and members of the *Sondergerichte.*[26] Every *Fragebogen* was investigated by a Special Branch Section of the Public Safety Division of the local U.S. military government detachment, in close cooperation with the Counter Intelligence Corps[27] as resources allowed.[28] The information provided in the *Fragebogen* was verified by all available evidence, such as the records from the German police, civil service, and the NSDAP. Falsification of answers would result in prosecution in a military government court and imprisonment of two to five years or longer.[29]

Following examination of the *Fragebogen,* individuals were classified into one of four categories: 1) Non-Employment Mandatory, 2) Employment Discretionary (No Adverse Recommendation), 3) No Evidence of Nazi Activity, and 4) Evidence of Anti-Nazi Activity.[30] New appointments were not to be made before a so-called "vetting," or screening, had been completed, except for those who had been reinstated before the denazification was underway under the present terms. Those persons would continue in their positions, pending their "vetting."[31]

Like all applicants for other forms of employment, candidates for legal office had to submit the *Fragebogen*, as well as a second *Fragebogen* for the legal profession, covering education, professional activities, and membership in political, official, and professional societies and organisations.[32] However, that approach merely served to draw a professional and political portrayal of an individual, based on an accumulation of elementary facts. The specialised questionnaire didn't reveal how a jurist had behaved in office or decisions the individual had been involved in, including cases of a political nature in which the law had been used as an instrument in the exercise of totalitarian political power. It also didn't reveal whether a person had represented National Socialist officials, had appeared before party courts, or whether the person's moral and intellectual attitudes indicated subservience or support for the National Socialist regime.[33]

Such questions regarding the denazification were addressed by German authorities. A group of political leaders in Marburg formed a political committee (*Staatspolitischer Ausschuß*) at the beginning of the occupation, to play an active role in the postwar reconstruction.[34] The committee chairman reported to the military government in June 1945, stating that anti–National Socialist Germans knew who had been politically implicated, but the committee wasn't given an opportunity to testify against them. In August 1945, a committee member reported that he and his colleagues couldn't understand why the military government had implicitly assumed that all Germans were National Socialists until they could prove otherwise. The committee produced a report for the *Oberbürgermeister* (mayor) of Marburg in November 1945, asserting that the military government denazification programme had demonstrated a misunderstanding of the National Socialist regime. The method of denazification, according to the questionnaire and prescribed scheme, was being carried out on the presumption of predetermined guilt, rather than on innocence. Fixing a date for determining a person's political implication didn't allow for individual consideration of every case, and didn't allow for the possibility that a member of the NSDAP wasn't necessarily a National Socialist.[35] According to the report, adopting another method of denazification would have addressed criticism of the military government's methods, and the programme would have been more effective if it had been transferred to German authorities, who had a greater understanding of local conditions and circumstances of the time.[36]

That flaw in the denazification programme was admitted by Professor Karl Loewenstein, Legal Advisor in the Office of Military Government for Germany. But he added that substantial scrutiny of personal factors was physically impossible for "overworked and unsophisticated" military government officials,[37] so the standard, based on date of entry, remained in place.

Military government authorities believed that an individual's support for the National Socialist regime could be determined by membership in a National Socialist organisation, and the earlier the date of entry, the greater the conviction. However, it could also be contended that an early member's enthusiasm could have dissipated, though they couldn't risk leaving the organisation.[38] The only defensible date put to use was considered to be 1 May 1937, after which officials could be coerced to join under the Public Officials Act, and those who had joined after that date were exempted from the automatic removal and exclusion categories.[39]

The 1 May 1937 date also served to expand the number of experienced candidates available and willing to serve in the restored justice system, since the denazification programme that was to drive out the influences of twelve years of National Socialist *Gleichschaltung* had created serious personnel shortages in the professional fields.[40] On the other hand, removal and suspension from office on the basis of membership in the NSDAP or an affiliated organisation, irrespective of the date of entry, often led to cases of injustice when one's former service to the National Socialist regime hadn't followed political motives. Judgment on the basis of entry into the NSDAP or an affiliated organisation, rather than providing evidence of politically oriented chargeable actions[41] conducted while in office, often served merely to indicate a lack of courage to avoid membership or an unwillingness to jeopardise one's career or position.[42]

The ideal situation for the restoration of justice was to reinstate jurists who had absolutely no association with the National Socialist regime[43] and had never been a member of the NSDAP or any of its affiliated organisations. The task of reorganising the German judiciary was charged to the Military Government Legal Officers in each area of local government (*Landkreis* and *Stadtkreis*). They made provisional appointments of jurists for local judicial positions and then notified the Legal Division of the Regional Military Government Office for the approval of those appointments.[44]

The establishment of the judicial organisation in Hesse followed an earlier reopening of German courts prior to the promulgation of Proclamation No. 2, which established the boundaries of the *Länder* of the U.S. zone. The U.S. military government emphasised reopening the *Amtsgerichte*, or county courts, functioning at the lowest level, and the *Landgerichte*, the appeals courts, during the early stages of the occupation, due to expected difficulty in finding qualified personnel for the Ministry of Justice and the *Oberlandesgerichte*[45]—the supreme courts of appeal. Military government legal officers accordingly sought to obtain the services of trained lawyers and retired judges without connections to the NSDAP or its affiliated organisations, and authorised them to reopen the first *Amtsgerichte*, subject to the approval of the Regional Legal Division, which was then followed by the reopening of the *Landgerichte*.[46]

The military government detachment in Frankfurt-am-Main instructed the leading judge of the local *Amtsgericht* and the local *Landgericht* president in July 1945 to select the necessary judicial personnel from candidates who had performed similar duties in the past, subject to approval by the military government.[47] The *Landgericht* president was to select staff for the *Landgericht* and the subordinate *Amtsgerichte*, and the lawyers and notaries in that area of jurisdiction (*Landgerichtsbezirk*). They would then be reinstated if their appointment was approved by the military government[48] on the basis of the denazification regulations.[49]

Local military government detachments also applied that procedure in the other reopened German courts in Hesse.[50] The presidents of the *Amtsgericht* and *Landgericht* in Frankfurt-am-Main initially selected jurists who hadn't been members of the NSDAP. However, it soon became necessary to rely on specialised clerks and judicial officials who were former members. As often as possible, the *Landgericht* president selected individuals for appointment who hadn't joined the NSDAP before 1 May 1937. Some judges and lawyers selected had been members of the NSDAP as early as 1933 or as late as 1940. The *Landgericht* president offered his personal guarantee that they weren't National Socialists, on the basis of their basic convictions. It was said that their entry into the NSDAP had been merely a formality, since they had feared grave disadvantages if they had refused to join.[51]

Although the military government conveyed freedom of action to German authorities at the higher levels of the judicial organisation, there was suspicion on the part of the military government concerning "class solidarity of the judiciary," which could have resulted in jurists resisting the denazification process by saving former colleagues from disbarment. On the other hand, members of the judicial profession could determine who had supported the regime, since they had the advantage of firsthand experience.[52]

Uniform regulations for the reinstatement of judicial personnel for *Land* judicial organisations in the U.S. zone were set forth in the Plan for the Administration of Justice. The appointment of judicial personnel was charged to the *Land* Minister of Justice as the administrative superior of the judicial organisations in the newly created *Länder* of the U.S. zone. Each *Land* minister of justice was made responsible for the appointment of judges,[53] and required the approval of the military government to appoint or remove judges from office.[54] *Landgericht* presidents were to select lawyers, notaries, and lay judges for their office or practice in the courts in their jurisdiction, or *Landgerichtsbezirke*. Their appointments were subject to prior approval from the military government.[55] Ministers of justice were responsible for the appointment of all judicial personnel, including those selected by the *Landgericht* presidents and leading public prosecutors (*Oberstaatsanwälte*) in Hesse.[56] The military government retained the function of screening and approving all applicants on the basis of the individual *Fragebogen* and denazification regulations[57] prior to their reinstatement into the *Land* judicial organisation.[58]

Disbarring legal personnel was initially governed by the necessity to comply with denazification directives, irrespective of the availability of personnel. Rather than emphasising the investigation of an individual's political record prior to removal from office, as was the practice for the denazification of personnel engaged in public office and in private industry in the British occupation zone, the policy in the U.S. zone was to carry out wide-sweeping dismissals, with the review of individual cases after dismissal.[59] Exceptions were made after 7 August 1945, when a Denazification Board was established to review appeals of persons who were considered more than "nominal Nazis," but were needed in essential functions until replacements for them could be found.[60] However, that could be considered an emergency measure, because the pace of denazification wasn't relaxed during the early stages of the occupation as the screening of legal personnel was progressing. The legal reconstruction was hampered by the lack of Germans qualified to serve as judges or other court personnel and also the lack of qualified Germans considered to be anti–National Socialists.[61]

Court backlogs increased at a considerable rate as a result of the removal of judicial officials, time-consuming statistical inquiries, reorganisation of the judicial organisation, and the number of criminal and civil cases to be heard. Those conditions resulted in an urgent necessity for judges and other judicial personnel to be reinstated to handle the increased workload.[62] Scarcely more than half of the lawyers in several cities in Hesse were considered eligible to retain their right to practice, solely on the basis of their political record by the time Military Government Law No. 8 had been promulgated[63] on 26 September 1945.[64]

The first decree specifically addressing the denazification of the legal profession was Article IV of the Control Council Law No. 4 of 30 October 1945 on the "Reorganization of the Judicial System." The Allied denazification policy provided in the Potsdam Protocol was restated in that law, stipulating that: "to effect the reorganization of the judicial system, all former members of the Nazi party who have been more than nominal participants in its activities and all other persons who directly followed the punitive practices of the Hitler regime must be dismissed from appointments as judges and prosecutors and will not be admitted to those appointments."[65]

Although it couldn't be denied that key positions in National Socialist organisations and offices at the highest levels could only have been held by ardent

National Socialists, there remained the problem of determining who had been a nominal National Socialist among the lower ranks of the judiciary. For example, an *Amtsrichter*, or president, of a *Landgericht* could have been an ardent National Socialist, while a judge in an *Oberlandesgericht* could have been a "nominal Nazi."[66] Evidence couldn't be established by evaluating cases solely on the basis of a person's date of entry into the NSDAP or an affiliated organisation. Moreover, jurists were generally treated with greater suspicion than members of other professions.

Although the denazification directive of 7 July 1945 applied to the personnel of the German justice system, the standards applying to judges and prosecutors were more rigid in comparison to other civil service personnel. Although individuals who had joined the NSDAP on or after 1 May 1937 fell into the category of "discretionary—no adverse recommendation," the unwritten practice was to exclude such applicants for judicial or prosecuting positions from appointment or reinstatement until December 1945,[67] by which time more than 250 judges and lawyers had been interviewed.[68]

One of the greatest obstacles to achieving an immediate and thorough denazification in all fields was securing trained and competent substitutes who were considered "free from Nazi taint" to take charge of essential functions.[69] The task of taking over the functions of removed personnel became burdensome for the reinstated German jurists. The U.S. military governor reported in November 1945 that approximately 80 percent of judges in the U.S. occupation zone who had been in office at the time of the surrender had been members of the NSDAP or its affiliated organisations, and, in keeping with denazification directives, had been dismissed from office. As a result, personnel shortages delayed the normal functioning of German courts, and in some cases, judges who had been cleared of National Socialist connections worked in several courts and handled various criminal and civil cases.[70] In addition to the personnel shortage, many of the remaining judicial personnel who were considered "politically acceptable" were of "relatively advanced age."[71]

The U.S. military government reported in June 1947 that it had become apparent from the outset of the occupation that maintaining rigid standards for the denazification of jurists would make the reestablishment of a German judicial organisation impossible, since some 80 to 90 percent of German judges and prosecutors had been members of the NSDAP or its affiliated organisations. Therefore, there were two alternatives: train politically acceptable laymen for judicial or prosecuting office within a few months, or readmit former members of the NSDAP who proved to have been only nominal members, thereby applying the same standard to judges and prosecutors that applied to other German civil servants.

The first approach was attempted in the Soviet zone, but was immediately rejected in the U.S. zone, since continental law required years of study and postgraduate work. It became apparent that the second alternative was the most logical, and measures were taken in December 1945 to put it into effect. The Legal Division of OMGUS *verbally* instructed the Legal Divisions of the *Land* military government offices to reinstate former NSDAP members who had joined on or after 1 May 1937, provided that the candidates had been classified under the category of "discretionary—no adverse recommendations" and were acceptable to *Land* ministers of justice.[72]

The initial phase of denazification was considered complete by the end of December 1945. The U.S. military governor reported that the German civil government in the U.S. occupation zone had effectively been purged of National Socialist control. More than 900,000 individuals had been investigated for "Nazi activity," and roughly 20 percent of those cases had been classified as "unfit to hold positions of responsibility."[73]

The removal of individuals at that time was solely based on membership in a National Socialist organisation. It was virtually impossible to determine whether an individual had served or supported the NSDAP, since the denazification programme, as set forth in JCS 1067, didn't allow for the assistance of the German population.[74] The failure of the application of Law No. 8 brought unnecessary interference to economic recovery and brought about individual injustices,[75] which contributed to the decision to transfer the denazification process to German authorities.[76]

An attempt at correcting the deficiencies that had been exposed in the initial denazification programme was the institution of a new comprehensive long-term programme, replacing the interim one that had been in place during the early period of the military occupation.[77] The U.S. military government Legal Division undertook a systematic study of the denazification process for the first time in November 1945, and recommended the formation of a central planning agency for denazification. General Clay, the U.S. deputy military governor, then approved the creation of a Denazification Policy Board to review the subject and "formulate a complete overall program for the denazification in the U.S. zone with as much responsibility as possible placed on the German officials for the long range."[78]

The new programme was to be drafted by this Denazification Policy Board that was appointed on 30 November 1945. The board was charged with the responsibility of formulating a comprehensive denazification programme that would transfer the greatest possible responsibility to German officials, who would then contribute to accomplishing the U.S. and Allied war aim of creating "genuinely democratic institutions" in Germany.[79] The U.S. military government at this time also lacked sufficient personnel to complete the denazification programme.[80]

A further step in reorganising the denazification programme was taken on 16 December 1945, when Denazification Review Boards were established in each *Land*, charged with accelerating the disposition of appeals and holding final jurisdiction in reviewing all reports dealing with individuals who might have been only "nominal" National Socialists.[81] Although the boards could deviate from the reliance on categories of office, positions, and membership in organisations that led to arbitrary results, their decisions were only final in mandatory removal cases in which an individual had been removed solely on the basis of membership in the NSDAP prior to 1 May 1937. The appeal process was also limited, since individuals affected by denazification had no right to appeal. The military government had sole authority to determine whether an individual could be reinstated if "no adequately qualified or politically reliable substitute could be found."[82]

The Denazification Policy Board completed its report on 15 January 1946, which reviewed the basic weaknesses of the present denazification programme in detail, citing five major criticisms: 1) certain cases had resulted in arbitrary consequences; 2) certain active National Socialists hadn't been affected; 3) the programme lacked long-term projection; 4) the programme lacked participation by Germans; and 5) the programme lacked coordination with other OMGUS programmes.

The board's recommendations were based upon an examination of the relationship between denazification and the broader objectives of the occupation, with the basic objective being to prevent Germany from becoming a threat to future peace. Germans needed to participate in the denazification programme, thereby giving them an opportunity to be involved in pursuing the political objectives of the programme and preventing the creation of a group of martyrs and social outcasts that could be exploited by agitators.[83] The report of the Denazification Policy Board included recommended legislation for providing an elaborate system of German administrative machinery that would operate under U.S. military government supervision. Each *Land* minister-president would appoint a denazification minister, with an adequate staff, serving the *Land* government. Denazification tribunals would be established at the *Kreis* and *Land* levels, trying the cases of individuals who were classified as offenders on the basis of presumptive guilt. The programme also followed earlier denazification legislation, including lists of ranks and organisations subject to trial proceedings, as well as stating that German denazification law would include the substance of Law No. 8, regardless of German proposals[84] being developed at that time.

Länder governments in the U.S. zone were working on a denazification law while the deliberations in the Denazification Policy Board were underway.[85]

General Clay instructed the *Länderrat* on 4 December 1945 to draft uniform guidelines for denazification in the U.S. zone by drafting a German denazification law.

A German draft of the law was completed in January 1946, while a U.S. military government committee was charged with the same task. The main principles of the new denazification law were to consist of the following: the responsibility for denazification was to be handled by German authorities, functioning under U.S. military government supervision; a minister for denazification was to be appointed in each *Land*; all individuals presumed to have been active National Socialists were to be registered; denazification tribunals, or *Spruchkammern*, were to be established, and prosecutors were to be appointed to determine "the degree of National Socialism" of those presumed to be National Socialists; accused persons would have the right to be heard, of exoneration, and of an appeal to an appellate tribunal; and every accused person would be classified into a category, with specified sanctions provided for each category.[86]

The last denazification enactment issued by the Allied military government before the German denazification law in the U.S. zone was Control Council Directive No. 24, of 12 January 1946, on "Removal from Office and From Positions of Responsibility of Nazis and of Persons Hostile to Allied Purposes,"[87] which reaffirmed the provisions of the U.S. Denazification Directive of 7 July 1945.[88] The purpose of the new directive was to establish a uniform denazification policy in the four occupation zones, as envisaged in the Potsdam Protocol.[89] The terms of the directive ordered the removal and exclusion of all individuals from public or semi-public office who had been defined as having been "more than nominal participants" in the activities of the NSDAP, and were thus considered active National Socialists, supporters of National Socialism, or militarists.[90] They were to be considered as such on the basis of designated offices and positions. Ninety-nine categories of ranks and positions were listed as the basis for compulsory removal from office or employment, including all senior judges and public prosecutors who had been employed or appointed at any time after 1 March 1933.[91]

An additional list of twenty-two categories provided for "discretionary removal" if an individual had been more than a nominal participant in National Socialist activities.[92] The most significant category in that list consisted of allegedly nominal members of the NSDAP who had joined after 1 May 1937. That date was a U.S. contribution considered of questionable value, since it was completely arbitrary, and didn't reflect the intricacies of personal situations under the National Socialist regime, especially for those who weren't civil servants.[93]

Although Directive No. 24 maintained the principle of presumptive guilt on the basis of official positions, it provided an improvement over the terms of former denazification legislation. The lists of offices initially presented in the *Handbook for Military Government* hadn't accurately reflected political affiliation with the National Socialist regime, including practically all of the leading administrative positions for which legal training was a traditional prerequisite, as well as ranking positions in the various courts. Hence, that measure also affected office-holders who had been appointed during the Weimar Republic. That error was remedied by Directive No. 24, which limited the exclusion of public officials to those who had been appointed after 30 January 1933 and those who had been incumbents on that date and had survived subsequent political purges.[94]

U.S. military government planning for a new denazification policy in early 1946 was based on Control Council Directive No. 24 and Military Government Law No. 8. The terms of those enactments were to serve as the framework for the task of denazification by German authorities, who were also in the process of drafting a German denazification law in the *Länderrat* that would be implemented in the three *Länder* of the U.S. zone.[95]

The ministers of justice of the U.S. zone completed a draft of the denazification law for the three *Länder* on 22 December 1945, which was accepted by the *Land* governments and then handed over to the military government for approval.[96] Both German and U.S. military government authorities agreed that the German draft was to serve as the basis for the new denazification law, with modifications based on the provisions of the military government draft. Both German and military government authorities were bound by the provisions of Control Council Directive No. 24.[97]

The German proposals that had been presented in that draft were then debated,[98] and points of variance emerged between the German draft denazification law and U.S. military government approach to denazification. The provisional government of Hesse had stated in November 1945 that a "*complete denazification*" had to be undertaken to cleanse the remnants of the former regime from all branches of the economy, the civil service, and all other spheres of society. Proceedings were to be instituted against individuals who had actively supported the National Socialist state, even if they hadn't been members of the NSDAP. Such individuals were to be dealt with more severely than those who had been forced to become formal members of the NSDAP, even if it had been against their personal convictions.[99] The denazification proceedings were thus to be focused on former actions, rather than formal membership.

German authorities at the *Länderrat* also objected to the date of 1 May 1937 for determining political implication, maintaining that when an individual had joined the NSDAP or its affiliated organisations and the duration of their membership was irrelevant. According to the German view, setting a key date to membership constituted a superficial and misleading indication of guilt, since it didn't provide evidence for actions or individual circumstances within the National Socialist regime.[100]

In contrast to U.S. military government denazification proceedings, the German draft denazification law also didn't include provisions for presumptive guilt or placing the burden of proof of innocence on the accused.[101] The German draft contended that the public prosecutor was responsible for proving the guilt of the accused. Prosecution was to be limited to more important National Socialists, and political implication was to be limited to those known to have taken an active part in the National Socialist regime.[102]

Whatever the reason a jurist had joined the NSDAP or an affiliated organisation, it would be difficult to prove that they had been guilty of criminal actions if they were applying the laws of the National Socialist regime, which were the laws of the state at that time. On the other hand, they could be judged on whether they had broken moral laws while involved in the National Socialist justice system.[103] Hence, German authorities intended to call individuals to account on the basis of their former actions, rather than broadly applying the principle of presumptive guilt solely on the basis of membership in a National Socialist organisation. Their proposed denazification legislation was based on a judicial rather than a political basis, detailing a series of crimes and acts, following the example of a criminal code. However, the law would declare that past actions were to be prosecuted *following* the enactment of the law, since the prosecution of those actions wasn't otherwise possible.[104]

That initial draft "Law for the Liberation from National Socialism and Militarism" was rejected by U.S. military government authorities, who believed it "contravened their basic policy objectives in Germany."[105] German authorities didn't accept the concept of removing individuals from office on the basis of broad categories, and recommended limiting the scope of denazification to the most notorious former National Socialists.[106] U.S. military government authorities at the *Länderrat* also instructed German authorities that the German denazification law was to include an appendix listing the categories of positions contained in Control Council Directive No. 24.[107] Those categories were to serve as evidence for determining the degree of affiliation with the National Socialist regime in individual cases, rather than on absolute criteria[108] of presumptive guilt. All former members of the National Socialist organisations were also to present themselves before denazification tribunals, where they could prove their innocence.[109]

Although the basic structure of the German denazification law draft wasn't changed, the U.S. military government ordered substantial provisions to be introduced. Tenure of membership, official position, or rank in the NSDAP or its affiliated organisations would justify the accusation of an individual being charged as a *Concerned Person*. The charge was presumptive, rather than final, until the accused disproved the charge in proceedings before a denazification tribunal, which could then place the accused in the category of *Follower* or *Non-concerned.* No one who had been a member of the NSDAP or its affiliated organisations could occupy a position of responsibility. The key date of 1 May 1937 was maintained, and anyone who had joined the NSDAP or an affiliated organisation before that date was automatically categorised as a *Concerned Person*[110] on the basis of presumptive guilt.

The German-drafted Law for Liberation from National Socialism and Militarism was adopted under strong U.S. military government pressure that disregarded the interests of German policy-makers.[111] That pressure was overwhelming, since the new German denazification law was to be approved by the U.S. military government.[112] The U.S. military government maintained that since Control Council Directive No. 24 was in force in Germany, it was also binding upon the administration of the U.S. zone. Hence, the Law for Liberation was to conform to the provisions of that directive.[113] German *Land* governments were entrusted with continuing the work of implementing the objectives of U.S. and Allied denazification policy,[114] which, in effect, restricted their freedom of policy-making.

Members of the cabinet of Hesse were reluctant to apply such an extensive denazification law. They feared that it would bring about a breakdown of the administration and negatively affect the economic reconstruction. They especially criticised the fact that the law affected too many people, and potentially could bring about opposition to democracy among a larger number of nominal former members of the NSDAP classified as *Followers.*[115] Cabinet members were particularly opposed to the automatic classifications under the denazification law draft and attached appendix[116] of categories.

In the face of military government pressure, however, the cabinet accepted the law, in conjunction with the cabinets of Bavaria and Württemberg-Baden, and officially adopted the law on 5 March 1946.[117] The implementation of the Law for Liberation through German authorities would attempt to bring about a political cleansing on the basis of common principles, in accordance with legally organised proceedings, in which the decisive factor of every case would be subject to an individual examination of overall conduct (*Gesamtverhalten*), rather than on external characteristics.[118] In addition to evaluating cases on an individual basis, the new law would attempt to address the mistakes of U.S. denazification policy,[119] stressing judicial penalties for crimes, using a scale of sanctions graded to the offence while maintaining the military government mandatory removal categories.[120]

Although the structure of the law followed the categories of presumptive guilt[121] in accordance with the guidelines provided by Control Council Directive No. 24, judgment also would be based on the investigation of individual cases, in addition to the basis of holding a certain office or membership in certain organisations.[122] The Law for Liberation thus represented a compromise between U.S. military government and German denazification approaches, treating cases on the basis of their merit, while maintaining the established principle of presumptive guilt on the basis of former membership.

The Second Phase of Denazification: The Law for Liberation from National Socialism and Militarism

Land governments assumed responsibility for applying the denazification programme in the U.S. zone following the enactment of the Law for Liberation from National Socialism and Militarism. *Länder* minister-presidents adopted the law on behalf of their respective governments, to be applied separately in each *Land* under the same terms.[123] German agencies would be established for the implementation of the Allied denazification policy.[124] The law would be put into practice beginning in June 1946,[125] following the creation of a Ministry of Political Liberation in each *Land* to enforce the law after the required tribunals and administrative and investigative machinery were established. The U.S. military government would continue its denazification operations under the current directives, including Law No. 8, which would remain in force until 1 June 1946,[126] when the new denazification procedure would be introduced under the German Liberation Law. All U.S. military government denazification directives were later rescinded on 14 June 1946, making German officials solely responsible for denazification operations, under the supervision of the U.S. military government.[127]

The promulgation of the Liberation Law set forth two main objectives for military government denazification officers: to reduce the number of cases to be processed before the programme would be handed over to the German authorities, and to assist German officials in establishing the administrative machinery through which the law would be implemented. The preparation for the transfer of responsibility, ensuring the uniform application and administration of the law in the U.S. occupation zone, took place in a series of meetings between denazification officials from the three *Länder* and military government officials affiliated with the *Länderrat* in March 1946. Procedures were established for registration through the *Meldebogen* (questionnaire)[128] that was to be filled out and submitted by every German adult,[129] the investigation and evaluation of that form, the enforcement of sanctions, and the proceedings of the tribunals.[130] The military government would confine its responsibilities to inspecting and supervising German authorities in the implementation of the law.[131]

It had been argued at the time that only an in-depth knowledge of the German language, along with an understanding of the political system and social life in the National Socialist era, could have provided individuals with the necessary context and background for making an accurate assessment of the role other individuals played in the former National Socialist regime. Whether the new German denazification programme could be implemented more successfully than the U.S. military government programme remained to be seen. Although the responsibility for denazification was transferred to German authorities, the Law for Liberation retained the pattern of the initial denazification programme, which required examining large numbers of individuals on the basis of presumptive guilt.[132]

The main similarity between the German programme and the U.S. military government programmes was that the Law for Liberation was designed to implement the Allied denazification policy as expressed under the terms of Control Council Directive No. 24. It provided for the creation of German tribunals, composed of "anti-Nazis of long standing," who would classify individuals appearing before the tribunals into specific categories of guilt and impose sanctions to the extent of the accused person's association with the National Socialist regime.[133]

The Law for Liberation was based on two primary insights: 1) it rejected the previously indiscriminate automatic removals from office, which had been based on the notion of collective guilt; and 2) it reaffirmed that individuals, rather than entire categories of individuals, could be held accountable for their degree of cooperation with the National Socialist regime.[134]

Being charged as a former National Socialist was defined according to a person's former office, in addition to their date of membership, thus introducing a more accurate, albeit theoretical, assessment of the personal circumstances surrounding one's level of activity in the regime. Individuals who had been removed from office could be reinstated. The law stated that all who were responsible would be called to account, while being afforded the opportunity to vindicate themselves. The evidence for judgment would be based on an individual's responsibility and their actual conduct as a whole. External appearances, such as membership in the NSDAP or its affiliated organisations, wouldn't be considered decisive in view of other evidence. Certain people, such as those possessing specialised knowledge, could be reinstated temporarily until they were replaced by another person who hadn't been politically implicated.[135]

Unlike automatic exclusion or removal from office, under the military government programme, specific penalties were set forth. Individuals were to be classified according to one of five categories: 1) Class I: Major Offenders; 2) Class II: Offenders (activists, militarists, and profiteers); 3) Class III: Lesser Offenders; 4) Class IV: Followers; and 5) Class V: Persons Exonerated.

Major Offenders included those who were guilty of committing crimes out of political conviction, crimes against humanity, or crimes in violation of international law. They were to be punished by sanctions, including imprisonment for up to fifteen years at hard labour, confiscation of property, permanent exclusion from public office, or death, in the most extreme cases. *Offenders* were those who had supported and/or contributed to the service of National Socialism and the National Socialist regime, and were subject to exclusion from public office and imprisonment for up to ten years.

Lesser Offenders included early participants in the NSDAP who had withdrawn from the party, members of the armed forces, or individuals who otherwise would be considered Offenders but merited milder penalties because of special circumstances or character, who had proven themselves capable of fulfilling their duties as citizens of a peaceful and democratic state during a period of probation. Their probation could last up to three years, during which time they were required to report periodically to the police in their place of residence, and as civil servants, they could face retirement or demotion.

Followers included those who were no more than nominal participants or insignificant supporters of National Socialism. They could be placed on probation, face restrictions of movement, or, as civil servants, face retirement or demotion and be expected to pay a single or a series of contributions to funds for reparations.

Persons Exonerated were those who despite their formal membership, candidacy, or other external association, had showed a passive attitude and had actively resisted the National Socialist regime to the extent of their powers and suffered disadvantages as a result.[136]

All cases were adjudicated by denazification tribunals (*Spruchkammern*) that determined the category to which an individual would be assigned, and then imposed appropriate sanctions. Cases could also be brought before a *Berufungskammer*, or appellate tribunal.[137] The individual under scrutiny could also appear before the tribunal with defence counsel.[138] Unlike in an ordinary law court, the burden of proof was borne by the individual.[139] An appendix to the law was included, upon the insistence of the U.S. military government, which listed ranks, organisations, and positions to be considered as incriminating evidence of National Socialist or militarist activity that would subject individuals to denazification proceedings.[140]

The most serious offenders in the legal profession were those considered to have been ardent National Socialists and holding high-ranking positions after 1 May 1937, based on the positions and offices listed in Control Council Directive No. 24. An appendix was included with the Law for Liberation, based on classifications set out in Control Council Directive No. 24, presenting an elaborate list of positions and judicial offices that automatically named accused persons as *Major Offenders*, or *Offenders*.[141]

Class I included the highest-ranking judicial and administrative officials of the national courts such as the *Reichsgericht*, judges and prosecutors of the *Volksgericht*, presidents of the *Oberlandesgerichte* appointed after 31 December 1938, and prosecuting attorneys and lawyers appointed to the *Oberlandesgerichte* after 31 March 1933.[142]

Class II included all members of the NSDAP who had joined prior to May 1937,[143] judges and prosecutors of the *Sondergerichte*, and presidents and chief prosecutors of the *Landgerichte*.[144]

Jurists who had been "nominal members" of the NSDAP or an affiliated organisation and had been readmitted to practice with the final approval of the military government maintained their practice. It was unnecessary for denazification proceedings to be initiated against them under the Law for Liberation, unless they could be classified in a category higher than *Follower* and there was evidence against them according to the results of an investigation.[145]

The relaxation of the policy of blocking politically implicated jurists from reinstatement made it possible for all German courts to be reopened by March 1946. Jurists who were reinstated following the change of the unofficial reinstatement policy possessed the complete confidence of the regional military government office and the *Land* minister of justice. Military government special branches applied the strictest possible standards for the classification of judicial personnel, while decisions in all cases that were doubtful were postponed under the German denazification procedure.[146]

Judicial personnel continued to be appointed by *Land* ministers of justice, subject to denazification procedures set forth under the Law for Liberation. The eligibility of judicial personnel appointed by the ministers of justice remained subject to prior investigation and approval by the military government, which verified individual *Fragebogen* that were submitted until June 1946. Approved jurists were then available for provisional appointment by the Ministry of Justice.[147]

Individuals who had been approved for reinstatement by the military government on the basis of an evaluation of their *Fragebogen* were to remain in their current office or occupation until their cases had been reevaluated by a *Spruchkammer*.[148] That included judicial personnel who previously had been selected to the *Amtsgerichte* affiliated with the appropriate *Landgerichtsbezirk* by local *Landgericht* presidents.[149] In the interest of maintaining the independence of the justice system and to facilitate the implementation of the Plan for the Administration of Justice (U.S. zone) in Hesse, each *Land* minister of justice was delegated sole authority to appoint and remove judicial officials within their *Land* government.[150] The appointments of jurists by ministers of justice were made permanent after an examination and judgment by a *Spruchkammer.*[151]

The power of the military government with regard to suspending and removing reinstated judicial officials was broadly defined as the right to remove officials whose actions were "in violation of the occupation objectives," lacked the necessary positive political qualities "to assist in the development of democracy in Germany," or were considered "detrimental to the achievements of U.S. military government objectives."[152] The U.S. military government insisted that appointments to certain key positions in the German justice system were to be kept clear of former members of the NSDAP. No such individual was to hold a position in the Ministry of Justice or an *Oberlandesgericht*, or to serve as a president or chief prosecutor at a *Landgericht.*[153] That policy was to be followed by German authorities when the U.S. military government divested itself of its power to approve new appointments in the German justice system on 21 September 1946.[154] In November 1946, the U.S. military government decreed that German judges and judicial officials, up to and including the minister of justice, could be appointed without prior approval of the U.S. military government.[155]

All key appointments in the *Land* justice system were filled upon the appointment of the General Prosecutor (*Generalstaatsanwalt*) of the *Oberlandesgericht* in Frankfurt-am-Main in October 1946.[156] Ministers of justice maintained the function of approving appointments of all other judicial personnel. Those appointments included individuals who had been reinstated on a temporary basis,[157] such as jurists who had been reinstated by the military government before the Law for Liberation went into force,[158] when the necessity for their services was pressing. They were to remain in office until the final status of their cases could be determined by a *Spruchkammer.*[159]

The integrity of the judicial profession as an aspect of implementing occupation policy was to be maintained by the *Land* Ministry of Justice while fulfilling the terms of denazification policy. The *Spruchkammer* was to determine whether or not a civil servant was eligible for reinstatement into office, which depended upon the sanctions the *Spruchkammer* imposed on the individual. Whether or not the individual would be reinstated after being declared eligible for reinstatement rested with the appointing authority of the governmental agency, which was to observe two policies: the civil servant being appointed or reinstated had to possess positive political, liberal, and moral qualities that would assist the development of democracy in Germany; and the appointment or reinstatement had to be subject to employment preferences and priorities favouring individuals who had been persecuted by the National Socialist regime and anti–National Socialists.[160]

In view of the experiences of German judges sabotaging democracy after 1919, it was particularly important to ensure that those key positions in the

German justice system were free of former National Socialists. The individuals selected for those key positions were responsible for the supervision of German courts and for checking potential "reactionary, legalistic and anti-democratic tendencies."[161]

The Ministry of Justice was mindful at the outset of denazification of the need to prevent former National Socialists from reentering the judicial organisation. The first individual in Hesse who presented himself to the Ministry of Justice for reappointment as a judge after being cleared by a German denazification tribunal "was refused appointment by the ministry on the grounds that not only cleared Nazis but also non-Nazis were desired as personnel for the administration of justice."[162] The minister of justice of Hesse reported to the U.S. military government that he had personally assumed the responsibility of verifying the political reliability of candidates for judicial office after they had been cleared by a *Spruchkammer* before their appointment as judges or prosecutors.

In addition to the problem of acquiring applicants with adequate political records, the professional qualities of available judicial personnel weren't always exemplary, since they were either over-age or had been out of practice for years as a result of the Second World War. On the other hand, ministers of justice attempted to employ former judges and prosecutors who'd had to leave Germany as a result of their racial, religious, or political persuasion, and had expressed a desire to return. There were three such judges among the staff of the Frankfurt-am-Main *Landgericht*. The Ministry also attempted to employ well-qualified judges from outside of Hesse.[163]

The success of the personnel reconstruction remained subject to the professional and political qualities of the available applicants. Their reinstatement was determined by denazification tribunals in Hesse, which were supplemented by recommendations for personnel submitted to *Land* ministers of justice through *Landgericht* presidents by leading authorities of the subordinate *Amtsgerichte*.[164] The decision for reinstatement was subject to further scrutiny by judicial officials and the final decision for reinstatement rested with the minister of justice.

The practice of evaluating jurists according to their political record, based on former membership in National Socialist organisations, severely hindered the personnel reconstruction of the judicial organisation as there were insufficient numbers of jurists to replace those who had been removed from office. Fifty percent of the regular positions in the justice system in Hesse that had been accounted for in the last *Reich* budget remained vacant in August 1946.[165] Removals from office had severely handicapped the justice system, and replacements were "too few, too old, and too inefficient," which resulted in long delays in criminal prosecutions and an increasingly large backlog of cases in the criminal and civil courts. In order to help alleviate the personnel shortage that was creating a serious burden on lawyers' offices, especially due to time being devoted to cases relating to denazification,[166] the personnel office of the Ministry of Justice in Hesse proposed employing jurists (judges, lawyers, and assessors) who had been removed from office due to political implication to serve as legal assistants.[167] Such individuals would be permitted to be employed in clerical functions, but couldn't offer legal advice, sign letters, or represent clients in court,[168] thus resigning them to the equivalent of "ordinary labour," since they were expressly forbidden to practice law.[169] However, that measure failed to remedy the shortage of court personnel, which was so acute that former National Socialist jurists had to be reinstated.[170] That was considered necessary, since the workload was continually increasing, and coping with the existing load could only be handled by assigning greater numbers of court personnel to remedy the situation.[171]

The work of the denazification tribunals, established by the Liberation Law, was also hampered by the personnel shortage. In addition to the problem of finding candidates who were "known opponents of National Socialism and Militarism, personally beyond reproach, and fair and just" as the law prescribed,[172] denazification authorities lacked legally trained personnel to serve with those tribunals.[173] The presidents of the *Landgericht* and the *Amtsgericht* in Frankfurt-am-Main informed the Ministry for Political Liberation that judges could hardly be spared to serve in the *Spruchkammer*, in view of the foreseen time that denazification proceedings would consume.

Judges who could fulfill that function were few (only eight out of forty-one), and some of those judges had come from other parts of Germany and were therefore unfamiliar with local conditions as prescribed by the Law for Liberation.[174] Others were unavailable to serve, or were ill-suited for the task because of age, ailments such as hearing loss, health considerations, or they were open to personal criticism due to events and circumstances in their past and therefore not considered politically irreproachable.

In spite of the fact that the number of the judges who could serve in the *Spruchkammer* was insufficient, since at least thirty would be required at the outset of the proceedings, judges who could serve couldn't devote all their time to that function, since law court staffs were completely insufficient. Other judges couldn't be spared at all, since they were engaged in specialised areas of the law.[175] The minister of justice instructed authorities of the judicial organisation that judges and prosecutors were not to be assigned to the *Spruchkammer* if their appointment to serve in denazification proceedings would impede the work of the justice system. If judicial personnel couldn't be spared for those tasks, the appointment of other suitable personnel would become the responsibility of local political administrators (the *Oberbürgermeister* and *Landräte*).[176]

Although the minister of justice pledged to assist denazification authorities in securing judges and other personnel for the denazification tribunals in return for providing priority to the clearance of judges and court personnel,[177] most qualified judges and lawyers were, in fact, unwilling to leave their practices to exercise the thankless function of serving in those tribunals.[178] Ninety-three percent of jurists in Hesse refused to participate in denazification functions.[179] Jurists were thus compelled to serve as public prosecutors under an ordinance issued by the cabinet of Hesse on 13 November 1946.[180] Jurists who avoided serving in the denazification tribunals included lawyers who had been victimised by the National Socialist regime since they weren't National Socialists. It was argued that serving in that capacity conflicted with their desired autonomy, and that lawyers were to be available to the greatest possible extent to serve the public as effective and suitable defenders during the denazification proceedings and its peculiarities.[181]

Jurists in Hesse serving as chairmen or prosecutors in the denazification tribunals repeatedly objected to having to take part in those tribunals. They declared that they couldn't reestablish their legal practices while serving in the tribunals. That left them at a disadvantage to former National Socialist jurists who had been classified as *Followers* or *Persons Exonerated* under the Liberation Law and could continue practicing in the legal profession thereafter.[182] Performing the function of prosecutor or judge was also likely to bring them into conflict with the local population or the military government.[183]

In addition to the problem of staffing the tribunals, the U.S. military government Special Branches that reviewed tribunal decisions[184] criticised their apparent tendency to pass excessively lenient sentences.[185] On the other hand, German politicians claimed they understood the term "National Socialists and Militarists" more realistically than the U.S. military government, and had reduced the number of individuals affected by the Law for Liberation in order to allow greater numbers of people to be reinstated in occupations that faced personnel shortages.[186]

That led to a conflict between German authorities and the U.S. military government over the rigour of the application of denazification.[187] The U.S. deputy military governor, General Clay, harshly criticised the work of the denazification tribunals at the Fourteenth Meeting of the *Länderrat* on 5 November 1946, accusing German authorities of lacking the political will and determination to mete out retribution to those deserving to be brought to justice. General Clay set forth that the Law for Liberation was designed as a basis for returning self-government, but the military government couldn't restore self-government to the German people if they proved unwilling to denazify their public life, since denazification was a "must" of U.S. policy. According to Clay, the U.S. military government would therefore pay special attention to the work of the denazification tribunals for the next sixty days, and no individual who had previously been removed from office by the military government could be reinstated on the basis of tribunal findings without prior approval from the military government.[188]

The military government in Hesse was under the impression that public prosecutors in Hesse weren't fully convinced of the justness of the Law for Liberation. Although there appeared to be unanimous acceptance of the need to prosecute the most notorious National Socialists as the real instigators, public prosecutors rarely supported the policy that all minor officials of the NSDAP and its affiliated organisations were to be regarded as guilty of perpetuating National Socialism. The individuals staffing the *Spruchkammern* appeared to regard the Law for Liberation as an unnecessary evil, and therefore felt justified in passing what the military government considered lenient penalties.[189] The U.S. military government reported to the Minister for Political Liberation in Hesse that in spite of written communications from the military government denazification division and oral statements made at the *Länderrat* by OMGUS officials, a review of the work of the *Spruchkammern* in Hesse had revealed that the sanctions imposed lacked severity.

The *Spruchkammern* continued to classify individuals who had held rank in the NSDAP or affiliated organisations in Class IV, such as those who had held non-commissioned ranks in the SA. In contrast, the U.S. military government maintained that such individuals had to be classified in Class III or higher, unless they had actively resisted and therefore could be placed in the Class V category. In other cases, the appellate tribunals generally tended to reduce verdicts. Judgments of cases that had been disapproved by the U.S. military government were ordered to be retried for corrective action following the submission of "Delinquency and Error" reports to the Ministry for Political Liberation.[190] However, those objections overlooked the central problem: the denazification proceedings extended too widely.[191]

The problem didn't lie with the trustworthiness of the German personnel charged with the responsibility of implementing the denazification programme. In spite of U.S. military government questions about how the Law for Liberation was being interpreted by German denazification authorities, General Clay later gave his approval for German denazification authorities to continue their functions on the basis of the results during the sixty-day probation period.[192]

While both German denazification authorities and the military government intended to implement the denazification programme, there remained the problem of the extent to which it was to be achieved, with German authorities seeking to reduce its scope while the military government insisted on an undiminished rigour.[193] General Clay had insisted on the implementation of policy without consideration for the circumstances of necessity. However, such a resumption of responsibilities ran counter to military government policy of restoring responsibility to German authorities, and the reduction of military government personnel also made a resumption practically impossible.[194]

It became evident that due to personnel shortages, the denazification policy as envisaged at the beginning of the occupation couldn't be fulfilled. The number of jurists who could be called upon to serve was limited by the application of denazification policy. That would lead to a modification of the policy to allow for greater numbers of trained and qualified jurists to serve.

The unanticipated personnel shortages that emerged during the reconstruction of the justice system undermined the occupation goal of a thorough political cleansing (Art. 22 of the Liberation Law) of every aspect of German public life in the postwar period. The Minister of Justice of Hesse, Georg-August Zinn, reported on 26 February 1946 that there had been a total number of 583 judges, public prosecutors, and *Amtsanwälte*[195] serving in the courts in Hesse before 1945, while only 235 had been appointed by that time. Zinn said that there was an urgent need for an additional 220 judges and prosecuting attorneys.[196] Causes of that shortage included the number of jurists who had been killed in the Second World War or were still interned in prisoner-of-war camps.[197]

An additional cause for the postwar shortage of trained lawyers may have originated before the war, when measures were taken to discourage university study and impose restrictions on admission to the Bar Association.[198] The shortage of jurists in Germany became evident during the Second World War because of a decline in the number of enrollments for the study of law,[199] as well as the large numbers of jurists called up for military service.[200] In the *Landgericht* in Frankfurt-am-Main and its subordinate *Amtsgerichte*, there were fifty judges employed at the *Landgericht* before 1 September 1939, twenty-six on 1 January 1943, and only twenty on 1 October 1943. There were sixty-one judges at the Frankfurt-am-Main *Amtsgericht* before 1 September 1946, compared to twenty-five on 1 January 1943. At the other *Amtsgerichte*: six in Frankfurt-am-Main-Höchst, two on 1 January 1943, and one on 1 October 1943. On the same dates, there were three in Homburg vs. two and none; two in Usingen vs. one and two.[201] Of the total number of judges who previously had been engaged in the *Landgericht* at Frankfurt-am-Main and the *Amtsgericht* at Bad Homburg, there were reported cases of judges who were deceased, killed, or missing, and there were many cases of individuals whose whereabouts were unknown, or were presumed to be awaiting their denazification proceedings, in addition to those who had been removed from office or were prisoners of war.[202]

Another possible cause that may have aggravated the shortage of jurists after the war was low salaries. Judges in the higher income brackets didn't retain more than RM 500 per month after taxes following the introduction of high income taxes[203] under Control Council Law No. 12 of 11 February 1946.[204] Personnel shortages were also evident outside the public sphere. Lawyers who were eligible to work in private practice didn't receive a fixed income and lost most of their earnings to taxes.[205]

The denazification "vintage principle" of political implication following enrollment in the NSDAP after 1 May 1937 may have theoretically widened the scope of judicial personnel made eligible for reinstatement, but in practice, it didn't alleviate the problem of finding the number of personnel to staff the postwar justice system.[206] The various causes for the shortage of judicial personnel weren't alleviated by modifying denazification legislation. There was simply a lack of qualified judicial personnel, irrespective of political record.

All courts authorised to function in the U.S. occupation zone were formally open by 30 March 1946, but proved unable to handle the existing cases on the dockets, in spite of the volume of cases having been reduced by the curtailing of cases within the jurisdiction of military government courts and the cessation of business transactions that left less corporate business to be handled by the courts.[207] Nevertheless, the shortage of jurists was so acute that politically implicated nominal National Socialists had to be reinstated if the courts were to continue to function.[208]

The implementation of the Liberation Law was overshadowed by the underlying problem of the acute personnel shortages in the legal profession. Whereas the Plan for the Administration of Justice in the U.S. Zone required five hundred judges and sixty-nine public prosecutors in Hesse, the personnel shortage was marked by the fact that only 233 judges, including assistant judges (*Hilfsrichter*), and fifty-three public prosecutors, including assistant public prosecutors (*Hilfsstaatsanwälte*), were appointed after the *Oberlandesgericht* of Hesse was opened.[209] There had been no urgency for reopening German courts in the initial phase of denazification, when military government courts were handling all criminal cases. Only German courts at the lowest level were authorised to be reopened during the military operations in the Rhineland, following a careful investigation of each potential candidate for reinstatement.[210]

The future personnel shortage was envisaged early in the occupation, soon after the first German courts were reopened. The first judges who were reinstated were over-age to a great extent, and several of them could no longer work at full capacity. The *Landgericht* president in Frankfurt-am-Main therefore recommended that the military government admit more judges as soon as possible, since court business was increasing quickly.[211] In view of the number of available jurists in September 1945 and the increase in court business, he advised that those numbers would be insufficient to staff the justice system. It was presumed that it would be necessary to rely on qualified personnel who had been members of the NSDAP before 1 May 1937, if they hadn't been politically implicated other than through simple party membership. Otherwise, normal court business would become impossible in the foreseeable future.[212]

Finding qualified personnel would become a more pressing consideration following the implementation of the Plan for the Administration of Justice of the U.S. zone, when greater responsibility was transferred to German courts. Hence, staffing a justice system that could operate at a prewar level remained a problem. In spite of the reduced jurisdiction of German courts, U.S. and British military government authorities chose to maintain politically implicated judges in office, rather than face the chaos of operating the justice system single-handedly.[213]

The readmission of jurists was initially limited to individuals considered politically untainted with regard to their affiliation with the National Socialist past. In practice, however, it became apparent that such a draconian denazification policy[214] wouldn't relieve the situation. The problem could be overcome either by rapidly training a new generation of jurists to meet the personnel requirement as soon as possible, as was attempted in the Soviet occupation zone,[215] or slacken denazification policy requirements to a more pragmatic level, which would adjust the demand for qualified jurists to the available number at hand. Hence, the critical shortage of qualified jurists was addressed by relaxing the standards, since the readmission of former civil servants and judges as soon as possible had become inevitable.[216]

The application of denazification policy was different in the U.S. and Soviet zones, but the cause for reinstating jurists without rehabilitation was the same: the reconstruction of the justice system wasn't possible without the necessary personnel.[217] The only solution to the problem appeared to be the reinstatement of the capable and qualified judges and prosecutors who had been removed from office under the denazification programme, and it soon became apparent that this would ultimately have to be done.[218]

The burden of increased caseload became increasingly apparent in 1947, as various types of cases, such as unauthorised border crossings and theft or illegal possession of U.S. property within a certain value, were transferred from military government courts to German courts. The caseload was to be absorbed by staffs that were well below peacetime strength.[219] German courts in Hesse at that time were handling about 2,000 criminal cases a month.[220] That influx of cases couldn't be handled by overworked staffs, many of whom were over-age, ill-housed, and poorly fed.[221]

The problem of immediately securing sufficient legal personnel considered suitable for appointment, with regard to their professional qualifications *and* political record, led to *Land* government institution of emergency measures to compensate for the shortfall. In order to compensate for the shortage of suitable personnel, individuals holding the professional qualifications of a judge or a prosecutor and "politically suitable" were to be enlisted for compulsory service for a period of three to six months. An ordinance for that purpose was prepared in January 1946, and all presidents of the *Landgerichte* and *Amtsgerichte* were asked to provide lists of such individuals to the ministers of justice.[222] That practice was then enacted as law.

The *Land* government required all individuals with judicial qualifications to be at the disposal of the *Land* justice system. Those people were obliged to register with the president of the local *Landgericht* to serve as a judge or prosecutor for an indefinite period, at the discretion of the minister of justice. Jurists who weren't civil servants, such as notaries and lawyers, could be enlisted to serve for a three-month term, which then could be repeated after a lapse of three months.

That ordinance didn't apply to those who presently held judicial office or were ineligible to do so after 8 May 1945, and it would remain in force for the duration of the emergency circumstances (*Notumstände*) that had necessitated its promulgation.[223] Nevertheless, the measures weren't sufficient to compensate for the shortfall in personnel.

In order to temporarily alleviate the difficulties arising from the shortage of judges,[224] the minister of justice ordered that every *Amtsgericht* judge was to function simultaneously as a *Hilfsrichter* at the respective superior *Landgericht*.[225] Additional judicial personnel were required as the workload of the courts increased. The criminal courts were barely capable of coping with the influx of cases due to the shortage of judges and an increased caseload after the military government transferred the power of the police to adjudicate in certain minor offences to German courts.[226]

As of June 1947, courts in the U.S. occupation zone as a whole possessed approximately 40 percent of the personnel they had employed in 1938,[227] while criminality in postwar Germany had increased between 500 and 600 percent compared to prewar years.[228] The Office of the Military Government in Hesse reported in November 1947 that the German justice system still had to manage with staffs that were 60 percent of the prewar numbers, while crime incidents were much higher than normal due to the severe economic and social conditions and the presence of a large migratory population.

German courts also had to absorb thousands of cases involving police ordinance violations that formerly had been adjudicated by the police, a practice which had been discontinued by the military government. The military government also began transferring groups of cases that couldn't be reversed from military government courts to German courts.[229] The *Land* Minister of Justice, Georg-August Zinn, stated on 8 March 1948 that there were 400 judges in Hesse, compared to 571 in the same territory in 1939. Meanwhile, the level of criminality in Hesse had increased dramatically, from about 50,000 criminal cases in 1938 to 115,715 in 1947.[230]

The *Länderrat* attempted to compensate for the shortage of jurists in the U.S. zone by drafting a law on 8 April 1948 to allow the appointment of refugee jurists from the *Sudetenland*.[231] In contrast to the officials of the other *Länder*, officials in the Hesse Ministry of Justice had long favoured introducing such a measure as a means to counterbalance the number of politically implicated individuals who had been admitted as a result of personnel shortages. The main difficulty lay in evaluating their professional qualifications and familiarising former Czech jurists with German legal practice.[232] The law was promulgated in Hesse on 21 June 1948 and went into force on 1 July 1948, allowing refugee jurists to resume their practices upon prior examination of their qualifications for office.[233]

In practice, none of those measures made a significant contribution toward alleviating the personnel shortage. Although the sharply rising number of criminal cases was handled expeditiously, no semblance of normal conditions was achieved while judicial personnel were blocked from service as they waited for their cases to be judged by the denazification tribunals.[234]

A shift in denazification policy for the legal profession thus took place to secure the required personnel, even if candidates had been considered politically implicated according to initial denazification standards. In order to address the problem, the military government maintained supervision of German court operations, as a safeguard against potential abuse of the justice system, which was necessary because the performance of reinstated jurists under the military government or German authorities couldn't be guaranteed.

Judicial independence was being restored to members of a judiciary in which there were few convinced democrats after a twelve-year absence of democratic government.[235] Since the military government hadn't made a thorough investigation of every jurist's professional record between 1933 and 1945, supervision of their work during the occupation indirectly compensated for that shortcoming. The reinstatement of jurists under the terms of denazification, which was based on evidence regarding former political affiliation, would be supplemented with evidence provided by their performance. Knowing that the numbers of anti– or non–National Socialist lawyers and judges had been exhausted, the military government adopted a more "realistic" view of the situation, based on expediency, and decided to reinstate jurists who were "nominal Nazis"[236] while simultaneously intensifying the supervision and inspection of German courts.[237] Inspections of the operation of German courts in Hesse revealed no significant violation of military government policies or laws, and according to one Legal Division report, nominal Nazis presented a problem only in that "they are scared and sometimes lean too heavily on Military Government in their hesitation to interpret the law freely and independently."[238]

Toward a Reevaluation of the Denazification Programme

Changes in the denazification policy allowed for greater numbers of jurists to be reinstated in understaffed courts. Modifications of the denazification policy loosened the standards in the U.S. occupation zone as certain clauses of the Law for Liberation were amended to accelerate the denazification process.[239] Modification of the Law for Liberation began with general amnesties, which resulted in great numbers of cases that didn't undergo denazification proceedings and weren't verified through individual investigations.[240]

As it soon became apparent that the Law for Liberation had been extended too widely, the first amnesty, which became known as the "youth amnesty,"[241] was introduced on 8 July 1946. The amnesty was extended to all individuals who had been born between 1 January 1919 and 5 March 1928, unless they were classified as Class I or II offenders under the Law for Liberation or there was sufficient evidence to warrant their possible classification into those categories in the future.[242]

To decrease the vast number of cases remaining to be adjudicated, the U.S. military government approved a *Länderrat* proposal in December 1946, which became known as the "Christmas amnesty," granting amnesty to former National Socialists in low income groups.[243] That included people whose yearly taxable income hadn't exceeded RM 3,600 during either 1943 or 1945 and whose taxable property hadn't exceeded RM 20,000 on 1 January 1945. It also included people with a physical disability of 50 percent or more according to social welfare or pension legislation. The amnesty didn't include those who were chargeable under the terms of Class I or II or the Law for Liberation.[244]

Of the 3,294,318 people who were affected by the Liberation Law, the two amnesties freed 1,861,483 of responsibility for the past (888,065 through the youth amnesty and 973,418 through the Christmas amnesty), thus reducing the denazification caseload by nearly 70 percent.[245] That represented an improvement in the application of denazification, but its weaknesses continued to be evident and as a consequence the scope of the programme continued to be reduced to accelerate its completion.

In addition to the problems involved in applying the provisions of the Law for Liberation, public opinion polls indicated that German acceptance of the denazification programme was gradually decreasing,[246] sinking from 57 percent in March 1946 to 32 percent in September 1947.[247] Criticism of the denazification procedure was generally directed at its implementation on the basis of former NSDAP membership, rather than on a person's conduct within the National Socialist regime. For example, the executive committee of the Bar Association (*Anwaltskammer*) in Frankfurt-am-Main argued that many more jurists would be able to serve in the justice system if their professional and personal suitability for reinstatement had been judged by their personal respectability rather than having the decisive factor be external characteristics, such as their date of entry into the NSDAP.[248]

German scholars led the way in criticising the U.S. military government denazification measures[249] that had been included in the Law for Liberation, maintaining that denazification should have been limited to the prosecution of *Major Offenders*,[250] in addition to prosecuting leading National Socialists. The scholars were respected by both the U.S. military government and the German population, and their opinions contributed significantly to the undermining the denazification programme.[251] German denazification authorities argued that the terms of the Liberation Law affected too many people, and that former National Socialists had already been blocked from occupying influential German public positions.

U.S. military government authorities who met with German denazification authorities agreed that the Liberation Law should be modified, since the originally intended thoroughness of denazification in the U.S. zone had proven to be an unwieldy task.[252] That view was also held by the political parties represented in the *Landtag* of Hesse, which presented a resolution on the denazification programme to the minister-president, requesting that the resolution then be forwarded to the Director of the *Land* Military Government and the U.S. Military Governor for Germany. The *Landtag* unanimously suggested that the Law for Liberation was too extensive. As a result, too many individuals who had been considered merely *Followers* had been penalised by a prohibition to work or other measures, while people who truly had been incriminated could avoid being brought to judgment rapidly, effectively, and justly due to the massive number of proceedings.

The *Landtag* requested that the U.S. military government amend the law to eliminate its existing shortcomings, and to improve implementation of the law by concentrating on the prosecution of truly influential National Socialists. Proposed amendments included: 1) allowing the public prosecutor to place ordinary members of the NSDAP and its affiliated organisations who had joined after 30 January 1933 into the category of *Follower*, regardless of their former office or rank, if the results of an investigation so merited and they weren't members of criminal organisations; 2) removing the employment prohibition of similar former cases immediately.[253]

Whereas the amnesties reduced the caseload of the denazification tribunals, further amendments were introduced to concentrate the efforts of the denazification programme on those people who had been more seriously implicated by their association with the National Socialist regime, thereby limiting the number of pending cases. Because the adjudication of the remaining cases would require many years, the U.S. military government requested the *Länderrat* in September 1947 to consider amending the Law for Liberation to accelerate the denazification process while maintaining its basic principles by allowing the tribunals to concentrate on the more incriminated and influential former National Socialists. It was the second important amendment to the Law for Liberation, if the enactment of the two amnesties was to be considered to be the first. Liberation Ministers in the U.S. zone intended to institute the amendment to the law, which was finally accepted after lengthy negotiations with the U.S. military government. According to the prior regulations, individuals had been subjected to the ponderous denazification procedure, even in cases in which all the participants had agreed beforehand that nothing would transpire from the case other than a classification of *Follower*.[254] Individual cases weren't prioritised for trial by the *Spruchkammern* according to their severity.

Three main points were recommended for the assessment of future cases: 1) the hitherto mandatory charges by the public prosecutor in the categories of *Major Offender*, *Offender*, and *Lesser Offender* were to be discretionary, unless the individual had been a member of an organisation found to be criminal by the International Military Tribunal or there was no evidence of activity in the NSDAP other than mere membership; 2) individuals who could be classified and charged as *Followers* could be reinstated prior to appearing before a denazification tribunal; 3) denazification tribunals were granted discretion in setting the length of time for probation for *Lesser Offenders*, which had previously required a period of two years.[255]

General Clay approved the measures proposed by the *Länderrat* for amending the Liberation Law on 3 October 1947, which were primarily designed to expedite denazification procedures for Class II cases, in which there appeared to be no evidence warranting a higher classification than that of *Follower*, thereby allowing public prosecutors and denazification tribunals to concentrate their efforts on more incriminated individuals.

Downgrading was to be effected upon the results of an investigation providing evidence that a respondent fell within the definition of *Follower* (Art. 12 of the Law for Liberation) and upon military government approval before the charge was submitted to a tribunal. Unless an individual had been a member of an organisation declared criminal by the International Military Tribunal,[256] the amendments made all people in Class II eligible for the category of *Follower* if the evidence indicated they had been only nominal members of the NSDAP and there was no evidence of active participation.[257]

The military government recognised that German criticism of denazification policy was justifiable in some respects, such as the modifying of judgments on those who had been automatically classified into Class II for having joined the NSDAP before 1 May 1937.[258] Individuals were thus to be charged according to the evidence in their case, at the discretion of the public prosecutor, rather than being summarily blocked from reinstatement until they were proven innocent. Apart from proceedings against individuals who had been members of those organisations, denazification trials of all former members of the NSDAP or its affiliated organisations became mandatory, based on the evidence presented, thus eliminating the principle of presumptive guilt.[259]

The acceleration plan went into effect as an amendment to the Law for Liberation on 7 October 1947.[260] Upon an investigation of the evidence in a case, a public prosecutor could classify an individual as a *Lesser Offender* or a *Follower*, provided they hadn't been a member of organisations declared criminal by the International Military Tribunal. Public prosecutors could exercise discretion in classifying individuals as *Followers* in cases of former nominal members of the NSDAP in which there was no evidence of active participation. Those cases included: 1) ordinary members of the NSDAP who had joined in 1933; 2) those who had joined the NSDAP after four years of service in the Hitler Youth (*Hitler Jugend*); and 3) block wardens (*Blockwalter*) of the *Nationalsozialistische Volkswohlfahrt* who had joined the NSDAP after 1933. Individuals classified as *Major Offenders* or *Offenders* remained subject to the employment restriction and could only be employed in ordinary labour[261] as defined by the provisions of Military Government Law No. 8. Individuals charged as *Followers* were allowed to resume their former occupations.[262]

The denazification tribunals in Hesse were instructed by the Minister of Political Liberation that the amendment to the Law for Liberation affected all cases of individuals suspected to be Class II offenders, regardless of the office, rank, or position they had held in the NSDAP or its affiliated organisations. Their classification into Class IV could be effected upon the institution of proceedings by the local public prosecutor. The only groups of cases that were not to be processed under the accelerated procedure were those suspected to be in Class I or II, those who had been members of organisations that were declared criminal by the International Military Tribunal, and those against which there was evidence of specific actions committed beyond their position, rank, or office.[263]

The Ministry for Political Liberation later decreed that accelerated proceedings were to apply to *all* individuals classified as Class II offenders. The U.S. military government would only query the judgments of the *Spruchkammern* if people classified as Class II offenders downgraded to Class IV were subject to trial by the International Military Tribunal or there was evidence that indicated they had been guilty of criminal actions.[264]

The new provisions were to contribute significantly to Germany's return to normal conditions by implementing a more prompt and efficient completion of the denazification programme in the U.S. zone. General Clay hoped that the changes to the Law for Liberation would enable denazification proceedings in the U.S. zone to be concluded by 1 July 1948.[265]

The changes had a significant effect on reducing the existing caseload. The monthly number of cases adjudicated by denazification tribunals tripled from November to December 1947. The revisions allowed for the disposal of about two-thirds of Class II cases. As with the previous amnesties for specific types of cases, public prosecutors didn't always stage a thorough investigation to uncover incriminating evidence, due to the pressure of the workload, the unavailability of evidence, and local pressure.[266]

Planning continued for the further acceleration of the denazification proceedings, which became the most significant factor in the development of the denazification programme. In order to enable public prosecutors and tribunals to concentrate on the more highly incriminated and influential National Socialists, local public prosecutors were to prepare a list of the pending cases of such individuals by 15 January 1948 and to prepare a court calendar from that list, including a trial date for each case. Those cases were to be completed by 30 May 1948.[267]

The U.S. military government sanctioned further revision of the Law for Liberation in response to criticism by Pastor Martin Niemöller and the Catholic Bishops of Mainz and Limburg.[268] An amendment introduced on 28 March 1948 gave public prosecutors complete discretion in filing charges against individuals who hadn't yet been tried. Pretrial employment restrictions on individuals classified as Class II offenders were removed to allow them to return to all but the most key positions in private industry and business.

In order to prevent injustices, tribunals were also able to consider pretrial restrictions when passing sentences, such as when individuals chargeable as *Lesser Offenders* or *Followers* had undergone a period of probation or internment as part of their penalty. Public prosecutors were also empowered with charging all individuals who had been classified as Class II offenders as Class IV without the prior approval of the U.S. military government. The new amendment also affected Class II offenders who had been nominal members of organisations declared criminal by the International Military Tribunal. They could be reclassified into Class IV under the usual proceedings, provided that there was no evidence that they'd had knowledge of criminal actions or intentions of those organisations while they were members or that they had committed criminal actions themselves.[269]

Cases of individuals classified as *Followers* according to the Part B appendix of the Law for Liberation were processed by publicly posting their names on lists. A Class IV classification would be maintained if a denunciation wasn't lodged with the public prosecutor within a specified time. Individuals affected by that provision would receive a written summons instructing them to pay a fine. The accelerated proceedings, known as the *B-Verfahren* (*beschleunigte Verfahren*),[270] also included cases of individuals classified in Class III under the Law for Liberation, who could be downgraded to Class IV.[271] Appeals for higher classifications were rare, and the procedure became the main method of liquidating the denazification process.[272]

A new system was introduced in April 1948 in response to continuing pressure to promote a speedier processing of cases. Unless there was sufficient evidence to prove that an individual was to be classified in Class III or Class IV, applications could be made to modify the classification. Individuals affected by the Law for Liberation immediately could be classified as *Followers* according to the evidence of overall conduct during a probationary period or if a misunderstanding in classification had resulted in penalties that had caused the individual to incur personal or economic restrictions.[273]

The amendments to the Law for Liberation also were extended to released prisoners of war who had taken up residence in the U.S. zone.[274] The U.S. military government would approve the downgrading of charges against an individual instituted by the public prosecutor unless the military government could present incriminating evidence from its files or could establish that the individual in question had falsified the *Meldebogen* or hadn't disclosed incriminating evidence.[275]

The emphasis of the denazification trials was thus further shifted toward dealing with the most seriously incriminated individuals more rapidly and thoroughly,[276] rather than maintaining the original standard of attempting to adjudicate the entire German adult population of the U.S. zone on a case-by-case basis. In view of the numbers of cases that were to be processed in Hesse, roughly 50,000, it appeared as if the *B-Verfahren* would allow the denazification proceedings to be concluded by the summer of 1948.[277]

The original standards were to be maintained for individuals occupying leading positions in the justice system. U.S. military government policy prescribed that only individuals who were "capable of assisting in the development of genuine democratic institutions in Germany" and could be relied upon to ensure "a correct solution to denazification problems" would be appointed as judges and prosecutors by virtue of "their moral and political qualities." The policy required that nominal National Socialists would be excluded from key positions that could exert an influence in developing personnel policies or exercise supervisory powers over personnel in the justice system. That policy also required that such individuals would also be excluded from positions in the *Oberlandesgerichte*, where interpretation of German law was made in the last instance.

In trials of National Socialist crimes against German law, the participation of judges and prosecutors who'd had any affiliation with the NSDAP were to be excluded, to maintain the impartiality of the proceedings. The director of each *Land* Office of Military Government upheld the policy by instructing local minister-presidents that no individual who had been a member of the NSDAP, the SA, the NSKK, or the NSFK could be appointed to the following positions: higher levels of the civil service in the Ministry of Justice, by which they would have the authority to issue orders in the name of the minister-president or minister of justice; judge or prosecutor in an *Oberlandesgericht*; president or chief prosecutor in a *Landgericht*; or senior judge of an *Amtsgericht* in cities with a population of more than 100,000.

No judge or prosecutor who had been a member of the aforementioned formations at any time could take part in the trial of a case involving "criminal offences against German law committed for the purpose of maintaining Nazi tyranny or militarism or to promote the realisation of Nazi ideology or tendencies." Those provisions didn't apply to individuals who had been "contributing members" of the aforementioned formations, or members of the SA Reserve II.[278]

The president of the court was to be an individual who hadn't been affected by the Law for Liberation. The justice system in Hesse agreed that only judges who hadn't been affected by the Law for Liberation could adjudicate in the aforementioned criminal cases involving National Socialist crimes. However, a departure from that policy became necessary, because of the limited number of judges. It wasn't possible to find suitable substitutes, due to the rigid policy in Hesse concerning positions at the *Oberlandesgericht* and other key positions that exhausted the number of judges not affected by the Law for Liberation.

That problem was exacerbated by the illness of several judges in Gießen and Frankfurt-am-Main.[279] In one such case, one judge had been a member of the NSDAP while the other had been a member of the SA. In another case, two judges were both former members of the SA.[280] The nature of the political cases heard by former nominal members of the NSDAP were minor, and the president of the court wasn't affected by the Law for Liberation. The Legal Division of the Military Government Office for Hesse would also examine the decisions in those cases.[281]

Although the U.S. military government had begun to approve the admission of nominal National Socialist jurists in 1946, since the reopening of German courts would otherwise have been impossible, the U.S. military government continued to affirm that key positions in the justice system within the U.S. zone, such as the Ministries of Justice, the *Oberlandesgerichte*, and the presidents and the chief prosecutors of the *Landgerichte*, not be held by even nominal National Socialists,[282] which amounted to more than 10 percent of the judges and prosecutors in the U.S. zone.[283] The *Land* military government legal division in Hesse affirmed that there were no nominal National Socialists at the *Oberlandesgericht* in Hesse. That was made possible by appointing a number of individuals from outside Hesse, in contrast to the practice in other *Länder*: "the staffs of Oberlandesgerichte in other Laender, particularly Bavaria, are so limited, largely because appointments have been governed by local patriotism as well as by the desire to keep positions open for the former Nazi incumbents thereof."[284]

The legal division therefore recommended that maintaining current standards and blocking even nominal former National Socialists from occupying key positions in the judicial organisation would ensure that any doubtful political judgments made by lower courts could be revised, thereby exercising an educational influence upon the lower courts at a time when military government controls were relaxed and supervision by the military government was limited.[285] The military government was also kept informed about reinstated officials and employees of the justice system in Hesse below the category of the upper level of the civil service (*höherer Dienst*) and classified as *Followers* under the Law for Liberation.[286] Although military government policy at that time was to admit former members of the NSDAP who had been classified by the *Spruchkammer* as either *Followers* or *Persons Exonerated* to certain positions in the civil service, such as judges and prosecutors, those individuals weren't reinstated automatically. The German administration of justice considered the merits of each case and determined whether the individual had been politically implicated.[287]

Corresponding consequences of accelerating the completion of the denazification programme followed for the legal profession, which was encompassed in the scope of the denazification programme along with all other professions. Individual jurists were either subject to amnesty or were classified below Class I or II of the Liberation Law and no longer subject to the initial penalties instituted under that law. In addition to reducing the caseload of the denazification tribunals by issuing amnesties for broad categories of individuals not classified into the top categories of the Law for Liberation, the severity of the penalties called for under that law were modified as demand increased for accelerating trial proceedings following criticism in the U.S. government concerning the cost of the military occupation and the need for rapid German economic recovery.[288] Industrial activity in western Germany in late 1947 hadn't reached 30 percent of 1938 levels, and representatives of the U.S. government considered the continued depression of the German economy to be "the single most important retarding element in the rehabilitation of western Europe."[289]

A shift in U.S. public opinion also played a role in the modification of denazification policy, which resulted from the cooling of relations with the Soviet Union, the introduction of the Truman Doctrine on 12 March 1947, and the draining cost of the military occupation.[290] The shift in world politics and the beginning of the Cold War led to a new assessment of relations with western Germany, since a new rise of fascism was no longer considered a threat.[291]

It's been argued that U.S. public opinion had a powerful impact on the formulation of U.S. denazification policy.[292] America's initial policy was more oriented toward appeasing public opinion in the U.S. than on the social realities of the National Socialist regime, and was thereby one of the causes for the extremely schematised and extensive application of the denazification programme.[293] In turn, a shift in the political climate and the corresponding force of public opinion contributed to the conclusion of the denazification programme.

The restoration of justice with personnel not implicated with the NSDAP *Unrechtsstaat* to any degree, as envisaged by the occupation powers in the Potsdam Protocol, couldn't be accomplished for two main reasons. First, the original denazification programme was soon undermined by various revisions. The original strident denazification standards and procedures were relaxed in view of the impracticability of its application. Second, the subject of denazification became awkward in view of the wider context of the Cold War. The threat of fascism was superseded by a fear of the extension of Communism to western Europe, which led to discussions among the western Allies concerning the future integration of a West German state into a defensive alliance.[294] The problems encountered in applying denazification policy and changes in international circumstances led to the American abandonment of the original denazification programme.

The critical personnel shortage made it evident that the original denazification programme would prevent the restoration of a functioning judicial organisation.[295] However, jurists were blocked from resuming their functions until after their denazification proceedings had been concluded. German denazification authorities agreed that the Liberation Law was extended too widely and that it affected too many people. The prohibition on employment was particularly criticised, since it imposed a lengthy penalty on hundreds of thousands of people suspected to be Class IV cases while the *Spruchkammer* couldn't deal with such cases rapidly enough.[296]

The U.S. House Select Committee on Foreign Aid reported in early 1948 that the rapid application of the denazification policy was excessively ambitious. It had become evident that too many individuals were being rigidly included into broad categorizations, causing uncertainty that hampered programmes for economic reconstruction and democratisation. It was also argued that the imposition of rigorous denazification standards conflicted with the U.S. military government objective of restoring responsibility to German authorities.[297]

The credibility of the denazification programme was undermined by focusing mainly on the formal criteria of membership in the NSDAP or one of its affiliated organisations, rather than on evidence of an individual's conduct in the National Socialist regime, which inevitably led to injustices and errors. Both German and U.S. authorities believed that the expectations of the denazification were responsible for the personnel shortages that obstructed the industrial and political recovery programme in Hesse, since skilled workers, technical experts, and professionals were greatly needed for the postwar economic reconstruction, regardless of individual personalities or political records that had been under suspicion as denazification proceedings took place. [298]

Three predominant conditions were cited for mitigating the original denazification standards: the need for granting German authorities greater responsibility for denazification; the growing chasm between the western Allies and the Soviet Union; the need to help western Germany begin making an important contribution to the economic recovery of western Europe. Changing situations provided opportunities for former National Socialists to return to influential positions in western Germany industry, either because of the need for their technical and commercial abilities or because higher production figures outweighed political considerations.[299]

In view of the inherent weaknesses of the denazification programme and a changing international situation, the House Select Committee recommended that denazification proceedings in the U.S. zone concerning all but *Major Offenders* and *Offenders* be closed by 8 May 1948. A full amnesty was to be issued for all *Lesser Offenders* and *Followers* whose clearance proceedings hadn't been completed by that date.[300]

The discrediting of the denazification programme and its subsequent liquidation corresponded to attempts to alleviate the personnel shortage in the justice system. Four hundred ninety judges were employed in the *Land* judicial organisation by the end of 1948, compared to 395 in 1947 (24. 1 percent), and 167 prosecutors, compared to 134 in 1947 (24. 7 percent). Although the increase in court personnel was far less than the increase of court business, the courts handled a 50 percent increase in cases. The number of civil service internships (*Referendare*) and clerical employees in the Ministry of Justice were also marked by increases: from 335 *Referendare* in 1947 to 390 in 1948 (16. 5 percent), and from 2,422 clerical employees in 1947 to 2,750 in 1948 (11. 9 percent).[301]

Further guidelines were introduced for the reinstatement of judges and prosecutors that combined legislation with new regulations. New applicants would be considered if: 1) they had held a position in the judicial organisation in postwar Hesse; 2) they possessed suitable professional qualifications and positions were open; 3) they hadn't been seriously implicated under the Law for Liberation, with priority granted to those who were less implicated; 4) they were residents of Hesse; 5) they hadn't been members of the NSDAP before 1 April 1933, members the *SS*, or officers of the *Waffen SS*; 6) they weren't politically implicated refugees from east of the Oder-Neisse Line; 7) they passed a legal training examination if they were refugee jurists from Czechoslovakia; 8) they were political refugees from the Soviet zone and had been granted political asylum in Hesse.[302]

The regulations for the reinstatement of jurists by that time were considerably more lenient than at the beginning of the occupation. Since the relaxation took place as the denazification programme was being concluded and the personnel shortage was no longer a severe impediment to the personnel reconstruction of the justice system, it may be inferred that the initial denazification regulations had been a primary cause of the shortage of highly specialised personnel.

The Conclusion of the Denazification Programme

The original denazification programme was effectively concluded in 1948.[303] By 7 May 1948, the cases pending trial under the Law for Liberation had been reduced to a relatively few highly incriminated and influential National Socialists. As a result, the military government would cease to review decisions of the denazification tribunals, except on an individual basis, in cases when the military government had new and substantial evidence that hadn't been available to the tribunal when it tried the case, or cases in which there had been a gross error.[304]

Military government supervision of German denazification proceedings ended when the Special Branches of the *Land* Military Government Office in Hesse were ordered to be disbanded in October 1948. The *Land* Special Branches were to be replaced by an Office of the Denazification Advisor in the Office of the Military Government. The new office was to advise the director of the *Land* military government on denazification matters, to assemble reports on the activities of German denazification authorities, to transfer those reports to OMGUS, and to establish a connection with the German denazification ministries. The Office of the Military Government for Hesse itself was to be closed on 1 July 1949, while the Office of the Denazification Advisor was to continue to function thereafter.[305] Although German authorities would continue to evaluate denazification cases, the function of the denazification ministries in the three *Länder* would be turned over to the permanent *Land* ministries. The Ministry for Liberation in Hesse was to cease functioning on 31 March 1949, and its tasks were to be assumed by either the Ministry of Justice or Labour, or a combination of both.[306]

The *Landtag* of Hesse promulgated a law concerning the completion of the political liberation in Hesse on 8 July 1949. All individuals classified in Class III by a denazification or appeal tribunal were to be downgraded to Class IV by 31 December 1949. Those who hadn't yet been tried by 31 December 1949 were only to be brought before a denazification tribunal if their case potentially warranted their being classified in Class I or II.[307] The law was to attempt to remedy the unjust inequalities within the denazification programme that had been evident from the beginning.

The scope of the denazification programme was considered to have been far too extensive, as indicated by the amnesties that were introduced to reduce the number of cases. Hence, public prosecutors were instructed to concentrate on Class III cases in which there was a greater probability of prosecution,[308] unless they had been downgraded.

The law ordering the conclusion of the political liberation in Hesse went into force on 23 November 1949,[309] effectively adjusting the denazification programme to what initially had been proposed by German policy-makers before the Law for Liberation was enacted and changing its application to the prosecution of former actions, while maintaining the categories within the legislation as an instrument of evaluating individual responsibility.

The reinstatement of former members of National Socialist organisations was practically completed after the conclusion of the denazification programme. All but some 2 percent of the original 34 percent of public officials in Hesse who had been removed from office had been reinstated by 8 July 1949.[310] By 27 October 1949, 3,222,922 people in Hesse had submitted a *Meldebogen*, of which 2,287,984 weren't affected by the Liberation Law.

The following decisions were made for the 934,938 who were affected by the law: 416 *Major Offenders*; 5,350 *Offenders* or *Activists*; 28,208 *Lesser Offenders*; 133,722 *Followers*; 5,279 *Persons Exonerated*; 663,273 amnesties. There remained 3,157 *Spruchkammer* proceedings and 2,749 appeals outstanding at that time,[311] 532 undecided cases by 30 June 1950,[312] and only 24 by 31 January 1954.[313] It became common practice for former members of National Socialist organisations to fill positions according to their skills, regardless of their political records. This practice was confirmed at the national level in May 1951, when the government of the Federal Republic of Germany passed a law that formally ended the denazification of civil servants. The legal status of civil servants who had been affected by the denazification, such as having been removed from office or not yet reinstated, was determined by law to fulfill the provisions of Art. 131 of the federal constitution. That measure marked the final stroke in the development of a civil service personnel reinstatement policy that had begun with the military occupation.[314]

All those who had been removed from office could make a legal claim for reinstatement, unless they had been ruled by a *Spruchkammer* to be unfit for public service, or had been employed by the *Gestapo*.[315] Hence, the goal of denazification to permanently block individuals from positions of influence, which already had been in decline toward the end of the denazification programme, was made virtually meaningless in the long term. The termination of the denazification programme during the military occupation was a tacit admission that the massive political cleansing of a nation wasn't feasible.[316]

A positive aspect of the postwar reconstruction of German political life was that incorrigible National Socialists who hadn't been prosecuted didn't control postwar democratic institutions, allowing the new democratic way of life in postwar Germany to take place. Resistance and sabotage scarcely occurred, since one's interests, even if that person was a former National Socialist, were better served by adhering to the postwar system.[317]

The decline in the enactment of the original denazification standards affected all occupations in each *Land* of the U.S. zone. No particular consideration was given to bringing former National Socialist jurists to account for their actions. In one case toward the end of the denazification programme, a jurist who had obviously been heavily incriminated according to the original denazification standards, having joined the NSDAP in 1930, the SS in 1933, and the SD in 1937, and having held a high rank in the *Luftwaffe*, and the position of *Oberstabsrichter* in a *Luftwaffe* military court (*Feldgericht*), was classified as a *Follower* and was penalised with a fine of RM 500. The evidence presented in that case indicated that the individual was an opportunist who had played a considerable role in the National Socialist regime, but judgments at that stage of denazification were less severe in comparison to previous earlier cases.[318]

Interest in implementing the denazification programme had greatly diminished by that time. In other cases of lenient penalties, it may be argued that the tribunals, staffed by Germans who had the benefit of firsthand experience of the conditions of the National Socialist regime, could justify their decisions by taking personal circumstances of each individual case into account, considering evidence of individual conduct and extenuating circumstances under the National Socialist regime.

In a case of overriding formal political guilt, a former judge who had been a member of the NSDAP from 1933 to 1945 was classified by an appeal tribunal as a *Follower*, downgraded from *Lesser Offender*, since she hadn't held a leading position in the NSDAP or the RAD, and her activity in office didn't reveal that she had supported the National Socialist dictatorship.[319] Taking individual circumstances into account as evidence was symptomatic of rejection of the concept of presumptive collective guilt that had been implied in the U.S. military government denazification procedure, which some Germans considered "a convenient over simplification and distortion of the circumstances."[320]

Judgment on the basis of NSDAP membership didn't accurately reflect the complexities of living in National Socialist Germany, since the theory of collective guilt failed to allow for discerning why individuals had joined the NSDAP, or whether they necessarily conducted themselves as National Socialists if they had been members of the NSDAP.[321] The denazification tribunals thereby passed judgment accordingly. For example, a judicial official (*Justizsekretär*) who had been a member of the NSDAP from 1 May 1933 was classified as a *Follower* and was penalised with a RM 540 fine since he had joined under strong pressure by his superior, and hadn't gained any advantages as a result of his membership.[322]

On the other hand, it may be argued that the denazification tribunals sometimes made what could be considered errors in judgment. For example, a former judge of a *Sondergericht* who wasn't only presumptively incriminated by virtue of having held that office, but according to the available evidence, had been personally involved in passing both death and prison sentences. He had been tried and classified in Class II in October 1946, but was later found to be in Class IV and penalised with a fine of RM 2,000 by an appellate tribunal in Hesse in February 1947.[323] Another example of what the *Land* legal branch considered "a common variety of Hessian white-wash,"[324] a *Spruchkammer* classified a former NSDAP *Blockleiter* who had joined the NSKK in 1933 and the party in 1942, and had served as assistant judge at a *Sondergericht* into Class IV and imposed a RM 100 fine. The *Spruchkammer* defended its judgment by stating that the individual had joined the NSDAP upon being advised to do so by his superior. The man was said to have attempted to resist National Socialist tendencies in his position as judge, and had therefore incurred disciplinary punishment and professional disadvantage. He had also served as an assessor at a *Sondergericht* for a year in 1941 against his wishes. Those facts formally placed the man in Class II, according to the terms of the Law for Liberation. On the other hand, the testimonies of several witnesses who were jurists supported the subject's claims that he hadn't supported National Socialism, and had thereby been relegated to a less important position. The *Spruchkammer* classified the accused as a *Follower* on the basis of his attitude and his economic circumstances.[325]

In another example, a former public prosecutor of the *Volksgerichtshof* was classified into Class IV.[326] The tribunals combined the task of denazification with rehabilitation in their judgments, by which it was tacitly assumed that the individual who had been called to account could become reformed. That practice led to them imposing sentences that were more lenient than what could have been expected from a stricter application of the law,[327] but may have been symptomatic of a widespread trend to repress and forget the details of the National Socialist past.[328] It was also argued, from the German point of view, that U.S. military government authorities had imposed the principle of presumptive collective guilt onto the denazification procedure because they distrusted all Germans, and hadn't considered the everyday realities of social life under the National Socialist regime, in which one was subject to political pressure and terror.[329]

The implementation of the denazification programme was also undermined by errors in judgment by the tribunals, due in part to the quality of denazification personnel, who hadn't been carefully selected because of the urgency of the task.[330] In addition to the quality of denazification tribunal personnel, the tribunals were sometimes intimidated by members of the communities in which denazification proceedings took place, and therefore imposed lenient judgments. Moreover, thorough investigation of individual cases was hindered by the fact that witnesses for the prosecution sometimes avoided that function, or were ostracised by members of their communities.[331]

Staging a thorough denazification at the local level was obstructed by both psychological and social impediments, since the denazification was carried out among neighbours and colleagues rather than by anonymous tribunals.[332] Members of the *Spruchkammer* were wary of trying *Major Offenders*, since they feared future reprisals from those influential individuals.[333] Prosecutors tended to base their indictments on the content of an individual *Meldebogen*, and tribunals tended to accept extenuating circumstances presented by the defence. As a result, many of the judgments made by these denazification tribunals were considerably more lax than those of the military government.[334]

In addition to tribunal judgment errors, amendments to the denazification law significantly reduced the number of individuals to be examined. A much larger number of individuals were retained in their employment than would have been expected from a strict application of the law.[335] A U.S. military government official revealed that approximately 85 percent of people removed from public service by the military government at the beginning of the denazification programme were later reinstated by German authorities.[336] But it had become apparent that the original policy, barring all former members of National Socialist organisations, couldn't be carried out without stultifying the normal functioning of the state.

Less serious cases were dealt with as rapidly as possible, to eliminate the vacuum that denazification was creating in the workforce. Serious cases (*grosse Fälle*), such as those concerning former members of the *Gestapo* and others who had taken part in the pogrom of November 1938, were postponed and later tried by criminal courts. The "Law on the Conclusion of the Political Liberation in Hesse" of 30 November 1949 called for the continued examination of cases involving individuals who could be considered Class I and II offenders on the basis of the evidence of former actions.[337] Such cases included: persecution of political opponents, murder or attempted murder of prisoners or political opponents, mistreatment or persecution of Jews, crimes against humanity, and serving as chairman (*Senatspräsident*) or prosecutor at the *Volksgerichtshof.* All other denazification proceedings were abandoned.[338]

Hence, only the worst offenders under the Law for Liberation could remain permanently excluded from the justice system. Former nominal members of National Socialist organisations wouldn't be affected in the long term. Deciding whether individual jurists were to be reinstated and could be expected to perform their functions according to acceptable standards was the responsibility of each *Land* minister of justice. For example, a heavily implicated former jurist wasn't severely penalised under the denazification procedure, but was blocked from future reinstatement as a jurist since he couldn't inspire the confidence of the minister of justice. He'd been classified into Class III by a *Spruchkammer* in January 1948, which had been upheld by an appeal tribunal in June 1948 and then modified to Class IV in February 1949. There was evidence indicating that he'd been a member and first chairman of a youth group of the *Schutz und Trutzbund* from 1919 until its dissolution in 1923. He'd also been a member of the NSDAP from 1 May 1933, had occupied a leading office in the NSRB as a *Gaufachgruppenwärter der Rechtsanwälte*, and had volunteered to serve with a unit of the SD, in which he was on friendly terms with a high official. His request for reinstatement was therefore refused by the Ministry of Justice because his former political conduct didn't guarantee that he could serve in a manner conducive to the requirements of a democratic justice system.[339]

It has been argued that the denazification programme could only have been successful if it had eliminated, or at least contributed toward the elimination of, National Socialist psychology and attitudes. On the positive side, the National Socialist organisation and its political and economic power were liquidated, and the legal system it had perpetuated was abolished during the military occupation. National Socialist ideology was virtually extinguished by the sheer force of the occupation, and perpetuating the ideology was no longer possible under those circumstances. The continuity of personnel from the National Socialist to a postwar democratic system also didn't threaten future political stability.

The shocking experiences of the Second World War and postwar period influenced the civil service and judicial professions, as well as the majority of the population, to adopt a positive attitude toward the new postwar political system. Acceptance of the transition from a monarchy to a republic in the Weimar period was marred by economic problems, while it was the successes in solving the social and economic problems in the Federal Republic of Germany that effectively sustained popular support for the new democratic state.[340] How effectively the U.S. military government had fulfilled the UN's aim of eradicating National Socialism from Germany, and reeducating Germany according to democratic principles[341] remains an open question.

Dealing with the Past and the Limitations of the Denazification Programme

The denazification programme eliminated National Socialist influences from postwar German institutions, but it didn't succeed in dealing with all the injustices that had been perpetrated during the National Socialist regime. Even though dealing with every individual on an equal basis wasn't practical, there remained the problem of dealing with actions committed under the regime and bringing the perpetrators to justice. Some of the injustices that had been committed under the National Socialist regime were prosecuted outside the scope of the Law for Liberation, while others that could have been considered injustices weren't brought under consideration.

The justice system in the National Socialist regime had undermined trust in the administration of criminal justice. Severe penalties were imposed for acts that weren't commonly considered criminal and didn't deserve such extreme penalties. In other instances, crimes weren't prosecuted due to political reasons. Confidence in the justice system only could be restored if the principles of the *Rechtsstaat* could be restored in that sphere, which would involve prosecuting the crimes committed under the National Socialist regime.[342]

Control Council Laws No. 1 of 20 September 1945 and No. 11 of 30 January 1946 rescinded the most notorious National Socialist laws, which contributed to the denazification of the law by prohibiting the further application of abolished National Socialist laws. But there remained the difficulty of dealing with sentences that had been passed while those laws were in force.[343]

In principle, an action is subject to prosecution according to the laws currently in force. That principle was set in Art. 8 of Military Government Law No. 1 and Art. 116 of the Weimar Constitution, but was breached by Control Council Law No. 10[344] of 20 December 1945 on "Punishment of Persons

Guilty of War Crimes,"[345] which the U.S. military government used to prosecute war criminals.[346]

The provisions of Law No. 10 called for four types of crimes to be adjudicated by the International Military Tribunal: 1) crimes against peace; 2) war crimes; 3) crimes against humanity; 4) membership in or association with an organisation that the International Military Tribunal declared to be criminal.[347] If so authorised by the respective occupation power, crimes committed by Germans against Germans or against displaced persons were to be transferred to a German court.[348]

In view of the inherent problems associated with a retroactive application of the law by German courts, the U.S. military government avoided granting the German judicial organisation the authority of a general application of Law No. 10,[349] such as the legal justification for applying legislation enacted following the perpetration of the action. Such cases were later admitted to German courts under special authorisation of the military government, as was provided for in paragraph 10 of Military Government Law No. 2.[350]

The most widespread discussion concerning the prosecution of National Socialist crimes centered on how to deal with German informers who had denounced other Germans to National Socialist authorities, out of loyalty to the regime or for personal gain.[351] When the government of Hesse issued a query about the prosecution of such cases, the military government responded with the following conclusions: 1) Those types of cases couldn't be adjudicated by German courts, since there was no German law covering such cases. Therefore, individuals who had denounced others couldn't be charged with such an offence. 2) Any law enacted by German authorities to make such actions open to prosecution would be retroactive and not be looked upon favourably.[352]

The perpetration of malicious denunciations theoretically could have come under Law No. 10, which specifically included "persecutions on political, racial or religious grounds" in Art. 2(c), but the question remained how the term "persecution" should be construed in such cases. Under German law, Art. 104 of the Criminal Code stated that denunciations weren't open to prosecution if the denunciations were true.[353] Art. 164 of the Criminal Code only allowed for prosecution for *false* denunciation, while those based on fact, such as when the denounced individual had listened to forbidden foreign broadcasts, were not chargeable.[354] Hence, if denunciation cases that had been reported by informers to the authorities were allegedly true, there was no legal basis for prosecution under existing German law. The informers in such cases could conceivably have been indicted on a charge of being an accomplice to murder or deprivation of freedom, but only if a new law was enacted to define the circumstances under which such an act would be made subject to prosecution.[355]

Since existing law didn't allow for criminal prosecution of indirect responsibility for the commitment of a crime, the ministers of justice in the U.S. zone drafted a law to prosecute those who had carried out the denunciations to help facilitate the denazification by prosecuting those who had willingly collaborated with the National Socialist regime at any level of society. Although the sanction of such a law would contradict the principle that criminal laws shouldn't possess retroactive power, there was public demand for the prosecution of informers, which hadn't been dealt with under the Law for Liberation from National Socialism and Militarism, since that law didn't specifically deal with criminal matters. The ministers of justice therefore recommended drafting a special criminal law for that purpose, which would be enclosed in a draft of the Law for the Punishment of National Socialist Crimes that was under discussion at that time. They proposed that whoever had directly or indirectly subjected another individual to political persecution as a result of a denunciation, whether deliberately or through negligence, which had caused serious consequences, particularly imprisonment in a concentration camp or death, would be sentenced to prison. Perpetrators who had acted out of self-interest, vengeance, or other reprehensible motives would be sentenced to imprisonment in a penitentiary.[356]

However, those provisions weren't introduced into any new German legislation. Since German legislation had to be approved by the military government, it may be surmised that the military government opposed the prosecution of denunciation cases, since it would have opened a floodgate of litigation. Such cases could still have been prosecuted under Art. 2(c) of Law No. 10, which specifically provided that prosecution of actions was possible "whether or not in violation of the democratic laws of the country where perpetrated." Prosecution was also technically possible under Law No. 10. Art. 3(d) of Law No. 10, provided the tribunal that could be charged with prosecution of a case could be a German court, in cases of crimes committed by Germans against other Germans, or if prior authorisation for the prosecution had been granted by the military government to a German court holding the appropriate jurisdiction.[357]

The U.S. military government ordered that cases involving informer denunciations would be authorised to be tried by German courts if the case revealed *prima facie* malicious intent by the informer, and "grave disadvantages were caused by the act of information to the person against whom it was directed."[358] In practice, the U.S. military government disapproved of overburdening the courts with minor cases that didn't involve principles of public interest or injustice. It was therefore ruled that German courts wouldn't be authorised to deal with denunciation cases under any circumstances until appropriate legislation had been enacted, since individual courts would otherwise have to handle cases with a wide divergence in principle, and justice could have been jeopardised.[359] Hence, the prosecution of informers wasn't authorised by the U.S. military government, which was concerned that either the volume of evidence on those informers would bring a proliferation of litigation, or cases of "minor" criminals would be considered low priority in view of "more important" work faced by understaffed courts, on the principle that such cases could be disregarded in lieu of more significant war criminal cases.[360]

German courts in the British, French, and Soviet zones were empowered with adjudicating denunciation cases according to the terms of military government ordinances, and courts in Berlin were empowered to hear such cases under the terms of Control Council Law No. 10 and German law. Although such cases couldn't be prosecuted in the U.S. zone, in exceptional cases, they could be tried upon special application if they also constituted a violation of German law.[361]

Although cases of denunciations conveying accurate information didn't violate any specific provision of the Criminal Code and Control Council Law No. 10 and couldn't be heard by German courts in the U.S. zone, the *Oberlandesgericht* in Hesse set the precedent for such cases to be tried under civil law. That court ruled that an individual who had denounced another for a political offence during the National Socialist regime had to have known about the possibility that the matter would be heard by an ordinary law court in an arbitrary manner, or possibly by the secret state police. Therefore, a denunciation to a public authority containing only accurate information couldn't be considered contrary to good morals under the conditions that had been prevalent under the National Socialist regime, rather than under the government of law. The *Oberlandesgericht* in Hesse therefore awarded damages to the plaintiff on the basis of paragraph 826 of the Civil Code. The *Land* military government's legal division agreed that the action of such denunciators constituted tort, even if they weren't a criminal offence.[362]

The German ministers of justice in the U.S. zone sponsored their own war crimes legislation through the *Länderrat* Legal Committee when they realised that authorisation for German courts to apply Law No. 10 wasn't forthcoming.[363] The adjudication and prosecution of individuals implicated with war crimes remained within the jurisdiction of the military government, and military courts were established for that purpose.[364] The ministers of justice in the *Länderrat* Legal Committee drafted laws dealing with crimes and injustices that had been committed during the National Socialist regime. Those included the "Law for the Punishment of National Socialist Crimes" of 29 May 1946,[365] and two other laws that dealt specifically with the redress of National Socialist injustices in the administration of criminal justice.[366]

The first, the "Law for the Redress of National Socialist Injustice in the Administration of Criminal Justice" of 29 May 1946, which went into force on 15 June 1946, stated that acts of political resistance against National Socialism and Militarism weren't punishable. The provisions of the law called for the annulment of sentences that had been passed according to National Socialist legislation, and justified previous acts of resistance against the National Socialist regime or the prosecution of total war.[367] The courts were empowered with adjudicating cases arising from crimes committed during the National Socialist regime involving political, racial, or religious persecution that hadn't been brought before a court prior to the occupation and had been considered criminal acts under German law prior to the enactment of National Socialist legislation that sanctioned actions contradicting the principles of justice.[368] The authority of the law was limited to the prosecution of actions that had been sanctioned by any National Socialist laws, enactments, or ordinances that had been abolished under occupation law. The enactment of the law removed the obstacle of a legal justification of applying the law retroactively.[369]

The second law, the "Law for the Compensation of National Socialist Injustice in the Administration of Criminal Justice," went into force simultaneously and translated the terms of Proclamation No. 3 into practical terms: overruling of judgments made by courts passing convictions according to National Socialist ideology, and requiring the sentences of persons convicted on political, racial, or religious grounds to be declared invalid.[370] The law thus reestablished the principle of equality of all in the eyes of the law.[371]

The "Second Law on the Compensation of National Socialist Injustice" of 13 November 1946 extended the provisions of the original law of 29 May 1946. Sentences pronounced by a *Sondergericht* between 31 January 1933 and 8 May 1945 that hadn't yet been served, either in whole or in part, and had been considered excessive in view of the act and the circumstances of the time were to be reduced to an appropriate extent, or suspended altogether. Such cases were to be reviewed by the *Landgericht* in the district where the *Sondergericht* formerly had been located. Each case would be reviewed on the basis of the evidence and the appropriate provisions of the Code of Criminal Procedure (*Strafprozeßordnung*). Decisions on those cases could be appealed to the *Oberlandesgericht* if a reduction of sentence had been refused.[372]

Supplementary provisions were later added to the two laws on 16 August 1947. Regarding the "Law on the Punishment of National Socialist Crimes," the new provisions stated that court proceedings could be resumed after a final verdict had been pronounced for cases in which the defendant had been judged unjustly. Those cases could be reopened if the defendant had been acquitted on grounds that could be considered offensive to the equality of race, religion, or political beliefs, when the defendant had received a disproportionately lenient sentence during the National Socialist regime, or when a crime constituted the subject of the investigation. Proceedings in such cases could be reopened until 31 December 1948.[373] Application of the provisions was to follow those stated in the law.

According to the "Law for the Compensation of National Socialist Injustice in the Administration of Criminal Justice," those who had been convicted of crimes violating criminal law that was in force at the time of the offence or had taken political actions that were considered criminal at the time remained subject to their sentences until their cases were reopened.[374]

German courts began a programme in the summer of 1946 for prosecuting cases of criminal actions committed between 1933 and 1945, instituting proceedings for political crimes or crimes against humanity involving actions that constituted offences under German criminal law. Such cases included trying individuals who had taken part in synagogue burnings or anti-Jewish riots shortly before the war.[375] The first such cases were authorised by the military government in Hesse in August 1946, which involved the burning of the synagogue in Wiesbaden-Schierstein, the desecration and destruction of the synagogue and the wrecking of Jewish homes and shops in Nachheim in November 1938.[376] By November 1946, the Darmstadt *Landgericht* had dealt with approximately ten such cases of atrocities committed against Germans in 1938, while approximately twenty other similar cases were pending in Gießen and fifteen others in Wiesbaden.[377]

The most notable case of political significance in Hesse was the trial of twenty-five physicians, nurses, and administrative staff members of the Hadamar, Eichberg, and Kalmenhof insane asylums, where some 20,000 Germans had been killed[378] as part of the National Socialist euthanasia programme. Two of the physicians were sentenced to death, and nine other defendants were sentenced to prison for periods ranging between two and a half years to eight years, with the head nurse receiving the longest sentence. The remaining fourteen people, mostly clerks in the administrative department, were acquitted.[379] The Frankfurt-am-Main *Landgericht* justified the sentencing of the accused by arguing that the euthanasia order hadn't been legally binding, since it neither had been enacted as law nor signed by an appropriate governmental minister. Thus, the order hadn't had the force of law,[380] so the accused hadn't been forced to comply with it.

The postwar judicial organisation adjudicated past offences to the extent that the law made it possible. It wasn't considered justifiable to administer justice retroactively, while some actions that were illegal when they were committed were prosecuted. That mainly applied to what could be considered major cases. The justification for prosecuting individuals in the euthanasia trials was based on the principle that the defendants weren't following the direct orders of the state, and were therefore responsible for their actions. The euthanasia orders didn't carry the status of law, since they had neither been promulgated as law, nor passed as state legislation, which removed any possible defence of being merely functionaries "following orders," like those who had taken part in organised violence, such as the anti-Jewish attacks. Though sentences passed under the National Socialist justice system were nullified, those who had administered the decisions weren't prosecuted. There were no special measures taken against the jurists who had passed such sentences, since they weren't considered to have been individually responsible for the injustices.

The effective prosecution of individual injustices was undermined by the denazification procedure, which failed to differentiate between actions committed by individuals from individual responsibility for the past. Failing to implement the original denazification programme didn't solve the problem of prosecuting individuals who had been implicated by their association with the National Socialist regime. Only the method of applying the denazification programme across a wide range of anonymous individuals was liquidated.

The criminal prosecution for judicial illegality in postwar Germany began with the Nuremberg Tribunal proceedings against seventeen leading jurists of the National Socialist regime on 17 February 1947,[381] Although there remained the question of how to deal with all other jurists who had taken part in the National Socialist justice system. It's been claimed that between two-thirds and three-quarters of the 15,000 judges and prosecutors who held office in the Federal Republic of Germany in 1950 were former National Socialists, and that some of them were likely to have taken part in judicial crimes.[382] It has also been maintained that no member of the People's Court (*Volksgerichtshof*), a Special Court (*Sondergericht*), or an ordinary court was called to account for administering "terror justice" or for their participation in judicial criminality under the National Socialist regime in the western occupation zones or the Federal Republic of Germany.[383]

An example of such a case in Hesse was that of two former *Sondergericht* judges who had sentenced Werner Höllander to death at the Kassel *Sondergericht* on 20 April 1943,[384] on the accusation of being a "dangerous habitual criminal" for having committed four cases of *Rassenschande* (sexual relations with a non-Aryan), thereby breaking the Nuremberg Law on the protection of "Aryan blood."[385] The two judges were tried by a jury court at the Kassel *Landgericht*, which pronounced its judgment on 28 June 1950. The court ruled that the accused were being prosecuted for a perversion of the course of justice by having pronounced the death sentence for alleged crimes committed according to the standard of National Socialist justice. However, although the accused were recognised to be "convinced and even fanatical National Socialists" who had both been members of the NSDAP since 1933,[386] they had applied the law that was in practice at the time, which wasn't a perversion of the course of justice, since courts were obliged to apply National Socialist legislation.[387]

The court therefore ruled that the accused were to be acquitted, since they hadn't broken the law according to the judicial basis of the case.[388] In other words, the accused couldn't be prosecuted under the existing law. The court merely acknowledged that the accused were morally guilty for sentencing Höllander to death,[389] since the death sentence was excessively severe in view of the facts of the case.[390] The court also rules that the accused shouldn't have been judged a "dangerous habitual criminal," and therefore the death sentence that had been passed was an error.[391]

The public prosecutor appealed the decision, which was then brought before the *Oberlandesgericht* in Frankfurt-am-Main, where the decision of the Kassel *Landgericht* jury court was quashed on 7 February 1951. The *Oberlandesgericht* ruled that the *Landgericht* hadn't considered prosecuting the accused for the charge of perversion of the course of justice on the basis of a deliberately unobjective application of formal law.[392] Since the Kassel *Landgericht* was said to have misjudged the definition of perversion of the course of justice, the *Oberlandesgericht* returned the case for a new trial at the Kassel *Landgericht* jury court after 1 October 1951.[393] The Kassel *Landgericht* pronounced its judgment on 28 March 1952, acquitting the two judges after maintaining its original decision and explaining that the court had made an error in the explanation of the facts of the case rather than in the conduct of the deliberations. The court ruled that the accused judges had acted inhumanely in passing the death sentence in the case. Although the accused could be considered "convinced" National Socialists, they believed that they had applied the existing law according to legal positivism, which convinced them that their decision corresponded to the law, in spite of its implications. Hence, the court maintained that the accused hadn't *willfully* committed a perversion of the course of justice. Prosecuting that case as a crime against humanity, through the application of Control Council Law No. 10, was also outside the jurisdiction of the court.[394] The court thus ruled that the accused hadn't acted illegally when they passed judgments according to existing law that was valid at the time, and were acquitted, since there was insufficient evidence to absolutely establish the fact that they willfully had acted illegally.[395]

Gustav Radbruch, a former Social Democratic minister of justice in the Weimar Republic, wrote that an instance of a perversion of justice was to be considered a criminal offence if the judge had consciously performed the act with "direct intent," but National Socialist justice had the status of law and was thus given a cover of legality.[396] Radbruch argued that the tradition of legal positivism in the German justice system effectively made the German judiciary defenceless against laws containing arbitrary or criminal content, regardless of the intrinsic value of justice[397] or whether they intended to uphold the interests of the National Socialist regime. Legal positivism dictated that what was legal at the time was automatically considered the legitimate embodiment of justice, without applying the ethical question of what was just.[398] Judges who had applied National Socialist law to the disadvantage of individuals who had acted against the regime weren't called to account for specific actions in having disregarded the principle of justice in applying the law, and the fact that a special criminal law for bringing judges of the National Socialist period to justice was never promulgated remained "a black mark in the history of postwar justice."[399]

It may be inferred that a law for prosecuting perversions of justice during the National Socialist regime, which would have, in effect, extended denazification to its original spirit, wasn't enacted, since it would have compromised vast numbers of an entire generation of jurists who had been reinstated into the denazified postwar justice system. Jurists weren't convicted for administering National Socialist justice in German courts in West Germany was a result of a pattern of legal argumentation concerning the theoretical legality of administering justice under the National Socialist regime. Judges administered justice on the basis of the law at the time. Theoretically, it could be argued that the independence of the judiciary in the National Socialist regime had been endangered, but was never *formally* abolished, even though the *Reichstag* resolution of 26 April 1942 allowed for the possibility of unlimited interference in the functions of the judiciary. The judges were responsible for committing those actions, since they maintained control over sentencing while operating within the context of circumstances beyond their control. Hence, a judge was responsible for passing sentences according to the legal standards of the time, in spite of the inhumane consequences of those sentences.

Judges could only be justly prosecuted if they had passed sentences that could be considered perversions of the administration of justice with direct intent.[400] As a consequence, they hadn't violated any law, and couldn't be prosecuted for what could be construed as the violation of undefined ethical standards of natural law. However, an accurate evaluation of how individual jurists behaved in office would have required a thorough investigation of their professional records, which could have revealed instances of resistance to the regime, as well as instances of conformity. Those who had been trained and had experience in the National Socialist justice system were henceforth responsible for upholding the standards of the postwar system, where knowledge of the law and the rule of law took precedence over all other considerations.

The question remained: to what extent could those jurists exercise a real or apparent threat to the new state? The denazification in the U.S. zone was applied widely and bureaucratically for jurists, but its results were just as unsatisfactory as with the other professions.[401] In spite of the failure of denazification to achieve a thorough reform of German public life to secure the postwar democracy, and the shortcomings of the denazification of the legal profession in Hesse and in the U.S. occupation zone, the former practices of the National Socialist regime were eliminated from the justice system. The terms of the Liberation Law absolved most of the legal profession from being brought to account for their role under the National Socialist regime, even if they had been involved in cases of a political nature, and the implementation of the Liberation Law in practice confirmed their absolution.

In spite of the shortcomings of the denazification programme, there were safeguards within the justice system to counteract potential abuses of judicial authority, such as the restored right to appeal lower court decisions and the administrative supervision of courts by the Ministry of Justice. Former members of the NSDAP and its affiliated organisations were reinstated into the judiciary, the Bar Association, and all other functions of the justice system, since permanently barring them from office was impossible. Postwar changes in the administration of justice prevented "politically unreliable" jurists from abusing their judicial office. In the final analysis, future generations of jurists, who hadn't had the experience of National Socialist antecedents, would fully consummate the democratisation of the justice system.[402]

Conclusion

The U.S. denazification programme lost its original impetus as a political purge and became increasingly narrower in its scope, as indicated by the constant redrafting of denazification policy until it was abruptly abandoned. The denazification programme failed after it became apparent that the scope of the programme was too broad and had become an impossible task to accomplish.[403] The denazification programme encountered various problems once it had been put into practice, and the denazification practice in the U.S. zone was widely criticised by both members of the Military Government and German jurists involved in implementing it.

Neither the U.S. military government nor German denazification authorities could arrive at a permanent solution to the problem of eliminating all politically implicated personnel, as had originally been envisaged in the Potsdam Protocol. It wasn't possible to permanently remove all such individuals from office, and it wasn't possible to change the attitudes of individuals, other than to force a change in the judicial system which would then force the jurists to adapt to the new situation. It also became evident that a permanent, legitimate definition of who had been an actual National Socialist would prove unworkable. An enormous amount of time and energy was spent on the denazification programme, but a smooth and just application of the programme for such large numbers in a short time "would have required supernatural powers of judgment and organization."[404] U.S. military government officers engaged in the denazification programme argued that the procedure should have begun by concentrating on prosecuting *Major Offenders* who had sought public office, rather than dealing with allegedly implicated parties at all levels and spending a large amount of time clearing the "little men" from the dockets.[405]

The Minister of Political Liberation for Hesse criticised the unsatisfactory results of the Law for Liberation. Too many people were being found to be formally incriminated under the law, and too many cases were to be disposed of in order to uncover a few guilty individuals, rather than utilising a process of instituting proceedings only against the guilty and responsible parties.

The deficiency of the denazification law in its original form was emphasised by the amnesties and amendments to the denazification law itself[406] that were introduced to reduce the caseload. From the viewpoint of the U.S. military government, on the other hand, there appeared to be no other procedure available for establishing an individual's political antecedents, thereby determining whether that person had been a National Socialist, except by screening the entire population on a common basis through a bureaucratic procedure, in spite of its shortcomings.[407]

The effort to completely purge German political and social life through an excessively ambitious and ill-considered programme was marked by good, if not naive, intentions.[408] The Control Council attempted to establish uniformity in denazification proceedings for the four occupation zones through Control Council Directive No. 38 of 16 November 1946, which extended the provisions of the Law for Liberation to the other occupation zones.[409] The Law for Liberation was considered an implementation of Directive No. 38 in the *Länder* of the U.S. zone.[410] However, in practice, the policy of the Soviet, British, and French military governments was to follow the principle of expediency.[411]

U.S. military government authorities undoubtedly pursued a denazification policy that was consistently more vigorous than that of the other occupation powers, attempting to screen the entire German population of the U.S. zone to determine the National Socialists among them. The Soviet military government either liquidated leading National Socialists or big "capitalists" or recruited them to Soviet agencies. The British military government concentrated on the criminal elements of the National Socialist regime and attempted to salvage talent from among the Germans to serve their purposes. The French military government didn't concentrate on whether a German was a National Socialist, provided that individual willingly accepted the occupation government's policies and programmes.[412] The denazification of members of all professions that would be entrusted with positions of responsibility involved five general problems:

First, who was to be removed from office? Was it possible to determine whether an individual had been a genuine National Socialist by conviction, or had merely been safeguarding personal interests, such as remaining in a position that entailed becoming a member of the NSDAP or of an affiliated organisation under the prevailing circumstances? Barring all such individuals from public offices according to automatic blacklisting would have meant disposing of about one-fifth of the population who had been members of the NSDAP,[413] which, in practice, would have meant barring 80 percent of German judges due to their political records before German courts had been reopened.[414]

Second, if certain broad categories could be defined under which individuals could be removed based on certain conditions, would it be possible to put those individuals through an accurate test to identify their guilt with complete and accurate justification? The number of Allied personnel versed in German language and the political conditions of National Socialist Germany was limited, and as a result could not be relied upon to accurately identify guilty parties. There was also the related question of who would have been considered to be suitable for handling the denazification process if it had been left to German authorities? It would have been practically impossible to employ judges for that function, since they had been required to become members of the NSDAP. Anti-Nazis couldn't automatically be accepted without prior screening, and the occupation authorities couldn't rely on them to provide evidence based on hearsay.

Third, since the great majority of individuals in senior administrative positions had been members of the NSDAP, whether out of conviction or as victims of circumstance, their automatic removal would have made the postwar administration of justice more difficult. How could a sufficient number of suitable replacements be found?

Fourth, what should have been done with the individuals removed from office? How would justice be served by imposing upon them what could be considered fair penalties if they had been guilty of offences related to their association with a National Socialist organisation? Establishing fairness in the process would involve introducing a sentence appropriate to the offence after guilt had been determined. That would have required considering each case, following a law and scale of penalties, and then establishing denazification machinery and collecting evidence on nearly eight million people.

Fifth, could denazification prevent recurring National Socialist sentiment in the individuals who had been tried under the process after the penalty had been served? Would individuals with important skills and abilities be able to exert a negative influence after the occupation? If they had been induced to change their way of thinking, what would constitute proof of their having acknowledged their guilt?[415]

The U.S. military government and German denazification authorities attempted to address those problems through legislation, which underwent modifications as difficulties were encountered in the implementation of the process. The Allies were generally convinced that all German civil servants and judges had been significantly implicated for having perpetuated the National Socialist *Unrechtsstaat*.[416] Therein could be found the problems that would arise regarding a thorough denazification.

The denazification programme was intended to serve as a political process in the form of a judicial purge, in which individuals residing in the U.S. zone were to be prosecuted for having joined the NSDAP or its affiliated organisations, which was declared an offence during the occupation, regardless of the person's conduct during their membership. After the collapse of the National Socialist regime, individuals were considered a National Socialist on the basis of having belonged to the NSDAP or one of its numerous organisations, regardless of their personal convictions and actions.[417] All former members were subject to screening by the U.S. military government, and then to trial by quasi-judicial German denazification courts, which were to administer a retroactive law against alleged offenders among the entire adult population of the U.S. zone.

It soon became apparent that the standards set at the beginning of the occupation went beyond the limits of the attainable. It's been argued that the denazification programme would have been more successful if less had been attempted[418]—for example, if the implementation of the programme had been focused on the most conspicuous cases, rather than on virtually the entire adult German population.

Membership in the NSDAP or one of its affiliated organisations wasn't necessarily motivated by acceptance of its tenets. It was forced upon the legal profession by various laws and regulations enacted by the National Socialist regime. Jurists in the National Socialist regime either accepted National Socialism out of conviction or were compelled to conform and pretend to pledge allegiance to the regime in order to maintain their positions. The latter became *Mußnazis*, who weren't necessarily National Socialists, since they had been coerced into joining the NSDAP or one of its affiliated organisations, and had demonstrated loyalty to the National Socialist regime out of circumstance rather than conviction.

Many people, regardless of their occupation, joined the NSDAP out of fear, to avert suspicion of being disloyal to the regime, or to maintain their means of livelihood, even though they were politically indifferent.[419] As a result of such pressures, the vast majority of the judiciary joined the NSDAP or demonstrated apparent allegiance to the regime by paying dues to National Socialist organisations. Apart from sheer opportunism, demonstrating allegiance to the National Socialist regime in that manner, as concrete outward evidence of political conformity, could be considered a form of an "insurance policy against dismissal," and helped maintain continued promotion within the civil service. That was especially important for older members of the profession, who needed to support families or whose tenures were at stake, while younger members entering the profession had virtually no chance of being promoted unless they held the requisite membership.[420]

In one example of political pressure, the Berlin *Gauleitung* (district office) of the NSDAP ordered that all law graduates would be required to join the NSDAP or one of its affiliated organisations. One such individual responded to that order by joining the *Reiter-SA* in October 1933, since that organisation emphasised sport rather than the "political" element.[421] In addition to those who joined the NSDAP or an affiliated organisation out of conviction or opportunism, many members of the legal profession were intimidated into joining a National Socialist organisation.

The question of readmitting former members of the NSDAP into judicial office was undermined by the force of circumstance—the reconstruction of justice faced a critical problem of achieving operational efficiency with a limited number of personnel. Hence, the denazification programme was only put into effect at the beginning of the occupation, until the personnel shortage problem became the most critical problem of denazification. Although not all of the jurists who were reinstated after 1945 had necessarily taken part in the lawlessness of the National Socialist regime, there were the exceptions who managed to evade the denazification procedure.[422] Since the need for expediency outweighed the completion of the denazification programme, some 90 percent of the judges and prosecuting attorneys who had been in office before 1945 had been reinstated into judicial office in western Germany by 1947–48.[423]

It became apparent by the time the denazification programme ended that it had failed to achieve its goal of cleansing all National Socialist influences from public life. By April 1947, approximately 35 percent of the acting legal personnel in Hesse who had been judged to be "nominal" National Socialists had been classified by denazification tribunals as either *Person Exonerated* or *Follower.*[424] Toward the end of the occupation, 70 percent of the reinstated judges and lawyers in Hesse were former members of the NSDAP.[425] The denazification division of the military government in Hesse found that 10 percent of the *politische Beamte*, 47.5 percent of the *höhere Dienst*, 50.6 percent of the *gehobene Dienst* (professional and executive levels of the civil service), and 33.7 percent of the *mittlere Dienst* had been incriminated under the Law for Liberation.

The number of individuals occupying high positions in the Ministry of Justice who had been formerly incriminated by the law was particularly large. Most judges had been to some extent incriminated under the Law for Liberation.[426] Thirty-four percent of the civil servants in Hesse were initially dismissed as a result of political implication, and all but some 2 percent of them had been reinstated by July 1949. The results were similar in Baden-Württemberg and Bavaria.[427]

The standard of incrimination under the Law for Liberation failed to accurately reveal whether an individual jurist was hostile to the standards of the postwar justice system. Uncovering the individual political and professional records of German jurists who had served under the National Socialist regime and had displayed cases of dubious actions would take place years after the end of the military occupation.[428] The process of screening judges according to the records of the *Sondergerichte* only began in West Germany when previously inaccessible records were made available by the East German government in the 1950s.[429]

Individuals who had served with the *Volksgerichtshof* remained in judicial office after the denazification programme had concluded. The Federal Ministry of the Interior sent the government of Hesse a list of the names of the former judges and prosecutors of the *Volksgerichtshof* on 28 January 1957. The Minister of the Interior intended to verify the extent to which the activity of those judges and prosecutors had breached contemporary principles of justice, and whether formal disciplinary proceedings would be required under Art. 9 of Art. 131 of the Basic Law. If those individuals had been reinstated without having disclosed information about their former service in the *Volksgerichtshof*,[430] their cases would have undermined the letter and spirit of the denazification.

In the case of the U.S. zone, the hastily implemented denazification followed a principle of collective presumptive guilt. Individuals were to be called to account for allegedly participating in crimes committed by the National Socialist organisations of which they had been members, regardless of their function within the organisation, rather than for their individual actions.[431] The theory of presumptive guilt encompassed those jurists who followed the line of least resistance against the regime by joining the NSDAP or affiliated organisations, as well as those who had promoted their own interests by actively and intentionally abetting the National Socialist regime.

The denazification programme opened the way for errors in judgment, since it didn't provide for a thorough examination of the professional and political records of every jurist who had served under the regime. The question posed to jurists by denazification authorities was whether they had been members of the NSDAP, rather than posing the more relevant question of whether they had administered National Socialist justice, thereby evaluating their *professional*, rather than political, records, and thus calling them to account for their actions accordingly. The denazification of the legal profession, and the broad-sweeping denazification process itself, was a dismal failure in that respect, since "it barely scratched the surface."[432] As a consequence, the effectiveness of judicial institutions took precedence over the political views of individual judicial personnel.

The reinstatement of dismissed former members of National Socialist organisations was characterised as "renazification," but that wasn't the case, since they generally became apolitical followers of the new system, and didn't create a neo-fascist political movement.[433] That also applies to the postwar judiciary. The jurists who served in postwar Germany couldn't all have been instilled with the National Socialist worldview. Many of them had received their judicial training before 1933, while a number of others who had begun their period of study after 1933 were decimated during the Second World War. Moreover, there was no manifestation of any form of bloc mentality among that total number. Therefore, it can be deduced that the postwar judiciary didn't possess a uniform National Socialist character.[434] The role and responsibility of the judiciary thus remained for individual jurists to carry out during the postwar administration of justice.

Implementing the reform of the German justice system required it to function according to the principles of the *Rechtsstaat*. The function of the *Rechtsstaat* was supported by established German court jurisdictions in the separate stages of appeals, which could lead to judgments at the highest courts that were provided for by constitutions[435] at the *Land* and national levels. It was also unlikely that the political opinions of reinstated jurists could jeopardise the function of the *Rechtsstaat*. Unlike the experience of the Weimar Republic, in which emotions opposing the democratic state were evident in the administration of justice, the transition to democracy in postwar Germany was much more successful.

Since there was no alternative after the collapse of the National Socialist regime, judges in the Federal Republic of Germany rapidly accepted the new state and its constitution.[436] The institutions of the justice system that would be operated by jurists, politically implicated or not, had been successfully denazified, in the sense that former National Socialist laws and practices had been eliminated.

Conclusion

THE ADMINISTRATION OF JUSTICE WAS A major bulwark of the National Socialist regime. Its reconstruction after the end of the Second World War was therefore an integral part of the reconstruction of postwar Germany. Allied policies regarding the reconstruction of the justice system in postwar Germany were governed by the principles of the rule of law, while maintaining the interests of the occupation powers. The postwar creation of *Land* Hesse in the U.S. zone, and the restoration of an independent justice system in that *Land* took place in the context of those objectives. The administration of justice was set upon the new foundation of a constitutional state at the *Land* level, which was developed under the supervision of the U.S. military government during the political reconstruction of postwar Germany. The justice system in Hesse became fully functional when an independent German justice system was established upon the creation of the Federal Republic of Germany, thereby completing the political transition from the National Socialist regime to democracy.

Political development of postwar Germany was influenced by two factors during the occupation: 1) the lack of a coherent German administration above the *Land* level; and 2) the zonal division of Germany and the failure of the four occupation powers to introduce a uniform territorial reorganisation of the *Länder*. As a result, the boundaries of the *Länder* were redrawn within the western zones, and later served as elements of a system of federal government in West Germany.[1]

The decentralisation of the German political administration was reinforced in the U.S. zone, where three separate *Land* governments were established in

Bavaria, Württemberg-Baden, and Hesse. The Allied Control Council for Germany and the U.S. military government in the U.S. zone maintained predominant authority for the duration of the military occupation. The function of government and the justice system in Germany at the beginning of the military occupation were assumed by military governments in the four occupation zones after the centralised National Socialist regime had collapsed. The Control Council was established as a military government for Germany as a whole, while zonal military governments were established in the four occupation zones, acting independently of that central authority. Each of the occupation powers carried out the various tasks of the postwar reconstruction in its respective occupation zone, while maintaining the principles for the reconstruction of Germany that had been set forth in the Potsdam Protocol and implementing decisions of the Control Council in matters affecting Germany as a whole.

Justice in postwar Germany was administered in accordance with Allied objectives for the restoration of the rule of law. The restoration of the postwar German justice system began with a complete standstill of justice, but was subsequently reconstructed separately in the four occupation zones. The reconstruction entailed eliminating National Socialist enactments from the body of German law, restoring the structure and functions of the justice system in each zone, and preventing the recurrence of National Socialist practices in the reconstituted German judicial organisations.

The German justice system in the U.S. zone was decentralised among the *Länder*, functioning at two separate levels of jurisdiction. The U.S. military government exercised its judicial authority through military government courts that maintained the interests of the occupation powers, reserving categories of cases for adjudication that had been excluded from the jurisdiction of German courts when they were reopened. The reopened German courts adjudicated under German law, subject to Control Council and U.S. military government legislation governing the functions of the German justice system.

The first *Amtsgerichte* and *Landgerichte* in what became *Land* Greater Hesse began to operate in the summer and autumn of 1945, adjudicating cases involving Germans outside the interests of the U.S. military government. The opening of those courts laid the foundation for the German justice system in what later became *Land* Hesse, prior to the establishment of that *Land* and its government. The *Land* governments in the U.S. zone operated as the highest level of German administration, cooperating with the U.S. military government in the various tasks of the postwar reconstruction.

The U.S. military government conferred responsibility for the reconstruction of the permanent *Land* judicial organisation to the *Land* government in Hesse through the "Plan for the Administration of Justice in the U.S. Zone" on

4 October 1945. That plan defined the composition and functions of the justice system in Hesse under the authority of the *Land* Minister of Justice, who served as the leading administrator of the *Land* justice system in the *Land* government. The provisions of the plan guided the reorganisation of the judicial organisation in Hesse until the construction of the ordinary courts was completed with the opening of the *Oberlandesgericht* on 23 May 1946.

The courts of the other branches of the *Land* justice system and their affiliated appeal courts, which weren't specifically addressed in the plan, were reestablished separately. Administrative courts were reestablished in Hesse to defend the constitutional rights of individuals by hearing cases involving disputes between individuals and public authorities. In addition to being a safeguard against potential arbitrary abuse of power by the state, those courts were made more effective than before by extending their former jurisdiction and the implementation of legislation that afforded greater protection to individuals. Cases of labour disputes were initially heard by courts in the ordinary judicial organisation until an independent labour court organisation was established in Hesse. While administrative courts defended the interests of all individuals before the state, labour courts ensured the impartial administration of justice in the workplace.

The reopened German courts in Hesse applied the law as it had been reformed after the collapse of the National Socialist regime. Control Council and U.S. military government legislation expressly forbade the application of National Socialist principles in the administration of justice from the beginning of the occupation. German law was reformed through Control Council, U.S. military government, and *Land* government legislation, which abolished National Socialist enactments or amendments and ensured that abuse of the justice system wouldn't be perpetuated.

The appeal courts, exercising appellate jurisdiction over the ordinary courts, administrative, and labour courts, ensured that misuses or abuses of the justice system would be rectified. The institution of jury courts in Hesse served as a further safeguard against abuses of authority in the justice system. The principle of the rule of law in the administration of justice and safeguards against abuse of authority by the state or the judiciary were entrenched in the *Land* constitution, which were upheld by the *Land* Supreme Constitutional Court, which was responsible for upholding its provisions. The institutions of the justice system in Hesse were thus reconstructed, but the complete restoration of their functions was precluded by the predominance of occupation law.

The ultimate authority for maintaining the rule of law rested with the U.S. military government, which retained supreme authority and the corresponding power to supervise and intervene in the functions of German courts, to ensure their compliance with occupation policies.

German courts functioned independently to the extent that their responsibilities had been established under German law and limited by occupation law, which represented the interests of the U.S. military government. Greater responsibility was conferred by the U.S. military government upon the *Land* judicial organisation in order to allow for a greater exercise of its functions and to alleviate the burden of cases that were waiting to be heard by U.S. military government courts. Occupation law was therefore amended to allow German courts to adjudicate a greater number of categories of cases than had initially been placed within their jurisdiction. The expediency of extending the responsibilities of German courts correspondingly led to the restoration of their jurisdiction, as defined by German law, until occupation law was no longer prevalent in the German justice system by the end of the military occupation.

Occupation law superseded the authority of German law by limiting the jurisdiction of German courts and by allowing for extraterritorial intervention in the administration of justice if German courts misused or abused their authority. The controls over the German justice system were lifted when the supreme judicial authority, exercised by the U.S. military government, was removed and transferred to German authorities. It was no longer in the interest of the occupation powers to exercise control over the German justice system once the occupation objectives had been accomplished, and the western Allies eventually conferred full-fledged state authority to the Federal Republic of Germany, under the provisions of the Occupation Statute.

The restrictions on the responsibilities and independence of German courts that had been imposed under occupation law were subsequently lifted. Judicial independence was fully restored, and the German judiciary was enabled to administer justice according to German law without any outside interference or control from the German government or the U.S. military government. The abolition of National Socialist practices in the administration of justice restored to the judiciary the role of upholding the law of the state in a manner that conformed to the principles of the rule of law. Justice was administered independently, to protect the interests of society and individuals, rather than solely serving the interests of a state that controlled the justice system.

There remained the question of whether the judiciary, which composed an integral part of the apparatus of the National Socialist regime, would accept the postwar justice system. As in every far-reaching political change involving people who had been involved in the former system, there was some question as to who could be considered trustworthy under the new political order.[2]

The personnel reconstruction in the U.S. zone and staffing of the reconstructed judicial organisation took place simultaneously with the reconstruction of the judicial organisation. German judicial personnel in the U.S. zone were initially treated as a politically suspect, anonymous bloc of individuals. They were subjected to the same wide-sweeping denazification procedures, instituted by the U.S. military government, that affected the members of all professions.

Military government legislation at the beginning of the occupation decreed that German jurists were to be suspended from practice and were to be reinstated only after the extent of their political implication with the National Socialist regime had been determined. The fundamental dilemma of the denazification policy was striking a balance between the divergent objectives of denazification and administrative efficiency. That dilemma gradually became apparent when the denazification policy was initially put in practice.[3]

The initial criterion for denazification in the U.S. zone was whether membership in the NSDAP or its affiliated organisations had been formal or superficial, active or nominal. But that didn't provide adequate grounds for passing a justifiable or decisive verdict for determining the moral, political and professional integrity of applicants for judicial positions. The ideal situation would have been to examine how each applicant had operated within the National Socialist regime, but that would have required extensive research while judicial personnel shortages continued to hinder the functions of the postwar justice system.[4]

The initial denazification policies were dropped, in view of the fact that the denazification programme was later considered to be an unrealistic enterprise, as indicated by the introduction of wide amnesties to reduce the scope of the denazification programme and modifications of denazification legislation in order to shift the emphasis toward highly implicated individuals. Other external factors that led to the rapid conclusion of the denazification programme were the onset of the Cold War, the impact of U.S. public opinion, and the problems associated with serious personnel shortages.

Restoring the German justice system required securing trained and qualified personnel, which conflicted with the premise that those people were also to be politically unimplicated. The ideal solution to the problem would have been either to rapidly train a new generation of politically acceptable jurists, as was initially attempted in the Soviet zone, or to lower the standards of denazification to allow the reinstatement of a larger number of jurists. The U.S. military government and the *Land* government had to reinstate former jurists on the basis of their professional qualifications rather than their political records in order to reconstruct the justice system as quickly as possible, because there weren't enough suitably qualified jurists to replace all those who'd been politically implicated.

A break from the past was made through the reconstitution of standards for the administration of justice in the Federal Republic of Germany, which were based on the principles of a democratic constitutional state, or *Rechtsstaat*. The judiciary was responsible for adhering to those principles in the discharge of their duties. Hence, the reconstructed judicial organisation was to take precedence over the personnel reconstruction in the justice system, which was the only way to neutralise potential abuses that could arise from any remaining National Socialist predilections among the postwar judiciary. The safeguards present in the justice system, such as the appellate courts, the *Land* constitutional court, and the guarantee of judicial independence contained in both the *Land* and the federal constitutions, served to compensate for the shortage of jurists who weren't implicated with the National Socialist regime. A *complete* break from the past would later be achieved through a new generation of jurists trained witin the postwar justice system in a democratic state.

Notes

Introduction

1. Elmar M. Hucko, ed., *The Democratic Tradition: Four German Constitutions* (Leamington Spa: Berg, 1987), 62.

2. John H. Herz, "Denazification and Related Policies," *From Dictatorship to Democracy: Coping with the Legacies of Authoritarianism and Totalitarianism* (Westport: Greenwood Press, 1982), 24.

3. Michael Stolleis, "Rechtsordnung und Justizpolitik: 1945–1949," *Europäische Rechtsordnung in Geschichte und Gegenwart: Festschrift für Helmut Coing*, ed. Norbert Horn, Vol. 1 (Munich: C. H. Beck'sche Verlagsbuchhandlung, 1982), 396.

4. Karl Loewenstein, "Law and the Legislative Process in Occupied Germany," *Yale Law Journal* Vol. 57 (1948): 1022.

5. The territories on the left bank of the Rhine were integrated into the French occupation zone.

6. Wolf-Arno Kropat. *Hessen in der Stunde Null, 1945–1947: Politik, Wirtschaft und Bildungswesen in Dokumenten* (Wiesbaden: Historische Kommission für Nassau, 1979): 20.

7. Harold Zink, "American Occupation Policies in Germany," *Review of Politics* Vol. 9 (July 1947): 285.

8. Ibid., 291.

9. Hucko, *The Democratic Tradition*, 63.

10. Georg-August Zinn, "Administration of Justice in Germany," *Annals of the American Academy of Political and Social Science* Vol. 260 (November 1948): 32.

11. Helmut Coing, "Zur Frage der strafrechtlichen Haftung der Richter für die Anwendung naturrechtswidriger Gesetze," *Süddeutsche Juristenzeitung* (1947): 61.

12. Albert Venn Dicey, *Introduction to the Study of the Law of the Constitution* (London: MacMillan & Co., 1960), 188.

13. Walter Clement, "Der Vorbehalt des Gesetzes, insbesondere bei öffentlichen Leistungen und öffentlichen Einrichtungen," (Diss.: Eberhard-Karls-Universität, 1987), 27.

14. Dicey, *Introduction to the Study of the Law*, 193.

15. Ibid., 195, 203.

16. Dieter Simon, *Die Unabhängigkeit des Richters* (Darmstadt: Wissenschafliche Buchgesellschaft, 1975), 9.

17. Dicey, *Introduction to the Study of the Law*, 337.

18. The exercise of those responsibilities differentiates the judicial organisation from the additional elements of the administration of justice, such as the police force, the civil service organisation within the Ministry of Justice, and the penal administration, which fulfill separate functions and lie outside the scope of this work.

19. Loewenstein, "Law and the Legislative Process in Occupied Germany," 734.

20. Eli E. Nobleman, "American Military Government Courts in Germany," *American Journal of International Law* Vol. 40 (1946): 804.

21. Rotberg, H. E. "Entpolitisierung der Rechtspflege," *Deutsche Rechts-Zeitschrift* (April 1947): 107.

22. Hodo von Hodenberg, "Zur Anwendung des Kontrollratsgesetz Nr. 10 durch deutsche Gesetze," *Süddeutsche Juristenzeitung* (1947): 113.

23. Eduard Kern, "Die Stunde der Justiz," *Deutsche Rechts-Zeitschrift* (April 1947): 105–106.

24. Wolfgang Friedmann, *The Allied Military Government of Germany* (London: Stevens & Sons, 1947), 3.

25. Wolfgang Benz, "Die Entnazifizierung der Richter," *Justiz Alltag im Dritten Reich* (Frankfurt-am-Main: Fischer Tagebuch Verlag, 1988), 115.

26. Richard Schmid, "Denazification: A German Critique," *American Perspective* Vol. 2 (1948): 238–239.

27. John Gimbel, *A German Community under American Occupation: Marburg, 1945–1952* (Stanford: Stanford University Press, 1961), 139.

Chapter 1

1. Friedrich Roetter, *Might is Right* (London, Quality Press, 1939), 131–132.

2. J. Walter Jones, *The Nazi Conception of Law* (Oxford: Oxford University Press, 1939), 5–6, 8–9.

3. Karl Loewenstein, *Hitler's Germany: The Nazi Background to War* (New York: Macmillan, 1944), 126.

4. "Verordnung des Reichspräsidenten zum Schutz von Volk und Staat," 28 February 1933, *Reichsgesetzblatt* I 1933: 83.

5. Karl Dietrich Bracher, *The German Dictatorship: The Origins, Structure and Effects of National Socialism*, trans. Jean Steinberg (New York: Praeger, 1971), 350–351.

6. "Verordnung des Reichspresidenten zum Schutze des deutschen Volkes. Vom 4. Februar 1933," *Reichsgesetzblatt* I 1933: 35–40.

7. "Gesetz zum Behebung der Not von Volk und Reich," 24 March 1933, *Reichsgesetzblatt* I 1933: 141.

8. Lothar Gruchmann, "Rechtssystem und nationalsozialistische Justizpolitik," *Das Dritte Reich: Herrschaftsstruktur und Geschichte*, eds. Martin Broszat and Horst Möller (München: Verlag C. H. Beck, 1983), 96.

9. "Gesetz gegen die Neubildung von Parteien vom 14. Juli 1933," *Reichsgesetzblatt* I 1933: 479.

10. "Gesetz zur Sicherung der Einheit von Partei und Staat vom 1. Dezember 1933," *Reichsgesetzblatt* I 1933: 1016.

11. "Gesetz über das Staatsoberhaupt des deutschen Reichs vom 1. August 1934," *Reichsgesetzblatt* I 1934: 747.

12. Hans Buchheim et al., "The SS—Instrument of Domination," Martin Broszat et al., *Anatomy of the SS State*, trans. Richard Barry (London: Collins, 1968), 127–128.

13. "Vorläufiges Gesetz zur Gleichschaltung der Länder mit dem Reich. Vom 31. März 1933," *Reichsgesetzblatt* I 1933, pp. 153–154; "Zweites Gesetz zur Gleichschaltung der Länder mit dem Reich. Vom 7. April 1933," *Reichsgesetzblatt* 1933 I: 173; "Gesetz zum Neuaufbau des Reichs. Vom 30. Januar 1934," *Reichsgesetzblatt* I 1934: 75.

14. Ernst Fraenkel, *The Dual State: A Contribution to the Theory of Dictatorship*, trans. E. A. Schils (New York: Oxford University Press, 1941), 40.

15. Carl Schmitt, "Der Weg des deutschen Juristen," *Deutsche Juristen-Zeitung* (1934): 695.

16. Werner Johe, *Die gleichgeschaltete Justiz: Organisation des Rechtswesens und Politisierung der Rechtsprechung 1933–1945 dargestellt am Beispiel des Oberlandesgerichtsbezirks Hamburg* (Frankfurt-am-Main: Europäische Verlagsanstalt, 1967), 29.

17. Klaus Marxen, "Strafjustiz im Nationalsozialismus: Vorschläge für eine Erweiterung der historischen Perspektive," *Justizalltags im Dritten Reich* (Frankfurt-am-Main: Fischer Taschenbuch Verlag, 1988): 101.

18. Lawrence Preuss, "Germanic Law Versus Roman Law in National Socialist Legal Theory," *Journal of Comparative Legislative and International Law* Vol. 16 (1934): 269.

19. Loewenstein, "Law in the Third Reich," *Yale Law Journal* Vol. 45 (1936): 785.

20. Jeremy Noakes and Geoffrey Pridham, *Documents on Nazism: 1919–1945* (New York: Viking Press, 1974), 265–266.

21. Wagner and Weinkauff, *Die Deutsche Justiz und der Nationalsozialismus* Vol. 1 (Stuttgart: Deutsche Verlags-Anstalt, 1968), 209.

22. Hugh R. Trevor-Roper, *Hitler's Secret Conversations: 1941–1944* (New York: Octagon, 1972), 247.

23. Hans Frank, *Nationalsozialistisches Handbuch für Recht und Gesetzgebung* (Munich: Zentralverlag der NSDAP, 1935), 3–6.

24. Johe, *Die gleichgeschaltete Justiz*, 3–6.

25. Dennis Leroy Anderson, *The Academy for German Law: 1933–1945* (New York: Garland Publishing, 1987), 18

26. Franz Neumann, *Behemoth: The Structure and Practice of National Socialism, 1933–1944* (New York: Oxford University Press, 1944), 447.

27. Loewenstein, *Hitler's Germany*, 120.

28. Noakes and Pridham, *Documents on Nazism*, 269–270.

29. Jerome Hall, "Nulla Poena Sine Lege," *Yale Law Journal* Vol. 47 (December 1937): 165.

30. "Reichsgesetz über die Staatsnotwehr," 3 July 1934, *Reichsgesetzblatt* I 1934: 529.

31. Noakes and Pridham, *Documents on Nazism*, 217.

32. Art. 2, "Gesetz zur Änderung des Strafgesetzbuchs. Vom 28. Juni 1935," *Reichsgesetzblatt* I 1935: 839.

33. W. Ward Fearnside, "Three Innovations of National Socialist Jurisprudence," *Journal of Central European Affairs* Vol. 16 (1956–1957): 150–151.

34. *Trials of War Criminals before the Nuremberg Military Tribunals under Control Council Law No. 10* (Green Series) Military Tribunal III: 44–45.

35. Bracher, *The German Dictatorship*, p. 363; Arno A. Herzberg, "The Situation of the Lawyer in Germany," *American Bar Association Journal* Vol. 27 (1941): 295.

36. Loewenstein, "Law in the Third Reich," 790.

37. Hugh Thomson Kerr, ed., *A Compend of Luther's Theology* (London: Student Christian Movement, 1943), 197.

38. Otto Kirchheimer, "Criminal Law in National-Socialist Germany," *Studies in Philosophy and Social Science*, ed. Max Horkheimer (Munich: Kosel-Verlag, 1970), 444.

39. Werner Johe, *Die Gleichgeschaltete Justiz*, 17–18.

40. Karl Loewenstein, "Law in the Third Reich," 797.

41. "Reichsbürgergesetz. Vom 15. September 1935," *Reichsgesetzblatt* I 1935, p. 1146; "Gesetz zum Schutze des deutschen Blutes und der deutschen Ehre. Vom 15. September 1935," *Reichsgesetzblatt* I 1935: 1146–1147.

42. Otto Kirchheimer, "The Legal Order of National Socialism," *Studies in Philosophy and Social Science*, Vol. 9 (1941): 456.

43. Wagner and Weinkauff, *Die Deutsche Justiz und der Nationalsozialismus*, 71.

44. "Vierzehnte Verordnung zur Durchführung und Ergänzung des Gesetzes über den Ausgleich bürgerlich-rechtlicher Ansprüche. Vom 18. März 1939," *Reichsgesetzblatt* I 1939: 614.

45. Roetter, *Might is Right*, 147.

46. Ibid., 148–149.

47. Wagner and Weinkauff, *Die Deutsche Justiz und der Nationalsozialismus*, 308.

48. Ibid., 67.

49. Diemut Majer, *Grundlagen des nationalsozialistischen Rechtssystems: Führerprinzip, Sonderrecht, Einheitspartei* (Stuttgart: Verlag W. Kohlhammer, 1987), 164–165.

50. Wagner and Weinkauff, *Die Deutsche Justiz*, 67.

51. Ibid., 66.

52. Section 1, Art. 4, Art. 5, "Gesetz zur Vereinheitlichung des Rechts der Eheschließung und der Ehescheidung im Lande Österreich und im übrigen Rechtsgebiet. Vom 6. Juli 1938," *Reichsgesetzblatt* I 1938: 807.

53. "Reichserbhofgesetz. Vom 29. September 1933," *Reichsgesetzblatt* I 1933: 685–692.

54. Art. 48(2), "Gesetz über die Errichtung von Testamenten und Erbverträgen. Vom 31. Juli 1938," *Reichsgesetzblatt* I 1938: 979.

55. Art. 2, "Gesetz über die Akademie für Deutsches Recht vom 11. Juli 1934," Art. 1, "Satzung der Akademie für Deutsches Recht," *Reichsgesetzblatt* I 1934: 605.

56. Anderson, *Academy for German Law*, 44–46.

57. Wagner and Weinkauff, *Die Deutsche Justiz und der Nationalsozialismus*, 56.

58. Anderson, *Academy for German Law*, 530.

59. Wagner and Weinkauff, *Die Deutsche Justiz und der Nationalsozialismus*, 110.

60. Ibid., 66.

61. Ibid., 110.

62. Anderson, *Academy for German Law*, 539–540.

63. Loewenstein, *Hitler's Germany*, 121.

64. "Erstes Gesetz zur Überleitung der Rechtspflege auf das Reich. Vom 16. Februar 1934," *Reichsgesetzblatt* I 1934: 91; "Zweites Gesetz zur Überleitung der Rechtspflege auf das Reich. Vom 5. Dezember 1934," *Reichsgesetzblatt* I 1934: 1214–1215; "Verordnung zur Überleitung der Rechtspflege auf das Reich. Vom 20. Dezember 1934," *Reichsgesetzblatt* I 1934: 1267; ""Drittes Gesetz zur Überleitung der Rechtspflege auf das Reich. Vom 24. Januar 1935," *Reichsgesetzblatt* I 1935: 68–69; "Verordnung zur Durchführung des Dritten Gesetzes zur Überleitung der Rechtspflege auf das Reich. Vom 18. März 1935," *Reichsgesetzblatt* I 1935: 381.

65. Wagner and Weinkauff, *Die Deutsche Justiz und der Nationalsozialismus*, 239.

66. Art. 2, "Erstes Gesetz zur Überleitung der Rechtspflege auf das Reich," 16 February 1934, *Reichsgesetzblatt* I 1934: 91.

67. Wilhelm Heuber, "Der Bund Nationalsozialistischer deutscher Juristen und die deutsche Rechtsfront," *NS Handbuch*, 1566–1571 *passim*.

68. This organisation was later known as the National Socialist League for the Maintenance of the Law (*Nationalsozialistischer Rechtswahrerbund*) in 1936, when it was expanded to include judges and all other legal personnel. Kenneth C. H. Willig, "The Bar in the Third Reich," *American Journal of Legal History* Vol. 20 (1976): 3.

69. Ibid., 3.

70. Wagner and Weinkauf, *Die Deutsche Justiz und der Nationalsozialismus*, 106.

71. Ibid., 107.

72. Ibid.

73. Roetter, *Might is Right*, 219.

74. Ibid., 218–219.

75. "Gesetz zur Sicherung der Einheit von Partei und Staat," 1 December 1933, *Reichsgesetzblatt* I 1933: 1016.

76. "Gesetz über die Zulassung zur Rechtsanwaltschaft. Vom 7. April 1933," *Reichsgesetzblatt* I 1933: 188.

77. Art. 19, "Zweites Gesetz zur Änderung der Rechtsanwaltsordnung. Vom 13. Dezember 1935," *Reichsgesetzblatt* I 1935: 1471.

78. Ibid., 1470–1471.

79. Loewenstein, "Law in the Third Reich," p. 806.

80. Ibid., pp. 805–806.

81. "Reichs-Rechtsanwaltsordnung," *Reichsgesetzblatt* I 1936: 113–114.

82. Wagner and Weinkauff, *Die Deutsche Justiz und der Nationalsozialismus*, 22.

83. Dieter Simon, "Waren die NS-Richter 'unabhängige Richter' im Sinne des § 1 GVG?," *Justizalltag im Dritten Reich*, eds. Bernhard Diestelkamp, Michael Stolleis (Frankfurt-am-Main: Fischer Taschenbuch Verlag, 1988), 14.

84. Gerhard F. Kramer, "The Influence of National Socialism on Courts of Justice and the Police," *The Third Reich* (London: Weidenfeld & Nicolson, 1955), 624.

85. Wagner and Weinkauff, *Die Deutsche Justiz und der Nationalsozialismus*, 221; Lühr, "Darf der Richter gegen das Gesetz entscheiden?," *Deutsche Richterzeitung* (1934): 35.

86. Loewenstein, "Dictatorship and the German Constitution," *University of Chicago Law Review* (1937): 566–567.

87. "Gesetz zur Wiederherstellung des Berufsbeamtentums. Vom 7. April 1933," *Reichsgesetzblatt* I 1933: 175–177.

88. Ibid. Art. 3(1), Art. 4: 175.

89. Wrobel, *Verurteilt zur Demokratie: Justiz und Justizpolitik in Deutschland 1945–1949* (Heidelberg: Decker & Müller, 1989), 14.

90. Roetter, *Might is Right*, 183.

91. "Deutsches Beamtengesetz," 26 January 1937, *Reichsgesetzblatt* I 1937: 41–70.

92. Art. 71, Ibid., 52.

93. Wagner and Weinkauff, *Die Deutsche Justiz und der Nationalsozialismus*, 122.

94. Art. 42, "Deutsches Beamtengesetz,": 47.

95. "Erlass des Führers und Reichkanzlers über die Ernennung der Beamten und die Beendigung des Beamtenverhältnisses," 10 July 1937, *Reichsgesetzblatt* I 1937: 769–770.

96. The introduction of this new form of oath followed the creation of the office of *Führer* on 2 August 1934, combining the offices of *Reich* President and Chancellor as part of the process of Hitler accumulating greater governmental power. Hans Buchheim et al., *Anatomy of the SS State*, 128.

97. Friedrich Roetter, "The Impact of Nazi Law," *Wisconsin Law Review* (July 1945): 535–536.

98. Roland Freisler, "Recht, Richter und Gesetz," *Deutsche Justiz* (1933): 695.

99. Majer, *Grundlagen des nationalsozialistischen Rechtssystems*: 101.

100. Wagner and Weinkauff, *Die Deutsche Justiz und der Nationalsozialismus*, 75.

101. Ibid., 93.

102. Ibid., 94.

103. Loewenstein, "Law in the Third Reich," 806.

104. Roper, Edith and Clara Leiser, *Skeleton of Justice* (New York: E. P. Dutton & Co., 1941), 81.

105. Roetter, "Impact of Nazi Law," 542.

106. Roper, *Skeleton of Justice*, 81.

107. Dietrich Güstrow, *Tödlicher Alltag. Strafverteidiger im Dritten Reich* (Berlin: Siedler Verlag, 1981), 260.

108. Roper, *Skeleton of Justice*, 83–85; Roetter, *Might is Right*, 216.

109. Hubert Schorn, *Der Richter im Dritten Reich: Geschichte und Dokumente* (Frankfurt-am-Main: Klostermann, 1959), 117.

110. Richard Grunberger, *The Twelve Year Reich: A Social History of Nazi Germany, 1933–1945* (New York: Holt, Rinehart & Winston, 1971), 110–111.

111. Güstrow, *Tödlicher Alltag*, 20, 92–93.

112. Ibid., 65.

113. Ibid., 47.

114. Weinkauff and Wagner, *Die Deutsche Justiz und der Nationalsozialismus*, 65.

115. Ibid., 364.

116. Wrobel, *Verurteilt zur Demokratie*, 58.

117. Section 3, Art. 20, Art. 21, "Verordnung über Maßnahmen auf dem Gebiete der Gerichtsverfassung und der Rechtspflege. Vom 1. September 1939," *Reichsgesetzblatt* I 1939: 1660.

118. Lothar Gruchmann, *Justiz im Dritten Reich 1933–1940: Anpassung und Unterwerfung in der Ära Gürtner* (München: R. Oldenbourg Verlag, 1988), 1069.

119. Ibid., 974.

120. Wagner and Weinkauff, *Die Deutsche Justiz und der Nationalsozialismus*, 228.

121. Section 3, Art. 13, "Verodnung über Maßnahmen auf dem Gebiete der Gerichtsverfassung und der Rechtspflege. Vom 1. September 1939," *Reichsgesetzblatt* I 1939: 1659.

122. Section 1, Art. 1, "Kriegswirtschaftsverordnung. Vom 4. September 1939" *Reichsgesetzblatt* I 1939: 1609.

123. "Verordnung gegen Volksschädlinge. Vom 5. September 1939," *Reichsgesetzblatt* I 1939: 1679.

124. "Gesetz zur Änderung von Vorschriften des allgemeinen Strafverfahrens, des Wehrmachtstrafverfahrens und des Strafgesetzbuchs vom 16. September 1939," *Reichsgesetzblatt* I 1939: 1841.

125. Ibid., 1843.

126. "Verordnung zur Ergänzung der Strafvorschriften zum Schutz der Wehrkraft des Deutschen Volkes. Vom 25. November 1939," *Reichsgesetzblatt* I 1939: 2319.

127. Weinkauff and Wagner, *Die Deutsche Justiz und der Nationalsozialismus*, 124.

128. "Verordnung über Maßnahmen auf dem Gebiete des Beamtenrechts. Vom 1. September 1939," *Reichsgesetzblatt* I 1939: 1603–1604.

129. "Die Rede des Führers vor dem Reichstag," *Völkischer Beobachter*, 27 April 1942.

130. "Beschluß des Großdeutschen Reichstags vom 26. April 1942," *Reichsgesetzblatt* I 1942: 247.

131. Hans Julius Wolff, "Criminal Justice in Germany," *Michigan Law Review* Vol. 42 (1944): 1068–1069.

132. Wagner and Weinkauff, *Die Deutsche Justiz und der Nationalsozialismus*, 365.

133. Ibid., 219.

134. *Trials of War Criminals*, Military Tribunal III, 51; "Erlaß des Führers über besondere Vollmachten des Reichsministers der Justiz. Vom 20. August 1942," *Reichsgesetzblatt* I 1942: 535.

135. Heinz Boberach, ed., *Richterbriefe: Dokumente zur Beeinflussung der deutschen Rechtsprechung 1942–1944* (Boppard am Rhein: Harald Boldt Verlag, 1975), 485.

136. *Trials of War Criminals*, Military Tribunal III, p. 53; Boberach, *Richterbriefe: Dokumente zur Beeinflussung der deutschen Rechtsprechung*, 1–3

137. Ilse Staff, ed., *Justiz im Dritten Reich: Eine Dokumentation* (Frankfurt-am-Main: Fischer Bücherei, 1964), 72.

138. Ibid., 69–70.

139. Ibid., 72.

140. Wagner and Weinkauff, *Die Deutsche Justiz und der Nationalsozialismus*, 166.

141. Boberach, *Richterbriefe: Dokumente zur Beeinflussung der deutschen Rechtsprechung*, 401.

142. See Hans Buchheim, *Anatomy of the SS State*, 146–167 and 291–292.

143. Gruchmann, *Justiz im Dritten Reich*, 583–584.

144. Bracher, *The German Dictatorship*, 364.

145. Friedmann, *The Allied Military Government in Germany*, 10–11. Documented examples of court judgments that were "corrected" by the state police are cited in: Martin Broszat, "Zur Perversion der Strafjustiz im Dritten Reich," *Vierteljahrshefte für Zeitgeschichte* Vol. 6 (1958): 390–445.

146. Wagner and Weinkauff, *Die Deutsche Justiz und der Nationalsozialismus*, 125, 197.

147. Martin Broszat, *Der Staat Hitlers: Grundlegung und Entwicklung seiner inneren Verfassung* (München: Deutscher Taschenbuch Verlag, 1969), 414–415; Heinrich Herfahrdt, "Der Streit um den Positivismus in den gegenwärtigen deutschen Rechtswissenschaft," *Deutsche-Rechtszeitschrift* (1949): 33.

148. Wagner and Weinkauff, *Die Deutsche Justiz und der Nationalsozialismus*, 174.

149. Ibid., 364.

150. Peter Schneider, ed., "Rechtssicherheit und richterliche Unabhängigkeit aus der Sicht des SD," *Vierteljahrshefte für Zeitgeschichte* Vol. 4 (1956): 409.

151. Ibid., 416.

152. Michael Stolleis, "Die Verwaltungsgerichtsbarkeit im Nazionalsozialismus," *Justizalltag im Dritten Reich* (Frankfurt-am-Main: Fischer Taschenbuch Verlag, 1988), 26–27.

153. Ibid., 28–29.

154. Hans Buchheim, *Anatomy of the SS State*, 154–155; Roetter, "The Impact of Nazi Law," 534–535.

155. Bracher, *The German Dictatorship*, 364.

156. Stolleis, "Die Verwaltungsgerichtsbarkeit im Nationalsozialismus," 30–31.

157. Frieda Wunderlich, *German Labor Courts* (Chapel Hill: University of North Carolina Press, 1946), 137–138.

158. Andreas Kranig, "Treue gegen Fürsorge: Arbeitsrichter unter dem Nationalsozialismus," *Justizalltag im Dritten Reich* (Frankfurt-am-Main: Fischer Taschenbuch Verlag, 1988), 64.

159. Loewenstein, "Law in the Third Reich," 800.

160. "Gesetz über Treuhänder der Arbeit vom 19. Mai 1933," *Reichsgesetzblatt* I 1933: 285.

161. Wunderlich, *German Labor Courts*, 138.

162. "Gesetz zur Ordnung der nationalen Arbeit. Vom 20. Januar 1934," *Reichsgesetzblatt* I 1934: 45–56.

163. Wunderlich, *German Labor Courts*, 138.

164. Ibid., 172.

165. "Arbeitsgerichtsgesetz," 10 April 1934, *Reichsgesetzblatt* I 1934: 319–340.

166. Wunderlich, *German Labor Courts*, 156.

167. Ibid., 175.

168. Kranig, "Arbeitsrichter unter dem Nationalsozialismus," 66.

169. Hucko, *The Democratic Tradition*, 173.

170. Fraenkel, *The Dual State*, 40.

171. Gruchmann, *Justiz im Dritten Reich*, 1132.

172. Noakes and Pridham, *Documents on Nazism*, 269.

173. "Gesetz zur Änderung von Vorschriften des Strafrechts und des Strafverfahrens. Vom 24. April 1934," *Reichsgesetzblatt* I 1934: 341–348.

174. William Sweet, "The Volksgerichtshof: 1934–1945," *Journal of Modern History* Vol. 46 (1974): 315.

175. Schorn, *Der Richter im Dritten Reich*, 102.

176. Roper, *Skeleton of Justice*, 94–95.

177. Ingo Müller, *Hitler's Justice: The Courts of the Third Reich*, trans. Deborah Lucas Schneider (Cambridge, Mass.: Harvard University Press, 1991), 142.

178. Loewenstein, *Hitler's Germany*, 122.

179. Schorn, *Der Richter im Dritten Reich*, 116.

180. "Verordnung der Reichsregierung über die Bildung von Sondergerichten. Vom 21. März 1933," *Reichsgesetzblatt* I 1933: 136–137.

181. Ibid.

182. "Gesetz zur Abwehr politische Gewalttaten. Vom 4. April 1933," *Reichsgesetzblatt* I 1933: 162.

183. 460/533, Wiesbaden. 3234—IV a/4 877/43. Betrifft: Entlastung der Sondergerichte. 5 July 1943.

184. Art. 1, "Gesetz gegen heimtückliche Angriffe auf Staat und Partei und zum Schutz der Parteiuniformen. Vom 20. Dezember 1934," *Reichsgesetzblatt* I 1934: 1269.

185. Art. 3(2), "Gesetz gegen heimtückliche Angriffe auf Staat und Partei und zum Schutz der Parteiuniformen. Vom 20. Dezember 1934," *Reichsgesetzblatt* I 1934: 1270.

186. "Gesetz zur Gewährleistung des Rechtsfriedens. Vom 13. Oktober 1933," *Reichsgesetzblatt* I 1933: 723–724.

187. "Verordnung über die Erweiterung der Zuständigkeit der Sondergerichte. Vom 20. November 1938," *Reichsgesetzblatt* I 1938: 1632.

188. Section 3, Art. 18, Art. 19, "Verordnung über Maßnahmen auf dem Gebiete der Gerichtsverfassung und der Rechtspflege. Vom 1. September 1939," *Reichsgesetzblatt* I 1939: 1659, 1660.

189. 460/533, Wiesbaden. 3234—IV a/4 877/43. Betrifft: Entlastung der Sondergerichte. 5 July 1943.

190. Art. 4, "Verordnung über außerordentliche Rundfunkmaßnahmen. Vom 1. September 1939," *Reichsgesetzblatt* I 1939: 1683; Section 1, Art. 19, Art. 20(1),

"Verordnung über Maßnahmen auf dem Gebiete der Gerichtsverfassung und der Rechtspflege. Vom 1. September 1939," *Reichsgesetzblatt* I 1939: 1660.

191. Art. 3, "Verordnung gegen Gewaltverbrecher. Vom 5. Dezember 1939," *Reichsgesetzblatt* I 1939: 2378.

192. Art. 14, "Verordnung über die Zuständigkeit der Strafgerichte, die Sondergerichte und sonstige Strafverfahrensrechtliche Vorschriften. Vom 21. Februar 1940," *Reichsgesetzblatt* I 1940: 405.

193. The penalty for listening to foreign radio broadcasts was a term of imprisonment (Art. 1). Circulating news of the those broadcasts was also penalised with imprisonment, unless the case was considered particularly serious (Art. 2). "Verordnung über außerordentliche Rundfunkmaßnahmen. Vom 1. 9.1939," *Reichsgesetzblatt* I 1939: 1683.

194. Art. 1(2), "Verordnung gegen Volksschädlinge," *Reichsgesetzblatt* I 1939: 1679.

195. "Verordnung gegen Gewaltverbrecher. Vom 5. Dezember 1939," *Reichsgesetzblatt* I 1939: 2378.

196. Gruchmann, "Rechtssystem und nationalsozialistische Justizpolitik," 100.

197. Cases to be presented before the ordinary judicial organisation were initially handled by the office of the public prosecutor.

198. Müller, *Hitler's Justice*, 153.

199. Werner Johe, *Die gleichgeschaltete Justiz*, 107.

200. 460/533, Wiesbaden. 3234—IV a/4 877/43. Betrifft: Entlastung der Sondergerichte. 5 July 1943.

201. Hans Wrobel, *Verurteilt zur Demokratie*, 8.

202. Ibid., 20.

203. 501/1199, Wiesbaden. Office of the Military Government for Germany (Denazification) HIT/Ij, APO 633. Subject: "Criteria for Membership in the NSDAP," 24 January 1947.

204. Art. 2, "Verordnung über die Vorbildung und die Laufbahnen der deutsche Beamten. Vom 28. Februar 1939," *Reichsgesetzblatt* I 1939: 371.

205. 501/1199, Wiesbaden. Office of the Military Government for Germany (Denazification) HIT/Ij, APO 633. Subject: "Criteria for Membership in the NSDAP," 24 January 1947.

206. Schorn, *Der Richter im Dritten Reich*, 41.

207. Wrobel, *Verurteilt zur Demokratie*, 79.

208. Schorn, *Der Richter im Dritten Reich*, 40.

209. Wrobel, *Verurteilt zur Demokratie*, 79.

210. Wagner and Weinkauff, *Die Deutsche Justiz und der Nationalsozialismus*, 233.

211. Güstrow, *Tödlicher Alltag*, 14.

212. Ingo Müller, *Hitler's Justice*, 192.

213. Gruchmann, "Rechtssystem und nationalsozialistische Justizpolitik," 101.

214. Ibid.

215. Wagner and Weinkauff, *Die Deutsche Justiz und der Nationalsozialismus*, 365.

216. Ibid., 364.

217. Ibid., 175.

Chapter 2

1. *Foreign Relations of the United States, Diplomatic Papers, 1943*, Vol. 1: *General* (Washington: U.S. Government Printing Office, 1963): 720–723.

2. Ibid., 755–756.

3. Hajo Holborn, *American Military Government: Its Organization and Policies* (Buffalo: William S. Hein, 1975), 22.

4. Ibid., 756–757.

5. See Harley Notter, *Postwar Foreign Policy Preparation: 1939–1945* (Westport: Greenwood Press, 1975), 69, 96, 124–133 *passim* for the development of the various U.S. State Department postwar policy planning committees.

6. Philip E. Mosely, "The Occupation of Germany: New Light on How the Zones were Drawn," *Foreign Affairs* Vol. 28 (July 1950): 583–585; Edwin J. Hayward, "Coordination of Military and Civil Affairs Planning," *Annals of the American Academy of Political and Social Science*, Vol. 267, (1950): 24–25.

7. *Foreign Relations of the United States, Diplomatic Papers: The Conferences of Malta and Yalta* (Washington: U.S. Government Printing Office, 1965), 113–118.

8. Ibid., 118–123.

9. Ibid., 124.

10. Ibid.

11. Holborn, *American Military Government*, 44.

12. *Foreign Relations of the United States: The Conference at Quebec, 1944* (Washington D.C.: U.S. Government Printing Office, 1971), 77–80.

13. Ibid., 77.

14. Paul J. Hammond, "Directives for the Occupation of Germany: The Washington Controversy," *American Civil-Military Decisions* (Birmingham: University of Alabama Press, 1963), ed. Harold Stein, 339.

15. Holborn, *American Military Government*, 26.

16. Hammond, "Directives for the Occupation of Germany," 357–358, 340.

17. Ray S. Cline, *United States Army in World War II; The War Department; Washington Command Post: The Operations Division* (Washington D.C.: Office of the Chief of Military History, Department of the Army, 1951), 325; U.S. Army, European Command, Historical Division, *Planning for the Occupation of Germany* (Frankfurt-am-Main: Office of the Chief Historian, 1947), 32–33.

18. Oliver J. Frederiksen, *The American Military Occupation of Germany: 1945–1953* (Historical Division Headquarters, U.S. Army, Europe, 1953), 1.

19. Forrest C. Pogue, *United States Army in World War II: The European Theater of Operations: The Supreme Command* (Washington D.C.: Office of the Chief of Military History, Department of the Army, 1954), 339.

20. Harold Zink, *The United States in Germany: 1944–1955* (New York: Van Nostrand, 1957), 21.

21. F. S. V. Donnison, *Civil Affairs and Military Government: North-West Europe, 1944–1946* (London: Her Majesty's Stationery Office, 1961), 8–15 *passim*.

22. Zink, *The United States in Germany: 1944–1955*, 20.

23. There were six editions of the *Handbook* amid controversy regarding the severity of denazification procedures, particularly President Roosevelt's intervention and insistence that the provisions of the *Handbook* were too lenient. Jill Jones, "Eradicating Nazism from the British Zone of Germany: Early Policy and Practice," *German History* Vol. 8 (1990): 153.

24. Earl F. Ziemke, *The U.S. Army in the Occupation of Germany: 1944–1946* (Washington D.C.: Center of Military History, United States Army, 1975), 80–81.

25. Holborn, *American Military Government*, 33.

26. Pogue, *The European Theater of Operations; The Supreme Command*, 77, 80.

27. Ibid., 347.

28. Holborn, *American Military Government*, 33, 135–139.

29. Donnison, *Civil Affairs and Military Government, North-West Europe*, 359.

30. Holborn, *American Military Government*, 36–37.

31. Ibid., 136–137.

32. *Handbook for Military Government in Germany: Prior to Defeat or Surrender* (Office of the Chief of Staff: Supreme Headquarters, Allied Expeditionary Force, December 1944), para. 562.

33. Ibid., para. 287.

34. Ibid., para. 78.

35. Ibid., paras. 81, 145.

36. Ibid., paras. 82, 86.

37. Ibid., para. 542.

38. Ibid., para. 84.

39. Ibid., para. 543.

40. Ibid., para. 85.

41. Ibid., paras. 1, 3.

42. Document II "Chapter V, Legal, from German Handbook, Document XII, "Military Government Instructions to Legal Officers and M.G.O's," *Military Government, Germany: Technical Manual for Legal and Prison Officers* Supreme Headquarters, Allied Expeditionary Force, G-5, 1944.

43. Document I "Military Government—Germany, Supreme Commander's Area of Control, Legal and Prison Policy," clauses 1, 2, *Technical Manual for Legal and Prison Officers.*

44. Document I, clauses 2, 3, 6, 7, 8, *Technical Manual for Legal and Prison Officers*

45. Z45F 11/3–1/24 RG 260 OMGUS, Koblenz. Annex XV Administration of Justice. 1945/3.

46. Joseph R. Starr, *U.S. Military Government in Germany: Operations during the Rhineland Campaign* (Karlsruhe: U.S. Army Historical Division, European Command, 1950), 3.

47. Pogue, *Supreme Command*, 356.

48. Hammond, "Directives for the Occupation of Germany," 376–377.

49. *Foreign Relations of the United States: The Conferences at Malta and Yalta*, 968–975.

50. Holborn, *American Military Government*, 41–42.

51. Velma Hastings Cassidy, "American Policy in Occupied Areas," *Department of State Bulletin*, vol. 15 (1946): 291–292.

52. Hammond, "Directives for the Occupation of Germany," 328, 362, 372, 390.

53. Leonhard Krieger, "The Inter-Regnum in Germany: March-August 1945," *Political Science Quarterly*, vol. 64 (1949): 517.

54. "Military Government of Germany: Directive to the Commander in Chief of the United States Forces of Occupation Regarding the Military Government of Germany," *Department of State Bulletin*, vol. 13 (21 October 1945): 598–599.

55. Ibid., 600.

56. *Enactments and Approved Papers of the Control Council and Coordinating Committee* 1945, Vol. 1, 125.

57. Eli E. Nobleman, "Quadripartite Military Government Organization and Operations in Germany," *American Journal of International Law*, Vol. 41 (July 1946): 652–653.

58. Herbert Feis, *Between War and Peace: The Potsdam Conference* (Princeton: Princeton University Press, 1960), 52.

59. *Foreign Relations of the United States, Diplomatic Papers: The Conference of Berlin (The Potsdam Conference)*: 1945, Vol. 2 (Washington D.C.: U.S. Government Printing Office, 1960), 1502–1505.

60. Ibid., 775–778.

61. Ibid., 750.

62. JCS 1067 defined "more than nominal participants" as individuals who: 1) had held offices in the NSDAP or its affiliated organisations; 2) had authorised or actively participated in National Socialist crimes or racial persecutions and discriminations; 3) were "avowed believers" in National Socialism or its racial and militaristic ideologies; or 4) had "voluntarily given substantial or material support or political assistance of any kind" to the NSDAP or National Socialist officials and its leaders. "Military Government of Germany: Directive to the Commander-in-Chief of the United States Forces of Occupation," *U.S. Department of State Bulletin* Vol. 13 (21 October 1945): 598–599.

63. *Foreign Relations of the United States, Diplomatic Papers: The Conference of Berlin*, 1945 Vol. 2, 1502–1503.

64. Ibid., 1503.

65. Loewenstein, "Law and the Legislative Process in Occupied Germany," 995.

66. Oliver J. Fredericksen, *The American Military Occupation of Germany: 1945–1953* (Karlsruhe: Historical Division, Hqs. USAEUR, 1953), 31; Ziemke, *U.S. Army in the Occupation of Germany: 1944–1946*, 93–94.

67. Zink, *United States in Germany: 1944–1955*, 26.

68. "Proclamation No. 1: Establishing the Control Council," *Official Gazette of the Control Council for Germany*, No. 1 (29 October 1945): 4–5.

69. *Monthly Report of the Military Governor, U.S. Zone*, 20 September, 1945, No. 2.

70. Loewenstein, "Law and the Legislative Process in Occupied Germany," 751.

71. Pogue, *Allied Military Government*, 353–354.

Chapter 3

1. Loewenstein, "Law and the Legislative Process in Occupied Germany," 733.

2. Lucius D. Clay, *Decision in Germany* (Garden City: Doubleday & Company, 1950), 17.

3. Helmut von Weber, "Der Einfluß der Militärstrafgerichtsbarkeit der Besatzungsmacht auf die deutsche Strafgerichtsbarkeit," *Süddeutsche Juristenzeitung* (1947): 65.

4. Z45F 11/5–2/1, Koblenz. Provenance: OMGUS, LD. Legal Division History.

5. Heinz Breuning, "Die Beschränkung der deutschen Gerichtsbarkeit durch die Besatzungsmächte" (Diss.: Eberhards-Karls-Universität zu Tübingen, 1952): 10.

6. Eli E. Nobleman, "American Military Government Courts in Germany," *American Journal of International Law* Vol. 40 (1946): 804.

7. Eli E. Nobleman, "The Administration of Justice in the United States Zone in Germany," *Federal Bar Journal* Vol. 8 (October 1946): 70.

8. *Military Government Gazette, Germany, United States Zone*, Issue A, 1 June 1946: 1.

9. Eli E. Nobleman, "Military Government Courts: Law and Justice in the American Zone of Germany," *American Bar Association Journal* Vol. 33 (1947): 851.

10. "Law No. 1: Abrogation of Nazi Law," *Military Government Gazette*, Issue A, 1 June 1946: 3–4.

11. "Regulation Under Law No. 1," *Military Government Gazette, Germany, United States Zone*, Issue A, 1 June 1946: 5–7.

12. "Law No. 2: German Courts," *Military Government Gazette* Issue A, 1 June 1946: 7–10.

13. Breuning, "Die Beschränkung der deutschen Gerichtsbarkeit," 25.

14. *Das Besatzungsregime auf dem Gebiet der Rechtspflege*, 5.

15. Ibid., 27–28.

16. "Ordinance No. 1: Crimes and Offences," *Military Government Gazette*, Issue A (1 June 1946): 57–60.

17. "Ordinance No. 2: Military Government Courts," *Military Government Gazette* Issue A (1 June 1946): 60–63.

18. "Law No. 6: Dispensation by Act of Military Government with Necessity of Compliance with German Law," *Military Government Gazette* Issue A (1 June 1946): 19.

19. von Weber, "Die Bedeutung der 'Allgemeinen Anweisung an Richter' Nr. 1," *Süddeutsche Juristenzeitung* (1946): 238.

20. The limitations on the jurisdiction of German courts as imposed by Military Government Law No. 2 included cases involving the military forces of the United Nations, or individuals either serving with or accompanying them; the United Nations or any national thereof; German law that was suspended or abrogated by the military government; any order of the Allied forces, any enactment of the military government, or "the construction or validity of any such order or enactment;" matters in which jurisdiction was assumed by a military government court; any case or groups of cases maintained under the exclusive jurisdiction of military government courts; or monetary claims against the German government or any legal entity that

existed under public law. Law No. 2, Art. 6, para. 10, *Military Government Gazette* Issue A, 1 June 1946: 9.

21. Z45F 117/56–7/7, Koblenz. Legal Form IJ 1 LA 9, Military Government—Germany, Supreme Commander's Area of Control, Instructions to Judges No. 1.

22. von Weber, "Die Bedeutung der 'Allgemeinen Anweisung an Richter' Nr. 1,", 238–239.

23. *Das Besatzungsregime auf dem Gebiet der Rechtspflege*, 4.

24. Joachim Reinhold Wenzlau, *Der Wiederaufbau der Justiz in Nordwestdeutschland: 1945 bis 1949* (Königstein: Athenäum, 1979), 53.

25. Nobleman, "Administration of Justice in the United States Zone of Germany," 74.

26. Breuning, "Die Beschränkung der deutschen Gerichtsbarkeit," 11. The Hague Conventions circumscribe extensive legislative powers to the occupant, which may be applied to ensure the safety of occupation troops and the welfare of the civilian population. Paul L. Weiden, "The Impact of Occupation on German Law," *Wisconsin Law Review* (1947): 334–335.

27. Breuning, "Die Beschränkung der deutschen Gerichtsbarkeit," 11, 14. See Eli E. Nobleman, "American Military Government Courts in Germany with Special Reference to Historic Practice and their Role in the Democratization of the German People" (Diss.: New York University, 1950), 2–13 *passim* for a discussion of the establishment of occupation courts on the basis of international law.

28. von Weber, "Der Einfluß der Militärstrafgerichtsbarkeit der Besatzungsmacht," 65.

29. Ibid., 66.

30. Document I, para. 3, *Technical Manual for Legal and Prison Officers.*

31. The military government courts in SHAEF-occupied Germany had tried 16,000 cases by 7 May 1945. Eli E. Nobleman, "American Military Government Courts in Germany," *American Academy of Political and Social Science*, Vol. 269 (1950): 90.

32. Nobleman, "American Military Government Courts," *Annals of the American Academy*, 88.

33. Clay, *Decision in Germany*, 247

34. Joseph R. Starr, *Denazification, Occupation and Control of Germany, March-July 1945* (Salisbury: Documentary Publications, 1977), 118.

35. "Ordinance No. 2: Military Government Courts," *Military Government Gazette* Issue A (1 June 1946): 60–63.

36. The term "United Nations" was defined in Military Government Law No. 3, in which 47 nations were cited. Hans Neidhard, "Die Rechtspflege in der Gesetzgebung der amerikanischen Zone," *Deutsche Rechts-Zeitschrift* (1946): 84.

37. Dexter L. Freeman, *Hesse: A New German State* (Frankfurt-am-Main: Druck und Verlaghaus, 1948), 135.

38. Ziemke, *U.S. Army in the Occupation of Germany*, 144.

39. *Report of the Military Government for Germany, U.S. Zone*, 20 August 1945, No. 1.

40. Nobleman, "American Military Government Courts," *American Journal of International Law*, 808.

41. Ibid., 807

42. Ibid., 806.

43. Military government detachments ordered the surrender of all firearms and ammunition once they were established in a German town. Starr, *Operations During the Rhineland Campaign*, 33.

44. *Monthly Report of the Military Governor, U.S. Zone*, 20 October 1945, No. 3.

45. Freeman, *Hesse: A New German State*, 38; problem of DPs: 39–40, 20, 23.

46. 463/945, Wiesbaden. Betr.: "Kriminalität der in Lagern zurückgebliebenen Ostarbeiter," 27. November 1945.

47. Freeman, *Hesse: A New German State*, 38; problem of DPs: 39–40, 20, 23.

48. Eli E. Nobleman. "American Military Government Courts in Germany," *Annals of the American Academy*, 87. It has been argued that military government courts served as an example for restoring democracy in Germany by promoting impartiality during the court proceedings in determining the facts of a case. Ibid., 804.

49. Nobleman, "American Military Government Courts," *Annals of the American Academy*, 95.

50. Foreign court jurisdiction in Germany having no legal meaning was considered a principle of German law. The effects of military court jurisdiction upon the competence of German courts signified an exception to this principle. von Weber, "Der Einfluß der Militärstrafgerichtsbarkeit der Besatzungsmacht," 70.

51. Loewenstein, "Law and the Legislative Process in Occupied Germany," 1001–1002.

52. Erhard Zimmer, *Studien zu Frankfurter Geschichte herausgegeben vom Frankfurter Verein für Geschichte und Landeskunde: Die Geschichte des Oberlandesgerichts in Frankfurt-am-Main* (Frankfurt-am-Main: Waldemar Kramer, 1976), 87.

53. Freeman, *Hesse: A New German State*, 19.

54. Conrad F. Latour and Thilo Vogelsang, *Okkupation und Wiederaufbau:Die Tätigkeit der Militärregierung in der amerikanischen Besatzungszone, 1944–1947* (Stuttgart: Deutsche Verlags-Anstalt, 1973), 97; Karlheinz Müller, *Preußischer Adler und Hessischer Löwe: Hundert Jahre Wiesbadener Regierung 1866–1966, Dokumente der Zeit aus den Akten* (Wiesbaden: Verlag Kultur und Wissen, 1966), 330, 337–339.

55. Freeman, *Hesse: A New German State*, 48.

56. *Report of the Military Government for Germany, U.S. Zone*, 20 August 1945, No. 1, 1–2.

57. Wolf-Arno Kropat, *Hessen in der Stunde Null, 1945–1947*, 19; Freeman, *Hesse: A New German State*, 49–50.

58. Latour, Volgelsang, *Okkupation und Wiederaufbau*, 98–99.

59. Loewenstein, "Political Reconstruction in Germany, Zonal and Interzonal," *Change and Crisis in European Government*, ed. James Kerr Pollock (New York: Rinehart & Company, 1949), 30; *Monthly Report of the Military Governor, U.S. Zone*, 20 October 1945, No. 3.

60. *Monthly Report of the Military Governor, U.S. Zone*, 20 October 1945, No. 3; James K. Pollock and James H. Meisel, *Germany under Occupation: Illustrative Materials and Documents* (Ann Arbor: George Wahr Publishing, 1947), 118–119.

61. Justus Fürstenau, *Entnazifizierung: Ein Kapitel deutscher Nachkriegspolitik* (Darmstadt: Luchterhand Verlag, 1969), 53.

62. "Proclamation No. 2," *Military Government Gazette*, Issue A, 1 June 1946, 2–3.

63. Bernard Diestelkamp, "Rechts- und verfassungsgeschichtliche Probleme zur Frühgeschichte der Bundesrepublik Deutschland," *Juristische Schulung* (1980): 793.

64. J. von Elmenau, "Aufbau und Tätigkeit des Länderrats der U.S.-Zone," *Deutsche Rechts-Zeitschrift* (1946): 113.

65. "Proclamation No. 2," Art. 3, *Military Government Gazette*, Issue A, 1 June 1946: 2–3.

66. Clay, *Decision in Germany*, 55.

67. "Staat und Verwaltung," *Süddeutsche Juristenzeitung* (1946), 18.

68. Wrobel, *Verurteilt zur Demokratie*, 111.

69. "Staat und Verwaltung," *Süddeutsche Juristenzeitung* (1946), 18.

70. Frederiksen, *American Military Occupation of Germany*, 31.

71. *Foreign Relations of the United States: The Conference of Berlin*, 1500–1501.

72. Zink, *The United States in Germany: 1944–1955*, 35–36.

73. Nobleman, "Administration of Justice in the United States Zone of Germany," 75.

74. Freeman, *Hesse: A New German State*, 49–51.

75. Adolf Arndt, "Die staats- und verwaltungsrechtliche Entwicklung in Groß-Hessen," *Deutsche Rechts-Zeitschrift* (1946): 183.

76. Kropat, *Hessen in der Stunde Null*, 28; Freeman, *Hesse: A New German State*, 50–51.

77. *Monthly Report of the Military Governor, U.S. Zone*, 20 December 1945, No. 5.

78. "Proclamation No. 2," *Military Government Gazette* Issue A, 1 June 1946, 2–3.

79. J. F. J. Gillen, *State and Local Government in West Germany, 1945–1953* (Bad Godesberg-Mehlem: Historical Division, Office of the U.S. High Commissioner for Germany, 1953), 48; "Staatsgrundgesetz des StaatesGroB-Hessen vom 22. November 1945," *Gesetz und Verordnungsblatt für Groß-Hessen* (1945): 23–26.

80. Arndt, "Die staats- und verwaltungsrechtliche Entwicklung in Groß-Hessen," 185

81. Clay, *Decision in Germany*, 86.

82. "Proclamation No. 2," Art. 3(2), *Military Government Gazette* Issue A, 1 June 1946: "Until such time as it is possible to establish democratic institutions it will be sufficient for the validity of state legislation that it be approved and promulgated by the Minister President."

83. Loewenstein, "Law and the Legislative Process in Occupied Germany," 1012; "Staatsgrundgesetz des Landes Groß-Hessen vom 22. November 1945" [Preliminary Constitution], Art. 9, *Gesetz—und Verordnungsblatt für das Land Groß-Hessen* (1946): 23.

84. Loewenstein. "Law and the Legislative Process in Occupied Germany," 1017.

85. Ibid., 1014.

86. Ibid., 1017.

87. "Gemeindewahlgesetz vom 15. Dezember 1945," *Gesetz—und Verordnungsblatt für das Land Groß-Hessen* (1946): 7–9.

88. "Grosshessische Gemeindeordnung vom 21. Dezember 1945," *Gesetz—und Verordnungsblatt für das Land Groß-Hessen* (1946): 1–11.

89. “Kreisordnung für das Land Hessen: Gesetz vom 24. Januar 1946,” *Gesetz—und Verordnungsblatt für das Land Groß-Hessen* (1946): 101–106.

90. “Kreiswahlgesetz vom 7. März 1946,” *Gesetz—und Verordnungsblatt für das Land Groß-Hessen* (1946): 73–75.

91. “Gesetz betr. den Volksentscheid über die Verfassung des LandesHessen,” *Gesetz—und Verordnungsblatt für das Land Groß-Hessen* (1946): 177, amended by “Gesetz zur Abänderung des Gesetzes betr. den Volksentscheid über die Verfassung des Landes Hessen vom 30. Oktober 1946,” *Gesetz—und Verordnungsblatt für das Land Groß-Hessen* (1946): 188.

92.”Wahlgesetz für den Landtag des Landes Hessen vom 14. Oktober 1946,” *Gesetz—und Verordnungsblatt für das Land Groß-Hessen* (1946): 177–180.

93. 501/927, Wiesbaden. “Programmatische Erklärung der Grosshessischen Staatsregierung,” 23/11/1945.

94. Report of the Military Government, U.S. Zone, 20 August, 1945, no 1.

95. Loewenstein, “Law and the Legislative Process in Occupied Germany,” 732.

96. “Law No. 1: Repealing of Nazi Laws,” *Official Gazette of the Control Council for Germany* No. 1 (29 October 1945): 6–8.

97. Loewenstein, “Law and the Legislative Process in Occupied Germany,” 734–735.

98. Z45F 17/199–3/41 RG 260/OMGUS, Koblenz. Provenance OMGUS: LD/AJ Br. Folder Title: Denazification of Judges and Prosecutors. Subject: “Denazification of Judges and Prosecutors in the German Ordinary Courts,” 4 June 1947.

99. Loewenstein, “Political Reconstruction in Germany,” 33.

100. “Law No. 5: Dissolution of the Nazi Party,” *Military Government Gazette*, Issue A, 1 June 1946: 17–19.

101. “Law No. 2: Providing for the Termination and Liquidation of the Nazi Organisations,” *Official Gazette of the Control Council for Germany* No. 1 (29 October 1945): 19–21.

102. “Proclamation No. 3: Fundamental Principles of Judicial Reform,” *Official Gazette of the Control Council* No. 1 (29 October 1945): 22–23.

103. Art. 1, “Law No. 4: Reorganization of the German Judicial System,” *Official Gazette of the Control Council for Germany* No. 2 (30 November 1945): 26.

104. The traditional jurisdictional powers of the *Amtsgericht* included civil litigation matters in which the disputed amount didn’t exceed 1,500 *Reichmarks*, and “over certain other matters, regardless of the amount involved, such as disputes between landlord and tenant . . . and claims for support between husband and wife.” It served as a court of first instance in criminal matters, while its jurisdiction to impose penalty “was limited to sentences of imprisonment not in excess of five years.” Nobleman, “Administration of Justice,” 92.

105. The *Landgericht* had civil jurisdiction in all matters in which the amount in controversy exceeded 1,500 *Reichmarks*, in cases that the *Amtsgericht* didn’t have any jurisdiction, and had appellate jurisdiction over disputed matters arising from the *Amtsgericht*. Its jurisdiction in criminal cases extended to all matters outside the power of sentence under the jurisdiction of the *Amtsgericht*. Ibid.

106. The *Oberlandesgericht* held appellate jurisdiction over decisions made by the *Landgericht* in both criminal and civil matters. Whereas the *Landgericht* heard appeals

from the *Amtsgericht* in criminal cases on the facts and the law, the *Oberlandesgericht* reviewed appeals only on matters of law. In addition, the *Oberlandesgericht* exercised supervisory administrative power over every *Landgericht* in the area under its jurisdiction, while the *Landgericht* exercised this power over every *Amtsgericht* under its appellate jurisdiction. Ibid.

107. Adolf Schönke, "Einige Fragen der Verfassung der Strafgerichte," *Süddeutsche Juristenzeitung* (1946): 63.

108. Art. 3, "Law No. 4: Reorganization of the German Judicial System," *Official Gazette of the Control Council for Germany* No. 2 (30 November 1945): 26.

109. Art. 2, "Law No. 4: Reorganization of the German Judicial System," *Official Gazette of the Control Council for Germany* No. 2 (30 November 1945), p. 26; "Rechtspflege: Gerichtsverfassung," *Süddeutsche Juristenzeitung* (1946): 19.

110. Art. 3(e), "Law No. 4: Reorganization of the German Judicial System," *Official Gazette of the Control Council*: 27.

111. Kurt Kleinrahm, "Rechtsnatur und Rechtswirkungen der Beschränkungen deutscher Gerichtsbarkeit durch das Besatzungsrecht," *Deutscher Rechts-Zeitschrift* (1948): 232.

112. Neidhard, "Die Rechtspflege in der Gesetzgebung der amerikanischen Zone," 84.

113. Friedmann, *Allied Military Government of Germany*, 174–175.

114. Heinrich Röhreke, "Die Besatzungsgewalt auf dem Gebiete der Rechtspflege," Diss.: Eberhard-Karls-Universität zu Tübingen, 1950, 44.

115. 1126/33, Wiesbaden. "Radio-Rede [Geiler] über Deutschland als Rechtsstaat" (n.d.).

116. Karl Loewenstein, "Justice," *Governing Postwar Germany*, ed. Edward H. Litchfield (Ithaca: Cornell University Press, 1950), 250.

117. Freeman, *Hesse: A New German State*, 134.

118. *Monthly Report of the Military Governor, U.S. Zone*, 20 November 1945, No. 4.

119. H. E. Rotberg, "Entpolitisierung der Rechtspflege," *Deutsche Rechts-Zeitschrift* (1947): 107.

120. Dicey, *Introduction to the Study of the Law*, xxv.

121. *Monthly Report of the Military Governor, U.S. Zone*, 20 December 1945, No. 5.

122. *Enactments and Approved Papers*, Vol. 1, 1945, 173–175.

123. Karl Loewenstein, "Reconstruction of the Administration of Justice in American-occupied Germany," *Harvard Law Review* Vol. 61 (1947–1948): 422.

124. Zimmer, *Die Geschichte des Oberlandesgerichts in Frankfurt-am-Main*, 88.

125. Latour and Vogelsang, *Okkupation und Wiederaufbau*, 78.

126. Starr, *Denazification, Occupation and Control of Germany, March-July, 1945*, 121–122.

127. Eckart G. Franz, Hans Hubert Hofmann, and Meinhard Schaab, *Gerichtsorganisation in Baden-Württemberg, Bayern und Hessen im 19. und 20. Jahrhundert* (Hannover: Akademie für Raumforschung und Landesplanung, 1989), 184.

128. Z45f 117/56–7/7, Koblenz. Legal Form IJ 1. Military Government—Germany; Supreme Commander's Area of Control; Instructions to Judges No. 1.

129. 460/568, Wiesbaden. Militärregierung—Deutschland; Kontroll-Gebiet des Obersten Befehlshabers. Dienstanweisung für Amtsrichter, 9 July 1945; Der aufsichtsführende Richter. Dienstanweisung Nr. 1, 31 August 1945.

130. 460/568, Wiesbaden. Betrifft: "Berichte an die Militärregierung," 28 July 1945.

131. 460/568, Wiesbaden. The *Landgericht* president, Frankfurt-am-Main, to the Military Government Legal Department at Frankfurt-am-Main, 6 August 1945.

132. *Monthly Report of the Military Governor, U.S. Zone*, 20 August 1945, No. 1.

133. "Der Aufbau der Justiz in der amerikanischen Zone: Groß-Hessen," *Deutsche Rechts-Zeitschrift* (1946): 120.

134. *Monthly Report of the Military Governor, U.S. Zone*, 20 September 1945, No. 2. Minor cases that were transferred to German courts as they reopened in the summer and autumn of 1945 included black market, curfew, and traffic violations. Z45F 11/5–2/1. OMGUS, LD. "Legal Division History," Koblenz.

135. Franz, Hofmann, Schaab, *Gerichtsorganisation*, 184.

136. 501/831 Wiesbaden. "Office of Military Government for Greater Hesse: Progress Report of Land Greater Hesse 1945," 21 December 1945.

137. 8/189–3/1, RG260 OMGUS, Wiesbaden. OMGH Historical Division. Monthly Historical Report, December 1945, Land Greater Hesse.

138. *Monthly Report of the Military Governor, U.S. Zone*, 20 October 1945, No. 3.

139. "Der Aufbau der Justiz in der amerikanischen Zone: Groß-Hessen," 120.

140. 463/929, Wiesbaden. "Headquarters, U.S. Forces, European Theater. Plan für die Justizverwaltung, amerikanische Zone," 4. Oktober 1945.

141. 463/929, Wiesbaden. "General Akten über Verfassung," 5. November 1945.

142. The policy of reconstructing separate judicial organisations in each *Land* following the reconstruction of the *Länder* and their governments in the U.S. occupation zone was in contrast to the policies of the occupiers in the British and the Soviet occupation zones. Rather than set up a Ministry of Justice operating within each *Land* government at the beginning of the occupation, a Central Justice Office (*Zentral Justizamt*) was established for the British zone on 1 October 1946 to deal with legislative and personnel functions. The judicial organisation in the Soviet occupation zone was also centralised at the zonal level. The newly created *Land* administrations included justice sections, which were directed by the superstructure of a German Central Administration for Justice (*Deutsche Zentralverwaltung für Justiz*). Bernhard Diestelkamp and Susanne Jung, "Die Justiz in den Westzonen und der frühen Bundesrepublik" *Aus Politik und Zeitgeschichte* Vol. 13 (24 March 1989): 19–20. The development of independent *Land* administrations in the U.S. zone also took place earlier than in the Soviet, French, and British zones. Lia Härtel, ed., *Der Länderrat des amerikanischen Besatzungsgebietes* (Stuttgart, Köln: W. Kohlhammer Verlag, 1951), xxi. This political development may have opened the way for the *Länder* of the U.S. zone to assume the responsibility for administering their individual judicial organisations at an early stage, rather than for the judicial organisation to be organised and administered at the zonal level.

143. 463/929 Wiesbaden. Headquarters, U.S. Forces, European Theater: Plan für die Justizverwaltung amerikanische Zone, 4. Oktober 1945.

144. *Monthly Report of the Military Governor, U.S. Zone*, 20 November 1945, No. 4.

145. 463/929 Wiesbaden. Headquarters, U.S. Forces, European Theater: Plan für die Justizverwaltung amerikanische Zone, 4. Oktober 1945.

146. Neidhard, "Die Rechtspflege in der Gesetzgebung der amerikanischen Zone,": 85.

147. 463/929 Wiesbaden. Headquarters, U.S. Forces, European Theater: Plan für die Justizverwaltung amerikanische Zone, 4. Oktober 1945.

148. 463/929, Wiesbaden. Headquarters, U.S. Forces, European Theater: Plan für die Justizverwaltung amerikanische Zone, 4. Oktober 1945.

149. Steidle, Hermann, "Der Plan für den Aufbau des Rechtspflegewesens in der amerikanischen Zone," *Süddeutsche Juristenzeitung* (1946): 14–15.

150. "Der Aufbau der Justiz in der amerikanischen Zone: Groß-Hessen": 120.

151. "Justizverwaltungsnachrichten: Großhessen," *Süddeutsche Juristenzieitung* (1946): 18.

152. 463/929 Wiesbaden. Headquarters, U.S. Forces, European Theater: Plan für die Justizverwaltung amerikanische Zone, 4. Oktober 1945.

153. This amount was later raised to 2,000 RM, in accordance with Control Council Law No. 4 Art. 2. Neidhard, "Die Rechtspflege in der Gesetzgebung der amerikanischen Zone," p. 85; 8/189–3/18 RG 260 OMGUS. APO 758. Subject: "Administration of Justice," 28 December 1945.

154. Steidle, "Der Plan für den Aufbau des Rechtspflegewesens in der amerikanischen Zone,": 14–15.

155. 463/929 Wiesbaden. Headquarters, U.S. Forces, European Theater: Plan für die Justizverwaltung amerikanische Zone, 4. Oktober 1945.

156. Nobleman, "Administration of Justice," 91.

157. Stolleis, "Rechtsordnung und Justizpolitik: 1945–1949," 396.

158. Clay, *Decision in Germany*, 248. Apart from Control Council enactments regarding the reform of justice in Germany, the restoration of the German administration of justice was organised differently in the four occupation zones. *Land* Ministries of Justice were established in the U.S. and French zones as the leading authority of the administration of justice at the *Land* level; the administrations of justice in the British and the Soviet zones were established at the zonal level. Friedmann, *Allied Military Government of Germany*, pp. 170–171; Wrobel, *Veruteilt zur Demokratie*, pp. 111–119.

159. Loewenstein, "Reconstruction of the Administration of Justice," 428;

160. RG 260 OMGUS, 17/210–2/6, Wiesbaden. APO 758. Subject: "Administration of Justice, Land Greater Hesse," 20 November 1945.

161. Loewenstein, "Reconstruction of the Administration of Justice," 429.

162. 502/919, Wiesbaden. Office of the Military Government for Greater Hesse. "Organisationsheft Nr. 2," 14. Oktober 1945.

163. 463/929 Wiesbaden. Headquarters, U.S. Forces, European Theater: Plan für die Justizverwaltung amerikanische Zone, 4. Oktober 1945.

164. Georg-August Zinn, "Administration of Justice in Germany," *Annals of the American Academy of Political and Social Science* Vol. 260 (November 1948): 35.

165. Heinz Guradze, "The Laenderrat: Landmark of German Reconstruction," *Western Political Quarterly*, Vol. 3 (June 1950): 191.

166. Pollock and Meisel, *Germany under Occupation*, pp. 126–127; *Monthly Report of the Military Governor, U.S. Zone*, May 1948, No. 35.

167. Ziemke, *U.S. Army in the Occupation of Germany*, 404.

168. von Elmenau, "Aufbau und Tätigkeit des Länderrats der U.S.-Zone," 113.

169. *Monthly Report of the Military Governor, U.S. Zone*, February 1949, No. 44.

170. Velma Hastings Cassidy, "The Beginning of Self-government in the American Zone of Germany," *Department of State Bulletin* Vol. 16 (1947): 231–232; Pollock and Meisel, *Germany under Occupation*, pp. 128–135.

171. *Monthly Report of the Military Governor, U.S. Zone*, 20 March 1946, No. 8; Pollock and Meisel, *Germany under Occupation*: 127–128.

172. Clay, *Decision in Germany*, 61.

173. Guradze, "Laenderrat," 195.

174. Härtel, *Der Länderrat des amerikanischen Besatzungsgebietes*, 210–211.

175. *Monthly Report of the Military Governor, U.S. Zone*, February 1949, No. 44.

176. Loewenstein, "Law and the Legislative Process in Occupied Germany," 1004.

177. Härtel, *Der Länderrat des amerikanischen Besatzungsgebietes*, 88.

178. Z1/1213 Koblenz. "Report on the meeting of the three Ministries of Justice of Württemberg-Baden, Bayern and Groß-Hessen." DR.H./1a, 18/12/46.

179. Loewenstein, "Law and the Legislative Process in Occupied Germany," p. 726, note 10.

180. Ibid., 1005.

181. von Elmenau, "Aufbau und Tätigkeit des Länderrats der U.S.-Zone," 116.

182. Loewenstein, "Law and the Legislative Process in Occupied Germany," 1006.

183. Härtel, *Der Länderrat des amerikanischen Besatzungsgebietes*, 88.

184. *Monthly Report of the Military Governor, U.S. Zone*, 20 March 1946, No. 8.

185. 502/1895, Wiesbaden. OMG for Germany (U.S.) Office of the Military Governor. APO 742. AG 010.1 (CA). Subject: "Relationship between the Military and Civil Government (U.S. Zone) Subsequent to Adoption of Land Constitutions," 30 September 1946.

186. Clay, *Decision in Germany*, 89.

187. 502/1895 Wiesbaden. OMG for Germany (U.S.) Office of the Military Governor. APO 742. AG 010.1 (CA). Subject: "Relationship between the Military and Civil Government (U.S. Zone) Subsequent to Adoption of Land Constitutions," 30 September 1946.

188. *Monthly Report of the Military Governor, U.S. Zone*, 20 February 1946, No. 7.

189. *Monthly Report of the Military Governor, U.S. Zone*, 20 July 1946, No. 12. The seats won by the various parties in Hesse were as follows: CDU/CSU 35; SPD 42; LDP/DVP/FDP 6; KPD 7.

190. Arndt, "Die staats- und verwaltungsrechtliche Entwicklung in Groß-Hessen," 186.

191. *Monthly Report of the Military Governor, U.S. Zone*, 31 October 1946, No. 16; Clay, *Decision in Germany*, 89.

192. *Monthly Report of the Military Governor, U.S. Zone*, 31 October 1946, No. 16.

193. Kropat, *Hessen in der Stunde Null*, 121.

194. Clay, *Decision in Germany*, 90. The name of the state was changed from "Greater Hesse" to "Hesse" upon the adoption of the constitution, since "Greater Hesse" was considered too reminiscent of the National Socialist "Greater Germany"

(Groß-Deutschland), Walter Mühlhausen, *Hessen 1945–1950: Zur politischen Geschichte eienes Landes in der Besatzungszeit* (Frankfurt-am-Main: Insel Verlag, 1985), 41.

195. Dieter Gosewinkel, *Adolf Arnt: Die Wiederbegründung des Rechtsstaats aus dem Geist der Sozialdemokratie, 1945–1961* (Bonn: Verlag J. H. W. Dietz Nachf., 1991), 97.

196. Adolf Arndt, "Status and Development of Constitutional Law in Germany," *Annals of the American Academy of Political and Social Science* (July 1948) Vol. 258: 5.

197. "Verfassung des Landes Hessen," VI. "Die Gesetzgebung" Arts. 116–125, *passim, Gesetz—und Verordnungsblatt für das Land Groß-Hessen* (1946): 237.

198. Härtel, *Der Länderrat des amerikanischen Besatzungsgebietes*, 88.

199. Zink, *The United States in Germany: 1944–1955*, 307.

200. Loewenstein, "Law and the Legislative Process in Occupied Germany," 1010.

201. "Verfassung des Landes Hessen," *Gesetz—und Verordnungsblatt für das Land Groß-Hessen* (1946), VII. "Die Rechtspflege," Art. 126: 237.

202. Gosewinkel, *Adolf Arndt: Die Wiederbegrüundung des Rechtsstaats aus dem Geist der Sozialdemokratie*, 134.

203. "Verfassung des Landes Hessen," *Gesetz—und Verordnungsblatt für das Land Groß-Hessen* (1946), VIII. "Der Staatsgerichtshof," Art. 131: 238.

204. Ibid., VII. "Die Rechtspflege," Art. 127: 237.

205. Z1/1283, Koblenz. Amt der Militärregierung für Hessen, Büro des Direktors, APO 633, Recht 312, EA/jh, Wiesbaden, 21.7.1947. "Betr.: Rechtsprechung"; Z45F 17/199–3/41 RG 260/ OMGUS, Koblenz. Office of Military Governor APO 742. "Subject: Administration of Justice," 13 June 1947.

206. Z1/1283, Koblenz. Amt der Militärregierung für Hessen, Büro des Direktors, APO 633, Recht 312, EA/jh, Wiesbaden, 21.7.1947. "Betr.: Rechtsprechung"; Z45F 17/199–3/41 RG 260/ OMGUS, Koblenz. Office of Military Governor APO 742. "Subject: Administration of Justice," 13 June 1947.

207. 463/929, Wiesbaden. 3200—Ia 1195, Betr.: "Sitz und Bezirk der Gerichte; Einteilung der Amts- und Landgerichtebezirke; Wiederöffnung von Voll- und Zweigsgerichten," 29 May 1947.

208. "Die Gesetzgebung der Länder (amerikanische Zone): Hessen," *Süddeutsche Juristenzeitung* (1946): 564.

209. "Verordnung über die Weitergeltung des Rechtspflege-Aufbauplans vom 14. April 1948"; "Anlage zur Verordnung über die Weitergeltung des Rechtspflege-Aufbauplans vom 14. April 1948," *Gesetz—und Verordnungsblatt für das Land Hessen* (1948): 71.

210. "Verfassung des Landes Hessen," *Gesetz—und Verordnungsblatt für das Land Groß-Hessen* (1946), VII. "Die Rechtspflege," Art. 127: 237.

211. 458/1021, Wiesbaden. 2052—Ib 2163. "Runderlass Über die Dienstbezeichnung der richterlichen Beamten," 9 September 1947.

212. "Verordnung über die Weitergeltung des Rechtspflege-Aufbauplans vom 14. April 1948"; "Anlage zur Verordnung über die Weitergeltung des Rechtspflege-Aufbauplans vom 14. April 1948," *Gesetz—und Verordnungsblatt für das Land Hessen* (1948): 71.

213. "Gesetz über den Staatsgerichtshof vom 12. Dezember 1947," *Gesetz—und Verordnungsblatt für das Land Hessen* 1948: 3–8; *Monthly Report of the Military Governor, U.S. Zone*, December 1947, No. 30.

214. Zinn, "Administration of Justice in Germany," 36.

215. Friedmann, *The Allied Military Government of Germany*, 82–83, 10.

216. Loewenstein, "Justice," 239.

217: "Law No. 36: Administrative Courts," *Official Gazette of the Control Council* No. 11 (31 October 1946): 183; *Monthly Report of the Military Governor, U.S. Zone*, 31 October 1946, No. 16.

218: Wilhelm Bauer, "Wierderaufbau der Verwaltungsrechtspflege," *Süddeutsche Juristenzeitung* (1946): 150.

219. Loewenstein, "Justice," 240.

220. *Monthly Reports of the Military Governor, U.S. Zone*, 20 October 1945, No. 3.

221. Bauer, "Wiederaufbau der Verwaltungsrechtspflege," 149.

222. Ibid., 152.

223. Clay, *Decision in Germany*, 248.

224. *Monthly Reports of the Military Governor, U.S. Zone*, 20 November 1945.

225. "Die Gesetzgebung der Länder: Verwaltungsrechtspflege," *Süddeutsche Juristenzeitung* (1946): 130.

226. Loewenstein, "Reconstruction of the Administration of Justice," 427.

227. 501/1892, Wiesbaden. Subject: "Reopening of Administrative Courts in Land Greater Hesse," 25.9.1946. Tgb: Nr. M845/46, Ku/St.

228. 1126/11, Wiesbaden. "Verordunung über die Wiedereinführung der Verwaltungsgerichtsbarkeit," 16. August 1946.

229. 1126/11, Wiesbaden. "Begründung zu dem Entwurf einer Verordnung über die Wiedereinführung der Verwaltungsgerichtsbarkeit."

230. *Monthly Report of the Military Governor, U.S. Zone*, 31 October 1946, No. 16.

231. "Die Gesetzgebung der Länder: Verwaltungsrechtspflege," p. 131.

232. Klaus Mehnert and Heinrich Schulte, eds. *Deutschland-Jahrbuch 1949* (Essen: West-Verlag, 1949), 33.

233. "Gesetz über die Verwaltungsgerichtsbarkeit vom 31. Oktober 1946," *Gesetz—und Verordnungsblatt für das Land Groß-Hessen* (1946): 194–203.

234. *Monthly Report of the Military Governor, U.S. Zone*, 31 January 1947, No. 19.

235. "Der Gesetzgebung der Länder (amerikanische Zone): Hessen," *Süddeutsche Juristenzeitung* (1947): 222; "Erste Ausführungs des Gesetzes über die Verwaltungsgerichtsbarkeit vom 26. Februar 1947," *Staats-Anzeiger für das Land Hessen*: 117.

236. Freeman, *Hesse: A New German State*, 69.

237. Günther Edelmann, "Der Einfluß des Besatzungsrechts auf das deutsche Staatsrecht der Übergangszeit (1945–1949), 46.

238. Diestelkamp, "Die Justiz in den Westzonen," 20.

239. "Arbeitsgerichtsgesetz vom 23. Dezember 1926," *Reichsgesetzblatt* I 1926: 507–524.

240. "Law No. 40: Repeal of the Law of 20 January 1934 on 'The Organization of National Labor,'" *Official Gazette of the Control Council for Germany* No. 12 (30 November 1947): 229.

241. "Law No. 56: Repeal of the Law of 23 March, on the Regulation of Labour in Public Administrations and Enterprises," *Official Gazette of the Control Council for Germany* No. 16 (31 July 1947): 287.

242. 458/1014, Wiesbaden. 7650. III 1299. Betr.: "Arbeitsgerichtliche Streitigkeiten," 30 September 1946.

243. Loewenstein, "Law and the Legislative Process in Occupied Germany," 755.

244. "Directive No. 14: Wage Policy" 12 October 1945, *Official Gazette of the Control Council for Germany* No. 3 (31 January 1946): 40–41.

245. "Directive No. 26: Regulation of Working Hours" 26 January 1946, *Official Gazette of the Control Council for Germany* No. 5 (31 March 1946): 115–116.

246. "Directive No. 31: Principles Concerning the Establishment of Federations of Trade Unions," 3 June 1946, *Official Gazette of the Control Council for Germany* No. 8 (1 July 1946): 160–161.

247. "Directive No. 29: Establishment of Advisory Committees (Beratungsausschüsse) at the Labor Offices," 17 May 1946, *Official Gazette of the Control Council for Germany* No. 7 (31 May 1946): 152.

248. "Law No. 22: Works Councils," 10 April 1946, *Official Gazette of the Control Council for Germany* No. 6 (30 April 1946): 133–135.

249. "Law No. 35: Conciliation and Arbitration Machinery in Labor Conflicts," 20 August 1946, *Official Gazette of the Control Council for Germany* No. 10 (31 August 1946): 174–177.

250. "Law No. 21: German Labour Courts," 30 March 1946, *Official Gazette of the Control Council for Germany* No. 5 (31 March 1946): 124–127.

251. "Rechtspflege: Gerichtsverfassung," *Süddeutsche Jursitenzeitung* (1946): 19.

252. RG 260 OMGUS. 8/188–2/5. APO 633. Subject: "Weekly Summary Report for Legal Division from 25 August to 31 August 1946," 30 August 1946.

253. Z1/674 Koblenz. "Stellungnahme der Unterschusses Arbeitsrecht vom 5.7.1946."

254. *Monthly Report of the Military Governor, U.S. Zone*, 31 December 1946, No. 18.

255. "Rechtspflege: Gerichtsverfassung," *Süddeutsche Juristenzeitung* (1946): 19.

256. Taylor Cole, "The Role of the Labor Courts in Western Germany," *The Journal of Politics* Vol. 18 (1956): 480.

257. "Die Gesetzgebung der Länder (amerikanische Zone): Hessen," *Süddeutsche Juristenzeitung* (1948): 344.

258. 458/1014, Wiesbaden. 7650. III 1299. Betr.: Arbeitsgerichtliche Streitigkeiten," 30 September 1946.

259. Arndt, "Die staats—und verwaltungsrechtliche Entwicklung in Groß-Hessen," 187.

260. "Gesetz vom 30. März 1948 zur Änderung des Arbeitsgerichtsgesetzes vom 27. August 1947," *Gesetz—und Verordnungsblatt für das Land Hessen* (1948): 57.

261. "Arbeitsgerichtsgesetz vom 27. August 1947 in der Fassung vom 30. März 1947 in der Fassung vom 30. März 1948," *Gesetz—und Verordnungsblatt für das Land Hessen* (1948): 57–64.

262. John B. Holt, "Corporative Occupational Organization and Democracy in Germany," *Public Administration Review* Vol. 8 (1948): 34.

263. 463/929, Wiesbaden. Headquarters, U.S. Forces, European Theater: Plan für die Justizverwaltung amerikanische Zone, 4. Oktober 1945.

264. 462/1308, Wiesbaden. Subject: Admission to the Bar, 12 November 1945.

265. 1126/11, Wiesbaden. "Abschrift" (n.d.).

266. *Monthly Report of the Military Governor, U.S. Zone*, 31 October 1946, No. 16.

267. Z45F 17/56–3/7 RG 260/OMGUS, Koblenz. Provenance OMGUS LD, LA Br., Folder Title: LA 91 The German Government, German Courts. Subject: Draft of the New Law on the Reconstruction of the German Bar (*Rechtsanwaltsordnung*) 10 June 1946 KL/nf.

268. 1126/11, Wiesbaden. "Abschrift" (n.d.).

269. *Monthly Report of the Military Governor, U.S. Zone*, 31 October 1946, No. 16.

270. "Gemeinsame Gesetzgebung der Länder," *Süddeutsche Juristenzeitung* (1947): 223.

271. Loewenstein, "Reconstruction of the Administration of Justice," 457.

272. "Gemeinsame Gesetzgegung der Länder: Stand vom 14.3.47," *Süddeutsche Juristenzeitung* (1947): 223.

273. "Rechtsanwaltsordnung 1946 vom 6. November 1946," Arts. 41(1), (2), *Bayerisches Gesetz—und Verordnungsblatt* (30 December 1946): 374.

274. Ibid., Arts. 41–103 *passim*, 374–379.

275. *Monthly Report of the Military Governor, U.S. Zone*, 31 October 1946, No. 16.

276. "Rechtsanwaltsordnung 1946," Art. 6 Übergangsbestimmungen, *Bayerisches Gesetz und Verordnungsblatt*: 380.

277. Ibid., Art. 4 Übergangsbestimmungen: 379.

278. Loewenstein, "Reconstruction of the Administration of Justice," 441.

279. Ibid.

280. "Rechtsanwaltsordnung 1946," Art. 28(a), *Bayerisches Gesetz und Verordnungsblatt* 1946: 373.

281. Loewenstein, "Law and the Legislative Process in Occupied Germany," 1018.

282. "Der Aufbau der Justiz in der amerikanischen Zone: Groß-Hessen," 120.

283. Mehnert and Schulte, *Deutschland Jahrbuch*, 98.

284. "Verordung über vorübergehende Maßnahmen in der Strafrechtspflege" vom 23.5.1946, *Gesetz—und Verordnungsblatt für das Land Groß-Hessen* (1946): 164.

285. "Verordnung über das Sofortverfahren in Strafsachen vom 4. April 1946," *Gesetz—und Verordnungsblatt für das Land Groß-Hessen* (1946): 99.

286. "Zweite Durchführungsverordnung vom 12. 6. 1946 zur Verordnung über das Sofortverfahren in Strafsachen," *Gesetz—und Verordnungsblatt für das Land Groß-Hessen* (1946): 164.

287. "Der Aufbau der Justiz in der amerikanischen Zone: Groß-Hessen," 120.

288. *Monthly Report of the Military Governor, U.S. Zone*, 20 March 1946, No. 8.

289. Loewenstein, "Law and the Legislative Process in Occupied Germany," 1012–1013.

290. Ibid., 1018–1019.

291. *Monthly Report of the Military Governor, U.S. Zone*, 20 October 1945, No. 3.

292. Loewenstein, "Law and the Legislative Process in Occupied Germany," 1018–1019.

293. *Monthly Report of the Military Governor, U.S. Zone*, 20 February 1946, No. 7.

294. RG 260 OMGUS, 17/210–2/6, Wiesbaden. APO 633. Subject: "Change of Existing Laws of the Länder to Deprive the German Police of their Legislative Powers and their Authority to Adjudicate Offences," 21 January 1946.

295. "Gesetz zur Überleitung des Strafverfügungsrechts der Polizeibehörden auf die Gerichte von 16. Mai 1946," *Gesetz – und Verordnungsblatt für das Land Groß-Hessen* (1946): 164.

296. Loewenstein, "Law and the Legislative Process in Occupied Germany," 1018–1019.

297. "Gemeinsame Gesetzgebung der Länder," *Süddeutsche Juristenzeitung* (1946): 17.

298. RG 260 OMGUS, 17/210–3/3, Wiesbaden. APO 633. Subject: Enactment of German Codes for Administration. 11 February 1946.

299. "1. Section III of the Ordinance on Measures in the Field of the Legal Constitution and of the Administration of Justice of 1 September 1939" *Reichsgesetzblatt* I: 1658; 2. "The Law for the Change of Regulations of the General Criminal Procedure, of the *Wehrmacht* Criminal Procedure and of the Resolution on Criminal Law of 16 September 1939" *Reichsgesetzblatt* I: 1841; 3. "The Ordinance on the Responsibility of the Criminal Courts, of the Special Courts and other Regulations on Criminal Proceedings of 21 February 1940" *Reichsgesetzblatt* I: 405; 4. "The Ordinance on further Simplification of the Administration of Criminal Justice of 13 August 1942" *Reichsgesetzblatt* I: 508; 5. "The Decree for the Further Adjustment of the Administration of Criminal Justice to the Requirements of Total War of 13 December 1944" *Reichsgesetzblatt* I: 339. "Einführungsgesetz zur Strafrechtspflegeordnung 1946 vom 21. Februar 1946," *Gesetz—und Verordnungsblatt für das Land Groß-Hessen* 1946: 13.

300. Ibid., 13–14.

301. "Proclamation No. 2" Art. 2, *Military Government Gazette* Issue A, 1 June 1946: 2–3.

302. Loewenstein, "Law and the Legislative Process in Occupied Germany," 736–737.

303. Z45F 11/5–2/1, Koblenz. RG 260 OMGUS, LD. Folder Title: Legal Division History. "Interview with Dr. Karl Loewenstein."

304. Loewenstein, "Law and the Legislative Process in Occupied Germany," 736–737.

305. 463/929, Wiesbaden. Headquarters, U.S. Forces, European Theater: Plan für die Justizverwaltung amerikanische Zone, 4. Oktober 1945.

306. Loewenstein, "Law and the Legislative Process in Occupied Germany," 737–738.

307. Ibid., 738–739.

308. Ibid., 739.

309. Elmer Plischke, "Denazification Law and Procedure," *American Journal of International Law*, Vol. 14 (October 1947): 811.

310. Lowenstein, "Law in Occupied Germany," 739–740.

311. *Monthly Report of the Military Governor, U.S. Zone*, 20 April 1946, No. 9.

312. Z45F 17/56–3/7 RG 260/OMGUS, Koblenz. Provenance: OMGUS, LD, LA Br., Folder Title: LA 91 The German Government, German Courts. Subject: Reform of German Law, APO 633, U.S. Army, 9 August 1946; request presented to Minister of Justice for Greater Hesse. Subject: Reform of German Law, APO 154, U.S. Army, 7 August 1946; request presented to Minister of Justice for Württemberg-Baden. Subject: Reform of German Law, APO 170, U.S. Army, 6 August 1946.

313. Ibid.

314. Ibid., 740–41.

315. "Law No. 11: Repealing of Certain Provisions of the German Criminal Law," 30 January 1946, *Official Gazette of the Control Council for Germany* No. 3 (31 January 1946): 55–57.

316. *Monthly Report of the Military Governor, U.S. Zone*, 20 February 1946, No. 7.

317. "Zur Auswirkung der Gesetzgebung der Besatzungsmächte auf das deutsche Strafgesetzbuch," *Süddeutsche Juristenzeitung* (1946): 121.

318. Z1/1230, Koblenz. Office of Military Government for Germany (U.S.), Legal Division APO 742, 27 September 1946. "Subject: Revision of German Criminal Code."

319. 463/929, Wiesbaden. Der Minister der Justiz, 1030—Ia 1126, 19 June 1946. An den Herrn Oberlandesgerichtspräsidenten in Frankfurt/Main, sämtliche Herren Landesgerichtspräsidenten, Oberstaatsanwälte, Generalstaatsanwalt in Frankfurt/Main, Amtsgerichtspräsidenten in Frankfurt/Main.

320. "Law No. 55: Repeal of Certain Provisions of Criminal Legislation," 20 June 1947, *Official Gazette of the Control Council for Germany* No. 16 (31 July 1947): 284–286.

321. Loewenstein, "Law and the Legislative Process in Occupied Germany," 752.

322. Ibid., p. 735; Bernhard Diestelkamp, "Kontinuität und Wandel in der Rechtsordnung: 1945 bis 1955," *Westdeutschland 1945–1955: Unterwerfung, Kontrolle, Integration*, ed. Ludolf Herbst, (München: R. Oldenbourg Verlag, 1986), 98.

323. Mehnert and Schulte, *Deutschland Jahrbuch 1949*, 88.

324. "Law No. 16: Marriage Law," 1 March 1946, *Official Gazette of the Control Council for Germany* No. 4 (28 February 1946): 77–94.

325. Loewenstein, "Law and the Legislative Process in Occupied Germany," fn. 50 737–738, 753.

326. Max Eisenberg, "Zur Gültigkeit der Durchführungsbestimmungen zum Ehegesetz 38," *Süddeutsche Juristenzeitung* (1946): 79.

327. Freeman, *Hesse: A New German State*, 135.

328. Z45 F 17/56–3/7 RG 260/ OMGUS, Koblenz. AJ 015.2, 18 November 1946 HMR/f, Subject: Report on Inspection of German Courts in Greater Hesse from 28 October to 4 November 1946.

329. Freeman, *Hesse: A New German State*, 135.

330. Mehnert and Schulte, *Deutschland-Jahrbuch 1949*, 88.

331. "Law No. 37: Repeal of Certain Statutory Provisions Relating to Successions," 30 October 1946, *Official Gazette of the Control Council* No. 11 (31 October 1946): 220.

332. Wilhelm Meiss, "Zur Frage der Weitergeltung des § 48 Abs. 2 des Testamentgesetzes und der Erbregelungsverordnung vom 4. Oktober 1944," *Süddeutsche Juristenzeitung* (1946): 66.

333. Law No. 45: Repeal of Legislation on Hereditary Farms and Enactment of other Provisions Regulating Agricultural Forest Lands," 20 February 1947, *Official Gaztte of the Control Council for Germany* No. 14 (31 May 1947): 256–261.

334. "Law No. 60: Repealing Nazi Legislation on Motion Pictures," 24 December 1947, *Official Gazette of the Control Council for Germany* No. 18 (31 January 1948): 296.

335. *Monthly Report of the Military Governor, U.S. Zone*, December 1947, No. 30.

336. "Law No. 62: Repealing Certain Laws, Ordinances, and Decrees Promulgated by the Nazi Government concerning Churches," 20 March 1948, *Official Gazette of the Control Council for Germany* No. 19 (31 August 1948): 104.

337. *Monthly Report of the Military Governor, U.S. Zone*, February 1948, No. 32.

338. Loewenstein, "Law and the Legislative Process in Occupied Germany,"; Clay, *Decision in Germany*, 154–155.

339. *Monthly Report of the Military Governor, U.S. Zone*, March 1948, No. 33.

340. Loewenstein, "Reconstruction of the Administration of Justice," 438–439.

341. 460/568, Wiesbaden. 313a E-Bl. 19. Betr.: Wochen und Monatsberichte, 16 February 1946.

342. Z1/1289, Koblenz. Office of Military Government for Germany (U.S.), Legal Division APO 742, 3 June 1946.

343. 460/570, Wiesbaden. U.S. Military Government for Germany; Instructions to Military Government; General. 1 January 1946.

344. Loewenstein, "Reconstruction of the Administration of Justice," 439.

345. Z45F 11/5–2/1, Koblenz. OMGUS, LD. Legal History. Interview with Dr. Karl Loewenstein.

346. Freeman, *Hesse: A New German State*, p. 135.

347. Z45F 11/5–2/1, Koblenz. OMGUS, LD. Legal History. "Interview with Dr. Karl Loewenstein."

348. *Monthly Report of the Military Governor, U.S. Zone*, 20 February 1946, No. 7.

349. *Monthly Report of the Military Governor, U.S. Zone*, 20 March 1946, No. 8.

350. Franz, Hofmann, Schaab, *Gerichtorganisation*, 184.

351. "Verordnung über die Errichtung eines Oberlandesgerichts für Groß-Hessen vom 23. Mai 1946," *Gesetz—und Verordnungsblatt für das Land Groß-Hessen* (1946): 137–138.

352. "Law No. 2: German Courts," Art. 6, para. 10(d), *Military Government Gazette* Issue A, 1 June 1946: 9.

353. Nobleman, "Administration of Justice in the United States Zone of Germany," 77.

354. Loewenstein, "Reconstruction of the Administration of Justice," 423.

355. Nobleman, "Administration of Justice," 96.

356. "Regulation No. 2 under Military Government Law No. 2: Testimony in German Courts by Persons Subject to United States Military Law and by Persons Associated with the United States Office of Military Government," *Military Government Gazette, Germany, United States Zone*, Issue B, 1 December 1946, pp. 3–4; *Monthly Report of the Military Governor, U.S. Zone*, 20 August 1946, No. 13.

357. Loewenstein, "Reconstruction of the Administration of Justice," 421–422.

358. "Amendment No. 2 to Military Government Law No. 2: Limitations Upon the Jurisdiction of German Courts," *Military Government Gazette, Germany, United States Zone*, Issue B, 1 December 1946: 1–3.

359. Z45F 17/56–3/7 RG 260/ OMGUS, Koblenz. Office of Military Government for Germany (U.S.), Office of the Military Governor, APO 742, AG 010 (LD), 2 October 1946.

360. Art. 1, "Amendment No. 2 to Military Government Law No. 2: Limitations Upon the Jurisdiction of German Courts," *Military Government Gazette* Issue B, 1 December 1946, p. 1.

361. Ibid., 2.

362. Ibid.

363. Military Government Ordinance No. 6 of 21 May 1946 originally set forth the terms for the composition and function of a military government court exercising the sole jurisdiction in such cases. *Monthly Report of the Military Governor, U.S. Zone*, 20 June 1946, No. 11; "Ordinance No. 6: Military Government Court for Civil Actions," *Military Government Gazette*, Issue A, 1 June 1946: 73–78 *passim*.

364. Art. 1, "Amendment No. 2 to Military Government Law No. 2: Limitations upon the Jurisdiction of German Courts," *Military Government Gazette* Issue B, 1 December 1946: 1.

365. Neidhard, "Die Gerichtsbarkeit der deutschen Gerichte und der Besatzungsgerichte in der amerikanischen Zone," 183–184.

366. Z1/1255 Koblenz. "Betr.: Erweiterte deutsche Gerichtsbarkeit," 13. Januar 1947.

367. Loewenstein, "Reconstruction of the Administration of Justice," 425.

368. "Amendment No. 1 to Military Government Law No. 2," *Military Government Gazette, Germany, United States Zone*, Issue A, 1 June 1946: 10.

369. Art. 2, "Amendment No. 2 to Military Government Law No. 2: Limitations Upon the Jurisdiction of German Courts," *Military Government Gazette* Issue B, 1 December 1946: 2.

370. Art. 3, "Amendment No. 2 to Military Government Law No. 2: Limitations Upon the Jurisdiction of German Courts," *Military Government Gazette* Issue B, 1 December 1946: 2–3; *Monthly Report of the Military Governor, U.S. Zone*, 20 September 1946, No. 15.

371. Breuning, "Die Beschränkung der deutschen Gerichtsbarkeit," 15.

372. Ibid., 18–19.

373. 463/1118 Wiesbaden. 9180—Ia 2283. U.S. Zone Ordinance No. 8: Military Tribunal for Security Violations, 29 November 1946.

374. *Monthly Report of the Military Governor, U.S. Zone*, 30 November 1946, No. 17.

375. 463/929, Wiesbaden. 3120—IIa 881, Betr.: "Die Zuständigkeit der deutschen Gerichte," 17 June 1947.

376. Z45F 17/56–3/7, Koblenz. RG 260/OMGUS, OMGUS LD, LA Br. LA 91, The German Government, German courts, 015 (AG), 20 November 1946, Subject: Supervision of German Courts.

377. Loewenstein, "Reconstruction of the Administration of Justice," 438–440.

378. Ibid., 440.

379. Ibid., 440–441.

380. Ibid., p. 440.

381. 1126/33, Wiesbaden. "Radio-Rede [Geiler] über Deutschland als Rechtsstaat" (n.d.).

382. 458/1014, Wiesbaden. 3222—II 511/45, Runderlaß Betr.: "Die Bildung von Schöffengerichtsbezirken," 22 October 1946.

383. 458/1015, Wiesbaden. 3220—Ia 548, Betr.: "Bildung von Schöffengerichten, Erlaß vom 22.10.1946," 25 April 1947.

384. "Anordnung über die Bildung von Schöffengerichten und Schwurgerichten vom 17. April 1947," *Gesetz—und Verordnungsblatt für das Land Hessen* (1947): 49–51.

385. 458/1015, Wiesbaden. Betr.: "Bildung der Schöffengerichte und Schwurgerichte," 30 October 1947.

386. Z1/1282, Koblenz. "Wieder Geschorene und Schöffen," Nr. 46588, *Frankfurter Rundschau* Nr. 132, 11.11.47.

387. *Das Besatzungsregime auf dem Gebiet der Rechtspflege*, 28–29; Heinrich Röhreke, "Die Besatzungsgewalt auf den Gebiete der Rechtspflege," 44.

388. Mehnert and Schulte, *Deutschland-Jahrbuch 1949*, 104.

389. Martin Broszat, "Siegerjustiz oder strafrechtliche 'Selbstreinigung': Aspekte der Vergangenheitsbewältigung der deutschen Justiz während der Besatzungszeit 1945–1949?" *Vierteljahrshefte für Zeitgeschichte* Vol. 29 (1981): 497–499.

390. Loewenstein, "Reconstruction of the Administration of Justice," 434–435.

391. Wolfgang Benz, "Die Entnazifizierung der Richter," *Justizalltag im Dritten Reich*, eds. Bernhard Diestelkamp and Michael Stolleis (Frankfurt-am-Main: Fischer Taschenbuch Verlag, 1988), 114.

392. Noakes and Pridham, *Documents on Nazism*, 226–227.

393. Loewenstein, "Justice," 252–254.

394. Gustav Radbruch, "Gesetzliches Unrecht und übergesetzliches Recht," *Süddeutsche Juristenzeitung* (1946): 105, 107.

395. Helmut Coing, "Zur Frage der strafrechtlichen Haftung der Richter für die Anwendung naturrechtswidriger Gesetze," *Süddeutsche Juristenzeitung* (1946): 61–62.

396. Edgar Bodenheimer, "Significant Developments in German Legal Philosophy since 1945," *American Journal of Comparative Law* Vol. 3 (1954): 380, 387.

397. Heinz Kleine, "Wiedergutmachungsrecht," *Süddeutsche Juristenzeitung* (1946): 36.

398. Adolf Arnt, "Das Strafmaß," *Süddeutsche Juristenzeitung* (1946): 30.

399. 8/216–1/12, RG OMGUS 260, Wiesbaden. APO 633. [letter to] Mr. ____ ____ ____, 15 June 1949.

400. Loewenstein, "Law and the Legislative Process in Occupied Germany," 727.

401. *Germany 1947–1949: The Story in Documents* (Washington D.C.: U.S. Government Printing Office, 1950), 157–158.

402. Arndt, "Status and Development of Constitutional Law in Germany," 6.

403. *Monthly Report of the Military Governor, U.S. Zone*, 31 March 1947, No. 21; Z1/218 Koblenz. Office of the Military Governor APO 742. "Subject: Revision of MGR Title 5, Section B, 'German Legislation,'" AG 010.6 (LD), 1 March 1947.

404. "Proclamation No. 2," Art. 3, *Military Government Gazette, Germany, United States Zone* Issue A 1 June 1946: 3

405. *Monthly Report of the Military Governor, U.S. Zone*, 31 March 1947, No. 21.

406. *Monthly Report of the Military Governor, U.S. Zone*, 30 April 1947, No. 22.

407. Z45F 11/5–2/1, Koblenz. OMGUS, LD. Legal Division History.

408. "Military Government of Germany: Text of Directive to Commander-in-Chief of U.S. Forces of Occupation, Regarding the Military Government of Germany, 11 July 1947," *U.S. Department of State Bulletin*, Vol. 17 (1947): 186.

409. "Third Session of the Council of Foreign Ministers, New York City, November 4–December 12: Preliminary Plans for Peace Settlements with Germany and Austria," *U.S. Department of State Bulletin* Vol. 16 (1947): 186.

410. Ibid., p. 188.

411. Loewenstein, "Law and the Legislative Process in Occupied Germany," 731–732.

412. "Preliminary Plans for Peace Settlements with Germany and Austria," *U.S. Department of State Bulletin* Vol. 16 (1947): 188.

413. Loewenstein, "Law and the Legislative Process in Occupied Germany," 1015.

414. "Preliminary Plans for Peace Settlements with Germany and Austria," *U.S. Department of State Bulletin* Vol. 16 (1947): 188.

415. Freeman, *Hesse: A New German State*, p. 135; RG 260 OMGUS, 8/188–2/5, Wiesbaden. APO 633. "Weekly Summary Report of Legal Division from 30 June 1946 to 28 December 1946," 20 December 1946.

416. *Monthly Report of the Military Governor, U.S. Zone*, 30 September 1947, No. 27.

417. Ibid.

418. *Monthly Report of the Military Governor, U.S. Zone*, 1 October 1947, No. 28.

419. 17/211–2/3, RG260 OMGUS, Wiesbaden. "Military Government, Germany; Regulation No. 3 Under Military Government Law No. 2, as amended."

420. 463/929, Wiesbaden. 3120—IIIa 1992. Betr.: "Deutsche Gerichtsbarkeit bei Verfehlungen gegen die Kennkartenpflicht, bei unerlaubten Grenzübertritt und bei bestimmten Fällen des Diebstahls zum Nachteil der Vereinten Nationen," 22 August 1947.

421. 463/929, Wiesbaden. Betr.: "Zuständigkeit deutsche Gerichte," 26 July 1947; 17/211–2/3; RG 260/OMGUS, Wiesbaden. Subject: "Jurisdiction of German Courts," 26 July 1947; "Allgemeine Ermächtigung gemäß Art. VI, Abs. 10 des Militärregierungsgesetzes Nr. 2," *Gesetz—undVerordnungsblatt für das Land Hessen* (1947): 99–100.

422. Freeman, *Hesse: A New German State*, 137.

423. *Monthly Report of the Military Governor, U.S. Zone*, 31 July 1947, No. 25.

424. 458/1015, Wiesbaden. 3206—Ia 2147. Betr.:"Rheinschiffahrtsgerichte," 5 September 1947.

425. *Monthly Report of the Military Governor, U.S. Zone*, 31 July 1947, No. 25.

426. Ibid.

427. *Monthly Report of the Military Governor, U.S. Zone*, October 1947, No. 28.

428. *Monthly Report of the Military Governor, U.S. Zone*, February 1948, No. 32.

429. 463/929, Wiesbaden. 3120—IVa 257. Betr.: "Zuständigkeit der deutschen Gerichte," 23 January 1948.

430. RG 260 OMGUS, 8/189–3/3. Subject: "1948 Historical Report of Legal Division, OMG Hessen."

431. Types of cases that lay within the jurisdiction of an *Amtsgericht.*

432. 463/929, Wiesbaden. 3120—IVa 1626. Betr.: "Zuständigkeit der deutschen Gerichte," 27 April 1948; 8/213–1/18, RG 260 OMGUS, Wiesbaden. APO 633. Legal 015. Subject: "Jurisdiction of German Courts," 12 June 1948.

433. 463/929, Wiesbaden. 3120—IVa 3927. Betr.: "Zuständigkeit der deutschen Gerichte Strafbefehle gegen Angehörige der Vereinten Nationen oder Staatenlose, die als Verschleppte einer der Vereinten Nationen gelten," 14 September 1948; 8/217–1/5 RG 260 OMGUS, Wiesbaden. Subject: "Jurisdiction of German Courts," 24 August 1948.

434. 260 OMGUS, 8/189–3/3. Subject: "1948 Historical Report of Legal Division, OMG Hessen."

435. *Monthly Report of the Military Governor, U.S. Zone,* June 1948, No. 36.

436. "Ausführungsverordnung Nr. 4 zum Militärregierungsgesetz Nr. 2 (geänderte Fassung)," *Gesetz—und Verordnungsblatt für das Land Hessen* 1948: 57.

437. *Monthly Report of the Military Governor, U.S. Zone,* July 1948, No. 37.

438. "Allgemeine Ermächtigung gemäß Art. VI Abs. 10 des Militärregierungsgesetzes Nr. 2," *Beilage Nr. 8 zum "Gesetz—und Verordnungsblatt für das Land Hessen" vom 27. September 1948*; 463/929, Wiesbaden. "Allgemeine Ermächtigung gemäß Art. VI Abs. 10 des Militärregierungsgesetzes Nr. 2," 19 September 1948.

439. Clay, *Decision in Germany,* 247.

440. Zink, *United States in Germany: 1944–1955,* 309.

441. *Monthly Report of the Military Governor, U.S. Zone,* January 1948, No. 31; "Ordinance No. 23: Relief from Unlawful Restraints of Personal Liberty," *Military Government Gazette, Germany, United States Area of Control,* Issue H, 16 January 1948: 7–14.

442. Art. 4, "Ordinance No. 23: Relief from Unlawful Restraints of Personal Liberty," *Military Government Gazette, Germany, United States Area of Control,* Issue H, 16 January 1948: 8–9; *Monthly Report of the Military Governor, U.S. Zone,* February 1949, No. 44.

443. Nobleman, "American Military Government Courts in Germany," *Annals of the American Academy,* 92.

444. Clay, *Decision in Germany,* 247.

445. Nobleman, "American Military Government Courts," *Annals of the American Academy,* 92.

446. Zink, *United States in Germany: 1944–1955,* 309.

447. Nobleman, "American Military Government Courts in Germany," *Annals of the American Academy,* 92–93.

448. *Report on Germany: September 21, 1949—July 31, 1952* (Office of the High Commissioner for Germany, 1952): 146.

449. There were five judicial districts established in Bavaria, two in both Württemberg-Baden and Hesse, one in Bremen, and one in the U.S. sector of Berlin. There were one or more district judges and magistrates within each district. The jurisdiction of

the magistrate corresponded roughly to the jurisdiction of the summary military government court, while the district judge had jurisdiction corresponding to the intermediate military government court. The district court, composed of three district judges or two district judges and a magistrate, corresponded to the general military government court. The district courts assumed the jurisdiction that was previously exercised by the military government court for civil actions. *Monthly Report of the Military Governor, U.S. Zone*, August 1948, No. 38.

450. "Ordinance No. 31: Code of Criminal Procedure for United States Military Government Courts for Germany," *Military Government Gazette, Germany, United States Area of Control* Issue K, 1 September 1948: 35–44.

451. "Ordinance No. 32: Code of Criminal Procedure for United States Military Government Courts for Germany," *Military Government Gazette, Germany, United States Area of Control* Issue K, 1 September 1948: 44–55.

452. "Ordinance No. 33: Code of Civil Procedure for United States Military Government Courts for Germany," *Military Government Gazette, Germany, United States Area of Control* Issue K, 1 September 1948: 55–60.

453. Breuning, "Die Beschränkung der deutschen Gerichtsbarkeit," 20–21.

454. "Law No. 59: Restitution of Identifiable Property," *Military Government Gazette, Germany, United States Area of Control* Issue G (10 November 1947): 1–25.

455. Art. 1, "Law No. 59: Restitution of Identifiable Property," *Military Government Gazette, Germany, United States Area of Control* Issue G (10 November 1947): 1–25.

456. Ibid.

457. "Regulation No. 4 under Military Govenment Law No. 59: Establishment of Board of Review," *Gesetz—und Verordnungsblatt für Verordnungsblatt für das Land Hessen* (1948), 3 September 1948: 58–61.

458. Breuning, "Die Beschränkung der deutschen Gerichtsbarkeit," 20.

459. "Gesetz zur Ausführung der Artikel 127 und 128 der Verfassung (Richterwahlgesetz) vom 13. August 1948," *Gesetz—und Verordnungsblatt für das Land Hessen* (1948): 95–96.

460. *Monthly Report of the Military Governor, U.S. Zone*, October 1948, No. 40.

461. RG 260 OMGUS, 8/189–3/3. Subject: "1948 Historical Report of Legal Division, OMG Hessen."

462. Herbert Brauer, "Die Neurordnung der Strafrechtspflege in Verfahren vor den Gerichten der amerikanischen Militärregierung," *Neue Juristische Wochenschrift* (1949): 131.

463. Elmer Plischke, *The Allied High Commission for Germany* (Bad Godesberg-Mehlem: Historical Division, Office of the High Commissioner for Germany, 1953): 4.

464. *Germany 1947–1949*, 275–276.

465. Elmer Plischke, *The Allied High Commission for Germany*, 14.

466. Press and Information Office of the Federal Government, "The Administration of Justice," *Germany Reports* (Wiesbaden: Franz Steiner, 1966), 287–288.

467. Diestelkamp, "Justiz in den Westzonen," 20.

468. Zink, *The United States in Germany: 1944–1955*, 44–45.

469. Elmer Plischke, *The Allied High Commission for Germany*, 26.

470. Friedrich Klein, "Das Besatzungsstatut für Deutschland," *Süddeutsche Juristenzeitung* (1949): 737.

471. Art. 1, "The Occupation Statute," *Official Gazette of the Allied High Commission for Germany* No. 1 (23 September 1949): 13.

472. Art. 2, "The Occupation Statute," *Official Gazette of the Allied High Commission for Germany* No. 1: 13–14.

473. Elmer Plischke, *The Allied High Commission for Germany*, 46–47, 197–206.

474. Diestelkamp, "Justiz in den Westzonen," 20.

475. Hucko, *The Democratic Tradition*, 201.

476. Ibid.

477. Rudolf Wassermann, "Richteramt und politisches System," *Revue d'Allemagne* (1973) Vol. 5: 903–904.

478. Hucko, *The Democratic Tradition*, 258.

479. Arnold Brecht, "Re-establishing German Government," *Annals of the American Academy of Political and Social Science* Vol. 267 (January 1950): 38.

480. Ibid., 239.

481. Hucko, *The Democratic Tradition*, 235–240.

482. "The Administration of Justice," *Germany Reports*, 288.

483. Unity of the administration of justice in western Germany was hitherto limited to the German High Court of Judicature for the Combined Economic Area, or the British-American Bizone, which held jurisdiction in legal matters in the economic sphere in keeping with maintaining legislative as well as economic unity in the Bizone. Proclamation No. 8 of 9 February 1948 provided for the establishment of the German High Court, with jurisdiction over disputes regarding the interpretation of bizonal economic legislation, and holding appelate jurisdiction over such cases arising from the ordinary courts in the individual *Länder* of the bizone. *Monthly Report of the Military Governor, U.S. Zone*, February 1948, No. 32; "Proclamation No. 8: Establishment of a German High Court for the Combined Economic Area," *Military Government Gazette* Issue I (16 March 1948): 6–10.

484. Zinn, "Administration of Justice in Germany," 42.

485. *Foreign Relations of the United States, 1949*: Vol. III, *Council of Foreign Ministers; Germany and Austria* (Washington: United States Government Printing Office, 1974), 321.

486. Härtel, *Der Länderrat des amerikanischen Besatzungsgebietes*, 84–87, 96

487. von Weber, "Der Einfluß der Militärgerichtsbarkeit der Besatzungsmacht," 65.

488. Loewenstein, "Justice," 237.

489. Klein, "Das Besatzungsstatut für Deutschland," 752.

490. Hellmut von Weber, "Das Ende der AAR Nr. 1," *Deutsche Rechts-Zeitschrift* (1950): 217.

491. Breuning, "Die Beschränkung der deutschen Gerichtsbarkeit," 38–39.

492. Elmer Plischke, *The West German Federal Government* (Bad Godesberg-Mehlem: Historical Division, Office of the High Commissioner for Germany, 1952), 127.

493. Broszat, "Siegerjustiz oder Strafrechtliche 'Selbstreinugung,'" 540; Plischke, *Allied High Commission for Germany*, 72.

494. Heinrich Röhreke, "Die Rechtsentwicklung in der Bundesrepublik Deutschland," *Deutsche Rechts-Zeitschrift* (1950): 34–35.

495. Breuning, "Die Beschränkung der deutschen Gerichtsbarkeit," 125.

496. "Law No. 13: Judicial Powers in the Reserved Fields," *Official Gazette of the Allied High Commission for Germany* No. 6 (9 December 1949): 54–58.

497. Loewenstein, "Justice," 244.

498. "Law No. 14: Offenses against the Interests of the Occupation," *Official Gazette of the Allied High Commission for Germany* No. 6 (9 December 1949): 59–63.

499. Loewenstein, "Justice," 244.

500. Röhreke, "Die Rechtsentwicklung in der Bundesrepublik Deutchland," 36.

501. 463/929, Wiesbaden. APO 757. "Direktive: Gemäss Gesetz Nr. 13 der allierter Hohen Kommission," 28 December 1949.

502. Criminal offences committed against persons or property of any person affiliated with the Allied forces or the Allied High Commission.

503. 463/929, Wiesbaden. 3120—IVa 141. Betr.: "Deutsche Strafgerichtsbarkeit nach dem Gesetz Nr. 13 der Allierten Hoher Kommission," 9 January 1950.

504. *Report on Germany: September 21, 1949—July 31, 1952* (Office of the U.S. High Commissioner for Germany, 1952): 148.

505. "Law No. A-37: Depriving of Effect and Repealing Certain Occupation Enactments," *Official Gazette of the Allied High Commission for Germany* No. 126 (5 May 1955): 3267–3270.

506. "Proclamation Revoking the Occupation Statute and Abolishing the Allied High Commission and the Offices of the Land Commissioners," *Official Gazette of the Allied High Commission for Germany* No. 126 (5 May 1955): 3272.

507. Loewenstein, "Law and the Legislative Process in Occupied Germany," 995.

508. Herbert Ruscheweyh, "Die Entwicklung der hanseatischen Justiz nach der Kapitulation bis zur Errichtung des Zentral-Justizamtes," *Festschrift für Wilhelm Kiesselbach* (Hamburg: Gesetz und Recht Verlag, 1947), 39.

509. Loewenstein, "Reconstruction of the Administration of Justice," 466.

510. Loewenstein, "Justice," 260.

511. Klaus Moritz and Ernst Noam, *NS-Verbrechen vor Gericht: 1945–1955* (Wiesbaden: Kommission für die Geschichte der Juden in Hessen, 1978), 355, fn. 122.

Chapter 4

1. *Monthly Report of the Military Governor, U.S. Zone*, 20 March, No. 8.

2. John Gimbel, *A German Community under American Occupation: Marburg, 1945–1952* (Stanford: Stanford University Press, 1961), 3.

3. Fürstenau, *Entnazifizierung*, 60.

4. "Law No. 5: Dissolution of the Nazi Party," *Military Government Gazette* Issue A, 1 June 1946: 17–19; Starr, *Operations During the Rhineland Campaign*, 78.

5. Starr, *Operations During the Rhineland Campaign*, 49.

6. Ibid., 58.

7. Z45F 17/199–3/41 RG 260/OMGUS, Koblenz. Provenance: OMGUS: LD/AJ Br. Folder Title: Denazification of Judges and Prosecutors. "Subject: Denazification of Judges and Prosecutors in the German Ordinary Courts," 4 June 1947.

8. Lutz Niethammer, *Entnazifizierung in Bayern: Säuberung und Rehabilitierung unter amerikanischer Besatzung* (Frankfurt-am-Main: S. Fischer Verlag, 1972), 65.

9. John Gimbel, "American Denazification and Local Politics, 1945–1949: A Case Study in Marburg," *American Political Science Review* Vol. 54 (1960), 85.

10. Starr, *Operations During the Rhineland Campaign*, 40–41.

11. Starr, *Denazification, Occupation and Control of Germany, March-July, 1945* (Salisbury: Documentary Publications, 1977), 46.

12. Elmer Plischke, "Denazification Law and Procedure," *American Journal of International Law* Vol. 41 (October 1947): 817.

13. Latour, Vogelsang, *Okkupation und Wiederaufbau*, 51.

14. Starr, *Operations During the Rhineland Campaign*, 77.

15. Latour, Volgelsang, *Okkupation und Wiederaufbau*, 51–52.

16. The initial work of the military government immediately following combat conditions was concentrated on emergency or negative tasks, such as securing shelter for the local population or denazification as part of the problem of arresting individuals who could represent a military danger to the occupation forces, before the various functions of reconstruction were exercised following the restoration of order and stability in the occupied areas. (Starr, *Operations During the Rhineland Campaign*, 59–60.) It may be argued that the military government didn't undertake reconstruction activities until after combat conditions, when Germans among the local population were required to assist the military government in the implementation of those functions.

17. Loewenstein, "Reconstruction of the Administration of Justice," 448, 455.

18. Starr, *Operations During the Rhineland Campaign*, 79.

19. Elmer Plischke, "Denazifying the Reich," *Review of Politics*, Vol. 9 (1947): 166–168; Gimbel, *A German Community under American Occupation*, 33.

20. William E. Griffith, "Denazification in the United States Zone in Germany," *Annals of the American Academy of Political and Social Science*, Vol. 269 (1950): 68.

21. Freeman, *Hesse: A New German State*, 28.

22. Harold Zink, "The American Denazification Program in Germany," *Journal of Central European Affairs*, Vol. 6 (October 1946): 233–234; Zink, *United States in Germany: 1944–1955*, p. 157; Joseph, R. Starr, *Denazification, Occupation and Control of Germany, March-July 1945*, 36.

23. "Final Report on Foreign Aid of the House Select Committee on Foreign Aid," 1 May 1948, 80th Congress, 2nd Session, 6 January—31 December 1948, *House Reports* Vol. 6 No. 1845 (Washington: U.S. Government Printing Office, 1948), 128.

24. Griffith, "Denazification in the United States Zone in Germany," 69.

25. Ibid., 68.

26. Rudolf Wassermann, *Auch die Justiz kann aus der Geschichte nicht aussteigen: Studien zur Justizgeschichte* (Baden-Baden: Nomos Verlagsgesellschaft, 1990), 188.

27. *Foreign Relations of the United States, Diplomatic Papers*, Vol. 1: *The Conference of Berlin*, 497.

28. There were deficiencies in the system in this respect, such as the possibility of establishing one's innocence by: bribing "reliable" Germans employed by the U.S. military government to undertake investigations to assist the Special Branches and Counterintelligence; purchasing black market certificates stating that a suspect had been a "fellow prisoner" in a concentration camp; or having colleagues vouch for one's innocence. Julian Bach Jr., *America's Germany: An Account of the Occupation* (New York: Random House, 1946), 171–172.

29. Plischke, "Denazification Law and Procedure," 815.
30. *Monthly Report of the Military Governor, U.S. Zone*, 31 October 1945, No. 16.
31. Zink, "The American Denazification Program," 237–238.
32. 460/645, Wiesbaden. "Special Questionnaire for Judges, Judicial Officials, Public Prosecutors and Amtsanwälte," 1 August 1945.
33. Loewenstein, "Reconstruction of the Administration Justice," 448.
34. Gimbel, *A German Community under American Occupation*, 67.
35. Ibid: 80, 148, 83–84.
36. Ibid: 3.
37. Loewenstein, "Reconstruction of the Administration of Justice," 419, 448.
38. Loewenstein, "Justice," 247.
39. Ibid.
40. Freeman, *Hesse: A New German State*, 35.
41. Chargeable actions are defined here as actions that would be subject to prosecution in law courts in ordinary circumstances.
42. Alvin Johnson (foreword; anonymous author), "Denazification," *Social Research* Vol. 14 (1947): 67–68.
43. Diestelkamp, "Die Justiz in den Westzonen," 21.
44. Nobleman, "Administration of Justice," 94.
45. Ibid., 93.
46. Ibid.
47. 460/568, Wiesbaden. Dienstanweisung für Amtsrichter, 9 July 1945; Betrifft: "Berichte an die Militärregierung," 28 July 1945.
48. 460/568, Wiesbaden. Betrifft: "Berichte an die Militärregierung," 28 July 1945.
49. 460/569, Wiesbaden. "The President of the Landgericht to MilitaryGovernment, Legal Department, Frankfurt-am-Main," 10 September 1945.
50. 462/1308, Wiesbaden. APO 756. Subject: Permission to practice law, 26 October 1945; Bescheinigung, Dem Rechtsanwalt Dr. E ____ R ____, 6 November 1945.
51. 460/568, Wiesbaden. The *Landgericht* president, Frankfurt-am-Main, to the Military Government Legal Department at Frankfurt-am-Main, 6 August 1945.
52. Loewenstein, "Reconstruction of the Administration of Justice," 449.
53. Arndt, "Die staats—und verwaltungsrechtliche Entwicklung in Groß-Hessen," 186.
54. 463/929, Wiesbaden. Headquarters, U.S. Forces, European Theater: Plan für die Justizverwaltung amerikanische Zone, 4 Oktober 1945.
55. 463/929, Wiesbaden. Headquarters, U.S. Forces, European Theater: Plan für die Justizverwaltung amerikanische Zone, 4 Oktober 1945; 460/645, Wiesbaden. Betrifft: "Fortzahlung von Gehältern und Lohnen an noch nicht beschäftigte der Justizbehörden," 20 September 1945.
56. 463/1118, Wiesbaden.—Az: 2010—I 22. "Rundverfügung über den Verkehr mit der Militärregierung und die Einstellung von Beamten, Angestellten usw. vom 7. Januar 1946," 7 January 1946
57. 460/645, Wiesbaden. Betr.: "Denazifizierung," 16 November 1945.

58. 462/1301, Wiesbaden. Office of the Military Government for Greater Hesse, APO 758. Subject: "Judicial Officials and Employees; Land Greater Hesse," 2 January 1946.

59. *Monthly Report of the Military Governor, U.S. Zone*, 20 October 1945, No. 3.

60. Ibid.

61. *Monthly Report of the Military Governor, U.S. Zone*, 20 September 1945, No. 2.

62. 458/670, Wiesbaden. Subject: "Employment of officials for the Amtsgericht," 17 September 1945.

63. Freeman, *Hesse: A New German State*, 35.

64. "Law No. 8: Prohibition of Employment of Members of Nazi Party in Positions in Business other than Ordinary Labor and for other Purposes," *Military Government Gazette*, Issue A, 1 June 1946: 20–21.

This law extended the denazification to private enterprise in order to eradicate National Socialist economic power and influence in addition to public and administrative life (Plischke, "Denazification Law and Procedure": 816), restricting the employment of former members of the NSDAP or one of its affiliated organisations to ordinary labour (*Monthly Report of the Military Governor, U.S. Zone*, 20 October 1945, No. 3), by which the implicated individual would not be allowed to act in supervisory or managerial capacity. Lawyers and notaries were not affected by this law since their offices did not qualify as business enterprises in the meaning of Law No. 8. RG 260 17/210–3/6, Wiesbaden. APO 633. Subject: "Law No. 8," 16 February 1946.

65. Art. 4, "Law No. 4: Reorganisation of the German Judicial System," *Official Gazette of the Control Council for Germany* No. 2 (30 November 1945): 27.

66. Loewenstein, "Reconstruction of the Administration of Justice," 445–446.

67. Z45F 17/199–3/41 RG 260/OMGUS, Koblenz. "Subject: Denazification of Judges and Prosecutors in the German Ordinary Courts," 4 June 1947.

68. 501/831 Wiesbaden. "Office of Military Government for Greater Hesse: Progress Report of Land Greater Hesse 1945," 21 December 1945.

69. *Monthly Report of the Military Governor, U.S. Zone*, 20 August 1945, No. 1.

70. *Monthly Report of the Military Governor, U.S. Zone*, 20 November 1945, No. 4.

71. *Monthly Report of the Military Governor, U.S. Zone*, 20 December 1945, No. 5.

72. Z45F 17/199–3/41 RG 260/OMGUS, Koblenz. Provenance: OMGUS: LD/AJ Br. Folder Title: Denazification of Judges and Prosecutors. "Subject: Denazification of Judges and Prosecutors in the German Ordinary Courts," 4 June 1947.

73. *Monthly Report of the Military Governor, U.S. Zone*, 20 January 1946, No. 6. Those numbers were extended to more than a million individuals in January 1946, of which 260,000 were considered "active Nazis and militarists" who were removed or excluded from public employment or important positions in the economic, social, and political life of the U.S. occupation zone. *Monthly Report of the Military Governor, U.S. Zone*, 20 February 1946, No. 7.

74. Fürstenau, *Entnazifizierung*, 29.

75. Griffith, "Denazification in the United States Zone in Germany," 69.

76. Loewenstein, "Law and the Legislative Process in Occupied Germany," 998.

77. Plischke, "Denazification Law and Procedure," 823.

78. John Gimbel, *The American Occupation of Germany: Politics and the Military, 1945–1949* (Stanford: Stanford University Press, 1968), 102; Charles Fahy, "The Lawyer in Military Government of Germany," *U.S. Department of State Bulletin*, Vol. 15 (1946): 858.

79. *Monthly Report of the Military Governor, U.S. Zone*, 20 January 1946, No. 6.

80. Karl Loewenstein, "Comment on Denazification," *Social Research* Vol. 14 (1947): 366–367.

81. *Monthly Report of the Military Governor, U.S. Zone*, 20 January 1946, No. 6.

82. John G. Kormann, *U.S. Denazification Policy in Germany: 1944–1950* (Historical Division, Office of the Executive Secretary; Office of the U.S. High Commissioner for Germany, 1952), 43.

83. Gimbel, *The American Occupation of Germany*, 103.

84. Kormann, *U.S. Denazification Policy in Germany*, 50–51.

85. "Kabinett-Sitzung vom 6.12.1945," Wiesbaden, 1126/19; Hans Ehard, "Das Gesetz zur Befreiung von Nationalsozialismus und Militarismus," *Süddeutsche Juristenzeitung* (1946): 7.

86. Z1/1213, Koblenz. Headquarters, Office of Military Government Württember-Baden, Dr.H./hb Leg., 20 February 1946, "Report of the Meeting of the Länderrat—Committee on Denazification, 7–16 February 1946."

87. "Directive No. 24: Removal from Office and from Positions of Responsibility of Nazis and of Persons Hostile to Allied Purposes," *Official Gazette of the Control Council for Germany* No. 5 (31 March 1946): 98–115.

88. Plischke, "Denazification Law and Procedure," 817; Kormann, *U.S. Denazification Policy in Germany*, 48.

89. Whereas denazification was a prime objective in the U.S. zone, the British occupation authorities maintained that denazification shouldn't interfere with the postwar reconstruction, and was therefore relegated to a secondary priority. Soviet authorities exploited denazification in their claim to foster social change, and the French made little effort on the whole. Kormann, *U.S. Denazification Policy in Germany*, 47–48; Carl J. Friedrich et al., *American Experiences in Military Government in World War II* (New York: Rinehart & Company, 1948) 259–261.

90. "Directive No. 24," Art. 2, *Official Gazette of the Control Council* No. 5: 98–100.

91. Art. 10, Ibid, 102–112.

92. Art. 12, Ibid, 113–114.

93. Friedmann, *Allied Military Government of Germany*, 116.

94. Loewenstein, "Justice," 247.

95. Latour, Vogelsang, Okkupation und Wiederaufbau, 137.

96. Gimbel, American Occupation of Germany, 104; Härtel, *Der Länderrat des amerikanischen Besatzungsgebietes*, 100.

97. Z1/1213, Koblenz. Headquarters, Office of Military Government Württemberg-Baden, Dr.H./hb Leg., 20 February 1946, "Report of the Meeting of the Länderrat—Committee on Denazification, 7–16 February 1946."

98. Gimbel, *American Occupation of Germany*, p. 104; Härtel, *Der Länderrat des amerikanischen Besatzungsgebietes*, 100.

99. 501/927, Wiesbaden. "Programmatische Erklärung der Grosshessischen Staatsregierung," 23/11/45.

100. Richard Schmid, "Denazification: A German Critique," *American Perspective* Vol. 2 (1948): 237.

101. Johnson, "Denazification," 71; Artur Sträter, "Denazification," *Annals of the American Academy of Political and Social Science*, Vol. 260 (1948): 47.

102. Kormann, *U.S. Denazification Policy in Germany*, 52; Friedrich, "Denazification, 1944–1946," 264.

103. Tom Bower, *The Pledge Betrayed: America and Britain and the Denazification of Postwar Germany* (Garden City, New York: Doubleday & Co., 1982), 145.

104. Johnson, "Denazification," 70.

105. Kormann, *U.S. Denazification Policy in Germany*, 55.

106. Ibid.

107. Ehard, "Das Gesetz zur Befreiung von Nationalsozialismus und Militarismus," 7.

108. "Final Report on Foreign Aid," 128.

109. Gimbel, *American Occupation of Germany*, 104.

110. Schmid, "Denazification: A German Critique," 236–237.

111. Härtel, *Der Länderrat des amerikanischen Besatzungsgebietes*, 98; Niethammer, *Entnazifizierung in Bayern*, 315.

112. Härtel, *Der Länderrat des amerikanischen Besatzungsgebietes*, 219.

113. 1126/17, Wiesbaden. "Erklärung Bowie vom 13.2.46."

114. *Monthly Report of the Military Governor, U.S. Zone*, 20 February 1946, No. 7.

115. Mühlhausen, *Hessen 1945–1950*, 315.

116. 1126/19, Wiesbaden. "Beschluß-Protokoll über die Sitzung des Kabinetts am 21. Februar 1946."

117. 1126/19, Wiesbaden. "Beschluß-Protokoll über die Sitzung der (sic) Kabinetts am 25. Februar 1946."

118. 1126/17, Wiesbaden. "Erklärung des Ministerpräsidenten von Gross-Hessen Prof. Dr. Karl Geiler zu dem Gesetz zur Befreiung vonNationalsozialisms und Militarismus," 4. März 1946.

119. Fürstenau, *Entnazifizierung*, 62.

120. Griffith, "Denazification in the United States Zone," 70.

121. Ehard, "Das Gesetz zur Befreiung von Nationalsozialismus und Militarismus," 8.

122. Dennis L. Bark and David R. Gress, *A History of West Germany*, Vol. 1: *From Shadow to Substance 1945–1963* (Oxford: Blackwell Publishers, 1993), 75.

123. *Monthly Report of the Military Government, U.S. Zone*, 20 March 1946, No. 8.

124. *Monthly Report of the Military Governor, U.S. Zone*, 20 February, No. 7.

125. Freeman, *Hesse: A New German State*, 160.

126. *Monthly Report of the Military Governor, U.S. Zone*, 20 March 1946, No. 8. Law No. 8 was only formally repealed by the U.S. military government on 11 May 1948, after its effective operation ceased to function upon the promulgation of the German Liberation Law. *Monthly Report of the Military Governor, U.S. Zone*, May 1948, No. 35.

127. *Monthly Report of the Military Governor, U.S. Zone*, 20 July 1946, No. 12.

128. *Monthly Report of the Military Governor, U.S. Zone*, 20 April 1946, No. 9. The *Meldebogen* was substantially the same as the earlier *Fragebogen*, except for slight differences in the form. A receipt was attached to the *Meldebogen* that had to be countersigned

and presented to the local authorities, the police, or a civil administration office before one could receive a ration card. In turn, the questionnaires were given to public prosecutors for processing and evaluation. Kormann, *U.S. Denazification Policy in Germany*, 68.

129. "Durchführungsverordnung Nr. 1 vom 5. März 1946 zum Gesetz zur Befreiung von Nationalsozialismus und Militarismus von 5. März 1946," *Gesetz—und Verordnungsblatt für das Land Groß-Hessen* (1946), pp. 71–72. The registration of all adult Germans in the U.S. occupation zone on Meldebogen forms was completed by 5 May 1946. *Monthly Report of the Military Governor, U.S. Zone*, 20 May 1946, No. 10.

130. *Monthly Report of the Military Governor, U.S. Zone*, 20 April 1946, No. 9.

131. *Monthly Report of the Military Governor, U.S. Zone*, 20 March 1946, No. 8.

132. Kormann, *U.S. Denazification Policy in Germany*, 68.

133. *Monthly Report of the Military Governor, U.S. Zone*, 20 March 1946, No. 8.

134. Kurt P. Tauber, *Beyond Eagle and Swastika: German Nationalism since 1945* Vol. 1 (Middletown: Wesleyan University Press, 1967), 29.

135. Arts. 1, 2, Section 1, Art. 60, Section 3, *Gesetz zur Befreiung von Nationalsozialismus und Militarismus vom 5. März 1946*, Erich Schullze, ed. (München: Biederstein Verlag, 1947), 4, 6, 59–60.

136. Arts. 4–18, Section 1, Ibid., 7–27.

137. Art. 24, Section 2, Ibid., 29.

138. Art. 35, Section 2, Ibid., 41–42.

139. Art. 34, Section 2, Ibid., p. 40.

140. Kormann, *U.S. Denazification Policy in Germany*, 68.

141. Loewenstein, "Reconstruction of the Administration of Justice," 450.

142. Schullze, *Gesetz zur Befreiung von Nationalsozialismus und Militarismus vom 5. März 1946*, 80–81.

143. Ibid., 67.

144. Ibid., 81–82.

145. Z45F 17/199–3/41 RG 260/OMGUS, Koblenz. Subject: "Denazification of Judges and Prosecutors in the Ordinary German Courts," 4 June 1947.

146. Z45F 17/199–3/41 RG 260/OMGUS, Koblenz. Subject: Denazification of Judges and Prosecutors in the German Ordinary Courts, 4 June 1947.

147. RG 260 OMGUS, 8/188–2/5. APO 633. Subject: "Weekly Summary Report for Legal Division from 11 to 17 August 1946," 16 August 1946.

148. 463/929, Wiesbaden. Betr.: "Weiterbeschäftigung der unter das Gesetz vom 5.3.1946 fallende Personen; Abschrift," 1050—I 850, 17 May 1946.

149. 462/1301, Wiesbaden. Betr.: "Wiedereinstellung des Justizinspektors K ____ und des Justizinspektors F ____, beide in Limburg/Lahn," 29 March 1946, 201 IE—54 -.

150. RG 260 OMGUS, 8/188–2/5, Wiesbaden. APO 633. Subject: "Weekly Summary Report for Legal Division from 18 to 24 August 1946," 23 August 1946.

151. 462/1301, Wiesbaden. Der Minister der Justiz, Ib AR 321/46. Herrn Landesgerichtspräsidenten in Limburg zu 201 IE—64 -., 15 May 1946.

152. Z45F 17/199–3/40 RG 260 OMGUS, Koblenz. Provenance: OMGUS, LD AJ Br. Folder Title: File No. H(g) Justice Ministry matters—organisation and functions of Justice Ministry. Description and Denazification of German Administration of Justice.

AGO 014.3, Subject: "Denazification of German Administration of Justice," 31 October 1947.

153. Z45F 17/199–3/40 RG 260 OMGUS, Koblenz. AGO 014.3. Subject: "Denazification of German Administration of Justice," 31 October 1947.

154. Ibid.

155. *Monthly Report of the Military Governor, U.S. Zone*, 30 November 1946, No. 17.

156. RG 260 OMGUS, 8/188–2/5, Wiesbaden. APO 633. Subject: "Weekly Report of Legal Division for week ending 5 October 1946."

157. 462/1302, Wiesbaden. Betr.: "Wiederanstellung des Justizinspektors H F ____ aus Gladenbach," 5 November 1946.

158. 501/42(1), Wiesbaden. APO 633. Subject: Request for Priority, 14 October 1947.

159. 460/545, Wiesbaden. 1050e—I 1060. Betr.: Genehmigung zur vorläufigen Weiterbeschäftigung nach Art. 60 des Gesetzes vom 5.3.1946, 2 October 1946; 501/42(1), Wiesbaden. APO 633. Subject: Request for Priority, 14 October 1947.

160. 501/831 Wiesbaden. Abschrift: "Extracts from Title 2 Military Government Regulations, Eradication of Nazism and Militarism."

161. Z45F 11/5–2/1, Koblenz. OMGUS, LD. Legal Division History. "Interview with Dr. Karl Loewenstein."

162. RG 260 OMGUS, 8/188–2/5, Wiesbaden. APO 633. Subject: "Weekly Summary Report for Legal Division from 6 July to 13 July 1946," 12 July 1946.

163. Z45 F 17/56–3/7 RG 260/OMGUS, Koblenz. AJ 015.2 18 November 1946 HMR/f, Subject: Report on Inspection of German Court in Greater Hesse from 28 October to 4 November 1946.

164. 462/1302, Wiesbaden. I M3. Betr.: Wiedereinstellung des Justizinspektors ____ in Wetzlar, 25 October 1946; I S2. Betr.: Wiedereinstellungsgesuch des Justizangestellten ____, 25 September 1946; IO. Betr.: "Anstellung des Justizinspektors ____, 22 July 1946.

165. RG 260. 8/188–2/5. APO 633, Wiesbaden. Subject: "Weekly Summary Report for Legal Division from 18 to 24 August 1946," 23 August 1946.

166. 501/831 Wiesbaden. I/St/Kö. Tageb. Nr. 20758/46. Betr.: "Juristische Hilfsarbeiter bei Rechtsanwälten," 13. Januar 1947; Der Vorstand der Anwaltskammer and der Herrn Minister für politische Befreiung, 26. Oktober 1946, Geschäftsnummer: 865.1196/46.

167. 501/831 Wiesbaden. I/St/Kö. Betr. "Beschäftigung belastete Juristen als Hilfsarbeiter beim Anwälten," 7.2. 1947.

168. 501/831 Wiesbaden. "Betr.: "Beschäftigung von Juristen als Hilfsarbeiter bei Anwälten, datiert 7.2.47."

169. 501/831, Wiesbaden. IX 9140. Betr.: "Beschäftigung in 'gewöhnlicher Arbeit' gemäß Art. 58, 63 des Säuberungsgesetzes vom 5.3.46."

170. Loewenstein, "Reconstruction of the Administration of Justice," 453.

171. 462/1302, Wiesbaden. Betr.: "Personalverhältnisse beim Amtsgericht in Biedenkopf," 15 November 1946.

172. Art. 28, Section 1, Schullze, *Gesetz zur Befreiung von Nationalsozialismus und Militarismus*, 32.

173. Loewenstein, "Reconstruction of the Administration of Justice," 451–452; Gustav Stolper, *German Realtities* (New York: Reynal & Hitchcock, 1948), 60.

174. Art. 25, Section 1, Schullze, *Gesetz zur Befreiung von Nazionalsozialismus und Militarismus*, 30.

175. 460/545, Wiesbaden. Betr.: Bildung von Kammern auf Grund des Gesetzes zur Befreiung vom Nazionalsozialismus und Militarismus vom 5.3.1946 im Landgerichtsbezirk Frankfurt-am-Main, 26 March 1946.

176. 463/929, Wiesbaden. Betr.: "Bildung vom Spruchkammer auf Grund des Gesetzes zur Befreiung von Nationalsozialismus und Militarismus," 25 March 1946.

177. *Monthly Report of the Military Governor, U.S. Zone*, 20 July 1946, No. 12.

178. Loewenstein, "Reconstruction of the Administration of Justice," 451–452.

179. Fürstenau, *Entnazifizierung*, 182.

180. 501/892, Wiesbaden. IV/Be/Re/Tgb.Nr. Betr.: "Verpflichtung zur Tätigkeit an einer Spruchkammer," 19.12.1946.

181. 501/843, Wiesbaden. Vorstand der Anwaltskammer Darmstadt, Darmstadt 3. Mai 1947. "Betr.: Dienstverplichtung von Rechtsanwälten."

182. 501/1586, Wiesbaden. "Betr.: Massnahmen zur Unterstützung der Juristen, die ihre Arbeitskraft der Durchführung des Gesetzes vom 5. März 1946 zur Verfügung stellen," 18 März 1946.

183. Johnson, "Denazification," 73.

184. *Monthly Report of the Military Governor, U.S. Zone*, 31 October 1946, No. 16.

185. Freeman, *Hesse: A New German State*, 162.

186. Fürstenau, *Entnazifizierung*, 73–74.

187. Ibid.

188. Z1/65, Koblenz. "Regional Government Coordinating Office," Speech of Lt. Gen. Lucius D. Clay delivered at the Fourteenth Meeting of the Laenderrat. Stuttgart, 5 November 1946; *Monthly Report of the Military Governor, U.S. Zone*, 30 November 1946, No. 17

189. 8/188–1/21 RG 260, OMGUS, Wiesbaden. APO 633, Subject: Weekly Summary Report, 15 November 1946.

190. 501/831 Wiesbaden. Office of the Military Government for Greater Hesse (Denazification). HIT/di. APO 633. Subj.: "Comments on Last Weekly Period," 2 December 1946.

191. Clemens Vollnhals, ed. *Entnazifizierung: Politische Säuberung und Rehabilitierung in den vier Besatzungszonen 1945–1949* (München: Deutscher Taschenbuch Verlag, 1991), 259.

192. *Monthly Report of the Military Governor, U.S. Zone*, 31 December 1946, No. 18.

193. Gimbel, *American Occupation of Germany*, 105–106.

194. John Herz, "Fiasco of Denazification," *Political Science Quarterly*, Vol. 63 December 1948: 573.

195. Public prosecutors who dealt with cases at the *Amtsgericht* level.

196. Moritz and Noam, *NS-Verbrechen vor Gericht: 1945–1955*, 18.

197. Diestelkamp, "Die Justiz in den Westzonen," 23; Bernhard Diestelkamp, "Kontinuität und Wandel in der Rechtsordnung: 1945–1955," *Westdeutschland 1945–1955: Unterwerfung, Kontrolle, Integration*, ed. Ludolf Herbst, (München: R. Oldenbourg Verlag, 1986), 94.

198. Herzberg, "The Situation of the Lawyer in Germany," 294.

199. Willig, "The Bar in the Third Reich," 6, 13.

200. Wagner and Weinkauff, *Die Deutsche Justiz und der Nationalsozialismus*, 257.

201. 460/568, Wiesbaden. Der Langerichtspräsident, Frankfurt/Main, an die Militärregierung—Legal—Frankfurt/Main. 9 November 1945.

202. 460/545, Wiesbaden. 105E -315. Betr.: Richtereinsatz (n.d.).

203. Loewenstein, "Reconstruction of the Administration of Justice," 458.

204. "Law No. 12: Amendment of Income Tax, Corporation Tax and Excess Profits Tax Laws," *Official Gazette of the Control Council for Germany* (No. 4), 28 February 1946: 60–68.

205. Loewenstein, "Reconstruction of the Administration of Justice," 458.

206. Diestelkamp, "Die Justiz in den Westzonen," 22.

207. Loewenstein, "Reconstruction of the Administration of Justice," 453.

208. Z45F 17/199–3/40 RG 260 OMGUS, Koblenz. Provenance: OMGUS LD AJ Br. Folder Title: File No. H(g) Justice Ministry matters—organisation and functions of Justice Ministry. Description and Denazification of German Administration of Justice. AGO 014.3. Subject: "Denazification of German Administration of Justice," 31 October 1947.

209. "Der Aufbau der Justiz in der amerikanischen Zone: Groß-Hessen," 120.

210. Starr, *Operations During the Rhineland Campaign*, 65–66.

211. 460/568, Wiesbaden. The *Landgericht* president, Frankfurt-am-Main, to the Military Government Legal Department at Frankfurt-am-Main, 6 August 1945.

212. 460/645, Wiesbaden. Betrifft: "Fortzahlung von Gehälten und Lohnen an noch nicht beschäftigte Bedienstete der Justizbehörden," 20 September 1945.

213. Bower, *The Pledge Betrayed: America and Britain and the Denazification of Postwar Germany*, 171, 173–176.

214. It has been noted that U.S. denazification policy was pursued with "high moral standards and expectations," while the other three occupation powers were more practical. Diestelkamp, "Kontinuität und Wandel in der Rechtsordnung," 93.

215. The problem of a serious shortage of jurists prevailed throughout Germany after the collapse of the National Socialist regime. The Soviet Union took advantage of the vacuum of qualified and employable jurists by staffing judicial positions with individuals who could be relied upon to serve as instruments of political policy. H.A. Himmelmann, "'Democratisation of Justice' in the Soviet Zone," *Contemporary Review* Vol. 176 (July 1949): 31–32.

216. Diestelkamp, "Die Justiz in den Westzonen," 21–22.

217. Benz, "Die Entnazifizierung der Richter," 124.

218. Z45F 17/199–3/41 RG 260/OMGUS, Koblenz. Subject: "Removal of Nazi Laws and Removal of Nazis from the Judicial System," 17 January 1947.

219. Freeman, *Hesse: A New German State*, p. 137. There were 384 judges and prosecutors in Hesse in June 1947 who were formally cleared by the military government, but the administration of justice remained greatly handicapped by a shortage of personnel. Z45F 17/199–3/41 RG 260/OMGUS, Koblenz. Subject: "Denazification of Judges and Prosecutors in the German Ordinary Courts," 4 June 1947.

220. Freeman, *Hesse: A New German State*, 137.

221. Ibid.

222. 460/639, Wiesbaden. 2200–1–240. Betr.: "Dienstverpflichtung der zum Richteramt befähigten Personen," 28 January 1946.

223. "Verordnung über Melde—und Dienstpflicht der zum Richteramt befähigten Personen vom 16. März 1946," *Gesetz—und Verordnungsblatt für das Land Groß-Hessen* (1946): 107; *Monthly Report of the Military Governor, U.S. Zone*, September 1946, No. 14.

224. RG 260 OMGUS 8/188–2/5. APO 633. Subject: "Weekly Summary Report for Legal Division from 30 June to 5 July 1946," 5 July 1946.

225. 458/1014, Wiesbaden. 3110—Ia 1031. Betr.: "Verwendung der Amtsrichter bei dem übergeordneten Landgericht," 6 June 1946.

226. Z45F 11/5–2/1, Koblenz. OMGUS, LD. Legal Division History. "Interview with Dr. Karl Loewenstein."

227. Loewenstein, "Reconstruction of the Administration of Justice," 454.

228. Adolf Schönke, "Criminal Law and Criminality in Germany of Today," *Annals of the American Academy of Political and Social Science*, Vol. 260 (1948): 140.

229. 8/213–1/18, RG 260 OMGUS, Wiesbaden. APO 633. Subject: "Proceedings in German Courts."

230. Zimmer, *Die Geschichte des Oberlandesgerichts in Frankfurt-am-Main*, 91.

231. "Gemeinsame Gesetzgebung: Stand vom 9.4.1948; Richteramtsbefähigung umgesiedelter und heimatvertriebener Juristen," *Süddeutsche Juristenzeitung* (1948): 220.

232. RG 260 OMGUS, 8/188–2/5, Wiesbaden. APO 633. Subject: "Weekly Summary Report for Legal Division from 1 September to 7 September 1946," 6 September 1946.

233. "Gesetz über Richteramtsbefähigung umgesiedelter und heimatvertriebener Juristen vom 21. Juni 1948," *Gesetz—und Verordnungsblatt für das Land Hessen* (1948): 79–80.

234. Loewenstein, "Reconstruction of the Administration of Justice," 454.

235. Ibid., 431, 433–434.

236. This was a common practice among the western Allies, due to the shortage of trained personnel. Friedmann, *Allied Military Government of Germany*, 174.

237. Freeman, *Hesse: A New German State*, 137.

238. Ibid.

239. Gimbel, *American Occupation of Germany*, 110, 159–162.

240. Herz, "Fiasco of Denazification," 573–574.

241. Kormann, *U.S. Denazification Policy in Germany*, 95–96.

242. "Amnestie-Verordnung vom 6. August 1946 zum Gesetz zur Befreiung von Nationalsozialismus und Militarismus vom 5. März 1946," *Gesetz—und Verordnungsblatt für das Land Groß-Hessen* (1946), 173.

243. Kormann, *U.S. Denazification Policy in Germany*, 113–114.

244. "Verordnung vom 5. Februar 1947 zur Durchführung der Weinachtsamnestie zum Gesetz zur Befreiung von Nationalsozialismus und Militarismus von 5. März 1946," *Gesetz—und Verordnungsblatt für das Land Hessen* (1948): 22–23.

245. Knappstein, "Die versäumte Revolution: Wird das Experiment der 'Denazifizierung' gelingen?" *Die Wandlung* (1947): 670.

246. Vollnhals, *Entnazifizierung: Politische Säuberung und Rehabilitierung in den vier Besatzungszonen*, 61.

247. Anna J. Merritt and Richard L. Merritt, eds. *Public Opinion in Occupied Germany: The OMGUS Surveys 1945–1949* (Urbana, Illinois, 1970), 304.

248. 460/639, Wiesbaden. Betr.: "Dienstverpflichtung der zum Richteramt befähigten Personen," 18 February 1946.

249. Kormann, *U.S. Denazification Policy in Germany*, 119–120.

250. Only individuals who were classified as *Major Offenders* were arraigned before the International Military Tribunal at Nuremberg. Michael H. Kater, "Problems of Political Reeducation in West Germany, 1945–1950," *Simon Wiesenthal Centre Annual* Vol. 4 (1984): 100.

251. Kormann, *U.S. Denazification Policy in Germany*, 119–120.

252. Fürstenau, *Entnazifizierung*, 77.

253. 501/803, Wiesbaden. "Gemeinsame Entschliessung aller Fraktionen des Hessischen Landtages zur Frage der politischen Befreiung, 4. Juli 1947."

254. 501/26, Wiesbaden. Die Änderung des Befreiungsgesetzes. Wichtiges Ziel: Beschleunigung des Verfahrens. Von Ministerialdirektor K. H. Knappstein (n.d.).

255. *Monthly Report of the Military Governor, U.S. Zone*, 30 September 1947, No. 27.

256. Those were: the SD, the *Gestapo*, the SS, and the Leadership Corps of the NSDAP. Loewenstein, "Reconstruction of Justice," 451. Former members of the SS were to be judged according to the provisions of the Law for Liberation, that differentiated between active and nominal members. Individuals who had joined after 31 December 1938 or had paid more than ten marks per month to the SS before this date, were to be classified in Class II. Those who had joined *before* 31 December 1938 or had paid less than ten marks per month weren't to be considered active supporters (*fördernde Mitglieder*) and weren't to be classified in Class I or II. They weren't considered full-fledged members of the SS since they hadn't been entitled to the rights of the SS, such as the uniform, etc., and hadn't been responsible for fulfilling the duties of SS members. Hence, such individuals weren't affected by the Law for Liberation. 462/1302, Wiesbaden. "Beglaubigte Abschrift. Der Minister für Wiederaufbau und politische Befreiung." M/Kn/Schoe/T.N. 6074/46. 20 June 1946.

257. 501/61, Wiesbaden. Office of the Military Government for Germany (U.S.), Office of the Military Governor. AG 010.6 (IA). Subject: "Amendments to the Law for Liberation and Expedited Procedures Thereunder," 23 October 1947.

258. Herz, "Fiasco of Denazification," 574.

259. Kormann, *U.S. Denazification Policy in Germany*, 127.

260. "Gesetz vom 18. Oktober 1947 über die Abänderung einzelner Vorschriften des Gesetzes zur Befreiung von Nationalsozialismus und Militarismus vom 5. März 1946," *Gesetz—und Verordnungsblatt für das Land Hessen* (1948): 91–92.

261. 501/61, Wiesbaden. "Law of 7 October 1947: Amending certain provisions of the Law for Liberation from National Socialism and Militarism of 5 March 1946."

262. 501/26, Wiesbaden. Die Änderung des Befreiungsgesetzes. Wichtiges Ziel: Beschleunigung des Verfahrens. Von Ministerialdirektor K. H. Knappstein (n.d.).

263. 501/1199, Wiesbaden. Office of the Military Government for Hesse ALY/di. Denazification Division. APO 633. Betr.: "Programm zur beschleunigten Erledigung der Entnazifizierung," 15 January 1948.

264. 501/1199, Wiesbaden. "Rundbrief an alle öffentlichen Kläger und Vorsitzenden der Spruch und Berufungskammern in Hessen," Betr.: Erweiterung des B-Verfahrens. Minister für politische Befreiung. Wiesbaden, 19. January 1948.

265. 501/1199, Wiesbaden. Office of Military Government for Hesse, Denazification Division. ALY/di, APO 633, U.S. Army, 15 January 1948, "Betreff: Programm zur beschleunigten Erledigung der Entnazifizierung."

266. Herz, "Fiasco of Denazification," 574–575.

267. 8/217–1/5, RG 260 OMGUS, Wiesbaden. Subject: "Priority for Trials involving highly incriminated and influential Nazis, Militarists and Profiteers," 11 December 1947.

268. Jack Raymond, "U.S. Backs Easing of Denazification: Official in Hesse declares that some German demands are worthy of acceptance," *New York Times* (21 March 1948): 26L+.

269. 501/26, Wiesbaden. Rundverfügung Nr. 119, An alle öffentlichen Kläger und Vorsitzenden der Spruchkammer, Betr.: "Zweites Änderungsgesetz," *Monthly Report of the Military Governor, U.S. Zone*, 1 March 1948, No. 33.

270. "Einführung des B-Verfahrens," *Amtsblatt des Hessischen Ministeriums für politische Befreiung*, 15 August 1947 (No. 22): 85–86.

271. 501/26, Wiesbaden. "Die Änderung des Befreiungsgesetzes. Wichtiges Ziel: Beschleunigung des Verfahrens. Von Ministerialdirektor K.H. Knappstein (n.d.); Kormann, *U.S. Denazification Policy in Germany*, 132–133; "Zweites Gesetz vom 9. April über die Abänderung einzelner Vorschriften des Gesetzes zur Befreiung von Nationalsozialismus und Militarismus vom 5. März 1946 (Zweites Änderungsgesetz)," *Gesetz—und Verordnungsblatt für das Land Hessen* (1948): 49.

272. Herz, "Fiasco of Denazification," 576.

273. "Zweites Gesetz vom 9. April über die Abänderung einzelner Vorschriften des Gesetzes zur Befreiung von Nationalsozialismus und Militarismus vom 5. März 1946 (Zweites Änderungsgesetz)," *Gesetz—und Verordnungsblatt für das Land Hessen* (1948): 19.

274. "Gesetz über die Anwendung des Gesetzes zur Befreiung von Nationalsozialismus und Militarismus (Befreiungsgesetz) auf Heimkehrer vom 15. April 1948," *Gesetz—und Verordnungsblatt für das Land Hessen* (1948): 65.

275. 501/26, Wiesbaden. Die Änderung des Befreiungsgesetzes. Wichtiges Ziel: Beschleunigung des Verfahrens. Von Ministerialdirektor K.H. Knappstein (n.d.).

276. Ibid.

277. Ibid.

278. Z45F 17/199–3/40 RG 260 OMGUS, Koblenz. AG 014.5. Subject: "Denazification of German Administration of Justice."

279. Z45F 17/217–3/4 RG 260 OMGUS, Koblenz. B/L Office of Military Government for Germany (U.S.) Administration of Justice Branch. APO 742 U.S. Army. Subject: Report Form Mg/Lg/10/F, 22 April 1948. Ka/gp. OMG for Hesse. Legal Division, APO 633. U.S. Army. 29 April 1948.

280. Z45F 17/217–3/4 RG 260 OMGUS, Koblenz. OMG for Germany (U.S.) Office of Military Governor APO 742. Subject: Report Form Mg/Leg/10/F. 22 April 1948.

281. Z45F 17/217–3/4 RG 260 OMGUS, Koblenz. B/L OMG for Germany (U.S.) Administration of Justice Br. APO 742 U.S. Army. Subject: Report Form Mg/Lg/10/F, 22 April 1948. Ka/gp. OMG for Hesse. Legal Division, APO 633. U.S. Army. 29 April 1948.

282. Z45F 17/199/40 RG 260 OMGUS, Koblenz. AGO 014.3. Subject: "Denazification of German Administration of Justice," 31 October 1947.

283. Z45F 17/217–3/4 RG 260 OMGUS, Koblenz. Memorandum. Subject: "Denazification of German Civil Service," 20 November 1947.

284. RG 260 OMGUS, 17/210–3/3, Wiesbaden. APO 633. Subject: "Personnel of German Courts," 27 February 1948.

285. Ibid.

286. Z45F 17/213–3/8 RG 260 OMGUS, Koblenz. "Former Nazis in Administration of Justice."

287. Z45F 17/217–3/4 RG 260 OMGUS, Koblenz. Memorandum. Subject: "Denazification of German Civil Service," 20 November 1947.

288. Griffith, "Denazification in the United States Zone," 72–73.

289. "Final Report on Foreign Aid," 8.

290. Latour, Volgelsang, *Okkupation und Wiederaufbau*, 143.

291. Moritz and Noam, *NS-Verbrechen vor Gericht: 1945–1955*, 14.

292. Zink, *United States in Germany: 1944–1955*, 167–168.

293. Klaus-Dietmar Henke, "Die Grenzen der politischen Säuberung in Deutschland nach 1945," *Westdeutschland 1945–1955: Unterwerfung, Kontrolle, Integration*, Ludolf Herbst, ed. (München: R. Oldenbourg Verlag, 1986), 130.

294. Diestelkamp, "Justiz in den Westzonen," 22.

295. Ibid.

296. 501/813, Wiesbaden. "Protokoll über die Sitzung des Denazifizierungs-Ausschusses beim Länderrat am 11./12. Februar in Wiesbaden: Hessische Vorschläge zur Überwindung der Denazifizierungskrise."

297. "Final Report on Foreign Aid," 128–129.

298. Freeman, *Hesse: A New German State*, 159–161.

299. Drew Middleton, "Many ex-Nazis re-enter German Political Life," *New York Times* (17 October 1948): 4E.

300. "Final Report on Foreign Aid," 127.

301. RG 260 OMGUS 8/189–3/3, Wiesbaden. Subject: "1948 Historical Report of Legal Division, OMG Hessen."

302. 458/1021, Wiesbaden. "Runderlaß wegen der Behandlung von Einstellungsgesuchen," 19 December 1948.

303. *Monthly Report of the Military Governor, U.S. Zone*, December 1948, No. 42.

304. 8/217–1/5, RG 260 OMGUS, Wiesbaden. Subject: "Military Government Policy in Denazification Matters," 7 May 1948.

305. 501/892, Wiesbaden. "Der Entnazifizierungsberater," Wiesbaden 23. June 1949.

306. *Monthly Report of the Military Governor, U.S. Zone*, 1 March 1949, No. 45.

307. 501/1204, Wiesbaden. "Gesetz über den Abschluß der politischen Befreiung in Hessen."

308. 501/1204, Wiesbaden. "Begründung zum Gesetz über den Abschluß der politischen Befreiung in Hessen."

309. 501/1072, Wiesbaden. Abwicklungsamt des ehemaligen Ministerium für politische Befreiung Ia—O5. Betr.: "Abschluss der politischen Befreiung im Lande Hessen," 25.11.49.

310. Niethammer, *Entnazifizierung in Bayern*, 531.

311. 501/892, Wiesbaden. M-Ia-05. "Betr.: Abwicklung des Ministeriums für politische Befreiung," 27. Oktober 1949.

312. 501/1212, Wiesbaden. Abwicklungsamt Ia-O5. Betr.: "Statistische Angaben über die Arbeit auf Grund des Gesetzes zur Befreiung von Nationalsozialismus und Militarismus," 12. August 1950.

313. 501/247, Wiesbaden. Betr.: "Stand der Entnazifizierung im Lande Hessen am 31.1.1954," 25. Februar 1954.

314. Rudolf Wassermann, *Auch die Justiz kann aus der Geschichte nicht aussteigen*, 187.

315. Klaus-Detlev Godau-Schüttke, *Ich habe nur dem Recht gedient: Die 'Renazifizierung' der Schleswig-Holsteinischen Justiz nach 1945* (Baden-Baden: Nomos Verlagsgesellschaft, 1993), p. 22; Diestelkamp, "Justiz in den Westzonen," pp. 27–28; Section 1, Art. 3, "Gesetz zur Regelung der Rechtsverhältnisse der unter Artikel 131 des Grundgesetzes fallenden Personen. Vom 11. Mai 1951," *Bundesgesetzblatt* I 1951: 308.

316. See Herz, "Fiasco of Denazification," 592, Latour, Vogelsang, *Okkupation und Wiederaufbau*, 179, and Diestelkamp, "Kontinuität und Wandel in der Rechtsordnung," 94.

317. Bark and Gress, *A History of West Germany*, 80–81, 85.

318. 501/662, Wiesbaden. Ermittlungszentrtalle, CII—Schw./Ti. Betr.: "Rechtsanwalt ____, Wiesbaden," 25 June 1949.

319. 501/465, Wiesbaden. Der Berufungskammer Fulda. Ber. Reg. Nr. 157/47. Aktenzeichen 1. Instanz Sch 27.

320. Schmid, "Denazification: A German Critique," 233.

321. Edward N. Peterson, *The American Occcupation of Germany: Retreat to Victory*, (Detroit: Wayne State University Press, 1977), 140; Stolper, *German Realities*, p. 59; Sträter, "Denazification," 47.

322. 462/1302, Wiesbaden. Der Spruchkammer Wetzlar; Aktenzeichen: We 15/14030 Fr. 2/46, 22 July 1946.

323. 501/39, Wiesbaden. Office of the Military Government for Greater Hesse. Denazification Division. ALY/gh. APO 633. Subject: "Disapproval of Reinstatement," 14 April 1947.

324. 8/79–1/4, RG 260 OMGUS, Wiesbaden. Denazification Branch, Legal Division, Administration of Justice, 15 January 1947.

325. 8/79–1/4, RG 260 OMGUS, Wiesbaden. Attested Copy, Spruchkammer Fritzlar-Homberg, Case record sign: FH/O 196, 10 August 1946.

326. 501/38, Wiesbaden. Office of the Military Government for Greater Hesse. Denazification Division. ECS/ivi. APO 633. Subject: "Prosecutor before the German People's Court," 10 March 1947.

327. Vollnhals, *Entnazifizierung: Politische Säuberung und Rehabilitierung in den vier Besatzungszonen*, 259–260.

328. Herz, "Fiasco of Denazification," 593. The syndrome of suppressing and forgetting the past affected the administration of justice to a significant extent. The implication of judges with National Socialism and the role of justice in the National Socialist regime only gradually began to be debated during the 1970s. Diestelkamp, "Justiz in den Westzonen," 23.

329. Schmid, "Denazification: A German Critique," 239.

330. 501/1212, Wiesbaden. Staatskanzlei, Abteilung Az LT/3c10/13. Drucksache I/382–. Betr.: "Geschäftsverkehr mit dem Landtag hier: Abschluß der Entnazifizierung; große Anfrage der Fraktion der BHE vom 7 März 1952," 13 März 1952.

331. Herz, "Fiasco of Denazification," 572.

332. Henke, "Die Grenzen der politischen Säuberung in Deutschland nach 1945," 130.

333. Delbert Clark, "Anti-Occupation Spirit Developing in Germany: Attack on U.S. denazification laws raise many questions of policy," *New York Times* (8 February 1948): 4E.

334. Herz, "Fiasco of Denazification," 572.

335. Friedmann, *Allied Military Government in Germany*, 119.

336. "OMGUS-Kritik an der Säuberung: Rund 85 Prozent Betroffene wieder eingestellt," *Frankfurter Rundschau* (11 April, 1948).

337. "Gesetz über den Abschluß der politischen Befreiung in Hessen vom 30. November 1949," *Gesetz—und Verordnungsblatt für das Land Groß-Hessen* (1949): 167.

338. 501/1212, Wiesbaden. Staatskanzlei Abteilung II Az LT/3c10/13. Drucksache I/382–. Betr.: Geschäftsverkehr mit dem Landtag hier: Abschluß der Fraktion der BHE vom 7. März 1952.

339. 462/1308, Wiesbaden. IIb AE 4309. Betr.: Gesuch um Zulassung als Rechtsanwalt, 9 January 1950.

340. Diestelkamp, "Die Justiz in den Westzonen," 23; "Kontinuität und Wandel in der Rechtsordnung," 96.

341. *Report of the Military Government for Germany, U.S. Zone*, 20 August 1945, No. 1.

342. Hodo von Hodenberg, "Zur Anwendung des Kontrollratsgesetzes Nr. 10 durch deutsche Gerichte," *Süddeutsche Juristenzeitung* (1947): 113.

343. Müller, *Hitler's Justice*, 290–291.

344. Mehnert and Schulte, *Deutschland-Jahrbuch 1949*, 103.

345. "Law No. 10: Punishment of Persons Guilty of War Crimes, Crimes against Peace and against Humanity," *Official Gazette of the Control Council for Germany* No. 3 (31 January 1946): 50–55.

346. von Hodenberg, "Zur Anwendung des Kontrollratsgesetzes Nr. 10 durch deutsche Gerichte," 114.

347. Art. 2 (1), "Law No. 10: Punishment of Persons Guilty of War Crimes, Crimes against Peace and against Humanity," *Official Gazette of the Control Council for Germany* No. 3 (31 January 1946): 50–51.

348. Art. 3 (1d), "Law No. 10: Punishment of Persons Guilty of War Crimes, Crimes against Peace and against Humanity," *Official Gazette of the Control Council for Germany* No. 3 (31 January 1946): 52–53.

349. Broszat, "Siegerjustiz oder strafrechtliche 'Selbstreinigung'," 496.

350. 8/216–1/12 RG 260 OMGUS, Wiesbaden. APO 633. Subject: "Jurisdiction of German Courts," 2 March 1949.

351. Grunberger, *The Twelve Year Reich*, 108–115.

352. RG 260 OMGUS, 17/210–2/6, Wiesbaden. APO 633, Subject: "Denouncements," 20 January 1946.

353. Z45F 17/56–3/7 RG 260/ OMGUS, Koblenz. Provenance: OMGUS, LD, LA Br., Folder Title: La 91 The German Government, German courts. Memo: to Lt.Col. A.S. Brown, Legal Division; Subject: Alleged Violations of Control Council Law No. 10, 4 March 1946.

354. Loewenstein, "Reconstruction of the Administration of Justice," 436–437.

355. Johnson, "Denazification," 71.

356. Z1/1235A, Koblenz. "Besprechungsgegenstand: Gesetz zur Ahndung nationalsozialistischer Straftaten," Stuttgart. 17 April 1946.

357. Z45F 17/56–3/7 RG 260/ OMGUS, Koblenz. OMGUS LD, LA Br. La 91 The German Government, German courts. Memo: to Lt. Col. A.S. Brown, Legal Division; Subject: Alleged Violations of Control Council Law No. 10, 4 March 1946.

358. Ibid.

359. Ibid.

360. Loewenstein, "Reconstruction of the Administration of Justice," 436–437.

361. Richard Lange, "Zum Denunziantenproblem," *Süddeutsche Juristenzeitung* (1948): 302. Part I, Art. 5, para. 9 defined a *Major Offender* as one who had actively denounced an opponent of the National Socialist dictatorship out of self-interest or personal gain in cooperation with the *Gestapo*, SS, SD, or similar organisation, or had contributed to their persecution. Schullze, *Gesetz zur Befreiung von Nationalsozialismus und Militarismus vom 5. März 1946*: 8.

362. RG 260 OMGUS, 17/210–3/3, Wiesbaden. APO 655. Subject: "Reports of Important Trials," 5 November 1947.

363. Loewenstein, "Reconstruction of the Administration Justice," 437.

364. "Ordinance No. 7: Organization and Powers of Certain Military Tribunals" (18 October 1946), *Military Government Gazette* Issue B December 1946: 10–15.

365. "Gesetz zur Ahndung nationalsozialistischer Straftaten vom 29. Mai 1946," *Gesetz—und Verordnungsblatt für Groß-Hessen* (1946): 136.

366. "Gesetz zur Wiedergutmachung nationalsozialistischen Unrechts in der Strafrechtspflege vom 29. Mai 1946," *Gesetz—und Verordnungsblatt für das Land Groß-Hessen* (1946): 136–137; "Zweites Gesetz zur Wiedergutmachung nationalsozialistischen Unrechts in der Strafrechtspflege vom 13. November 1946," *Gesetz—und Verordnungsblatt für das Land Groß-Hessen* (1946): 223.

367. Neidhard, "Die Rechtspflege in der Gesetzgebung der amerikanischen Zone," 119.
368. Ibid.
369. Broszat, "Siegerjustiz oder Strafrechtliche 'Selbstreinigung,'" 496.
370. Loewenstein, "Reconstruction of the Administration of Justice," 437.
371. "Gemeinsame Gesetzgebung der 3 Länder," *Süddeutsche Juristenzeitung* (1946): 101.
372. "Zweites Gesetz zur Wiedergutmachung nationalsozialistischen Unrechts in der Strafrechtspflege vom 13. November 1946," *Gesetz—und Verordnungsblatt für das Land Groß-Hessen* (1946): 223.
373. "Ergänzungsgesetz vom 16. August 1947 zum Gesetz zur Ahndung nationalsozialistischer Straftaten vom 15. Juni 1946," *Gesetz—und Verordnungsblatt für das Land Hessen* (1947): 64.
374. "Ergänzungsgesetz vom 16. August 1947 zum 1. Gesetz zur Wiedergutmachung nationalsozialistischen Unrechts in der Strafrechtspflege vom 15. Juni 1946," *Gesetz—und Verordnungsblatt für das Land Hessen* (1947): 64.
375. *Monthly Report of the Military Governor, U.S. Zone*, 31 October 1946, No. 17.
376. RG 260, 8/188–2/5, Wiesbaden. APO 633. Subject: "Weekly Summary Report for Legal Division from 18 August to 24 August 1946," 23 August 1946.
377. Z45 F 17/56–3/7 RG 260/ OMGUS, Koblenz. AJ 015.2 18 November 1946, Subject: "Report on Inspection of German Courts in Greater Hesse from 28 October to 4 November 1946."
378. Freeman, *Hesse: A New German State*, 135.
379. *Monthly Report of the Military Governor, U.S. Zone*, 30 April 1947, No. 22.
380. Broszat, "Siegerjustiz oder Strafrechtliche 'Selbstreinigung,'" 500.
381. Bernhard Diestelkamp, "Die Justiz nach 1945 und ihr Umgang mit der eigenen Vergangenheit," *Justizalltag im Dritten Reich*, eds. Bernhard Diestelkamp and Michael Stolleis (Frankfurt-am-Main: Fischer Taschenbuch Verlag, 1988), 134.
382. Theo Sommer, "The Nazis in the Judiciary," *The Politics of Western Germany* (New York: Frederick A. Prager, 1963) ed. Walter Stahl, 241–242.
383. Diestelkamp, "Die Justiz in den Westzonen," 26; Diestelkamp, "Die Justiz nach 1945 und ihr Umgang mit der eigenen Vergangenheit," 133, 145.
384. Ernst Noam and Wolf-Arno Kropat, eds., *Juden vor Gericht, 1933–1945: Dokumente aus hessischen Justizakten* (Wiesbaden: Kommission für die Geschichte der Juden in Hessen, 1975), 168–173.
385. Moritz, Noam, *NS-Verbrechen vor Gericht: 1945–1955*, 309–310.
386. Ibid., 315.
387. Ibid., 310.
388. Ibid., 315.
389. Ibid., 316.
390. The penalty for extra-marital relations between Jews and German nationals or individuals of "related blood" was imprisonment in a jail (*Gefängnis*) or prison for capital offenders (*Zuchthaus*). Art. 5(2), "Gesetz zum Schutz des deutschen Blutes und der deutschen Ehre. Vom 15. September 1935," *Reichsgesetzblatt* I 1935: 1147.
391. Mortiz, Noam, *NS-Verbrechen vor Gericht: 1945–1955*, 311–312.

392. Ibid., 316–317.

393. Ibid., 318.

394. Ibid., 321–324.

395. Ibid., 326–327; Diestelkamp, "Die Justiz nach 1945 und ihr Umgang mit der eigenen Vergangenheit," 137.

396. Müller, *Hitler's Justice*, 276.

397. Gustav Radbruch, "Gesetzliches Unrecht und übergesetzliches Recht," *Süddeutsche Juristenzeitung* (1946): 107.

398. Sommer, "The Nazis in the Judiciary," 247.

399. Diestelkamp. "Die Justiz in den Westzonen," 27; Ingo Müller, *Hitler's Justice*, 283; Moritz, Noam, *NS-Verbrechen vor Gericht: 1945–1955*, 336–337.

400. Diestelkamp, "Die Justiz in den Westzonen," 27; "Die Justiz nach 1945 und ihr Umgang mit der eigenen Vergangenheit," 140–145 *passim*.

401. Stolleis, "Rechtsordnung und Justizpolitik: 1945–1949," 396.

402. Loewenstein, "Reconstruction of the Administration of Justice," 465–466.

403. Joseph F. Napoli, "Denazification from an American's Viewpoint," *Annals of the American Academy of Political and Social Science* Vol. 264 (July 1949): 121.

404. Gimbel, *A German Community under American Occupation*, 7.

405. Clark, "Anti-Occupation Spirit Developing in Germany,": 4E.

406. 8/217–3/13, RG 260 OMGUS, Wiesbaden. APO 633. Subject: Monthly Report, 10 July 1948.

407. Loewenstein, "Comment on Denazification," 366.

408. Bower, *The Pledge Betrayed: America and Britain and the Denazification of Postwar Germany*, 155–156.

409. 501/831, Wiesbaden. Office of Military Government for Greater Hesse (Denazification) APO 633. Betr.: "Ausfuerung d. Kontrollratgesetzes No. 38," 23 November 1946. It has been argued that Control Council Directives Nos. 24 and 38 were promulgated largely as a result of American pressure, and that serious effort to implement those directives in full was only made in the U.S. zone. Zink, *United States in Germany: 1944–1955*, 166.

410. 501/37, Wiesbaden. Office of Military Government for Germany (U.S.), Office of Military Governor, APO 742. AG 010 (CO). Subject: "Implementation of Control Council Directive No. 38 in the U.S. Zone," 19 October 1946.

411. Loewenstein, "Political Reconstruction in Germany," 34.

At the end of October 1945, British occupation authorities led the way in reinstating former National Socialists to judicial office under the so-called piggy-back policy, allowing a jurist formally charged with having been a former member of the NSDAP, along with every jurist who wasn't charged with a guilty political record under the denazification procedure. This restriction was lifted in June 1946, allowing any jurist to be considered for judicial appointment after having been through denazification. Wenzlau, *Der Wiederaufbau der Justiz*, 103, 130.

The practice in the Soviet zone was to rapidly train people's judges and people's prosecutors, without consideration for the quality of education. Those new jurists were to be adapted to the planned reorganisation of the administration of justice, in which the traditional professionalised handling of the law was considered unnecessary, or even a nuisance. The elimination of the legal and economic order wasn't intended in the western occupation zones, and therefore such a radical programme for training a new generation of jurists was inadmissible. Diestelkamp, "Die Justiz in den Westzonen," 22; Georg-August Zinn, "Administration of Justice in Germany," 39; Hilde Benjamin et al., *Zur Geschichte der Rechtspflege in der DDR: 1945–1949* (Berlin: Staatsverlag der Deutschen Demokratischen Republik, 1976), 90–96 *passim.*

See Reinhard Grohnert, *Die Entnazifizierung in Baden, 1945–1949: Konkeptionen und Praxis der "Epuration" am Beispiel eines Landes der französischen Besatzungszone* (Stuttgart: W. Kohlhammer Verlag, 1991), pp. 99–102 for the example of the denazification of jurists in French-occupied Baden.

412. "Final Report on Foreign Aid," 128.

413. Michael Balfour and John Mair, *Four Power Control in Germany and Austria: 1945–1946*, ed. Arnold Toynbee (London: Oxford University Press, 1956), 171–172.

414. Harol Zink, *American Military Government in Germany* (New York: MacMillan, 1947), 125.

415. Balfour and Mair, *Four Power Control in Germany and Austria*, 171–172.

416. Diestelkamp, "Kontinuität und Wandel in der Rechtsordnung," 93.

417. Knappstein, "Die versäumte Revolution: Wird das Experiment der 'Denazifizierung gelingen?,'" 668.

418. Earl F. Ziemke, *The U.S. Army in the Occupation of Germany*, 445–446.

419. Sträter, "Denazification," 45, 50.

420. Loewenstein, "Reconstruction of the Administration of Justice," 443–444; Sträter, "Denazification," 50.

421. 462/1308, Wiesbaden. Subject: Admission to the Bar, 12 November 1945.

422. Diestelkamp, "Kontinuität und Wandel in der Rechtsordnung," 95.

423. Diestelkamp, "Die Justiz nach 1945 und ihr Umgang mit der eigenen Vergangenheit," 145.

424. Loewenstein, "Reconstruction of the Administration of Justice," 452.

425. 501/1592, Wiesbaden. "Das Ende der Denazifizierung" (n.d.).

426. 8/217–3/13, RG 260, OMGUS, Wiesbaden. APO 633. Subject: Monthly Division Report, 10 May 1948.

427. Niethammer, *Entnazifizierung in Bayern*, 531–532.

428. Sommer, "The Nazis in the Judiciary," 240–241.

429. Ibid., 244–245; Diestelkamp, "Die Justiz nach 1945 und ihr Umgang mit der eigenen Vergangenheit," 137–138.

430. 501/4886. Wi/Tr., II/1—Az: 25aO2. "Betr.: "Richter und Staatsanwälte des früheren Volksgerichtshofs und der dortigen Reichsanwaltschaft," 22 February 1957; II3—23 330-3609/57. "Richter und Staatsanwälte des früheren Volksgerichtshofs und der dortigen Reichsanwaltschaft," 28 January 1957.

431. Gimbel, *A German Community under American Occupation*, 209.

432. Sommer, "Nazis in the Judiciary," 244.

433. Vollnhals, *Entnazifizierung: Politische Säuberung und Rehabilitierung in den vier Besatzungszonen*, 63.

434. Diestelkamp, "Kontinuität und Wandel in der Rechtsordnung," 94–95; "Die Justiz nach 1945 und ihr Umgang mit der eigenen Vergangenheit," 145–148.

435. "Das Besatzungsregime auf dem Gebiet der Rechtspflege," 45–46.

436. Rudolf Wassermann, "Richteramt und politisches System," *Revue d'Allemagne* Vol. 5 (1973): 904.

Conclusion

1. Friedmann, *The Allied Military Government of Germany*, 68.

2. Klaus-Dietmar Henke, "Die Grenzen der politischen Säuberung in Deutschland nach 1945," p. 127.

3. Jones, "Eradicating Nazism from the British Zone of Germany: Early Policy and Practice," 148–149.

4. The problem of reinstatement or removal from office of incumbents in the administration of justice who had served in a dictatorship was later considered during the reconstruction of the administration of justice in the former *Länder* of the German Democratic Republic following the reunification of Germany on 3 October 1990. The initial consideration of the problem included the option of removing all jurists who had been members of the former ruling SED, drawing a parallel to the postwar denazification. It was decided that the criterion for reinstatement would be based on their performance in office—whether a judge had administered justice on the basis of fairness and impartiality in cases of a non-political nature. Conversation with Herr Dr. Jr. Rolf Faber, Leitender Ministerialrat at the Thüringen Justizministerium. Hessisches Hauptstaatsarchiv, 7 April 1994.

Bibliography

Archival Sources

Bundesarchiv: Koblenz

Z1/14
Z1/16
Z1/65
Z1/92
Z1/168
Z1/218
Z1/279
Z1/639
Z1/674
Z1/958
Z1/1213
Z1/1230
Z1/1231
Z1/1232
Z1/1235A
Z1/12.36
Z1/1237
Z1/1255
Z1/1259
Z1/1282
Z1/1283
Z1/1286A
Z1/1289
Z1/1319

Z45F 11/3–1/24 RG 260 OMGUS
Z45F 11/5–2/1 RG 260 OMGUS
Z45F 17/56–3/7 RG 260 OMGUS
Z45F 17/199–3/40 RG 260 OMGUS
Z45F 17/199–3/41 RG 260 OMGUS
Z45F 17/213–3/8 RG 260 OMGUS
Z45F 17/217–3/4 RG 260 OMGUS

Hessisches Hauptstaatsarchiv: Wiesbaden

8/19–1/13 RG 260 OMGUS
8/79–1/4 RG 260 OMGUS
8/79–3/6 RG 260 OMGUS
8/187–1/1 RG 260 OMGUS
8/188–1/21 RG 260 OMGUS
8/188–2/5 RG 260 OMGUS
8/189–3/1 RG 260 OMGUS
8/189–3/2 RG 260 OMGUS
8/189–3/18 RG 260 OMGUS
8/189–3/25 RG 260 OMGUS
8/213–1/18 RG 260 OMGUS
8/216–1/2 RG 260 OMGUS
8/216–1/12 RG 260 OMGUS
8/217–1/5 RG 260 OMGUS
8/217–3/13 RG 260 OMGUS
17/210–2/6 RG 260 OMGUS

8/189–3/3 RG 260 OMGUS
8/189–3/10 RG 260 OMGUS
17/210–3/3 RG 260 OMGUS
17/211–2/3 RG 260 OMGUS

458/179	461/11073	501/42(1)	501/1071
458/670	461/11074	501/42(1)	501/1072
458/725	461/11095	501/42(2)	501/1169
458/773	461/11103	501/42(2)	501/1175
458/775	461/11107	501/42(1)	501/1199
458/1014	461/11112	501/61	501/1202
458/1015	461/11139	501/97	501/1204
458/1016	461/11158	501/247	501/1212
458/1017	462/1293	501/276	501/1234
458/1021	462/1295	501/409(1)	501/1586
458/1024	462/1301	501/465	501/1592
460/525	462/1302	501/468(1)	502/919
460/528	462/1308	501/530	502/1892
460/533	462/1311	501/561(2)	502/1895
460/540	462/1330	501/662	502/2773A
460/545	463/945	501/803	502/2773B
460/568	463/929	501/813	502/3203
460/569	463/935	501/822	502/4882
460/570	463/1118	501/823	502/4886
460/571	501/18	501/831	1126/4
460/573	501/25(1)	501/843	1126/10
460/608	501/26	501/884	1126/11
460/632	501/37	501/892	1126/17
460/639	501/38	501/927	1126/19
460/645	501/39	501/960	1126/33
460/826	501/40		

Published Sources and Documents

Amtsblatt des Hessischen Ministeriums für politische Befreiung. 15 August 1947, No. 22.

Bayerisches Gesetz—und Verordnungsblatt 1946

Bundesgesetzblatt I 1951

Documents on Germany: 1944–1961. New York: Greenwood Press, 1968.

Enactments and Approved Papers of the Control Council and Coordinating Committee: Allied Control Authority, Germany. 1945, Vol. 1. Legal Division: Office of Military Government for Germany.

Enactments and Approved Papers of the Control Council and Coordinating Committee: Allied Control Authority, Germany. January 1, 1946–February 28, 1946, Vol. 2. Legal Division: Office of Military Government for Germany.

"Final Report on Foreign Aid of the House Select Committee on Foreign Aid," 1 May 1948, 80th Congress, 2nd Session, 6 January–31 December 1948, *House Reports* Vol. 6 No. 1845. Washington: U.S. Government Printing Office, 1948.

Foreign Relations of the United States, Diplomatic Papers, Vols. 1 and 2: *The Conference of Berlin (The Potsdam Conference) 1945.* Washington: U.S. Government Printing Office, 1960.

Foreign Relations of the United States, Diplomatic Papers, 1949, Vol. 3, *Council of Foreign Ministers; Germany and Austria.* Washington: U.S. Government Printing Office, 1974.

Foreign Relations of the United States, Diplomatic Papers, 1943. Vol. 1: *General.* Washington: U.S. Government Printing Office, 1963.

Foreign Relations of the United States, Diplomatic Papers: The Conferences of Malta and Yalta. Washington: U.S. Government Printing Office, 1965.

Foreign Relations of the United States: The Conference at Quebec, 1944. Washington: U.S. Government Printing Office, 1971.

Germany 1947–1949: The Story in Documents. Washington: U.S. Government Printing Office, 1950.

Gesetz- und Verordnungsblatt für das Land Hessen: 1946–1949.

Handbook for Military Government in Germany Prior to Defeat or Surrender. Office of the Chief of Staff: Supreme Headquarters, Allied Expeditionary Force, December 1944.

Judgment of International Military Tribunal for the Trial of German Major War Criminals (30 September and 1 October 1946). London: His Majesty's Stationery Office, 1946.

Military Government Gazette, Germany, United States Zone. Issues A–O.

Official Gazette of the Allied High Commission for Germany. Nos. 1–126 (23 September 1949–5 May 1955).

Official Gazette of the Control Council for Germany. Nos. 1–19. (October 1945–August 1948).

Reichsgesetzblatt I: 1926, 1933–1945.

Report on Germany: September 21 1949–July 31, 1952. Office of the U.S. High Commissioner for Germany, 1952.

Technical Manual for Legal and Prison Officers. Supreme Headquarters, Allied Expeditionary Force, G-5 Division. 1945.

Trial of War Criminals before the Nuremberg Military Tribunals under Control Council Law No. 10 (Green Series) Military Tribunal III.

Primary Sources

Acheson, Dean, John J. McCloy, Henry Parkman, Sterling Fisher. "Our Military Government Policy in Germany." *U.S. Department of State Bulletin* 13 (2 September 1945): 310–318.

Arndt, Adolf. "Die staats–und verwaltungsrechtliche Entwicklung in Groß-Hessen." *Deutsche Rechts-Zeitschrift* (1946): 185–188.

———. "Das Strafmaß." *Süddeutsche Juristenzeitung* (1946): 30–31.

———. "Status and Development of Constitutional Law in Germany." *Annals of the American Academy of Political and Social Science* Vol. 260 (1948): 1–9.

———. "Zur Auslegung des Ges. 13 der Allierten Hohen Kommission." *Neue Juristische Wochenschrift* (1950): 212–213.

Arndt, Adolf and Professor Herrfahrdt. "Gereichtigkeit gegen jedermann: Die Eröffnung des Landgerichts Marburg." *Marburger Presse* (2 October 1945).

"Der Aufbau der Justiz in der amerikanischen Zone: Groß-Hessen." *Deutsche Rechts-Zeitschrift* (1946): 120.

Auld, F.C. "Law Reform in Germany." *Canadian Bar Review* 12 (1934): 26–29.

"Zur Auswirkung der Gesetzgebung der Besatzungsmächte auf das deutsche Strafgesetzbuch." *Süddeutsche Juristenzeitung* (1946): 121–124.

Bach, Julian, Jr. *America's Germany: An Account of the Occupation.* New York: Random House, 1946.

Bauer, Wilhelm. "Wiederaufbau der Verwaltungsrechtspflege." *Süddeutsche Juristenzeitung* (1946): 149–152.

Becker. "Der Richterliche Widerstand." *Süddeutsche Juristenzeitung* (1947): 480–490.

Benjamin, Hilde et al., *Zur Geschichte der Rechtspflege der DDR: 1945–1949.* Berlin: Staatsverlag der Deutschen Demokratischen Republik, 1976.

Das Besatzungsregime auf dem Gebiet der Rechtspflege. Tübingen: Institut für Besatzungsfragen Tübingen, 15 November 1949.

Boberach, Heinz, ed. *Richterbriefe: Dokumente zur Beeinflussung der deutschen Rechtsprechung, 1942–1944.* Boppard-am-Rhein: Harald Boldt Verlag, 1975.

Bodenheimer, Edgar. "Significant Developments in German Legal Philosophy since 1945." *American Journal of Comparative Law* Vol. 3 (1945): 379–396.

Brauer, Herbert. "Die Neuordnung der Strafrechtspflege in Verfahren vor den Gerichten der amerikanischen Militärregierung." *Neue Juristische Wochenschrift* (1949): 127–131.

Brecht, Arnold. "Re-establishing German Government." *Annals of the American Academy of Political and Social Science* 267 (January 1950): 28–42.

Brinkmann, Werner. "Die Ungleichheit der Strafmessung." *Deutsche Justiz* (1936): 1653–1657.

Broderson, Uwe, and Ingo von Münch. *Gesetze des NS-Staates: Dokumente eines Unrechtssystems.* Paderborn: Ferdinand Schöningh, 1982.

Brown, John Mason. "The Judicial System of the Nazi Party." *American Political Science Review* 38 (1944): 96–103.

Buchheim, Hans. "Ein NS-Funktionär zum Niemöller-Prozess." *Vierteljahrshefte für Zeitgeschichte* 4 (1956): 307–315.

Buchheim, Hans et al., *Anatomy of the SS State,* trans. Richard Barry. London: Collins, 1968.

Cassidy, Velma Hastings. "American Policy in Occupied Areas." *U.S. Department of State Bulletin* 15 (1946): 291–296.

———. "The Beginnings of Self-Government in the American Zone of Germany," *U.S. Department of State Bulletin* 16 (1947): 223–233.

Clark, Delbert. "Anti-Occupation Spirit Developing in Germany: Attack on U.S. denazification laws raise many questions of policy." *New York Times* (8 February 1948): 4E.

Clay, Lucius D. *Decision in Germany.* Garden City: Doubleday & Company, 1950.

Coing, Helmut. "Zur Frage der strafrechtlichen Haftung der Richter für die Anwendung naturrechtswidriger Gesetze." *Süddeutsche Juristenzeitung* (1946): 61–64.

Cole, Taylor. "National Socialism and the German Labor Courts." *Journal of Politics* 3 (1941): 169–167.

———. "National Socialism and the German Labor Courts in Western Germany." *Journal of Politics* 18 (1956): 479–498.

Cook, J. J. "The Judicial System of Germany." *The Juridical Review* 1 (1889): 70–80, 184–192, 298–306.

Dernedde, Dr., Oberregierungsrat a.D., Oldenbourg. "Die Gerichtsbarkeit auf den vorbehaltenen Gebieten." *Justiz und Verwaltung* (1950): 27–31.

Deutsch, P. Eberhard. "Military Government: Administration of Occupied Territory." *American Bar Association Journal* 33 (1947): 133–136, 208.

Dorn, Walter L. "The Debate over American Occupation Policy in Germany in 1944–1945." *Political Science Quarterly* 72 (December 1957): 481–501.

Ehard, Hans. "Das Gesetz zur Befreiung von Nationalsozialismus und Militarismus." *Süddeutsche Juristenzeitung* (1946): 7–9.

Eisenberg, Max. "Zur Gültigkeit der Durchführungsbestimmungen zum Ehegesetz 38." *Süddeutsche Juristenzeitung* (1946): 79.

von Elmenau, J. "Aufbau und Tätigkeit des Länderrats der U.S.-Zone." *Deutsche Rechts-Zeitschrift* (1946): 113–117.

Euler, August Martin. "Unser Rechtsspiegel." *Hessische Nachrichten* (3 November 1945): 5.

Fahy, Charles. "The Lawyer in Military Government of Germany." *Department of State Bulletin* Vol. 15 (1946): 852–859.

Feis, Herbert. *Between War and Peace: The Potsdam Conference.* Princeton: Princeton University Press, 1960.

Figge, Robert. "Die Verantwortlichkeit des Richters." *Süddeutsche Juristenzeitung* (1947): 179–184.

Fraenkel, Ernst. *The Dual State: A Contribution to the Theory of Dictatorship*, trans. E. A. Shils. New York: Oxford University Press, 1941.

Frank, Hans. *Nationalsozialistisches Handbuch für Recht und Gesetzgebung.* München: Reichsrechtsamt der NSDAP, 1935.

———. *Nationalsozialistische Leitsätze für ein neues Strafrecht.* Berlin: Reichsrechtsamt der NSDAP, 1935.

———. *Rechtsgrundlegung des naionalsozialistischen Führerstaates.* München: Zentralverlag der NSDAP, 1938.

Frederiksen, Oliver J. *The American Military Occupation of Germany, 1945–1953.* Karlsruhe: Historical Division of the U.S. High Commission for Germany, 1953.

Freeman, Dexter L. *Hesse: A New German State.* Frankfurt-am-Main: Druck und Verlaghaus, 1948.

Freisler, Roland. "Recht, Richter und Gesetz." *Deutsche Justiz* (1933): 694–696.

———. "Richter, Recht und Gesetz." *Deutsche Justiz* (1934): 1333–1335.

———. "Volk, Richter und Recht" *Deutsche Justiz* (1935): 1160–1163.

Friedmann, Wolfgang. *The Allied Military Government in Germany.* London: Stevens & Sons, 1947.

Friedrich, Carl J. "Military Government and Dictatorship," *Annals of the American Academy of Political and Social Science* 267 (January 1950): 1–7.

———. "Rebuilding the German Constitution," *American Political Science Review* 43 (1949): 461–482, 704–720.

Friedrich, Carl J. et al. *American Experiences in Military Government in World War Two.* New York: Rinehart & Company, 1948.

Garner, James W. "The Judiciary of the German Empire." *Political Science Quarterly* 17 (1902): 490–514.

———. "Recent German Nationality Legislation." *American Journal of International Law* 30 (1936): 96–99.

"Gemeinsame Gesetzgebung der 3 Länder." *Süddeutsche Juristenzeitung* (1946): 101–102.

"Gemeinsame Gesetzgebung der Länder." *Süddeutsche Juristenzeitung* (1946)" 15–17.

"Gemeinsame Gesetzgebung der Länder: Stand vom 14. 3. 47." *Süddeutsche Juristenzeitung* (1947): 223–224.

"Gemeinsame Gesetzgebung der Länder: Stand vom 9. 4. 1948." *Süddeutsche Juristenzeitung* (1948): 219–220.

"Die Gesetzgebung der Länder (amerikanische Zone): Grosshessen." *Süddeutsche Juristenzeitung* (1946): 242.

"Die Gesetzgebung der Länder (amerikanische Zone): Hessen." *Süddeutsche Juristenzeitung* (1947): 222–223.

"Die Gesetzgebung der Länder (amerikanische Zone): Hessen." *Süddeutsche Juristenzeitung* (1948): 343.

"Die Gesetzgebung der Länder (amerikanische Zone): Hessen." *Süddeutsche Juristenzeitung* (1948): 562.

"Die Gesetzgebung der Länder: Verwaltungsrechtspflege." *Süddeutsche Juristenzeitung* (1946): 131.

Gillen, J. F. J. *State and Local Government in West Germany, 1945–1953.* Bad Godesberg-Mehlem: Historical Division, Office of the High Commissioner for Germany, 1953.

Griffith, William E. "Denazification in the United States Zone of Germany." *Annals of the American Academy of Political and Social Science* 269 (1950): 68–76.

Guradze, Heinz. "The Laenderrat: Landmark of German Reconstruction." *Western Political Quarterly* 3 (June 1950): 190–213.

Güstrow, Dietrich. *Tödlicher Alltag. Strafverteidiger im Dritten Reich.* Berlin: Siedler Verlag, 1981.

Hall, Jerome. "Nulla Poena Sine Lege." *Yale Law Journal* 47 (December 1937): 165–193.

Härtel, Lia, ed. *Der Länderrat des amerikanischen Besatzungsgebietes.* Stuttgart: W. Kohlhammer Verlag, 1951.

Harvey, C. P. "Sources of Law in Germany." *Michigan Law Review* Vol. 11 (1948): 196–213.

Hayward, Edwin J. "Co-ordination of Military and Civilian Civil Affairs Planning." *Annals of the American Academy of Political and Social Science* 267 (1950): 87–97.
Heneman, Harlow J. "American Control Organization in Germany." *Public Administration Review* 6 (1946): 1–9.
Herrfahrdt, Heinrich. "Der Streit um den Positivismus in der gegenwärtigen deutschen Rechtswissenschaft." *Deutsche Rechts-Zeitschrift* (1949): 32–33.
Herz, John H. "The Fiasco of Denazification in Germany." *Political Science Quarterly* 63 (December 1948): 569–594.
———. "German Administration under the Nazi Regime." *American Political Science Review* 40 (1946): 682–702.
Herzberg, Arno A. "The Situation of the Lawyer in Germany." *American Bar Association Journal* 27 (1941): 294–295.
Himmelman, H.A. "'Democratisation of Justice' in the Soviet Zone." *Contemporary Review* 176 (July 1949): 29–33.
von Hodenberg, Hodo. "Zur Anwendung des Kontrollratsgesetzes Nr. 10 durch deutsche Gerichte." *Süddeutsche Juristenzeitung* (1947): 113–124.
Holborn, Hajo. *American Military Government: Its Organization and Policies.* Buffalo: William S. Hein, 1975.
Holt, John B. "Corporative Occupational Organization and Democracy in Germany." *Public Administration Review* 8 (1948): 34–40.
Hubbard, Ralph B. "G-5 in Germany," *Infantry Journal* (November 1946): 27–30.
Hudson, Richard. "The Judicial System of the German Empire." *Michigan Law Review* 1 (1902): 121–126.
Hull, Cordell. *The Memoirs of Cordell Hull*, Vol. 2. New York: MacMillan, 1948.
Ipsen, Hans Peter. "Deutsche Gerichtsbarkeit unter Besatzungshoheit." *Festschrift zu Ehren von Rudolf Laun.* Hamburg: Verlag Hamburg, 1948.
Jerusalem, Franz W. "Zum Verfassungsproblem." *Süddeutsche Juristenzeitung* (1946): 108–111.
Johnson, Alvin (foreword; anonymous author), "Denazification," *Social Research* 14 (1947): 59–74.
Jones, J. Walter. Oxford Pamphlets in World Affairs, No. 21: *Nazi Conception of Law.* Oxford: Oxford University Press, 1939.
"Justizverwaltungsnachrichten: Großhessen." *Süddeutsche Juristenzeitung* (1946): 17–18.
Kern, Eduard. "Die Stunde der Justiz." *Deutsche Rechts-Zeitschrift* (April 1947): 105–107.
Kirchheimer, Otto. "Criminal Law in National-Socialist Germany." *Studies in Philosophy and Social Science*, ed. Max Horkheimer. Munich: Korel-Verlag, 1970: 444–463.
———. "The Legal Order of National Socialism." *Studies in Philosophy and Social Science* 9 (1941): 456–475.
———. *Political Justice: The Use of Legal Procedure for Political Ends.* Princeton University Press, 1961.
Klein, Friedrich. "Das Besatzungsstatut für Deutschland." *Süddeutsche Juristenzeitung* (1949): 737–753.

Knappen, Marshall. *And Call it Peace.* Chicago: University of Chicago Press, 1947.
Köhler, Walter. "Die Generalklauseln im Neuaufbau des deutschen bürgerlichen Rechts." *Süddeutsche Juristenzeitung* (1946): 165–168.
Kramer, Gerhard F. "The Influence of National-Socialism on the Courts of Justice and the Police." *The Third Reich.* London: Weidenfeld and Nicolson, 1955: 595–632.
Kleine, Heinz. "Wiedergutmachungsrecht." *Süddeutsche Juristenzeitung* (1946): 36.
Kleinrahm, Kurt. "Rechtsnatur und Rechtswirkungen der Beschränkungen deutscher Gerichtsbarkeit durch das Besatzungsrecht." *Deutsche Rechts-Zeitschrift* (1948): 232–235.
Koch, H. Wolfgang. *In the Name of the Volk: Political Justice in Hitler's Germany.* New York: St. Martin's Press, 1989.
Kogon, Eugen. "Das Recht auf den politischen Irrtum." *Frankfurter Hefte* (1947): 641–655.
Knappstein, Karl Heinrich. "Die versäumte Revolution: Wird das Experiment der 'Denazifizierung' gelingen?" *Die Wandlung* (1947): 663–677.
Krieger, Leonhard. "The Interregnum in Germany: March–August 1945." *Political Science Quarterly* 64 (1949): 507–532.
Lange, Richard. "Zum Denunziantenproblem." *Süddeutsche Juristenzeitung* (1948): 302–311.
Loewenstein, Karl. "Comment on 'Denazification.'" *Social Research* 14 (1947): 365–369.
———. "Dictatorship and the German Constitution: 1933–1937." *University of Chicago Law Review* (1937): 537–574.
———. *Hitler's Germany: The Nazi Background to War.* New York: MacMillan, 1944.
———. "Justice," *Governing Postwar Germany* ed. Edward H. Litchfield. Ithaca: Cornell University Press, 1950: 236–262.
———. "Law and the Legislative Process in Occupied Germany." *Yale Law Review* 57 (1948): 724–760, 994–1022.
———. "Law in the Third Reich." *Yale Law Review* 45 (1936): 779–815.
———. "Political Reconstruction in Germany, Zonal and Interzonal" *Change and Crisis in European Government,* ed. James Kerr Pollock. New York: Rinehart & Company, 1949: 29–43.
———. "Reconstruction of the Administration of Justice in American-Occupied Germany." *Harvard Law Review* 61 (1947–1948): 419–467.
Löschhorn, Werner. "Rechtsweg und Befreiungsgesetz." *Süddeutsche Juristenzeitung* (1946): 111–113.
Lühr [Amts- und Landrichter]. "Darf der Richter gegen das Gesetz entscheiden?" *Deutsche Richterzeitung* (1934): 33–35.
Mannzen, Walter. "Die Bindung des Richters an Gesetz und Recht." *Süddeutsche Juristenzeitung* (1948): 646–650.
McIlwain, C. H. "Government by Law." *Foreign Affairs* 14 (1936): 185–198.
Meisel, James H., and James K. Pollock. *Germany under Occupation: Illustrative Materials and Documents.* Ann Arbor: George Wahr Publishing, 1947.
Meiss, Wilhelm. "Zur Frage der Weitergeltung des § 48 Abs. 2 des Testamentgesetzes und der Erbregelungsverordnung vom 4. Oktober 1944," *Süddeutsche Juristenzeitung* (1946): 65–66.

Middleton, Drew. "Many ex-Nazis re-enter German Political Life." *New York Times* (17 October 1948): 4E.

"Military Government of Germany: Directive to the Commander in Chief of the United States Forces of Occupation Regarding the Military Government of Germany." *U.S. Department of State Bulletin* 13 (1945): 596–601.

"Military Government of Germany: Text of Directive to Commander-in-Chief of U.S. Forces of Occupation, Regarding the Military Government of Germany, 11 July 1947." *U.S. Department of State Bulletin* 17 (1947): 186–193.

Morgan, Sir Frederick. *Overture to Overlord.* Garden City: Doubleday & Co., 1950.

Moseley, Harold W., Charles W. McCarthy and Alvin F. Richardson. "The State-War-Navy Coordinating Committee." *U.S. Department of State Bulletin* 13 (1945): 745–747.

Mosely, Philip E. "Dismemberment of Germany: The Allied Negotiations from Yalta to Potsdam." *Foreign Affairs* 28 (April 1950): 487–498.

———. "The Occupation of Germany: New Light on How the Zones Were Drawn." *Foreign Affairs* 28 (July 1950): 580–604.

Murphy, Robert D. *Diplomat Among Warriors.* Garden City: Doubleday & Co., 1964.

Napoli, Joseph F. "Denazification from an American's Viewpoint." *Annals of the American Academy of Political and Social Science* Vol. 264 (July 1949): 115–123.

Natter, E. "Der Wiederaufbau der Rechtsanwaltschaft." *Deutsche Rechts-Zeitschrift* (1946): 46–48.

Nehlert, Gerhard, ed. *Die Beschränkung der deutschen Gerichtsbarkeit: Die Gesetzgebung der Besatzungsmächte insbesondere Gesetze Nr. 2 und Nr. 52 und Befehl 124 nebst Ausführungsbestimmungen.* Berlin: Walter de Gruyter & Co., 1948.

Neidhard, Hans. "Die Gerichtsbarkeit der deutschen Gerichte und der Besatzungsgerichte in der amerikanischen Zone." *Deutsche Rechts-Zeitschrift* (1946): 183–185.

———. "Die Rechtspflege in der Gesetzgebung der amerikanischen Zone: I. Die Gesetzgebung der Besatzungsmacht." *Deutsche Rechts-Zeitschrift* (1946): 84–86.

———. "Die Rechtspflege in der Gesetzgebung der amerikanischen Zone: II. Die gemeinsame Gesetzgebung der drei Länder Bayern, Württemberg-Baden und Großhessen," *Deutsche Rechts-Zeitschrift* (1946): 117–120.

Neumann, Franz. *Behemoth: The Structure and Practice of National Socialism, 1933–1945.* New York: Oxford University Press, 1944.

Neumann, Robert G. "New Constitutions in Germany" *American Political Science Review* 42 (1948): 448–468.

Noakes, Jeremy and Geoffrey Pridham. *Documents on Nazism: 1919–1945.* New York: Viking Press, 1974.

Noam, Ernst and Klaus Moritz, eds. *NS-Verbrechen vor Gericht: 1945–1955.* Wiesbaden: Kommission für die Geschichte der Juden in Hessen, 1978.

Nobleman, Eli E. "The Administration of Justice in the United States Zone of Germany." *Federal Bar Journal* 8 (1946): 70–97.

———. "American Military Government Courts in Germany." *American Academy of Political and Social Science* 269 (1950): 87–97.

———. "American Military Government Courts in Germany." *American Journal of International Law* 40 (1946): 803–811.

———. "American Military Government Courts in Germany with Special Reference to Historic Practice and their Role in the Democratisation of the German People." Diss.: New York University, 1950.

———. "Military Government Courts: Law and Justice in the American Zone of Germany." *American Bar Association Journal* 33 (1947): 777–780, 851–852.

———. "Quadripartite Military Government Organization and Operations in Germany." *American Journal of International Law* 41 (July 1946): 650–655.

Notter, Harley. *Postwar Foreign Policy Preparation: 1939–1945.* Westport: Greeenwood Press, 1975.

"OMGUS-Kritik an der Säuberung: Rund 85 Prozent Betroffene wieder eingestellt." *Frankfurter Rundschau* (11 April 1948).

Pendleton, H. M. "The European Civil Affairs Division." *Military Review* 26 (April 1946): 49–51.

Plischke, Elmer. "Denazification Law and Procedure." *American Journal of International Law* 41 (October 1947): 807–827.

———. "Denazifying the Reich." *Review of Politics* 9 (1947): 153–172.

———. *The West German Federal Government.* Bad Godesberg-Mehlem: Historical Division, Office of the U.S. Commissioner for Germany, 1952.

———. *The Allied High Commission for Germany.* Bad Godesberg-Mehlem: Historical Division, Office of the U.S. High Commissioner for Germany, 1953.

———. "Denazification in Germany: A Policy Analysis." Wolfe, Robert, ed. *Americans as Proconsuls: U.S. Military Government in Germany and Japan, 1944–1952.* Carbondale and Edwardsville: Southern Illinois University Press, 1984: 198–225.

Pollock, James Kerr. "Germany under Military Occupation." *Change and Crisis in European Government,* ed. James Kerr Pollock. New York: Rinehart & Company, 1949: 45–61.

Preuss, Lawrence. "Germanic Law versus Roman Law in National Socialist Legal Theory." *Journal of Comparative Legislation and International Law* 16 (1934): 269–280.

Radbruch, Gustav. "Gesetziches Unrecht und übergesetzliches Recht." *Süddeutsche Juristenzeitung* (1946): 105–108.

Raymond, Jack. "U.S. Backs Easing of Denazification: Official in Hesse declares that some German demands are worthy of acceptance." *New York Times* (21 March 1948): 36L+.

"Rechtspflege: Gerichtsverfassung." *Süddeutsche Juristenzeitung* (1946): 19–20.

"Die Rede des Führers vor dem Reichstag." *Völkischer Beobachter* (27 April 1942).

Roetter, Friedrich. *Might is Right.* London: Quality Press, 1939.

———. "The Impact of German Law." *Wisconsin Law Review* (1945): 516–562.

Römer, Walter. "Wiederaufbau des Rechts: Ein Rückblick." *Süddeutsche Juristenzeitung* (1947): 93–101.

Roper, Edith, and Clara Leiser. *Skeleton of Justice.* New York: E. P. Dutton & Co., 1941.

Rotberg, H. E. "Entpolitisierung der Rechtspflege." *Deutsche Rechts-Zeitschrift* (1947): 107–110.

Ruhm von Oppen, Beate. *Documents on Germany under Occupation: 1945–1955.* London: Oxford University Press, 1955.

Ruscheweyh, Herbert. "Die Entwicklung der hanseatischen Justiz nach der Kapitulation bis zur Errichtung des Zentral-Justizamtes." *Festschrift für Wilhelm Kiesselbach zu seinem 80. Geburtstag.* Hamburg: Gesetz und Recht Verlag, 1947: 37–71.

Schmid, Richard. "Denazification: A German Critique," *American Perspective* 2 (1948): 231–242.

Schmitt, Carl. "Der Weg des deutschen Juristen," *Deutsche Juristen-Zeitung* (1934): 691–698.

Schneider, Peter, ed. "Rechtssicherheit und richterliche Unabhängigkeit aus der Sicht der SD." *Vierteljahrshefte für Zeitgeschichte* 4 (1956): 599–422.

Schöllingen, Werner. "Der Richter und das Gesetz" *Frankfurter Hefte* (1947): 656–664.

Schönke, Adolf. "Einige Fragen der Verfassung der Strafgerichte." *Süddeutsche Juristenzeitung* (1946): 63–65.

———. "Criminal Law and Criminality in Germany of Today." *Annals of the American Academy of Political and Social Science* 260 (1948): 137–143.

Schullze, Erich, ed. *Gesetz zur Befreiung von Nationalsozialismus und Militarismus von 5. März 1946.* München: Biederstein Verlag, 1947.

Schwenk, Edmund H. "Legislative Power of the Military Occupant under Article 43, Hague Regulations." *Yale Law Journal* 54 (1944–1945): 393–416.

Shartel, Burke and Hans Julius Wolff. "Civil Justice in Germany," *Michigan Law Review* Vol. 12 (1944): 863–908.

"Staat und Verwaltung." *Süddeutsche Juristenzeitung* (1946): 18–19.

Staats-Anzeiger für das Land Hessen. 1947.

Staff, Ilse, ed. *Justiz im Dritten Reich: Eine Dokumentation.* Frankfurt-am-Main: Fischer Bucherei, 1964.

Starr, Joseph R. *U.S. Military Government in Germany: Operations During the Rhineland Campaign.* Karlsruhe: Historical Division, European Command, 1950.

———. *Denazification, Occupation and Control of Germany, March–July 1945.* Salisbury: Documentary Publications, 1977.

Steidle, Hermann. "Der Plan für den Aufbau des Rechtspflegewesens in der amerikanischen Zone." *Süddeutsche Juristenzeitung* (1946): 14–15.

Stimson, Henry L., and McGeorge Bundy. *On Active Service in Peace and War.* New York: Harper & Brothers, 1948.

Stolper, Gustav. *German Realities.* New York: Reynal and Hitchcock, 1948.

Strang, William. *Home and Abroad.* London: Andre Deutsch, 1956.

Sträter, Artur. "Denazification." *Annals of the American Academy of Political and Social Science.* 260 (1948): 43–52.

Taylor, Telford. *Nuremberg Trials: War Crimes and International Law.* New York, 1949.

Trevor-Roper, H.R., ed. *Hitler's Secret Conversations: 1941–1944.* New York: Octagon, 1961.

"Übersicht über die Gesetzgebung der Länder: Großhessen." *Süddeutsche Juristenzeitung* (1946): 16–17.

von Weber, Helmut. "Die Bedeutung der 'Allgemeinen Anweisung an Richter' Nr. 1." *Süddeutsche Juristenzeitung* (1946): 65–70.

———. "Der Einfluß der Militärgerichtsbarkeit der Besatzungsmacht auf die deutsche Strafgerichtsbarkeit: 1. Beitrag." *Süddeutsche Juristenzeitung* (1947): 65–70.

———. "Das Ende der AAR Nr. 1." *Deutsche Rechts-Zeitschrift* (1950): 217–219.

Wedderburn, E. A. M. "Criminal Law in the Third Reich.". *The Juridical Review* 48 (1936): 373–382.

Weiden, Paul L. "The Impact of Occupation on German Law." *Wisconsin Law Review* (1947): 332–356.

Wells, Roger H. "The Liquidation of the German *Länder*." *American Political Science Review* 30 (1936): 350–361.

Wengler, Wilhelm. "Betrachtungen zum Besatzungsstatut." *Neue Juristische Wochenschrift* (December 1949): 881–886.

Wolff, Hans-Julius. "Criminal Justice in Germany." *Michigan Law Review* 42 (1943): 1067–1088; 43 (1944): 155–178.

Wunderlich, Frieda. *German Labor Courts.* Chapel Hill: University of North Carolina Press, 1946.

Zink, Harold. "American Military Government Organization in Germany." *The Journal of Politics* 8 (August 1946): 329–349.

———. "The American Denazification Program in Germany." *Journal of Central European Affairs* 6 (October 1946): 227–240.

———. *American Military Government in Germany.* New York: MacMillan, 1947.

———. "American Occupation Policies in Germany." *Review of Politics* 9 (1947): 284–296.

———. *The United States in Germany: 1944–1955.* New York: Van Nostrand, 1957.

Zinn, Georg-August. "The Administration of Justice in Germany." *Annals of the American Academy of Poltical and Social Science* 260 (1948): 32–42.

———. "Der politische Mord," *Süddeutsche Juristenzeitung* (1948): 141–142.

Secondary Sources

Anders, Helmut. "Die Demokratisierung der Justiz beim Aufbau der antifaschistisch-demokratischen Ordnung 1945 bis 1949." *Jahrbuch für Geschichte* Vol. 9 (1973): 385–438.

Anderson, Dennis Leroy. *The Academy for German Law, 1933–1944.* New York: Garland Publishing, 1987.

Bachof, Otto. "Die 'Entnazifizierung.'" *Deutsches Geistesleben und Nationalsozialismus.* Tübingen: Rainer Wunderlich Verlag, 1965.

Bader, Karl S. "Strafverteidigung vor deutschen Gerichten im Dritten Reich." *Juristenzeitung* 27 (1972): 6–12.

Balfour, Michael, and John Mair. *Survey of International Affairs, 1939–1946: Four-Power Control in Germany and Austria, 1945–1946*, ed. Arnold Toynbee. London: Oxford University Press, 1956.

Bark, Dennis L., and David R. Gress. *A History of West Germany*, Vol. 1: *From Shadow to Substance 1945–1963.* Oxford: Blackwell Publishers, 1993.

Benz, Wolfgang. "Die Entnazifizierung der Richter." *Justizalltag im Dritten Reich*, eds. Bernhard Diestelkamp and Michael Stolleis. Frankfurt-am-Main: Fischer Taschenbuch Verlag, 1988.

Bower, Tom. *The Pledge Betrayed: America and Britain and the Denazification of Postwar Germany*. Garden City, New York: Doubleday & Co., 1982.

Bracher, Karl Dietrich. *The German Dictatorship: The Origins, Structure and Effects of National Socialism*, trans. Jean Steinberg. New York: Praeger, 1971.

Breuning, Heinz. "Die Beschränkung der deutschen Gerichtsbarkeit durch die Besatzungsmächte." Diss.: Eberhard-Karls-Universität zu Tübingen, 1952.

Broszat, Martin. "Zur Perversion der Strafjustiz im Dritten Reich." *Vierteljahrshefte für Zeitgeschichte* 6 (1958): 390–445

Broszat, Martin. *Der Staat Hitlers: Grundlegung und Entwicklung seiner inneren Verfassung*. München: Deutscher Taschenbuch Verlag, 1969.

———. "Siegerjustiz oder Strafrechtliche 'Selbstreinigung': Aspekte der Vergangenheitsbewältigung der deutschen Justiz während der Besatzungszeit 1945–1949," *Vierteljahrshefte für Zeitgeschichte* 29 (1981): 477–544.

Broszat, Martin, Hand Buchheim, Hans-Adolf Jacobsen, and Helmut Krausnick. *Anatomy of the SS State*, trans. Richard Barry. London: Collins, 1968.

Clement, Walter. "Der Vorbehalt des Gesetzes, insbesondere bei öffentlichen Leistungen und öffentlichen Einrichtungen." Diss.: Eberhard-Karls-Universität, 1987.

Cline, Ray S. *United States Army in World War II; The War Department; Washington Command Post: The Operations Division*. Washington D.C.: Office of the Chief of Military History, Department of the Army, 1951.

Cohn, E. J. *Manual of German Law*, Vol. 1. London: British Institute of International and Comparative Law, 1968.

Coles, Harry L., and Albert K. Weinberg. *Civil Affairs: Soldiers Become Governors*. Washington D.C.: Office of the Chief of Military History, Department of the Army, 1964.

Dicey, Albert Venn. *Introduction to the Study of the Law of the Constitution*. London: MacMillan & Co., 1960.

Diestelkamp, Bernhard. "Rechts- und verfassungsgeschichtliche Probleme zur Frühgeschichte der Bundesrepublik Deutschland." *Juristische Schulung* (1980): 401–405, 481–485, 790–796; (1981): 96–102, 409–413, 488–494.

———. "Kontinuität und Wandel in der Rechtsordnung: 1945 bis 1955," *Westdeutschland 1945–1955: Unterwerfung, Kontrolle, Integration*. ed. Ludolf Herbst. München: R. Oldenbourg Verlag, 1986: 85–105.

———. "Die Justiz nach 1945 und ihr Umgang mit den eigenen Vergangenheit." *Justiz im Dritten Reich*, ed. Bernhard Diestelkamp and Michael Stolleis. Frankfurt-am-Main: Fischer Taschenbuch Verlag, 1988: 131–149.

Diestelkamp, Bernhard, and Susanne Jung. "Die Justiz in den Westzonen und der frühen Bundesrepublik." *Aus Politik und Zeitgeschichte* 13 (24 March 1989): 19–29.

Donnison, F. S. V. *Civil Affairs and Military Government: North-West Europe, 1944–1946*. London: Her Majesty's Stationery Office, 1961.

———. *Civil Affairs and Military Government Central Organization and Planning*. London: Her Majesty's Stationery Office, 1966.

Dotterweich, Volker. "Die Entnazifizierung." *Vorgeschichte der Bundesrepublik Deutschland: Zwischen Kapitulation und Grundgesetz*, eds. Josepf Becker, Theo Stammen, and Peter Waldmann. München: Wilhelm Fink Verlag, 1979: 123–161.

Edelmann, Günther. "Der Einfluß des Besatzungsrechts auf das deutsche Staatsrecht der Übergangszeit (1945–1949)." Diss.: Johann Wolfgang Goether-Universität, 1955.

Eisenberg, Carolyn Woods. *Drawing the Line: The American Decision to Divide Germany, 1944–1949.* New York: Cambridge University Press, 1996.

Eschenburg, Theodor. *Geschichte der Bundesrepublik Deutschland* Vol. 1: *Jahre der Besatzung 1945–1949.* Stuttgart: Deutsche Verlags-Anstalt, 1983.

Fearnside, W. Ward. "Three Innovations of National Socialist Jurisprudence." *Journal of Central European Affairs* 16 (1956–1957): 146–155.

Fitzgibbon, Constantine. *Denazification.* London: Michael Joseph, 1969.

Franz, Eckart G., Hans Hubert Hoffmann, and Meinhard Schaab. *Gerichtsorganisation in Baden-Württemberg, Bayern und Hessen im 19. und 20. Jahrhundert.* Hannover: Akademie für Raumforschung und Landesplanung, 1989.

Friedlander, Henry. "The Judiciary and Nazi Crimes in Postwar Germany." *Simon Wiesenthal Centre Annual* 1 (1984): 27–44.

Friedrich, Carl J. "The Development of the Executive Power in Germany," *American Political Science Review* 27 (1933): 185–203.

Friedrich, Carl J., ed. *American Experiences in Military Government in World War II.* New York: Rinehart & Co., 1948.

Fürstenau, Justus. *Entnazifizierung: Ein Kapitel deutscher Nachkriegspolitik.* Darmstadt: Luchterhand Verlag, 1969.

Gaab, Jeffrey S. *Justice Delayed: The Restoration of Justice in Bavaria under American Occupation, 1945–1949.* New York: Peter Lang, 1999.

Gimbel, John A. "American Denazification and German Local Politics, 1945–1949: A Case Study in Marburg." *American Political Science Review* 54 (1960): 83–105.

———. *A German Community under American Occupation: Marburg, 1945–1952.* Stanford: Stanford University Press, 1961.

———. *The American Occupation of Germany: Politics and the Military, 1945–1949.* Stanford: Stanford University Press, 1968.

Godau-Schüttke, Klaus-Detlev. *Ich habe nur dem Recht gedient: Die 'Renazifizierung' der Schleswig-Holsteinischen Justiz nach 1945.* Baden-Baden: Nomos Verlagsgesellschaft, 1993.

Gosewinkel, Dieter. *Adolf Arndt: Die Wiederbegründung des Rechtsstaats aus dem Geist der Sozialdemokratie, 1945–1961.* Bonn: J. H. W. Dietz Nachf., 1991.

Grohnert, Richard. *Die Entnazifizierung in Baden, 1945–1949: Konzeptionen und Praxis der "Epuration" am Beispiel eines Landes der französischen Besatzungszone.* Stuttgart: W. Kohlhammer Verlag, 1991.

Gruchmann, Lothar. "Hitler über die Justiz: Das Tischgesprache von 20. August 1942," *Vierteljahrshefte für Zeitgeschichte* Vol. 12 (1964): 86–101.

———. "Rechtssystem und nationalsozialistische Justizpolitik," *Das Dritte Reich: Herrschaftsstruktur und Geschichte*, eds. Martin Broszat and Horst Möller. München: Verlag C. H. Beck, 1983: 83–103.

———. "Ein unbequemer Amtsrichter im Dritten Reich: Aus den Personalakten des Dr. Lothar Kreyßig". *Vierteljahrshefte für Zeitgeschichte* 32 (1984): 463–488.

———. *Justiz im Dritten Reich 1933–1940: Anpassung und Unterwerfung in der Ära Gürtner.* München: R. Oldenbourg Verlag, 1988.

Grunberger, Richard. *The Twelve Year Reich: A Social History of Nazi Germany, 1933–1945.* New York: Holt, Rinehart and Winston, 1971.

Hammerschmidt, Helmut, ed. *Zwanzig Jahre Danach: Eine Deutsche Bilanz, 1945–1965.* Munich: Verlag Kurt Desch, 1965.

Hammond, Paul Y. "Directives for the Occupation of Germany: The Washington Controversy." *American Civil-Military Decisions: A Book of Case Studies,* ed. Harold Stein. Birmingham: University of Alabama Press, 1963: 314–460.

Hansen, Reimer. *The Fourth Richest Reich.* New York: MacMillan, 1980.

Hege, Hans. "Recht und Justiz." *Die Bundesrepublik Deutschland* Vol. 1, ed. Wolfgang Benz. Frankfurt-am-Main: Fischer Taschenbuch Verlag, 1984: 92–121.

Henke, Klaus-Dietmar. "Die Grenzen der politischen Säuberung in Deutschland nach 1945." *Westdeutschland 1945–1955: Unterwerfung, Kontrolle, Integration,* ed. Ludolf Herbst. München: R. Oldenbourg Verlag, 1986: 127–133.

Hucko, Elmar M. *The Democratic Tradition: Four German Constitutions.* Leamington Spa: Berg, 1987.

Johe, Werner. *Die gleichgeschaltete Justiz: Organisation des Rechtswesens und Politisierung der Rechtsprechung 1933–1945 dargestellt am Beispiel des Oberlandesgerichtsbezirks Hamburg.* Frankfurt-am-Main: Europäische Verlagsanstalt, 1967.

Johnson, Julia E., ed. *The Dilemma of Postwar Germany.* New York, 1948.

Jones, Jill. "Eradicating Nazism from the British Zone of Germany: Early Policy and Practice." *German History* 8 (1990): 145–162.

Kater, Michael H. "Problems of Political Reeducating in West Germany, 1945–1960." *Simon Wiesenthal Centre Annual* 4 (1987): 99–123.

Kerr, Hugh Thomson, ed. *A Compend of Luther's Theology.* London: Student Christian Movement, 1943.

Kormann, John G. *U.S. Denazification Policy in Germany: 1944–1950.* Historical Division: Office of the High Commissioner for Germany, 1952.

Kranig, Andreas. "Treue gegen Fürsorge: Arbeitsrichter unter dem Nationalsozialismus." *Justizalltag im Dritten Reich,* eds. Bernhard Diestelkamp and Michael Stolleis. Frankfurt-am-Main: Fischer Taschenbuch Verlag, 1988.

Kropat, Wolf-Arno, *Hessen in der Stunde Null 1945–1947: Politik, Wirtschaft und Bildungswesen in Dokumenten.* Wiesbaden: Historische Kommission für Nassau, 1979.

Kropat, Wolf-Arno and Ernst Noam, eds. *Juden vor Gericht, 1933–1945: Dokumente aus hessischen Justizakten.* Wiesbaden: Kommission für die Geschichte der Juden in Hessen, 1975.

Latour, Conrad F., and Thilo Vogelsang. *Okkupation und Wiederaufbau: Die Tätigkeit der Militärregierung in der amerikanischen Besatzungszone Deutschland, 1944–1947.* Stuttgart: Deutsche Verlags-Anstalt, 1973.

MacDonald, Charles B. *United States Army in World War II, The European Theater of Operations: The Last Offensive.* Washington D.C.: Office of the Chief of Military History, 1973.

Maginnis, John J. *Military Government Journal*, ed. Robert A. Hart. University of Massachusetts Press, 1972.

Majer, Diemut. "Zum Einfluß der NSDAP auf die Organisation und Personalpolitik der Justiz 1933–1945." *Deutscher Richterzeitung* (1978): 47–51.

———. *Grundlagen des nationalsozialistischen Rechtssystems: Führerprinzip, Sonderrecht, Einheitspartei.* Stuttgart: Verlag W. Kohlhammer, 1987.

Marx, Fritz Morstein. "Germany's New Civil Service Act." *American Political Science Review* 31 (1937): 878–883.

Marxen, Klaus. "Strafjustiz im Nationalsozialismus: Vorschläge für eine Erweiterung der historischen Perspektive." eds. Bernhard Diestelkamp and Michael Stolleis. *Justialltag im Dritten Reich.* Frankfurt-am-Main: Fischer Taschenbuch Verlag, 1988: 101–111.

Mehnert, Klaus, and Heinrich Schulte, eds. *Deutschland-Jahrbuch 1949.* Essen: West-Verlag, 1949.

Merritt, Anna J., and Richard L. Merritt. *Public Opinion in Occupied Germany: The OMGU.S. Surveys, 1945–1949.* Urbana: University of Illinois Press, 1970.

Mühlhausen, Walter. *Hessen 1945–1950: Zur politischen Geschichte eines Landes in der Besatzungszeit.* Frankfurt-am-Main: Insel Verlag, 1985.

Müller, Ingo. "Die Verwendung des Rechtsbeugungstatbestands zu politischen Zwecken," *Kritische Justiz* (1984): 119–141.

———. *Hitler's Justice: The Courts of the Third Reich*, trans. Deborah Lucas Schneider. Cambridge, Mass.: Harvard University Press, 1991.

Müller, Karlheinz. *Preußischer Adler und Hessischer Löwe: Hundert Jahre Wiesbadener Regierung 1866–1966, Dokumente der Zeit aus den Akten.* Wiesbaden: Verlag Kultur und Wissen, 1966.

Niethammer, Lutz. *Entnazifizierung in Bayern: Säuberung und Rehabilitierung unter amerikanischer Besatzung.* Frankfurt-am-Main: S. Fischer Verlag, 1972.

Ostendorf, Heribert, and Heino ter Veen. *Das „Nürnberger Juristenteil": Eine kommentierte Dokumentation.* Frankfurt-am-Main: Campus Verlag, 1985.

Pappe, H. O. "On the Validity of Judicial Decisions in the Nazi Era." *Modern Law Review* 23 (May 1960): 260–274.

Peterson, Edward N. *The American Occupation of Germany: Retreat to Victory.* Detroit: Wayne State University Press, 1977.

Pogue, Forrest C. *United States Army in World War II: The European Theater of Operations, The Supreme Command.* Washington D.C.: Office of the Chief of Military History, Department of the Army, 1954.

Press and Information Office of the Federal Government. "The Administration of Justice," *Germany Reports.* Wiesbaden: Franz Steiner, 1966.

Pünder, Tilman. *Das Bizonale Interregnum: Die Geschichte des Vereinigten Wirtschaftsgebietes, 1946–1949.* Waiblingen: Grote'sche Verlagsbuchhandlung, 1966.

Reifner, Udo, and Bernd-Rüdeger Sonnen, eds. *Strafjustiz und Polizei im Dritten Reich.* Frankfurt-am-Main: Campus Verlag, 1984.

Röhreke, Heinrich. "Die Besatzungsgewalt auf dem Gebiete der Rechtspflege." Diss.: Eberhard-Karls-Universität zu Tübingen, 1950.

———. "Die Rechtsentwicklung in der Bundesrepublik Deutschland," *Deutsche Rechts-Zeitschrift* (1950): 34–37.

Rückerl, Adalbert. *The Investigation of Nazi Crimes, 1945–1978: A Documentation*, trans. Derek Rutter. Hamdon: Archon Books, 1980.

Schmid, Richard. *Justiz in der Bundesrepublik*. Pfullingen: Wiske, 1967.

Schorn, Hubert. *Der Richter im Dritten Reich: Geschichte und Dokumente*. Frankfurt-am-Main: Vittorio Klostermann, 1959.

Schrenck-Notzing, Caspar. *Charakterwäsche: Die amerikanische Besatzung in Deutschland und ihre Folgen*. Stuttgart: Seewald Verlag, 1965.

Simon, Dieter. "Waren die NS-Richter 'unabhängige Richter' im Sinne des § 1 GVG?" *Justizalltag im Dritten Reich*, eds. Bernhard Diestelkamp and Michael Stolleis. Frankfurt-am-Main: Fischer Taschenbuch Verlag, 1988.

Sommer, Theo. "The Nazis in the Judiciary." *The Politics of Postwar Germany*, ed. Walter Stahl. New York: Frederick A. Praeger, 1963: 240–248.

Stolleis, Michael. "Rechtsordnung und Justizpolitik: 1945–1949." *Europäische Rechtsdenken in Geschichte und Gegenwart: Festschrift für Helmut Coing zum 70. Geburtstag* Vol. 1, ed. Norbert Horn. Munich: C. H. Beck'sche Verlagsbuchhandlung, 1982: 383–407.

———. "Die Verwaltungsgerichtsbarkeit im Nationalsozialismus." *Justizalltag im Dritten Reich*, eds. Bernhard Diestelkamp and Michael Stolleis. Frankfurt-am-Main: Fischer Taschenbuch Verlag, 1988.

Sweet, William. "The Volksgerichtshof: 1933–1945." *Journal of Modern History* 46 (1974): 314–329.

Tauber, Kurt P. *Beyond Eagle and Swastika: German Nationalism since 1945*, Vols. 1 and 2. Middletown: Wesleyan University Press, 1967.

U.S. Army, European Command, Historical Division. *Planning for the Occupation of Germany*. Frankfurt-am-Main: Office of the Chief Historian, 1947.

Vogt, Timothy R. *Denazification in Soviet-occupied Germany. Brandenburg 1945–1948*. Cambridge, Mass.: Harvard University Press, 2000.

Vollnhals, Clemens, ed. *Entnazifizierung: Politische Säuberung und Rehabilitierung in den vier Besatzungszonen 1945–1949*. München: Deutscher Taschenbuch Verlag, 1991.

Wagner, Walter. *Die Deutsche Justiz und der Nationalsozialismus*, Vol. 3: *Der Volksgerichtshof im nationalsozialistischen Staat*. Stuttgart: Deutsche Verlags-Anstalt, 1974.

Wassermann, Rudolf. *Auch die Justiz kann aus der Geschichte nicht aussteigen*. Baden-Baden: Nomos Verlagsgesellschaft, 1990.

———. "Richteramt und politisches System." *Revue d'Allemagne* 5 (1973): 901–913.

Weinberg, Albert K. *Civil Affairs: Soldiers Become Governors*. Washington D.C.: U.S. Government Printing Office, 1964.

Weinkauff, Hermann, and Albrecht Wagner. *Die Deutsche Justiz und der Nationalsozialismus* Vol. 1. Stuttgart: Deutsche Verlags-Anstalt, 1968.

Wenzlau, Joachim Reinhold. *Der Wiederaufbau der Justiz in Nordwestdeutschland, 1945–1949*. Königstein: Athenaum, 1979.

Willig, Kenneth C. H. "The Bar in the Third Reich." *American Journal of Legal History* 20 (1976): 1–14.

Wolfe, Robert, ed. *Americans as Proconsuls: United States Military Government in Germany and Japan, 1944–1952.* Carbondale and Edwardsville: Southern Illinois University Press, 1984.

Wrobel, Hans. *Verurteilt zur Demokratie: Justiz und Justizpolitik in Deutschland 1945–1949.* Heidelberg: Decker & Müller, 1989.

Ziemke, Earl F. *The U.S. Army in the Occupation of Germany: 1944–1946.* Washington D.C.: Center of Military History, United States Army, 1975.

———. "The Formulation and Initial Implementation of U.S. Occupation Policy in Germany." *U.S. Occupation in Europe after World War II*, Hans A. Schmitt, ed. Lawrence: Regents Press of Kansas, 1978.

Zimmer, Erhard. *Studien zur Frankfurter Geschichte herausgegeben vom Frankfurter Verein für Geschichte und Landeskunde: Die Geschichte des Oberlandesgerichts in Frankfurt-am-Main.* Frankfurt-am-Main: Waldemar Kramer, 1976.

Index

About the Author

Andrew Szanajda is assistant professor in the Applied Foreign Languages Department at the Overseas Chinese Institute of Technology in Taichung, Taiwan. He received his M.A. and his Ph.D. from McGill University in Montreal, Canada.

www.ingramcontent.com/pod-product-compliance
Lightning Source LLC
Chambersburg PA
CBHW051253200926
51612CB00001B/29